EGYPT

From ALEXANDER
to the EARLY CHRISTIANS

EGYPT

From ALEXANDER to the EARLY CHRISTIANS

An Archaeological and Historical Guide

Edited by Roger S. Bagnall
and Dominic W. Rathbone

The J. Paul Getty Museum
Los Angeles

First published in 2004 by
The British Museum Press
A division of The British Museum Company Ltd
46 Bloomsbury Street, London WC1B 3QQ

First published in the United States of America in 2004 by
Getty Publications
1200 Getty Center Drive, Suite 500
Los Angeles, California 90049-1682
www.getty.edu

Christopher Hudson, *Publisher*
Mark Greenberg, *Editor in Chief*

Library of Congress Control Number: 2004110573

ISBN 0-89236-796-2

Maps by David Cox
Plans by Will Foster (Monitos)
Designed and typeset in Weiss and Stone Sans by Martin Richards

Printed in Spain by Grafos SA, Barcelona

CONTENTS

6 Middle Egypt

7 The Theban region

8 Upper Egypt

9 The western oases

10 The Eastern Desert

PREFACE

The aim of this guide is to enable the traveller to Egypt, or anyone interested in the archaeology and history of ancient Egypt, to appreciate the rich material legacy of the Hellenistic, Roman and Late Antique (or Byzantine) periods, roughly the millennium from 332 BC to AD 641. This ancient Egypt is not as familiar in general, or as immediately obvious on the ground, as the monuments and civilization of the preceding two millennia and more of pharaonic rule which have always dominated the Western image of Egypt. Most guidebooks focus on the pharaonic past, although there is an enormous amount from this later period to see and study, and much of exceptional beauty and interest.

From 525 to 399 BC, and again from 343, Egypt was part of the Persian Empire. After its conquest by Alexander the Great in 332 BC, it was ruled for the next 300 years by the Ptolemaic dynasty founded by Ptolemy I, one of Alexander's generals. With the defeat of Cleopatra VII in 30 BC, Egypt became a province of the Roman Empire, and subsequently of the Byzantine Empire. For a thousand years, from 332 BC to the Arab conquest in AD 641, Egypt was one of the most prosperous lands of the variegated Mediterranean civilization which developed under Greek and Roman rule. While the Egyptian heritage, especially in religion and art, continued to be vital, Greek and other settlers from all over the Hellenistic and Roman worlds brought with them their own cultural traditions. Christianity then added new influences. The result was a remarkably vibrant and diverse material and intellectual culture.

The visible legacy of this period includes the remains of cities and villages, temples, tombs, churches and monasteries, forts, statues and reliefs, paintings, decorated mummies, craft objects, inscriptions on stone and documents. Some of the most impressive surviving monuments in the Egyptian tradition, like the great temples of Dendera and Edfu, were built in the name of Ptolemaic and Roman rulers. Alexandria and other sites have produced superb Hellenistic mosaics and statuary, and occasional traces of the monumental civic buildings of the Roman period. The so-called 'Fayyum' portraits from mummies are a unique and striking survival from the Roman world. Egypt today remains home to Coptic Christianity with its rich and distinctive architectural and artistic traditions. Tens of thousands of documents of all types, public and private, written on papyrus in Greek and other languages, have survived by accident and give us, in random bursts, a wealth of detailed historical information about events and daily life which is unparalleled in earlier Egyptian history or in any other area of the Greek and Roman worlds. In this guide we include major finds of documents as part of the archaeology, just as we try to place the archaeological remains in their historical context.

We have had to be selective in our choice of sites and objects, and in the amount of detail given. Over 150 sites are described, from Marina el-Alamein on the Mediterranean to Berenike on the Red Sea. We have included major sites and monuments which have now been destroyed or moved, where possible with photographs and reconstructions of how they once appeared. We also cover the objects of our period displayed in the principal museums of Egypt at the present time. The eventual contents of the new museums currently being opened in Alexandria, Cairo and elsewhere are not yet certain; some objects may be moved between museums, and many new objects will be put on display. We include a brief historical introduction and some illustrative glimpses of the world of the papyrus documents. Readers who want more can turn to the fuller, illustrated, historical survey of A. K. Bowman, *Egypt after the Pharaohs, 332 BC–AD 642* (1986; 2nd edn 1996), and the collection of translated and commented papyrus documents in J. L. Rowlandson (ed.), *Women and Society in Greek and Roman Egypt. A Sourcebook* (1998).

We give some advice on how to visit sites outside the main tourist areas, and provide GPS co-ordinates for oasis and desert sites, but travellers should consult a recently updated tourist guide for the practicalities of transport, accommodation and health. From time to time security concerns lead the police to forbid or restrict travel by foreigners in some areas of Egypt, particularly Middle Egypt and the Eastern Desert; anyone planning to visit areas off the normal tourist circuit should seek advice first from their Consulate. Access to ancient sites in Egypt is controlled by the Supreme Council for Antiquities (SCA) and the Tourist and Antiquities Police. Entrance tickets are sold at the gate of sites and museums open to the public; churches and monasteries in current use normally allow visitors. Other sites should not be visited without permission from the Cairo or local headquarters of the SCA. Sites decay easily and must be treated with respect. The acquisition, by any means, of antiquities in Egypt is illegal and subject to severe penalties.

ACKNOWLEDGEMENTS

In addition to the twelve main contributors to this book, Sarah Clackson contributed 6.5 shortly before her untimely death, and Todd Hickey provided material for ch.1, and Herbert Verreth for 2.7. The complete first draft was read by Don Bailey, who made many valuable suggestions, and parts by Elizabeth S. Bolman. The plans were drawn by Will Foster, the maps by David Cox, and two pictures by Sue Testar. Judith McKenzie contributed her maps of Alexandria and the late Sheila Gibson's axonometric drawings. Martin Richards, the book designer, cheerfully assisted with several illustrations. Help in finding and providing photographs was also given by Sally-Ann Ashton, Elizabeth S. Bolman, Annie Cottry, Sue Davies, Mark Depauw, Darlene Brooks Hedstrom, Marie-Hélène Marganne (Cedopal), Robin Meador-Woodruff, Paul Nicolson, Harry Smith, Thelma K. Thomas, Bart Van Beek and Beatriz Waters. Coralie Hepburn was production editor, and Leslie MacCoull compiled the index. In the writing and editing of this book Dominic Rathbone benefited from a Leverhulme Trust Research Professorship, and Roger Bagnall had research support from Columbia University, and was assisted by Jinyu Liu and Giovanni Ruffini. To all these, and to Nina Shandloff of the British Museum Press, the editors are extremely grateful.

MAIN CONTRIBUTORS

Roger S. Bagnall (9; 10)
Columbia University, New York

Alan Bowman (2.1–5)
University of Oxford

Willy Clarysse (2.7; 8.3, 4, 6, 8, 9)
Katholieke Universiteit Leuven

Ann Ellis Hanson (1.2, 3, 7)
Yale University, New Haven

James G. Keenan (1.1, 4, 6)
Loyola University, Chicago

J. G. Manning (6.2.e, 4.d; 8.1, 2, 7, 10–12)
Stanford University

Dominic Rathbone (2.6; 3.3; 5)
King's College London

Jane Rowlandson (6.1–2)
King's College London

Dorothy J. Thompson (3)
Girton College, Cambridge

Peter van Minnen (1.5; 6.3–4)
University of Cincinnati

Katelijn Vandorpe (7.1–4; 8.5)
Katholieke Universiteit Leuven

T. G. Wilfong (4; 7.5)
University of Michigan, Ann Arbor

1 GENERAL INTRODUCTION

1.1 HISTORICAL BACKGROUND

1.1.a A new era

In 332 BC Alexander the Great of Macedon entered Egypt, then part of the Persian Empire, and gained control of it without opposition. Alexander stayed only for one eventful winter, in which he travelled to the oracle of Zeus-Ammon in Siwa and founded the city of Alexandria. In 331 BC he left, never in his brief lifetime to return, but his establishment of Macedonian rule in Egypt initiated a new era in Egyptian history. By the time Alexander died in Babylon in 323 BC, his conquests stretched from Greece eastwards to modern Afghanistan. The fiction of his empire was maintained in recognition as king of, successively, Philip III Arrhidaios, Alexander's half-brother, and Alexander IV, his infant son. Real power, however, resided with some of Alexander's generals, who soon seized control of major parts of the empire. Among them, the late-blooming but cunning Ptolemy, son of Lagos, chose Egypt.

Egypt had been known to Greeks as far back as Homer as a region of fabulous wealth. Herodotus, 'the father of history', claimed to have visited Egypt in the fifth century BC. He called the Delta 'the gift of the river' to Egypt. Indeed, all Egypt was 'the gift of the Nile' (as Herodotus is often misquoted), for its renowned agricultural bounty and the rhythm of its years were dependent upon the great river's annual flood. The Nile also lay behind the administrative, and sometimes political, division of Egypt into 'Upper' and 'Lower' halves. Lower Egypt was the Nile Delta, with Memphis at its apex as its chief political and religious centre. Upper Egypt lay to the south, and the region around Thebes was its major centre of power. South of Egypt, and providing a link with sub-Saharan Africa, lay the region known as Nubia. Beyond the limits of the Nile's floodplain lay deserts, their edges sharply defined: the stony, mountainous Eastern Desert with its exceptional mineral wealth and network of roads to ports on the Red Sea (Chapter 10), the sandy Western, or Libyan, Desert with its extensive oases (Chapter 9), and the fertile depression called the Fayyum (Chapter 5).

Bibliography: Bowman 1986; Watterson 1997.

1.1.b Before the Ptolemies

Macedonian rule certainly brought innovations to Egypt, but there were important continuities from the pharaonic past. In the spheres of administration, religion and architecture, change occurred over centuries rather than decades. Egypt after Alexander can only be understood properly through appreciation of thousands of years of pharaonic antecedents. We start, however, with the first significant Greek involvement in Egypt, during Dynasty 26 (664–525 BC). Dynasty 26 arose in the wake of four centuries of fragmentation and foreign domination after the end of the New Kingdom and marks the beginning of the 'international' epoch of Egyptian history which is called the Late Period. Its founder was Psammetichos I, whose base was Sais in the western Delta; hence this dynasty is called the Saite period. While the Assyrian king, whose client he originally was, was preoccupied closer to home, Psammetichos gained control of the entire Delta by 660 BC, and by 656 BC he had become master of all of Egypt.

Although Psammetichos relied on diplomacy more than force, foreign mercenaries – principally Greeks, Jews and Phoenicians – played a critical role in his advance. Throughout the Saite period, these troops protected the state not only from external threats, but also from the strong, indigenous warrior class (the *machimoi*), which was predominantly of Libyan ancestry. Of course mercenaries can cause problems: there were revolts under the pharaoh Apries, and the resentment of the *machimoi* towards the privileged position of Greeks and Carians contributed to his overthrow by Amasis. Egypt's trade links with Greece and Phoenicia also developed significantly during the Saite period. Greek settlement was permitted at Naukratis, which was made the designated trading centre for all Greek commerce. An increase in the importance of Eastern trade is suggested by the canal from the Nile to the Red Sea that the pharaoh Necho II began to construct, which was completed under the Persian king Darius I.

Despite a web of alliances with Near Eastern and Aegean states, Amasis and his son Psammetichos III were not able to fend off the new 'world power', Persia. The Great King Cambyses defeated Psammetichos III at the battle of Pelousion in 525 BC, and Egypt became a part of the Achaemenid Empire. On Cambyses' death in 522 BC, Egypt revolted, but Cambyses' successor Darius I was able to regain control by 519/18 BC. Rebellions continued sporadically throughout the Persian occupation, but Egypt still contributed resources to the empire, including men and material for the attacks on Greece by Darius and his successor, Xerxes. Herodotus' *Histories*, which recount these attacks and the background to them and devote a whole chapter to Egypt, are an important, though sometimes controversial, source for the history of the Late Period.

Although Egypt was a 'satrapy' (province) of the Persian Empire, the Great King was defined there in much the same vocabulary as a pharaoh. Under Cambyses and Darius, we find sensitivity to Egyptian traditions in administration and religion, although Xerxes seems to have been less tactful. In 404 BC another ruler originating from Sais, Amyrtaios, was able to free Egypt from Persian rule and inaugurate the last ancient period of Egyptian independence. The rule of Dynasties 28 to 30 was characterized by instability and the struggle for survival, both internally and externally. Inside Egypt, the Greek mercenaries and the native priests vied for power. All but one of the pharaohs in Dynasty 29 were overthrown. Beyond Egypt's borders, Persia remained an omnipresent threat, and despite Egypt's diplomatic and military efforts, there were frequent attacks, including at least three by Artaxerxes III. In 343 BC Artaxerxes defeated the last indigenous pharaoh, Nektanebo II, and by 341 BC he had conquered all Egypt. However, Persian control was fragile, and after Alexander the Great had defeated Darius III's forces at Issos in 333 BC, he had no difficulty in taking over Egypt.

Bibliography: Kienitz 1953; Lloyd 2000; Myśliwiec 2000.

Fig. 1.1.1 Ptolemy I, Greek-style basalt head (British Museum EA 1641).

1.1.c The Ptolemaic period

After Alexander's death in 323 BC, his generals at first claimed merely to be satraps, nominally under the authority of his heirs, but in 306 BC one of them, Antigonus, called himself 'king', and Ptolemy at once followed suit. The royal line thus established in Egypt lasted for nearly three centuries and was the longest-lived successor kingdom to Alexander's empire.

The first century of Ptolemaic rule saw expansion abroad and stability and growth at home. Following the battle of Ipsos in 301 BC, the Ptolemies controlled Coele Syria ('Hollow Syria'), roughly modern Palestine. Ptolemy I added Cyrene, Cyprus and a number of Aegean islands. Ptolemy II added some coastal cities and territories in Asia Minor and fought the neighbouring Seleucid Empire to maintain control over Coele Syria. Ptolemy III invaded Syria proper during one of the Seleucid kingdom's times of troubles (246–241 BC) and even occupied Seleucia in Pieria, the port city of the Seleucid capital, Antioch. For a brief moment, the Ptolemaic Empire reached its greatest territorial extent. The Seleucid king Antiochus III attempted to regain control of the Ptolemaic possessions in Syria but was surprisingly defeated by Ptolemy IV in 217 BC at Raphia, famous as the first battle in which the Ptolemies made extensive use of native Egyptian troops. This innovation born of desperation was thought by the Greek historian Polybius to mark the beginning of the end of Egypt's internal social cohesion.

In Egypt the first Ptolemies encouraged the immigration of Greeks, attracting military settlers (cleruchs) from all over the eastern Mediterranean through grants of land. In place of pharaonic Memphis, Ptolemy I made Alexandria his capital city, and established in Upper Egypt a second chief city named Ptolemais Hermeiou. Greek soon became the official language of government. The Ptolemies retained the traditional division of Egypt into forty or so administrative districts called 'nomes'. Irrigation was extended and new villages founded in the Fayyum and the eastern Delta (Chapters 2, 4 and 5). Alexandria (Chapter 2) became the largest city of the eastern Mediterranean, a commercial entrepôt whose colossal lighthouse, the Pharos, was one of the wonders of the ancient world. Alexandria also became the leading Mediterranean city of arts and sciences under royal patronage of its Museum, Library and zoological gardens.

While the Ptolemies fostered Greek cultural and scientific endeavours, to legitimate their rule to Egyptians they also promoted native cults and their priesthoods by sponsoring and supporting the repair and restoration of existing temples and the construction of new ones, including some of the finest surviving examples. The temples remained wealthy landholders and enjoyed other privileges. As part of their religious policy, the Ptolemies encouraged worship of themselves and their queens as divinities and also fostered worship of the hybrid Graeco-Egyptian god Sarapis, whose cult became popular well beyond Egypt itself, especially in the Roman period (1.4).

In the historical tradition, the second century of Ptolemaic rule is a tale of contraction, disarray and decline. In 204 BC Ptolemy IV was assassinated in a palace coup, which was followed months later by the accession of his son Ptolemy V, barely six years old. Shortly before, the upper part of Egypt, the Thebaid, had revolted, and remained independent under a native dynasty until its recovery in 186 BC. Another long-term revolt, in the Delta, was finally crushed in 185 BC. On the foreign front, in 200 BC, the young Ptolemy's regents lost Coele Syria to Antiochus III at the battle of Panion. The loss of all the other Ptolemaic foreign possessions followed. Soon Rome began intervening in Egyptian politics. In 168 BC Egypt became, loosely, a Roman protectorate, when Roman diplomatic intervention forced the Seleucid king Antiochus IV, who had invaded in 170 BC and begun to rule Egypt, to withdraw. In 163 BC the Romans restored the ousted Ptolemy VI and his sister-wife Cleopatra II and assigned Cyrenaica to Ptolemy's opponent and younger brother, Ptolemy VIII. The latter eventually, in 145 BC, succeeded to his brother's throne in a reign that our sources describe as a disaster in every way. A late attempt to restore harmony to the land

Fig. 1.1.2
Ptolemy II, Egyptian-style calcite bust (British Museum EA 941).

is seen in the long series of royal amnesty decrees of the year 118 BC. A major force in these years, from her marriage to her uncle, Ptolemy VIII, in 140/39 BC down to her violent end in 101 BC, was Cleopatra III, daughter of Ptolemy VI and Cleopatra II.

In the following century, the by now familiar troubles, including civil wars and dynastic assassinations, continued to plague Egypt. There was a second major revolt in the Thebaid in the early 80s. Finally, Egypt became one of the settings for the civil wars that were tearing the Roman Republic to pieces. In 58 BC Rome annexed the Ptolemaic kingdom of Cyprus. After years of exile, Ptolemy XII died in 51 BC, leaving Egypt to his children, Cleopatra VII (col. pl. 1.1.3) and her younger brother Ptolemy XIII. In 49 BC they began waging war against one another. In 48 BC, after his defeat by Julius Caesar at the battle of Pharsalus, Pompey fled to Egypt and was assassinated on the orders of Ptolemy XIII. Caesar entered Alexandria, where he was besieged by Ptolemy, but gained victory – in which Ptolemy XIII died – by allying himself with Cleopatra. Caesar cohabited with Cleopatra and had a son by her, Ptolemy Caesar, known as Caesarion (Little Caesar). Cleopatra followed Caesar to Rome, where she lived until his assassination in 44 BC. Later, at Ephesos, Cleopatra met Caesar's henchman, Mark Antony, who from 41 BC, when not on military campaign, lived with her in Alexandria. Cleopatra supported Antony in the civil war against Octavian, the great-nephew of Caesar and his adopted son and heir. After the defeat of their fleet at the battle of Actium in 31 BC, they fled to Egypt and committed suicide. Cleopatra's daughter by Antony was spared by Octavian and was married to Juba, the Roman client king of Numidia.

Bibliography: Chauveau 2000, 2002; Hölbl 2001a, 2001b; Lewis 1986; Turner 1984; Walker and Higgs 2001.

1.1.d The Roman period

Octavian, later known as Augustus, dated his rule of Egypt from 1 August 30 BC, the day he entered Alexandria. As he himself tersely put it in his *Res Gestae*: 'I added Egypt to the empire of the Roman people'. Egypt became an imperial province: Augustus, like the Ptolemies, was portrayed in art with the trappings of pharaoh, but Egypt was now directly governed by a Roman 'prefect' resident in Alexandria, a distinguished man of the equestrian class appointed by and directly responsible to the emperor. Roman senators, as potential rivals to the emperor, were barred from the wealthy province. Garrisoned by three legions (later reduced to two), Egypt became an important source of imperial revenue, especially of wheat shipped to feed the population of the city of Rome.

The years of Roman rule in Egypt were relatively peaceful and uneventful, not so much a history of 'events' as of 'structures'. Nevertheless, the first prefect, the poet-soldier C. Cornelius Gallus earned the emperor's displeasure for his military campaign beyond the First Cataract of the Nile into the region known as Nubia, and, more offensively, for vaunting his successes by inscriptions and statues throughout Egypt. Gallus was recalled to Rome, and only escaped judicial condemnation by the Senate through suicide. Military operations on the southern frontier against the kingdom of Meroe occupied Petronius, the second prefect, and resulted in the Roman occupation of Primis (Qasr Ibrim). By a treaty with Meroe,

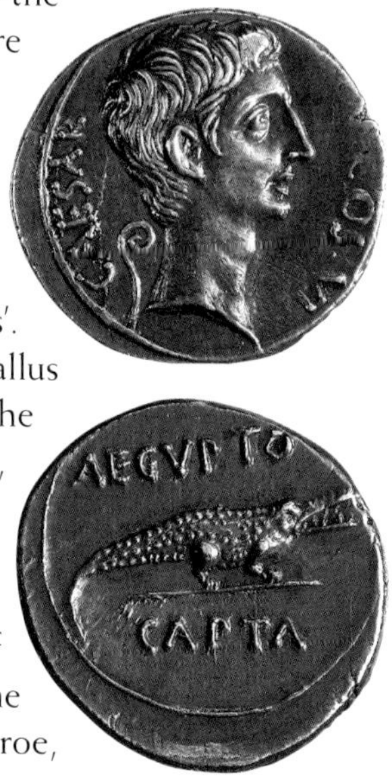

Fig. 1.1.4
Silver denarius of Octavian (Caesar), 28 BC: 'Egypt captured' (British Museum C650).

Egypt's southern boundary was set at Hiera Sykaminos, well south of the First Cataract.

In AD 38, under Gaius, anti-Jewish riots broke out in Alexandria. Subsequently, following another(?) outbreak of violence in AD 41, the emperor Claudius, in his well-known 'Letter to the Alexandrians', attempted to end the conflict between the Jewish and Greek inhabitants. Claudius' successor Nero never acted on his plans to visit Egypt but in AD 61 sponsored an exploration of the 'Ethiopian' lands south of Egypt. In the civil war after Nero's suicide in AD 68, the prefect Tiberius Julius Alexander, scion of an eminent Alexandrian-Jewish family, sided with the victorious Vespasian, who was proclaimed in Alexandria on 1 July 69. Vespasian spent the winter in Alexandria before progressing to Rome, and so did his son Titus after the capture of Jerusalem in AD 70, the decisive event in the Jewish revolt of AD 66–73.

The crushing of another Jewish uprising in AD 115–17 spelled the effective end of the Jewish community in Alexandria. The emperor Hadrian visited Egypt in AD 129–30, touring the country and witnessing the installation of an Apis bull at Memphis. He hunted lions in the desert, visited the site of the Colossus of Memnon, and, following the death by drowning in the Nile of his beloved Antinoos, founded the city of Antinoopolis (6.3.c). He also initiated the development of the Red Sea coastal road known as the Via Hadriana (Chapter 10). The first two-thirds of the second century were a time of great prosperity in Egypt. Drastic change came with an outbreak of plague (likely to have been smallpox) in AD 167, in the reign of Marcus Aurelius (AD 161–80), which lasted through the 170s and was a major demographic catastrophe. In AD 175 a revolt in the Delta by so-called Boukoloi (Cowherds) was crushed by the Roman governor of Syria, Avidius Cassius. Hearing, falsely, that Marcus had died, Cassius proclaimed himself emperor but was overthrown after only three months' rule.

The year AD 193 produced problems of imperial succession similar to those of AD 68. After a series of short-lived emperors, the victor this time was a North African-born general, Septimius Severus, whose dynasty lasted until AD 235. Severus visited Egypt in AD 200–1, heard legal cases in Alexandria, and granted city councils to Alexandria and to the capitals (*metropoleis*) of all of Egypt's nomes. The cities thereby became autonomous Greek-style cities with the same rights as the existing cities of Alexandria, Ptolemais, Naukratis and Antinoopolis. Severus' son and successor, Caracalla, is famous for his *Constitutio Antoniniana* of AD 212, a grant of Roman citizenship to all free inhabitants of the empire. Caracalla visited Egypt in AD 215; he ruthlessly quashed a demonstration in Alexandria, expelling Egyptian natives from the city and slaughtering many in the process.

The mid-third century is traditionally portrayed as an age of anarchy in Roman history. Egypt, because of its strategically secure situation, was spared much of the external turmoil that afflicted the rest of the empire but seems to have experienced some internal decline. In AD 250 there was some persecution of Christians under the emperor Decius. Confusion spread in Egypt, and Alexandria in particular, following the capture of the emperor Valerian by the Persian King Shapur I in AD 260, but by the latter half of AD 262 order was restored in the person of Valerian's co-ruler and son, Gallienus. Through many of these years Egypt was sporadically threatened on its southern border by a nomadic people known as the Blemmyes. In AD 270–2 Egypt was occupied and ruled by potentates from the Syrian caravan city of Palmyra, only to be recovered for the Roman Empire by the energetic emperor Aurelian. Diocletian restored the administrative stability of the empire. He crushed the revolt of Domitius Domitianus in Egypt and in AD 298 fought against the nomadic Nobades on the southern frontier, where he drew back the frontier to the island of Philae at the First Cataract. As part of an empire-wide reform, Diocletian sub-divided the province of Egypt into a number of smaller provinces to increase administrative efficiency. Persecution of Christians late in his reign left its legacy in hagiographic literature and in datings by 'the era of Diocletian', later called 'the era of the martyrs', which ensured that his reputation with Christian posterity would be dark.

Following Diocletian's retirement in AD 305, the eastern part of the Roman Empire came to be ruled by Licinius – until his defeat in AD 324 by Constantine, who reunited an empire that had been divided. His reign may be said to usher in another new period in Egyptian, and indeed Roman imperial, history.

Bibliography: Alston 2002; Bagnall 2001b; Bowman 1996; Lewis 1983; Ritner 1998; Willems and Clarysse 2000.

1.1.e Christian Egypt

As applied to Egypt in this new period, 'Christian' stresses the eventual and nearly total conversion of Egypt to Christianity, especially in the course of the fourth and fifth centuries. The period is also often referred to as 'Byzantine', after Byzantium, the site of the new imperial capital of Constantinople, by papyrologists who study the Egyptian documents, although for historians of Byzantium this period is usually considered too early to be truly 'Byzantine'. Among other labels, 'Late Antique' suggests to modern scholars Egypt's ties with the full Mediterranean world, while 'Coptic' alludes to the rise of the Coptic script and writings (1.3.a), and also highlights the native culture of Egypt in its Late Antique form.

In AD 395 the old Roman Empire was severed into eastern and western halves, and it was only briefly patched together again by Justinian in the mid-sixth century. A treaty between the emperor Marcian and the Blemmyes in AD 451 attempted to bring peace to Egypt's southern frontier. In AD 539 Egypt's provinces were once more restructured by Justinian. In the early seventh century Egypt sided with the unsuccessful usurper Phocas. In AD 619 the Sasanian Persians under Chosroes II's general Shahrbaraz occupied Egypt and ruled it until their withdrawal was negotiated in AD 629. In AD 639, seven years after the death of Mohammed, Egypt was invaded by the Arabs under Amr ibn al-As. Two years later, the country was in Arab hands, and in AD 642 the Byzantines abandoned Alexandria to the victorious Arabs.

Bibliography: Alston 2002; Bagnall 1993, 2001b; Heinen 1998; Keenan 2001; Ritner 1998; Watterson 1988; Wilfong 1989.

1.1.f Early Islamic Egypt

The new Arab government established its headquarters just north of the Roman fortress of Babylon in a place that came to be called Fustat. Greek retained its importance as an administrative language for another century or so. The conversion of the population to Islam was gradual and never complete, as the presence today of a substantial Coptic Christian minority shows. At first there were few Arabs in Egypt, and they dwelt in the cities, not the countryside. Documentation on the Arabic land tax (*kharâj*) and the poll tax imposed on the Christian population is fairly extensive. A certain amount is known about the Arab administration of Middle Egypt through the early eighth-century correspondence between Egypt's governor, Qorrah ibn Sharîk, and a regional official, Flavius Basilius, discovered at Aphrodito, which counterbalances the decidedly negative portrayal of Qorrah in the literary sources.

Little is known about specific events in this neglected period of Egyptian history. In AD 705 Arabic was made the official language for all state affairs. The AD 720s were marked by a series of tax revolts by Copts. In the decade AD 727–37 many Arabs were relocated from Syria into Egypt. Gradually Muslims replaced Copts as village headmen. And in AD 750 the original Umayyad ruling dynasty, based in Damascus, was replaced by the Abbasid dynasty, based in Baghdad. The Arabization and Islamicization of Egypt proceeded over centuries as evolutions rather than revolutions but lie beyond the chronological scope of this book.

Bibliography: Fraser 1991; Kaegi 1998; Kennedy 1998; Watterson 1988; Wilfong 1998, 2002.

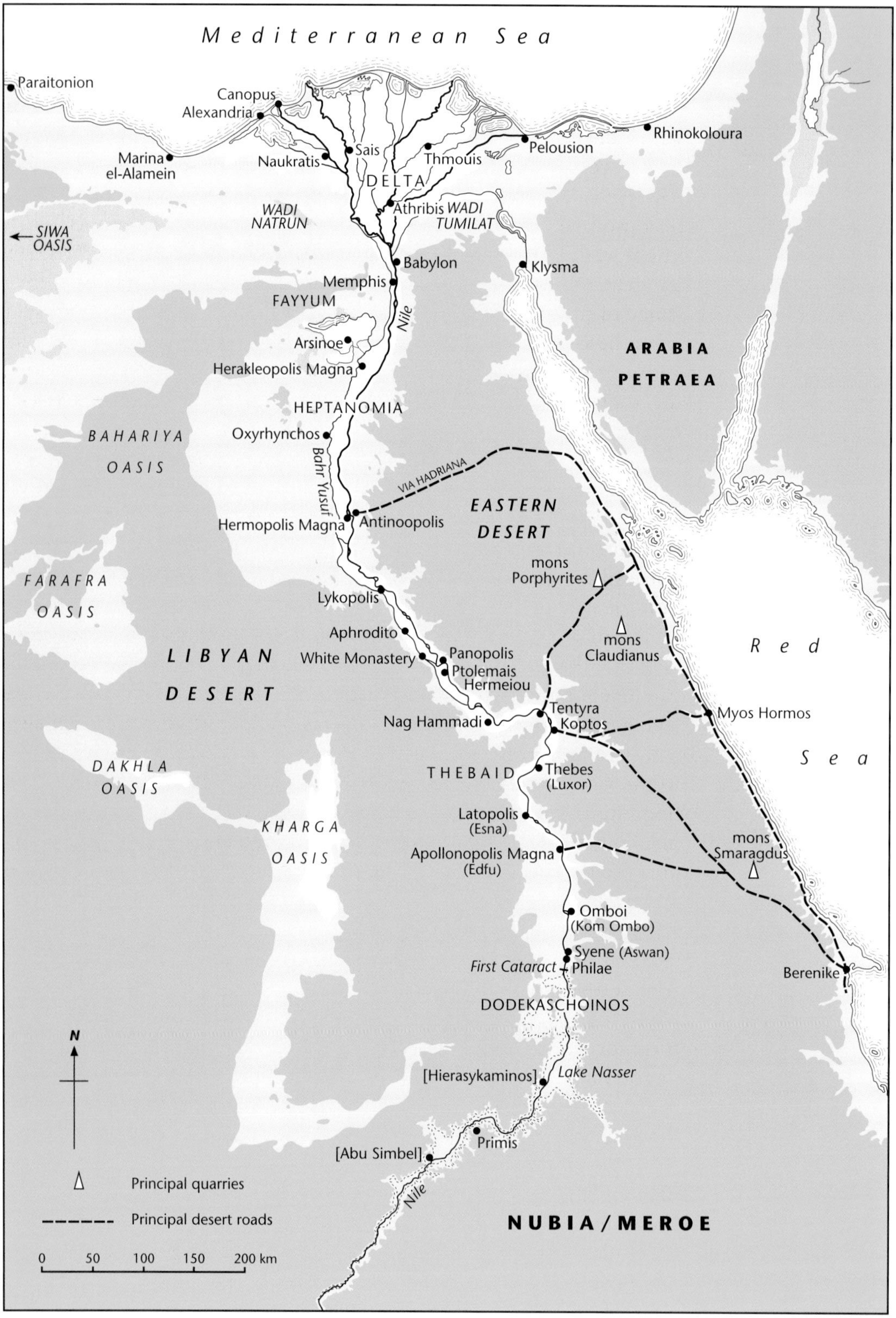
Mediterranean Sea
Paraitonion
Canopus
Alexandria
Marina el-Alamein
Naukratis
Sais
Thmouis
Pelousion
Rhinokoloura
DELTA
WADI NATRUN
SIWA OASIS
Athribis
WADI TUMILAT
Babylon
Klysma
Memphis
FAYYUM
Nile
Arsinoe
Herakleopolis Magna
ARABIA PETRAEA
HEPTANOMIA
BAHARIYA OASIS
Oxyrhynchos
Bahr Yusuf
VIA HADRIANA
EASTERN DESERT
Hermopolis Magna
Antinoopolis
FARAFRA OASIS
mons Porphyrites
Lykopolis
mons Claudianus
Aphrodito
LIBYAN DESERT
White Monastery
Panopolis
Ptolemais Hermeiou
Red Sea
Nag Hammadi
Tentyra
Koptos
Myos Hormos
DAKHLA OASIS
THEBAID
Thebes (Luxor)
KHARGA OASIS
Latopolis (Esna)
Apollonopolis Magna (Edfu)
mons Smaragdus
Omboi (Kom Ombo)
Syene (Aswan)
First Cataract
Philae
Berenike
DODEKASCHOINOS
N
[Hierasykaminos]
Lake Nasser
Primis
[Abu Simbel]
Nile
Principal quarries
Principal desert roads
NUBIA/MEROE
0 50 100 150 200 km

1.2 ECONOMY AND SOCIETY

Throughout Egyptian history the Nile has played a dominant role in the lives of the people. Its annual risings endowed the Egyptian year with a distinctive rhythm – inundation, planting, harvest, a fallow period or second cropping, followed by the new inundation, repetitious and regular. The copious flow of the river's waters deposited a new layer of topsoil yearly, enabling the land to produce the surpluses for which Egypt was already fabled before the arrival of the Greeks. From an aerial view, the Nile appears as a shining stripe in the middle of a green fringe of the alluvial plains on either of the river's banks; further distant from the river are the browns and yellows of the arid desert plateaux, and, at many points behind them, mountainous regions. Year after year, the summer rains from the Ethiopian highlands and tropics rushed northward, bringing the flood-crest in mid-August and September, but receding directly thereafter, as the Nile's waters carried mud and suspended matter from the volcanic rocks of the east African highlands in the south. This mineral-rich silt created and expanded the new lands that formed the Delta, the great fanning out of the Nile's branches north of modern Cairo, as the river's channels pushed ahead to empty into the Mediterranean.

The main pillar of Egypt's economy has always been the arable farmland that depended upon the yearly inundation to lay down silt and fill catchment basins with water for irrigation. Pigeon droppings were collected for fertilizer from the dovecotes that peppered farming villages. The strength of the inundation determined whether feast or famine would visit the land at the next harvest season, and an excessively high flooding that retarded the planting of new crops was as disastrous as one that failed to irrigate all the fields. The levels of a flood were measured from pharaonic times onward by Nilometers strategically placed at crucial points along the river.

The encouragement of immigration by the first two Ptolemies brought many Greeks from the mainland and the coast of Asia Minor, who settled not only in the new city of Alexandria, but also in areas whose capacities for agricultural production were being improved by the monarchs through irrigation and drainage projects. Particularly important were the new lands created by the draining of Lake of Moiris in the natural depression of the Fayyum (Chapter 5). While feeder and drainage canals continued to rely on gravity, as they had in times past, the waterwheel and Archimedean screw were introduced into those plots of land in the Arsinoite nome that lay close to the canals, so that the water could be lifted throughout the year and perennial irrigation be available for gardens, orchards and vineyards. This made the area attractive for settlement by the Greeks who had been soldiers in the army of Ptolemy I, and the land was allotted to them for their lifetime,

Fig. 1.2.1
Egypt.

provided they were willing to serve the king in military and other capacities when need arose. The efforts of individuals in developing the Fayyum at the middle of the third century BC are readily apparent from the papers they left behind: two engineers, Kleon and his successor Theodoros, who worked on the drainage projects, and Zenon, estate manager for the 10,000-*aroura* plot granted to Apollonios, minister of finance for Ptolemy II, in and around the new village of Philadelphia. After the battle of Raphia in 217 BC, the Egyptians who had gained entry into the armed services were also given allotments, although generally smaller in size than those given to Greeks. However, much of the arable land in the Fayyum, and other nearby nomes, remained in the possession of the monarch, and it was leased in relatively small plots to Egyptian peasants, called 'royal farmers'. In Upper Egypt farmlands were often under the control of the great temples, which arranged their cultivation through leases of this so-called 'sacred land' to the local peasantry.

Before the arrival of the Greeks the main cereal grains produced in Egypt were barley and a husked emmer wheat called *olyra*, both of which were pounded down and boiled into porridge or baked into coarse loaves. Both were also made into beer. Greeks introduced the wheat to which they were accustomed, most probably the naked tetraploid hard variety (*Triticum durum*) that yielded a higher grade of flour, and, to Greek tastes, more appetizing breads. This wheat speedily came to be the dominant crop throughout Egypt. Cereal grains constituted a major part of the agricultural production; they were taxed in kind, and surpluses were sold to the benefit of the royal treasury. The early Roman emperors were dependent upon Egyptian wheat for about a third of the supply needed to feed the population of the city of Rome. The early Greek settlers were also accustomed to drinking wine in their homelands, and vineyards soon became a prominent feature of the Arsinoite nome, with surplus quantities sold to wine merchants, licensed by the government, for dispatch to Alexandria and throughout Egypt. Native Egyptian beer continued to be produced, and even tiny farming communities were likely to house at least one brewer, also licensed to brew by the central government. It was only in later antiquity that beer gave way to wine as the national drink. Under the early Ptolemies the traditional oils of Egypt continued to be produced – a type of castor oil, known as *kiki* and extensively used in lamps, and sesame-seed oil for cooking – along with an expansion of the range of oil crops, such as linseed and safflower. Olive cultivation developed rather more slowly, perhaps because olive trees are difficult to establish and require years of maturation before reaching full production. Although olive orchards had been established by Zenon on Apollonios' estate, this third pillar of the Mediterranean diet became a regular feature in the Fayyum only in the early Roman period. New varieties of plants and fruit trees were introduced from different parts of the Mediterranean and the territories Alexander the Great had conquered from the Persians – figs, walnuts, peaches, plums and apricots. Flax, grown mainly for its fibres that were turned into linen, was cultivated on land where water was abundant, and the export of the cloth increased with encouragement from the central government. Fodder crops and lentils were grown in summer months, prior to the new inundation, and various legumes rotated with the cereal grains and flax to replenish soil nutrients. The papyrus plants that grew in the Delta had for millennia provided Egyptians with the raw materials for manufacture of rolls for writing down literature and priestly records, and may have been a royal monopoly in pharaonic times. Under the Ptolemies production for export expanded, so that papyrus rolls became the writing paper of the entire Mediterranean world. Some experiments with new crops succeeded, while others, such as the attempt to grow poppies for oil on Apollonios' estate, did not and were abandoned.

The Ptolemies founded trading posts along the western coast of the Red Sea, although the lion's share of trade with India and the East seems to have remained in Seleucid hands, for their war elephants were of the Indian variety; the Ptolemies, in contrast, were forced to acquire theirs from the Nubian tribe of Blemmyes, living at the southern extremes of Upper Egypt, and trade with sub-Saharan east Africa flourished under the Ptolemies. The Romans soon turned their attention to expanding and exploiting the province's mineral assets, including the fine ornamental stones from quarries in the Eastern Desert that were shipped to Rome to decorate its monumental buildings. The speckled grey-and-white columns of Trajan's Forum and the Pantheon were quarried at Mons Claudianus, and gold, silver, emeralds and turquoise were mined in the region. Under Roman rule Egypt became the main conduit for seaborne trade in products from India – spices, incense, tortoiseshell and pepper (Chapter 10).

The interest of the first Ptolemaic monarchs had been to maximize agricultural and other profits from the land of Egypt while minimizing risk to the royal treasury. This meant that the Greeks whom they appointed to bureaucratic positions displayed keen interest not only in the collection of taxes in money and in kind, but also in the production of saleable commodities and their conveyance to market. What had been largely a redistributive economy in pharaonic times was converted into a market economy, with surpluses available for sale internally and as exports. A silver and bronze currency was introduced, and monetization of transactions became a regular feature, as copies of contracts and leases, loans and repayments, preserved for us on papyrus, make clear. The great mass of their subjects were the Egyptian peasants who cultivated the land and dwelt in the villages. The Ptolemies followed their pharaonic predecessors in fostering the interests of the upper classes of Egyptian society, particularly the priestly elite of the great temples. By casting themselves as successors to the native pharaohs and observers of native traditions, their visits up and down the countryside and their parades of royal power conciliated the Egyptian masses and made it easier for the new rulers to impose their will. The Ptolemies turned a Greek face, however, when dealing with their Greek populations, for the latter expected material rewards and positions of authority within the new regime in return for their support. Greeks remained a minority group within Egypt, even as 'being Greek' was slowly redefined as more a cultural and linguistic phenomenon than an ethnic one, and after a century of Ptolemaic rule, Hellenized Egyptians began to fill posts in the military and the bureaucracy. The individuals of greatest privilege lived in the so-called 'Greek cities' that possessed Greek-style governmental institutions and gymnasia that saw to local affairs: Naukratis, already a Greek enclave and market town in the seventh century BC, and the great Ptolemaic foundations of Alexandria and Ptolemais Hermeiou. By the time of the Roman conquest, the many ethnic groups of Greeks from the mainland, Asia Minor, and the islands, as well as Carians and others, who had advertised their origins in the early years, were ceasing to identify themselves as such – with only the Jewish communities being an exception to the rule, for they continued to be labelled as *Ioudaioi* by themselves and others. To the Romans, the bulk of the population could be considered '(Graeco-) Egyptian', and they lumped the inhabitants of the province into this single category for political and judicial purposes. At the same time, the Romans privileged urban residents above villagers and thus extended the drive toward urbanization that had begun with the early Ptolemies. Egypt became one of the most urbanized areas in the Roman Empire, with perhaps as much as a quarter of its population living in the cities and metropoleis. Papyri from Oxyrhynchos, for example, provide a vivid picture of the urban elite in the Roman and Late Antique periods, as they benefited their community through public works, providing spectacles and service as magistrates. In their private lives, these wealthy landowners leased their rural properties to managers in the villages to subcontract out to individual tenant farmers; as parents they arranged schooling for their children and married their daughters through contracts that stipulated in great detail the dowry of clothing, jewellery, utensils, furniture and slaves; as responsible family members they wrote up wills, giving their sons their share of the family's wealth in the form of property.

Ownership of land was the principal basis of wealth and status throughout antiquity, and by right of conquest and then inheritance Ptolemaic monarchs remained the largest landholders. Traditional forms of tenure by small farmers in Upper Egypt amounted almost to private ownership, while royal grants to Greeks of land in Middle Egypt, intended to insure availability of a fighting force and a source of bureaucratic officials loyal to the regime, were gradually treated as heritable property, and eventually alienable as well. Plots as small as 5 *arouras* (less than 1.4 hectares) dominate the landscape under Roman rule, even at a time when the very wealthiest were accumulating estates as large as 2,000 *arouras*. A family's holdings, even the smallest ones, might be geographically spread, and it made sense to lease out to others isolated plots. Thus a family of modest means might be both lessors and lessees, in order to consolidate their efforts in one area. Families without land of their own had to lease from others or hire themselves out as labourers. Their struggles to avoid poverty are documented in the papers they left behind them, which often show them to be chronically in debt.

In Egyptian history it is normally the powerful and wealthy about whom we are best informed. The description of Cleopatra VII as she sailed up the River Cydnus to meet Mark Antony mirrors the pharaonic image of extravagant expenditure by the ruler of Egypt: her barge was gold-prowed with purple sails, rowed along by silver oars, while she lay beneath a gold-spangled canopy, adorned like Aphrodite. However, the archaeology of village sites, plus the relative abundance of papyri from the Greek and Roman periods, permit us to gain a vivid picture of Egyptian society at a wide variety of economic levels and social statuses, because it was not just the rich who made use of written records for their many activities. There are gaps in our knowledge, for example because very few papyri survive from Alexandria and the Delta, but the inhabitants of Egypt during the thousand years from which papyri in Greek and Egyptian languages have survived are far better known to us than any other group from the ancient world. We know many of their habits and preferences, as well as the harsh mortality functions that kept life expectancy at birth hovering in the mid-twenties, owing largely to the high rate of infant mortality. We are able to tell individual life stories through their own words, and to draw conclusions about the way these men and women led their lives day to day in ways that are better documented and more secure than for other Greeks and Romans.

Bibliography: Bagnall 1993, 1995; Bagnall and Frier 1994; Bowman 1986; Bowman and Rogan 1999; Jackson 2002; Lewis 1983, 1986; Meskell 2002; Rowlandson 1998.

1.3 LANGUAGES AND SCRIPTS

1.3.a Egyptian

Like most of the main languages of the ancient and modern Near East, the native language of Egypt belongs to the group known as Afroasiatic, or Hamito-Semitic, and represents an autonomous branch of this group. In the course of the nearly four millennia of history of the Egyptian language as a medium of communication, significant shifts in phonology, morphology and syntax occurred. The earlier form of the language found in the Pyramid Texts of the Old Kingdom and the Coffin Texts, wisdom literature, tales and hymns of the Middle Kingdom, differs from Egyptian of the Late Period, which saw a blossoming of narrative texts and new genres of entertainment literature such as myths and love poetry, and later the introduction of Christian texts. Dialect differences from the various regions of the country also become evident in the writing of Late Antiquity, mainly in orthographic conventions and sometimes in word-formation and lexicon.

The Egyptian language was represented in a number of different scripts. The earliest and most basic graphic system was the hieroglyphs, or 'sacred incised letters'; it acquired this name only in the Ptolemaic period, to distinguish it from 'demotic', the 'popular writing' system then in common use. Hieroglyphs began to be inscribed on monuments about 3000 BC and continued to be written until their demise in the fourth century AD; the latest-known hieroglyphic inscription is dated AD 394. Hieroglyphs are a variable set of graphemes, ranging from some 1000 signs employed in the Old Kingdom of the third millennium BC to about 750 signs in the classical language of the second millennium, only to increase to many thousands in the Late Period and under Greek and Roman rule. While the hieroglyphs are pictographic signs in that they represent categories of people, gods, animals, parts of the body, plants, buildings, furniture, astronomical entities and so on, they were never organized simply as ideographs in which a picture and its meaning were inevitably the same. Rather, a single sign could represent a sound in one context but in another retain the pictorial meaning, thus combining phonological and semantic principles. In the earlier hieroglyphs a mark that Egyptologists call a determinative stroke was invariably added to indicate when the hieroglyph meant what it pictured. The finding of the so-called Rosetta Stone in 1799 enabled scholars to compare an Egyptian text in hieroglyphs and demotic script with a Greek version that could be read and understood (box 1.3.1). The discovery that the hieroglyphs in which Ptolemaic royal names were written had phonetic values that could be applied to other words led to the full decipherment of the hieroglyphic script.

The normal orientation of Egyptian hieroglyphic writing was from right to left, as Herodotus knew. But symmetry and artistic composition

Cartouches of Ptolemy v on the Rosetta Stone

In Egyptian hieroglyphic writing the primary names of kings and queens were enclosed in ovals representing tied ropes which modern Egyptologists call 'cartouches'. This practice is first attested in Dynasty 4 (*c.* 2600 BC) and continues through the Graeco-Roman period, appearing in some of the latest hieroglyphic texts of the fourth century AD. The Rosetta Stone, found in 1799, was inscribed with versions in hieroglyphic and demotic Egyptian and in Greek of the decree of 196 BC by the Egyptian priesthood in honour of king Ptolemy V (see box 2.6). The cartouches of the king (illustrated here) were instrumental in the early decipherment of hieroglyphs. By 1816 the British researcher Thomas Young had recognized them as enclosures for the royal name 'Ptolemy' (the third, longer, cartouche includes the epithets 'living forever, beloved of Ptah') and correctly identified the phonetic values of five of the hieroglyphs they contained. A cartouche of Cleopatra III on the Bankes obelisk from Philae provided additional clues. Jean-François Champollion built on Young's research to produce his first systematic publication of the decipherment of hieroglyphs in 1822. The highlighting of these cartouches in white against the black background was shown to be the result of modern intervention when a recent cleaning restored the Rosetta Stone, with its inscription, to its natural colour of dark grey with a pink vein. (Parkinson 1999; Quirke and Andrews 1988)

Box 1.3.1
Fig. 1.3.1

could cause the signs to be written in vertical columns, with individual signs turned so that they faced the reader, or even ranged in line from left to right. Aesthetic considerations also governed the placement of hieroglyphs in relation to one another. In order to group signs in balanced rectangles, or ideal squares, flat signs could be placed horizontally, one on top of the other, or vertically, parallel to one another, and all signs could be enlarged or reduced in size.

The painstaking task of drawing the detailed hieroglyphic signs was suitable for walls of temples and tombs. A cursive form of the writing, known as 'hieratic', was also developed. Although hieratic was a direct rendering of the hieroglyphic signs, it was designed to be written quickly, and it employed ligatures to join sequences of signs. Hieratic was more manually suited for writing texts on a roll of papyrus with a brush made of rushes, and so it was used for documents and legal texts, as well as literary productions. In the course of time hieratic script created its own conventions in orthography and grammar, following more closely the language as it was actually being spoken.

During the seventh century BC a new system of cursive writing, called 'demotic', emerged, with vastly simplified versions of the hieroglyphic signs. Demotic was an instrument of the Saite unification of Egypt and an effective tool in the hands of royal officials and priests, who used the script for administrative documents, literature and magic texts. Although Greek gained ground throughout the Ptolemaic period, demotic remained in everyday use until the early Roman period, when it virtually disappeared as a language of business. However, it still flourished until the third century among the Egyptian priesthoods as a literary and scholarly language. In the sanctuary of Philae the last dated text in demotic is from AD 452.

If the upper classes of Egyptian society in the towns and cities had come to use Greek during Ptolemaic and Roman times for everyday purposes, Egyptian persevered as a spoken language among the general populace and was the dominant language throughout the countryside. A new script for Egyptian, 'Coptic', appeared by the end of the third century AD, written in the Greek alphabet with the addition of six

Hieratic script

This example of hieratic script is taken from Papyrus Bremner-Rhind (British Museum EA 10188). Its colophon (scribal label) dates it to 'Year 12 of Alexander, son of Alexander' – the deceased child king Alexander IV – which is 306/5 BC. The papyrus is one of a set of funerary and ritual papyri compiled for a fourth-century BC priest called Nesmin. The text shown here comes from the 'Book of Overthrowing Apophis', a ritual directed against an archetypal enemy of the sun god Re in earlier Egyptian cosmological legend. The elegant script illustrates how hieratic signs adapt and simplify hieroglyphs. (Faulkner 1933; Verhoeven 2001)

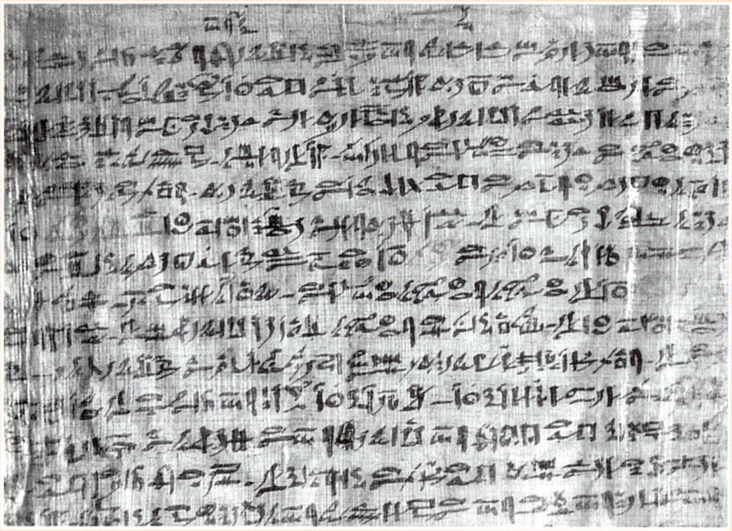

Box 1.3.2

Fig. 1.3.2

or seven signs from demotic to indicate Egyptian phonemes absent from Greek. It developed a range of handwritings closely parallel to those in Greek, from a fast documentary cursive to legible letterhands and uncial bookhands. For the first time in the history of written Egyptian, vowels were regularly written and many loan-words from Greek appear. Much of early Coptic literature is in Sahidic, a standardized literary dialect used throughout the Nile valley. The development of Coptic was closely connected with the Christian church. Translations from Greek originals, including the Bible, Apocrypha and Church Fathers, are common, but within a century a corpus of original Christian literature was taking shape. The other major dialect, Bohairic, representing the spoken language of the west Delta, ultimately came to dominate in the liturgy of the Coptic church. As a spoken language Coptic was gradually superseded by Arabic from the ninth century onward, although it survives to the present day as a liturgical language among Egyptian Christians.

1.3.b Greek

Greeks began to arrive and settle in Egypt in considerable numbers under the first Saite rulers, both as mercenaries and for trade. They brought their language with them, and because most of them hailed from Ionia (now western Turkey) and the nearby islands, the Greek they wrote was a mixture of Ionian and East Greek Doric dialects and letter forms.

The Greek language itself changed considerably after this first wave of settlement. Alexander the Great and his Macedonians spread what had been the dialect of the city of Athens ('Attic' Greek) over the entire eastern Mediterranean and inland to the borders of India. Thereafter, many whose native language was not Greek needed to learn it as the language of government, commerce and socio-economic advancement. While the Greek alphabet and the writing conventions of Hellenistic Greek remained essentially the same as those employed in Attic Greek towards the end of the fifth century BC, phonetic changes ensued in the first in a series of alterations due in part to contact with non-native speakers. In this later Greek called 'Koine', or 'Common' Greek, pitch accent was replaced by stress, the number of vowel sounds was considerably reduced, and many morphological and lexical anomalies disappeared.

Opportunities for a Greek education, particularly in the Roman period, were more plentiful in the towns and cities than in the villages, and parents who could afford private tutoring for their children were more likely to see superior results. The less wealthy might combine together to hire a teacher for a group of children, but education was always privately arranged. Ptolemaic monarchs and Roman emperors provided funds almost exclusively for those who taught advanced pupils. As in

Graffito of 591 BC

Graffito inscribed in 591 BC by Archon, son of Amoibichos, and Peloqos, son of Eudamos, on the leg of a colossus of Ramesses II in front of the great temple at Abu Simbel in Nubia. Other soldiers, likewise in the service of Psammetichos II when he campaigned in Nubia, also inscribed their names in the vicinity (Meiggs and Lewis 1969, 12–13, nos 7a–c, f):

(a) When King Psamatichos came to Elephantine, those who sailed with Psamatichos, son of Theocles, wrote this; and they came above Kerkis as far as the river allowed; and Potasimto had command of those of foreign speech, and Amasis of the Egyptians...
(b) Helesibios from Teos.
(c) Telephos from Ialysos wrote me.
(f) Pabis from Qolophon, with Psammat(ichos).

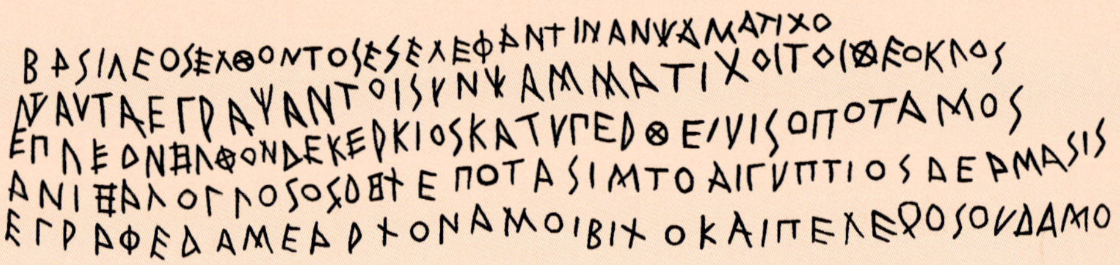

the case of the Egyptian scripts, fast cursives were developed by professional scribes, writing essentially for themselves and their fellows, while carefully articulated 'bookhands' were used for works of Greek literature. The mass of the population was illiterate in Greek, though the ability to write and read the language was expected of the upper classes. The number of literates within the population was low by our standards, but illiterates were not cut off from the daily activities that required reading and writing to the extent they are in modern times, for there seem to have been sufficient literates to assist them.

Box 1.3.3
Fig. 1.3.3

Most Greek writing was essentially without word division (*scriptio continua*), although writers of documents were more likely to articulate names and otherwise format their texts than the scribes copying works of literature. Fashions in the fast cursive and also in bookhands changed over the some thousand years Greek was employed in Egypt.

1.3.c Latin

Under Roman rule there was little pressure to learn Latin, and the number of Latin papyri unearthed in Egypt is many times smaller than those in Greek, and the uses of Latin far more circumscribed. There are a few elegant copies of Latin literary texts and limited evidence for schooling in Latin. A fast cursive also developed for Latin, which was used principally for the wills of Roman citizens, documents dealing with the Roman army and private letters of soldiers and veterans.

Bookhand and cursive script

On the left is an example of a carefully written bookhand from a now-mutilated papyrus roll of Homer's *Iliad* VI (*P.Yale* I 8), probably copied early in the first century AD. On the right are the opening lines of a petition to the epistrategus Vedius Faustus, sent by priests of the Egyptian deity Sokonopis at Narmouthis in AD 160/1; although the name of the epistrategus and his title are carefully articulated, the cursive script in the rest of the text was written very quickly. (*Zeitschrift für Papyrologie und Epigraphik* 134 [2001] 183–90)

Box 1.3.4
Fig. 1.3.4a–b

Bibliography: Braun 1982; James 1991; Loprieno 1995; Meiggs and Lewis 1969; Thomson 1960; Zauzich 1992.

1.4 RELIGION

1.4.a Egyptian religion

When the historian Diodorus the Sicilian visited Egypt around 59 BC, he was stunned by the Egyptian reverence for animals, and the mummification and mourning of them. He says that killing a sacred animal was treated as a capital crime, and that he witnessed the immediate lynching of a Roman ambassador who had accidentally killed a cat. Other ancient outsiders commented negatively on Egyptian 'theriolatry' (animal worship). All Egyptian gods and goddesses had their corresponding animal alter egos, such as Horus and the falcon, Thoth and the baboon, Amun and the ram, Anubis and the jackal. Despite this, Greeks as far back as Herodotus had sought to identify Egyptian deities with Greek equivalents. Aphrodite, for example, was identified and then merged with Hathor and Isis, Zeus with Amun-Re, Hermes with Thoth. There were mixtures and confusions of identities and shapes, and combinations of deities in particular cults.

This syncretism, or fusion, of deities may seem as bewildering to some modern sensibilities as it was to some ancient ones, but the manifest power of the local gods led the incoming Greeks to adopt Egyptian cults as their own. Age-old religious traditions continued to flourish, with their focus on the cycle of death and rebirth as symbolized by sunrise and sunset and the Nile's flood and ebb. The annual inundation, a matter of life and death, was celebrated in a great festival, the *Nileia*. Funerary belief persisted in viewing the afterlife as a perilous journey, needing detailed instructions, which led to a Hall of Judgment where the deceased's heart would be weighed and judged. The soul could remain immortal as long as it had a body in which to dwell, so well into the Roman period mummification was practised by Greeks and Romans as well as Egyptians. Sacred animal corpses were mummified too. The catacombs of the Apis bulls at Saqqara (3.4.b), the cemetery of sacred crocodiles at Tebtunis in the Fayyum (5.4.d), and the cemetery of sacred cats at Boubastis (2.6.c) are well-known examples. Because of the profusion of surviving funerary monuments and materials, it is easy to forget that this was also a religion for the living, with oracles, healing cults, and an ever-expanding calendar of festivals, some lasting weeks, with processions and shows. Egyptian temples were centres of life, not just static buildings (see box 1.6). Guardian deities such as Bes, the dwarf-like protector of mothers and infants, were especially popular.

Whatever the Ptolemies initially thought of Egyptian religion, they quickly recognized the importance of the Egyptian temples and their priests. They granted privileges to both, showed personal reverence to Egyptian deities, and fostered the hybrid cult of the Graeco-Egyptian god Sarapis, in origin a local god of Memphis (Osiris-Apis), as their own patron deity. Although Sarapis was worshipped in Greek style in Alexandria, site of the god's most famous temple, and in Egyptian style at Memphis, he quickly became in some sense a 'national' divinity whose worship spread throughout the Ptolemaic Empire and thence the Mediterranean world. Often identified with Zeus or Pluto, the Greek god of the Underworld, Sarapis had associations with fertility and was traditionally represented wearing a headdress of a basket (*kalathos*) with ears of grain.

For the ideological unity of Ptolemaic rule in Egypt, it was important that from the beginning the Ptolemies, though foreigners, were portrayed as pharaohs, and therefore recognized as divine according to Egyptian practice: they were living incarnations of the god Horus, son of Amun-Re. The kings were also honoured as gods in a dynastic cult of Hellenistic inspiration which generated its own special cult names such as *Soter* (Saviour)

Fig. 1.4.1
Stucco mummy of Artemidoros, Hawara, second century AD (British Museum EA 21810).

Fig. 1.4.2
The god Bes, terracotta figurine (British Museum EA 22378).

and *Euergetes* (Benefactor), eponymous priesthoods, and ceremonies, especially in the Greek cities of Alexandria and Ptolemais. A striking example is the institution by Ptolemy II of a regular festival ostensibly to honour his father Ptolemy I, but also to buttress his own claims to power. Called the Ptolemaieia, it was first held with extraordinary pageantry in Alexandria in 279/8 BC. The intended audience seems to have been the whole Greek world, for all the Greek cities were invited. There were grand processions with exotic animals, sacrifices, banquets, games and athletic and musical contests, lasting perhaps a full month.

Around 268 BC, after the death of his sister-wife Arsinoe II, Ptolemy II deified her and established a cult in her honour. Statues of Arsinoe II

Fig. 1.4.3
Bust of Sarapis
(Alexandria, Graeco-Roman Museum 22158).

Fig. 1.4.4
The priest Pasherbastet, first century BC (British Museum EA 34270).

were to be set up in temples throughout the land alongside the already resident deities. The living king and deceased queen came to be worshipped together as 'brother-sister gods'. Arsinoe II and subsequently deified queens were identified with goddesses, most often Aphrodite-Hathor. Normally they received cult with their husbands, but Arsinoe II was treated as an individual deity, and so perhaps much later was Cleopatra VII, whose memory seems to have been worshipped privately by some Egyptians into the fourth century of the Roman period.

When the Roman emperors replaced the Ptolemies as pharaohs, they introduced their own, less spectacular, imperial cult. They also introduced their own divinities, adding yet another layer to the already complex religious amalgam, but there is little evidence for the worship of purely Roman gods in Egypt. The Egyptian temples and priests retained most of their privileges, but the Romans controlled them more closely. Priests had to submit regular inventories (in Greek) of temple personnel and property. Entry to the priesthoods, in theory hereditary and sometimes conferring certain tax advantages, was carefully scrutinized. Candidates for the priesthood had to show priestly descent or prove their knowledge of 'sacred and Egyptian letters'. Priests were circumcised and were meant to shave their heads and wear linen garments. In the Roman period, Egyptian cults became popular throughout the Mediterranean. Above all Isis, goddess of the many names and functions, including fertility and healing, attested in the demotic and Greek hymns in her honour, was worshipped throughout the Roman Empire (including Rome, Pompeii and London). Her cult was one of several 'mystery cults', like the Perso-Syrian cult of Mithras and Christianity, that gained great popularity by offering initiates access to the secrets of the cosmos and hope of a blessed afterlife.

1.4.b Christianity

Despite the strength of its own religious institutions and cults, native and Hellenized, Egypt came early to be associated with Christianity. Tradition held that the Holy Family took refuge in Egypt to escape Herod's persecution, and people from Egypt are among the many listed in Acts 2: 7–12 as present in Jerusalem for Pentecost. Egypt's large Jewish community provided a fertile milieu for Christianity. Coptic tradition attributes the coming of Christianity to Alexandria to St Mark the Evangelist. Papyrus fragments of the New Testament suggest a significant Christian presence in Egypt by the second century, but it is only in the fourth century that Christianity can be shown to have made serious inroads into the countryside. Now the papyri show the existence of churches and an ecclesiastical hierarchy of bishops, priests and deacons, and a shift in naming patterns in which biblical and other Christian personal names come to displace pagan ones.

Also in the fourth century, the monastic movement began to flower from its third-century roots. Early anchoritic monasticism is associated with figures like St Antony and St Paul the Hermit. Its spirit is wonderfully captured in contemporary writings with their vignettes of solitary holy men moving ever deeper into the desert to escape the secular world, often without success as their fans pursued them (Chapter 4). Communal (cenobitic) monasticism is associated with St Pachomios, whose set of rules, in Latin translation, became so influential in the West. The White Monastery across the river from Panopolis was especially famous in the fifth century under its flamboyant head Shenoute (6.5.b). Although paganism showed resilience in both elite and popular circles and Christianization was a gradual process, by the fifth century Egypt had become a Christian land. Even modest villages boasted several churches, and monasteries were ubiquitous. Somewhere behind major controversial events such as the destruction by monks of the temple of Sarapis in Alexandria in AD 391, the lynching of the philosopher Hypatia in AD 415, and Justinian's supposed sixth-century closing of the Temple of Isis on Philae, lurks the true story of the conversion of Egypt to Christianity.

The history of Egyptian Christianity, as told in the literary and patristic sources, also entailed near-constant internal conflict between the 'orthodoxy' promoted from Constantinople, especially as a result of the Council of Chalcedon in AD 451, and regional schisms and heresies: Gnosticism, Meletianism and Arianism in the fourth century, Nestorianism in the fifth, and lasting longest, from the mid-fifth century, Monophysitism, the belief that Christ had but one nature. This led in Alexandria to a dual patriarchate, one Greek Orthodox (later known as Melkite or 'royal'), the other Coptic Orthodox (and monophysite), both lasting beyond the Arab conquest and both claiming descent from St Mark. Coptic Christianity survived and flourished well beyond the conquest, remaining an important factor in Egypt down to the present day. The conversion of Egypt to Islam was even more gradual than its earlier conversion to Christianity, and likewise never complete.

Bibliography: Bagnall 1993: Chapter 8; Bell 1953; Fowden 1993; Frankfurter 1998c; Hölbl 2001b; Pearson and Goehring 1986; Quaegebeur 1988; Rousseau 1985; Thompson 2000; Wilfong 2002; Witt 1971.

1.5 LITERATURE

1.5.a Greek literature in Alexandria

The earliest contacts between Greek literature and Egypt are found in the Homeric poems and Herodotus, in the eighth and fifth centuries BC. The Homeric poets knew Egypt only from hearsay, but Herodotus claimed to have travelled there himself. The Greek cemetery at Memphis, the capital of Egypt before the foundation of Alexandria, has given us the earliest extant Greek book, a private fourth-century copy on papyrus of a poem by Timotheus of Miletus. Once Alexandria was founded, contacts between Egypt and the rest of the Mediterranean world increased, and a common Greek culture developed, which we label 'Hellenistic'.

Thanks to monarchy, Greek culture in the Hellenistic period differed from that of classical Greek city states. Earlier Macedonian kings had patronized the arts by attracting cultural luminaries to their court, but Alexander's successors fostered the arts on an unprecedented scale. Starting with Ptolemy I, who wrote an account of Alexander's conquests, the Ptolemies were in competition with their royal rivals the Antigonids and Seleucids and, later, Attalids. Alexandria attracted stars from all over the Greek world, whom the Ptolemies supported individually with cash, and as a group with tax benefits. They institutionalized support of the arts and sciences by founding the Museum, which was a shrine for the Muses and a support system for educators and literati, providing food for the body, and for the soul in the form of books. The Library associated with the Museum expanded apace, for funds were unlimited (2.1.b).

An author of the early Hellenistic period, Callimachus, originally came from Cyrene. He was employed as a reference librarian in the Museum to draw up *pinakes* or tables of contents of all the books in the Library, but he is most famous for his short poems, which later inspired Roman poets such as Catullus and Horace. A contemporary, Posidippus from Pella in Macedonia, is known for his epigrams, of which over a hundred have recently been found on an early Hellenistic papyrus. Another contemporary was Apollonius Rhodius, who wrote a Homeric-style epic on the voyage of the Argonauts. Bucolic ('pastoral') poetry was composed by Theocritus, who spent some time in Alexandria, while Herodas wrote mimiambs with scenes from Alexandrian everyday life, which survive only on a papyrus from the Roman period. The Septuagint, a translation of the Hebrew Scriptures in Greek, is said to have been made for the Alexandrian Library, although it was more likely made for members of the Jewish community in Alexandria. Another non-Greek contribution to Greek literature was the history of Egypt in Greek written by Manetho, an Egyptian priest, whose chronological framework of dynasties is still used, as in this book. The Ptolemies fostered the sciences, too. They had particular interest in areas of technology useful for warfare, but their engineers also invented many devices with civil potential, albeit mostly not realized in this period. Medicine was also favoured by the Ptolemies, who provided condemned criminals for vivisection, thus promoting advances in anatomy. One of the Museum's librarians, Eratosthenes, calculated the circumference of the earth almost precisely.

An interesting literary figure from the Roman period is Athenaeus from Naukratis, who wrote a lengthy work in the form of dialogues at the dinner table in which the participants display their erudite knowledge on a variety of topics – mostly related to food. His contemporary Claudius Ptolemy compiled a geography of the world and also perfected the astronomical view of the cosmos which survived until Galileo. From astronomy it was an easy step to astrology. Many astrological works preserved in the Byzantine and Arab traditions go back to Alexandrian models.

Bibliography: Aujac 1993; Bagnall 2002; Braund and Wilkins 2000; Collins 2000; Fraser 1972; Hutchinson 1988; Pfeiffer 1968.

1.5.b Demotic literature in Graeco-Roman Egypt

Egyptian literature from the Graeco-Roman period is known to us only through papyri. The Christianization of Egypt cut the cultural ties with the past, so that no Egyptian literature was transmitted the way Greek literature was. Major texts from individual finds include the Demotic Chronicle, the later parts of which read more like a prophecy than a history; a series of stories about magic featuring the high priests of Memphis with Setne, the son of Ramesses II, as the main protagonist; another narrative text featuring the popular king Amasis of the Saite Period; and the Myth of the Eye (daughter) of the Sun, in fact a narrative framework for a series of animal fables. More strictly religious texts include the 'script' for the ritual of embalming the Apis bull at Memphis. Two important wisdom texts, which provide moral instruction like the book of Proverbs in the Old Testament, are also extant. There is even an invective about a shabby harpist, and another against women.

In the late nineteenth century hundreds of demotic manuscripts from the Roman period, together with business documents in Greek and demotic, were found in the houses of their one-time owners, the priests of the Fayyum village of Soknopaiou Nesos. In 1931 thousands of manuscript fragments, in hieroglyphic, hieratic, demotic and Greek, were found crammed into two storage bins on the edge of the sacred precinct in Tebtunis. They may have been discarded from the private libraries of the priests there. The pièce de résistance, in several copies, is an onomasticon containing traditional Egyptian lore in the form of a lexicon followed by a systematic encyclopaedia. Between the lines of the hieratic, text glosses in demotic and sometimes in Greek, for the correct pronunciation of unusual Egyptian words, were added. The demotic material ranges from religious works about the gods and wisdom texts to adventure narratives which, in the Egyptian tradition, involve gods, and also incorporate Greek elements such as Amazons.

Technical literature, such as astrology, astronomy, mathematics, medicine and law, is also represented. The more specifically religious works in hieratic include the so-called Book of the Fayyum, an illustrated 'religious guide' to the Fayyum, which identifies the local cult centres in a unifying regional mythology. Other illustrated texts include Greek herbals, which identify plants by pictures and descriptions to avoid mistakes when gathering them for medical preparations.

Bibliography: Hoffmann 2000; Lichtheim 1980; Van Minnen 1998.

1.5.c Christian, Jewish and pagan writings

Jewish scholars in Alexandria were responsible for translating the Hebrew Scriptures into Greek. They borrowed techniques of reading, such as etymology and allegory, from the Greek interpretation of the text of Homer, to develop the hermeneutical strategies still used in reading the Old Testament. One such exegete from the early first century AD was Philo, whose writings on the Pentateuch blend Greek philosophy, Platonic and Stoic, with traditional Jewish views.

Building on these traditions, some Christians such as Valentinus elaborated allegorical and symbolical readings of the Scriptures, especially of the Gospel of St John, and developed 'Gnostic' systems which typically pit physical, material experience against divine, spiritual experience. Egyptian Gnosticism is illustrated by the Nag Hammadi Library, named after its findspot in Upper Egypt, of early Gnostic texts translated into Coptic in papyrus codices (books) of the fourth century. A special brand of Gnosticism was Manichaeism. Mani founded a new religion in Mesopotamia in the third century, but presented it as an updated version of Christianity. He claimed to be the Paraclete, a New Testament designation for the Holy Spirit. Coptic translations of some of his works, made in Upper Egypt, have been found in Narmouthis in the Fayyum, and more Manichaean literature has been found at Kellis, in the Dakhla Oasis (see box 9.3). However, this kind of dualism of evil and good did not become the dominant form of Christianity in Egypt.

The earliest Christians from Alexandria to leave substantial works, Clement and Origen in the first half of the third century, also adopted allegorical and symbolical readings of the Scriptures. They were lay teachers at the so-called *didaskaleion*, an institution for the instruction of new believers, especially the more educated ones. Clement wrote several works on Christianity as a philosophy. He still grappled with Gnosticism and was at pains to present his 'philosophy' as the true Gnosticism. His successor Origen wrote apologetic and speculative works as well as commentaries on books of the Bible. Origen thought that his views would make Christianity palatable to members of the educated public. Most of his works are preserved only in Latin, because the Eastern Church eventually condemned him and his works for heretical views. The work of another fourth-century biblical commentator from Alexandria, Didymos the Blind, survives mainly on papyrus codices found in a cave near Cairo.

The dominant literary figure of fourth-century Egyptian Christianity was Athanasius, who was Bishop of Alexandria for forty-five years from AD 328. Much of his work is devoted to his defence of the doctrines of the Council of Nicaea (AD 325) and the legitimacy of his episcopate against a host of foes, including the schismatic Meletians, but principally the followers of Arius, whose view of the nature of Christ he condemned. His struggles with emperors and other bishops made him a larger-than-life figure whom succeeding generations venerated and tried to claim for their own causes. His most influential work, however, was the *Life of Antony*, a spiritual biography of an Egyptian hermit, which has inspired ascetics everywhere.

In Late Antiquity Greek philosophy also flourished in Alexandria. The major proponents now often came from Egypt, and some went on to Rome. In the third century Plotinus from Lykopolis founded Neoplatonism; Christians used his theology to underpin theirs. Other philosophers worked on more practical topics such as mathematics and astronomy, among them Hypatia and her father Theon. The alchemist Zosimus of Panopolis (c. AD 300) was a Christian Gnostic. A special blend of pagan theology and philosophy is represented by Hermetism: the Greek 'Hermetic' texts are mainly dialogues between an inspired teacher, often the Egyptian god Thoth, or Hermes in Greek, and a willing pupil.

The Christian ascetic movement also contributed to literature. Pachomios provided rules for the conduct of cenobitic monks, which in a form elaborated after his death became the literary model for Benedict's *Rule*. Shenoute, abbot of the White Monastery, produced the most important extant corpus of original Coptic literature. His writings, which were removed from his monastery in modern times, are now scattered worldwide. They include many homilies in which he addresses his own congregation or the general public, and a substantial collection of letters.

The Coptic martyrologies of later date are often inauthentic, stereotyped and full of gruesome details. The most famous Egyptian martyr was Menas from Alexandria. His martyrology was written in the fifth century in Greek by Cyrus from Panopolis, who, along with fellow Upper Egyptian littérateurs, played a large role in the cultural and political world of Late Antiquity. Many panegyrists, composers of speeches and poems of praise honouring the emperors on special occasions, came from Egypt, including the Latin poet Claudian. A prominent family of pagan philosophers traced its roots to Panopolis as well. The last of the line, the younger Horapollon, wrote a treatise on

Egyptian hieroglyphs and eventually became a Christian. A copy of a petition he wrote was found among the papers of Dioskoros of Aphrodito, a village in Upper Egypt. This sixth-century notary public found the petition in the archives in Antinoopolis, where he spent several years. Dioskoros also tried his hand at writing poems for public occasions. The aesthetic merits of his poems are debatable, but they illuminate the culture of an educated provincial of the period.

Bibliography: Cameron 1965; Dawson 1992; Fournet 1999; MacCoull 1988; Mirecki and BeDuhn 1997; Orlandi 1997; Quasten 1953–2000; Rousseau 1985; Sandmel 1979; Turner and McGuire 1997.

1.6 ARCHITECTURE AND ART

1.6.a Architecture

The most imposing architectural remains of the Graeco-Roman period are temples, notably the new Ptolemaic temples of Horus at Edfu and Hathor at Dendera, and those at Kom Ombo, Esna and Philae (Chapter 8). In building new temples and refurbishing existing ones, despite some innovations, the Ptolemies and Romans followed Egyptian style as it had developed in the New Kingdom and the Late Period. Temple construction continued into the mid-second century AD, and decoration and repairs into the early or mid-third century. Like medieval cathedrals, temples were works in progress, being repaired, extended or adapted over hundreds of years. They were abodes of the gods, places of religious power, but also centres of intellectual, social and economic life.

Normally, a temple was approached by a processional way (*dromos*) lined with statuary, often sphinxes. Its core consisted of its pylon gateway, open-air colonnaded courtyard, and inner sanctum. The entrance pylon, flanked by obelisks and colossal statues, and the courtyard were open to the public. The hypostyle (colonnaded) halls and inner sanctuaries with their shrines, often divided for multiple divine occupants, were closed to the public, but sometimes visible through chapel niches and openings for the submission and receipt of oracles. Characteristic features of late temples were the *pronaos* (a colonnaded hall added to the front of the temple), entrance porches, kiosks (freestanding canopies), and entrance kiosks abutting temple gates. Late temples, unlike their predecessors, tend to be enclosed by a massive outer wall, creating an internal ambulatory around most of the temple proper. Temples were liberally decorated with painted sculptures in relief, often labelled with historically and religiously significant hieroglyphic inscriptions, including cartouches of Ptolemaic royalty and Roman emperors. The relief scenes remained within the Egyptian artistic tradition, portraying priests or pharaohs (Ptolemaic kings, Roman emperors) in procession or performing rituals in the presence of human-shaped, but often animal-headed divinities, and mythological dramas like 'the Triumph of Horus' on the inner face of the enclosing wall at Edfu. Associated with large temple complexes at Edfu, Dendera and Philae were small, specialized temples known as *mammisis* (see box 8.2.1).

In contrast to the temples, city centres became Hellenized and Romanized under Roman rule through the construction of temples in classical style, triumphal arches and colonnades along major streets, and tetrastyla (sets of four honorific columns) to monumentalize important street intersections. The scarce physical remains, supplemented by evidence from the documentary papyri, suggest that cities throughout the province of Egypt were architecturally similar to cities elsewhere in the Roman Empire. They had gymnasia, baths, fountain houses, theatres, odea (roofed 'music halls'), and hippodromes ('race tracks'). The best recorded sites for classical urban architecture are Hermopolis Magna and Antinoopolis, across the Nile from one another in Middle Egypt (6.3). Domestic architecture is best known from houses excavated at Kellis, a village of the Dakhla Oasis in the Western Desert (9.3.c), at Karanis in the Fayyum (5.2), and at Kom el-Dikka in central Alexandria (2.2.d). A considerable amount about houses, their occupancy patterns and tendency to be legally sub-divided into 'shares', sometimes very minute, is known from the documentary papyri. The papyri also yield a vocabulary for the various rooms and other housing components. Archaeology and papyrology also testify to buildings like dovecotes and granaries.

As Christianity gained ground, many temples and their precincts were adapted to other uses. An enormous Roman military camp was built at Luxor in the late third century, for example, while other temples were converted into churches or monasteries, often after periods of abandonment. Some temple precincts, like those at Elephantine and Jeme (Medinet Habu) were filled with the dense housing of Christian villages. Late Antique architecture is best represented by the remains of Coptic churches, whether independent or in monastic complexes. The favoured form of church was the basilica, a shape invented by the Romans for secular buildings. It was an oblong structure, with an internal double colonnade running lengthways to create a large central 'nave' and two narrower side aisles, with a central semicircular apse at the end. Monastic architecture is well illustrated by the four monasteries at Wadi Natrun (albeit largely of later date) and the partly ruined monastery of St Simeon at Aswan: churches, living quarters (two-chambered suites, reminiscent of hermits' cells), kitchens, granaries, dovecotes and towers, in case of attack.

The monumental catacombs in and around Alexandria are architecturally unique. Dating from the late fourth century BC until the second century AD, and perhaps beyond, they attest diverse burial traditions:

Egyptian, Greek, Jewish and Christian. Their layouts are complex and difficult to classify (2.4). They often have striking architectural features, such as the Doric columns in the tombs at Mustapha Pasha. Their immensely varied painted decoration includes richly detailed *trompe l'oeil* paintings of doors, depicting nails, ring handles, locks and keys, on the removable limestone slabs that sealed the individual burial niches (*loculi*). The designers of the catacombs used architectonic paintings

Box 1.6

Life in a temple of the Graeco-Roman period

To a certain degree temples were organized according to local customs, traditions and cult practices, and into three classes according to size and importance. The temple and priesthood of Ptah at Memphis was the chief religious institution of the Ptolemaic state and played an important political and economic role. Ptolemaic temples were often centres of industry, especially textile manufacturing, and animal husbandry.

There were many persons who were attached in service to the local temple, from the high priest, to lesser levels of priesthood, organized into rotating 'tribes', to personnel such as scribes and herdsmen who supported the economic functions of the temple. The priests were distinguished by observance of ritual purity and their knowledge of a canonical group of ancient texts, a list of which is preserved in the temple at Edfu. Each temple also provided local economic and legal functions – it was the place to go for drawing up legal instruments and adjudicating disputes before priestly tribunals. One such dispute over the inheritance of property between a sister-in-law and brother who served in the temple of the god Wepwawet at Asyut in the middle of the second century BC is recorded verbatim on a papyrus now in the British Museum.

One of the novelties in Egyptian temples built during the Graeco-Roman period is that more of the daily cult ritual is recorded on the temple walls, in text and in image. The temple of Horus at Edfu is especially rich in such texts and scenes. This allows scholars to reconstruct temple life and ceremonies in some detail. There were two main types: the daily ritual, which served to guarantee cosmic order in Egypt, of care of the cult statues, performed and witnessed by a select group of priests; and the annual public festivals, which re-enacted the principal mythic narratives. The priests served a variety of functions within the temple and included those who were responsible for cleansing and clothing the cult statue of the local god each day, astronomers who kept watch over the heavens and the timing of annual festivals, and priests who carried the cult image in the sacred processions. The main daily ritual consisted of purifying the temple and preparing food offerings for the cult statues within the temple. The highlight of each day was the singing of a hymn to the god while the chief officiant approached the inner sanctum of the temple in which stood the image of the god. The god was believed to inhabit the statue and was offered myrrh, anointed with unguent, presented with ritual cloths and purified with water before the shrine door was closed once again for the day. Each temple had an 'endowment' of land and animals to provide for the cult activities and the temple staff.

Public festivals were an important part of the life of temples and were times when the public could observe the local ritual. These events also reinforced social and religious ties between temples. The main public festivals at Edfu, lasting from one to fifteen days, were the New Year's festival, which celebrated the rising of the Nile, the Coronation of the Sacred Falcon (Horus), the Festival of Victory of Horus over Seth, and the Festival of the Sacred Marriage, when the goddess Hathor of Dendera visited Edfu. This was one of the most dramatic festivals of the Ptolemaic period, which brought together cults and officials from Dendera to Elephantine. (Alliot 1949–1954; Fairman 1954; Frankfurter 1998c; Thompson 1988) and other devices to transform two-dimensional walls into three-dimensional space and to give the illusion of location above ground: clever changes of colour to suggest shading, engaged columns made to look freestanding, half-shuttered windows looking out upon a simulated blue sky. This 'illusionism' is one of the stylistic hallmarks of the Alexandrian catacombs.

1.6.b Art

The painted decoration in the Alexandrian catacombs reflects both Greek and Egyptianizing traditions and is not limited to architectural motifs. The funerary scenes in the Ptolemaic tombs at Anfushy exemplify Egyptianizing work. The most remarkable paintings in the classical style are those on a large slab from the Saqiya Tomb on display in the Graeco-Roman Museum in Alexandria, which include a landscape scene after which the tomb was named: two oxen turning a waterwheel (*saqiya*), encouraged by a boy playing the pipes; equally naturalistic is the foreground scene of waterfowl in a pond (col. pl. 2.4.3).

However, the most distinctive paintings produced in Graeco-Roman Egypt are the mummy portraits, often associated with the Fayyum because that was where most were first found (col. pls 5.2.3 and 5.5.1). They range in date from the early Roman period to about AD 250. Many of the earlier portraits, with notable examples from burials at Akhmim, were painted on the gesso (plaster) casings of their mummies and were sometimes gilded, like the mummies recently uncovered in the Bahariya Oasis (9.4.b). These 'portraits' in Egyptian style are not veristic representations of the deceased. The later paintings on linen or wooden tablets (imported limewood being especially prevalent for the Hawara portraits), in tempera or encaustic medium (pigments mixed with beeswax and resin, applied, then affixed by heat), are quite different. They strike the viewer as true-to-life portraits of their subjects, even in one case reproducing an unflattering facial tic. These later portraits are also valuable for, and often dated by, the apparently realistic details of hairstyles, clothing and jewellery. Some of the subjects are seen in three-quarters view (a perspective poorly suited to incorporation into a mummy). This characteristic, and the holes found in some of the wooden boards, may indicate that the portraits were meant to be hung on walls in their houses, as Greek- or Roman-style portraits of living persons, perhaps for long periods of time. On the person's death, the portrait could have been trimmed and fitted into the mummy, which was otherwise decorated in Egyptian style. Unfortunately, the mummies associated with most of the Fayyum portraits have been destroyed; the best-known survivor is the mummy of Artemidoros, from Hawara, now in the British Museum (fig 1.4.1).

Coptic-period painting is highly stylized, perhaps from ancient

Egyptian roots or in close association with the style of Byzantine icons. Portraits tend toward stereotypical shapes for facial features; bodies tend to be given in outline; all available space is filled with decorative elements. Surviving art is almost exclusively religious, associated with churches and monasteries. Mural scenes from the Old and New Testaments abound (Adam and Eve, the Virgin and Child), as do representations of Egyptian saints like the warriors George and Theodore. Sculpture is represented by architectural remains such as column capitals, sometimes decorated naturalistically with acanthus and vineleaf scrolls, sometimes geometrically. All sculpture is now relief sculpture in limestone or sandstone; freestanding sculpture was no longer made.

Statues and fragments of statues from Graeco-Roman Egypt come in a variety of styles and stone types – black and green basalt, green basanite, porphyry, schist, marble, granite, calcite and limestone. They can be purely Egyptian, purely Greek or, later, Roman, or hybrids, such as Egyptian with Greek hairstyles and dress, more realistically modelled faces, or 'iconographic' props like the cornucopia. Egyptian-style sculptures tend to be highly stylized and uniform, Greek-style sculptures more varied and realistic. To take the case of the Ptolemaic kings (figs 1.1.1 and 1.1.2), statues in Egyptian style are typically bare-torsoed with a kilt and in a striding posture (male), or in a sheath dress (female), with wigs rather than natural hair, and wearing the distinctive Egyptian crown or *nemes* headdress with one or two uraei (cobras). Faces may show some apparently individualized features, including artificial beards, but these tend to be traditional and stylized rather than realistic. Greek-style statues have more natural poses and individualized, though not necessarily veristic, faces and hair. Since the statues are rarely identified by inscriptions, identifications as this or that Ptolemy or Cleopatra are often controversial. The picture is further complicated by deliberate imitation; for instance, Cleopatra VII took Arsinoe II as her model.

Statues of gods and goddesses, whether oversize or in miniature, are much more easily identifiable, especially when they appear in hybrid animal-human form. The goddess Isis can be identified by the distinctive central knot of her tunic, and her crown of a solar disc between horns topped by feathers; she may hold a *situla* (special jar) for sacred Nile water in one hand with a serpent wrapped around the other, and rest her foot upon a crocodile. Sarapis is usually depicted as a bearded Zeus with long hair in sumptuous curls, crowned with a grain basket. The popular Bes, protector of mothers and infants, is depicted as a grimacing, bearded dwarf, sometimes naked and squatting, or crowned with feathers, or sword and shield in hand. Some divinities are regularly portrayed in pairs, such as Sarapis and Isis, or Isis nursing the infant Horus (Harpokrates), or in threes, such as Sarapis, Isis and Harpokrates.

Fig. 1.6.1
Isis nursing Horus, bronze statuette (British Museum EA 60756)

Museum collections contain an amazing variety of other artefacts: inscribed temple and funerary reliefs; pottery; coins; glassware; statuettes of gods, worshippers and animals carved in wood or made from terracotta, faience (glazed quartz frit), or bronze; jewellery, especially gold rings, earrings, bracelets and necklaces, sometimes inset with semi-precious stones. Objects of little artistic merit are valuable for the impression they convey about daily life: oil lamps made from terracotta and glass; children's toys; bronze mirrors; models of houses, boats, temples and altars; agricultural implements (winnowing shovels, sickles, pitchforks); doors and doorlocks; tables and reading stands; toiletries (combs, hair pins, kohl sticks); baskets; spindles, whorls, crochet hooks, sewing needles; boxed pairs of dice; writing materials and products (pens, inkpots, papyri, ostraka, tablets).

Alexandria was famous for its glassware in antiquity. Some techniques were ancient, like pouring hot glass around moulds. The art of glassblowing, apparently introduced into Egypt from Phoenicia at the end of the Ptolemaic period, revolutionized manufacture. Products of Egyptian glassmaking include perfume vials, flasks, pitchers, cups, basins, plates and mosaic tiles, in a wide variety of colours. Even in fragments, the fineness and colour of millefiori objects still impress.

Egyptian pottery was mostly produced for everyday use, to provide storage or transport containers, and tends to be artistically undistinguished. The cooking pots, amphoras, cups, vases and storage jars are infrequently decorated. Occasionally they were painted with simple floral or geometric motifs. The potsherds (ostraka) from the inevitably frequent breakages furnished an ubiquitous and free medium for brief written records, especially tax receipts.

Coptic art is especially famous for its decorated linen and woollen textiles, which probably served originally as wall hangings, before deposition with corpses in cemeteries like those at Akhmim and Antinoopolis (col. pl. 1.6.2). Coptic arts and crafts also include highly skilled minor productions of metal- and woodwork, glassware and decorated ceramics, including the well-known St Menas bottles from Abu Mina (4.3.a).

Bibliography: Alston 2002; Badaway 1978; Bailey 1990; du Bourguet 1991; Doxiadis 1995; Gazda 1983; Grossmann 2002; Hawass 2000; Thomas 2000; Walker and Bierbrier 1997; Walker and Higgs 2001; Watterson 1988; Wilfong 1997; Wilkinson 2000; Willems and Clarysse 2000.

1.7 TOURISM IN ANTIQUITY

To the Greeks of the seventh century BC Egypt was a land of great antiquity and riches, and after the founding of Naukratis (2.6.6), Greek merchants and mercenaries frequented Egypt in ever-increasing numbers. The historian Herodotus of Halicarnassus claimed to have visited the Memphis area, Thebes and Elephantine in the mid-fifth century BC, and wrote at length about Egypt and its customs in his *Histories*, because 'Egypt has more wonders than any country in the world and more works beyond description than anywhere else'. Much of the information in Herodotus seems to derive ultimately from Egyptian priests. Occasional mentions of an interpreter might indicate a nascent tourist industry catering to foreign visitors.

Alexander the Great's conquest opened Egypt to Greek intellectuals. Hecataeus of Abdera (*c.* 360–290 BC), who went up the Nile to Thebes and saw the mortuary temple of Ramesses II, in his lost work (*Aegyptiaca*) gave a Greek paraphrase of the inscription behind Keats' 'I am Ozymandias, King of Kings'. Eratosthenes of Cyrene (*c.* 285–194

Letter regarding the visit of a Roman senator in 112 BC

To Asklepiades. Lucius Memmius, a Roman senator, who occupies a position of great dignity and honour, is making the voyage from Alexandria to the Arsinoite nome to see the sights. Let him be received with special magnificence, and take care that at the proper spots the guest-chambers be prepared and the landing-places to them be got ready with great care, and that the gifts of hospitality mentioned below be presented to him at the landing-place, and that the furniture of the chamber, the customary bites of food for Petesouchos [the crocodile god] and the crocodiles, the necessaries for the view of the Labyrinth, and the victims to be offered and the supply for the sacrifices be properly managed; in general take the utmost pains in everything that the visitor may be satisfied. . .

(Bagnall and Derow 2004: 118 no. 69)

Box 1.7.1

BC), head of the Alexandrian Library when he wrote his lost *Geographica*, introduced more precise descriptions and more accurate measurement of distances.

Romans also visited Egypt, beginning with embassies to the Ptolemaic kings. Julius Caesar spent several months in 48/7 BC in the vicinity of Alexandria and took a Nile cruise with Cleopatra. Strabo's *Geography* provides our most complete description of the city of Alexandria. Strabo also journeyed up the Nile with the prefect Aelius Gallus (26–24 BC) as far as Philae and into Ethiopia, and at Thebes heard the cry made by the so-called Colossus of Memnon (7.3). In AD 19 Augustus' great-nephew Germanicus began his tour by greeting crowds in Alexandria and visiting the pleasure resort of Canopus. He then sailed up the Nile to Elephantine and Syene, stopping at Memphis and the pyramids, the Fayyum and Thebes. The emperor Hadrian's tour of the provinces brought him to Pelousion in AD 130. He spent some six months in Egypt, visiting Alexandria and the Libyan Desert before journeying up-river with his wife Sabina and their extensive entourages. No other emperor visited until Septimius Severus spent a portion of AD 199 in Alexandria and apparently also on the Nile journey to Philae.

Less important visitors also commemorated their visits. Hermogenes of Amaseia carved a graffito about his personal inspection of the Colossus of Memnon, claiming he was overcome with wonder, for the statue was even more splendid than the tombs in the Valley of the Kings. More than 2000 graffiti were found there, although Tomb 9, said to be the tomb of Memnon, contains nearly half of them. The temple of Hatshepsut was the destination of pilgrims searching for a cure or an oracle from Imhotep-Asklepios, the syncretistic healing deity of the shrine from the third century BC to the fifth century AD, when the temple was converted into a Coptic monastery. Although many graffi-

An epigram by Julia Balbilla

This is one of four poems Julia Balbilla wrote to commemorate the visit of Hadrian and his empress Sabina to Thebes in November AD 130. Her poems were carved on the left leg of the Colossus of Memnon.

Yesterday Memnon was silent as he received the wife,
in order that the fair Sabina would return here,
for the exquisite beauty of our queen pleases you.
At her arrival you uttered your divine cry,
lest our Emperor be angry with you; for too long a time in your boldness
you constrained his holy and legitimate wife.
And Memnon, terrified of the power of great Hadrian
suddenly cried out, and she, hearing, was pleased.

(Bernand and Bernand 1960: 93–6, no. 30)

Box 1.7.2

ti were inscribed by visitors resident in adjacent areas, a few came from further afield (7.3.a).

The Western tourists who visited Egypt in the centuries after the Arab conquest were mostly Christian pilgrims like those of Late Antiquity (Chapter 4), eager to trace the travels of the Holy Family. The establishment of Ottoman rule (1517) saw an increase in antiquarian tourism, as collectors began to carry back to European homelands mummies and manuscripts. Scholars also arrived: the English astronomer John Greaves, who spent time at Giza in 1638–9 measuring the pyramids and consulting medieval Arabic sources in addition to ancient Greek authors; the French Jesuit Claude Sicard (1677–1726), who reached Upper Egypt, identifying the site of Thebes, Memnon, and Valley of the Kings on the basis of ancient descriptions; the Dane Frederik Norden (1708–42), whose account of his travels in Egypt, lavishly illustrated, enjoyed considerable popularity. Nonetheless, it was the impetus of another military invasion that marked the beginning of Egypt as a tourist destination for the modern world. Napoleon

A visitor to the Colossus of Memnon

The Roman Celer, apparently strategus of the Ombite nome, visited the Colossus of Memnon for the first time on 30 June 123 at about 6 a.m., claiming in his graffito that 'he had come to see the sites and to pay reverence'. Because he heard no cry from Memnon, he came again two days later and was rewarded with the 'sound of the god' (*SB* V 8339). Celer also made the pilgrimage to Imhotep-Asklepios, inscribing the fact that 'Celer the strategus made obeisance *(proskynema)* together with his children' (Bataille 1951: 84, no. 124). Only the name of the first child is preserved, Archibias.

Box 1.7.3

Napoleonic graffiti

Napoleon's soldiers also carved graffiti on monuments. In a chamber up in the west pylon of the Ptolemaic temple at Edfu, Corporal Poudrat left a remembrance of his guard duty there on 8 May 1799, despite the fact that he forgot to record the name of his home town. (Brégeon 1991: 624)

Box 1.7.4
Fig. 1.7.1

Bonaparte's occupation of Egypt was short-lived (July 1798 to September 1801), but the cohorts of scientists, technicians, writers and artists who accompanied him, his Commission for Arts and Sciences of the Army of the Orient, quickly set to work, eventually expanding their activities to include the whole of Egypt. Despite military setbacks and the departure of Napoleon, the Commission continued their work, and its creation, the magnificent volumes of the *Description de l'Égypte*, were published between 1809 and 1826. The illustrations provided a permanent record of the antiquities as they found them.

Egyptomania quickly pervaded England and the Continent, and those who could travel to Egypt did so, as the trickle of tourists became a flood. In the letter Gustave Flaubert posted to his mother from Esna on 26 April 1850, he observed:

> We stop at all the ruins. We tie up the boat and go ashore. There is always some temple buried to its shoulders in the sand, partially visible, like an old dug-up skeleton. Gods with heads of ibises and crocodiles are painted on walls white with the droppings of the birds of prey that nest between the stones. We walk among the columns, ... we stir up the old dust... (quoted in Foertmeyer 1989: 1)

Bibliography: Anderson and Fawzy 1987; Baines and Malek 2000; Bataille 1951; Beaucour 1990; Bernand and Bernand 1960; Bowersock 1984; Brégeon 1991; Foertmeyer 1989; Lloyd 1975; Raymond 2000.

2 ALEXANDRIA, THE DELTA AND NORTHERN SINAI

2.1 HISTORY OF THE SITE

2.1.a Introduction

Alexandria was by far the largest and most important city in the eastern Mediterranean, politically, culturally and economically, from the third century BC until Late Antiquity, when it was rivalled and politically overshadowed by Constantinople. Tradition dates its foundation by Alexander the Great to 7 April 331 BC. Its Egyptian name was Rakote, 'Construction (site)'; this may indicate that Alexandria was built on an existing settlement. The name remained attached to an area in the south of the metropolis, which remained an enclave of the native Egyptian inhabitants of the city. After an initial period with the seat of government at Memphis, by about 320 BC Alexandria had become the capital of the new Ptolemaic state, with a privileged and exclusive Greek citizen population and an 'autonomous' civic administration modelled on the institutions of the Greek city-state (*polis*), particularly Athens. It was endowed with a dependent territory in the Delta but lay outside the Nile Valley proper and was never quite integrally Egyptian. For the whole of the period when the country was under Ptolemaic, Roman and Byzantine domination, Alexandria looked both outwards towards Greece and the Mediterranean and inwards towards Egypt.

At its peak the population of Alexandria may have reached 500,000, mainly descendants of settlers originally drawn from Greece, the Aegean Islands, Asia Minor, Thrace, Macedonia, Persia, Syria and Judaea. The city was divided into five quarters designated by the first five letters of the Greek alphabet. By the early Roman period one of them (Delta) and a substantial part of another (Beta) were occupied by the large Jewish community established there in Ptolemaic times. The privileges of the Greek citizen body were jealously guarded, and alleged attempts to encroach on them by members of the Jewish population led to tension and violence between the two communities in the first century AD. In any case, the Alexandrian populace had from Ptolemaic times earned a reputation for volatility and violence which was periodically manifested throughout the Roman period.

Alexandria was the most important commercial centre in the eastern Mediterranean. This position it owed in part to its natural advantages. There were two magnificent harbours, the Great Harbour to the east and the Eunostus ('Harbour of Fortunate

Return') to the west, with a smaller, artificially excavated harbour (Kibotos) to its rear. The two main harbours were divided by a dyke (the Heptastadion) which linked the mainland to the Island of Pharos, on which stood the famous lighthouse. The area between the ancient coastline and the island, where the dyke was constructed, has been completely silted up in the course of the modern period. The harbours accommodated an immense amount of maritime trade with the Mediterranean and also made Alexandria a major centre of the shipbuilding industry. To the south of the city, Lake Mareotis, which itself had an important and thriving port on its southern shore (2.5.b), was linked by canals to the Canopic branch of the Nile, giving access to the river valley. Alexandria was thus in a good position to avail herself of as much of Egypt's domestic produce as she required – the large-scale transport of grain from the valley was an essential constituent of the city's own food supply, as well as that of Rome – and the Nile also linked her, through the entrepôt of Koptos, to the ports of the Red Sea coast and a network of trading

Fig. 2.1.1 The city of Alexandria (after McKenzie 2003: 42–3).

relations with India and Arabia (Chapter 10). Spices, perfumes, precious stones and other luxury goods found their way to Alexandria where manufacturing, processing and marketing facilities developed, alongside the artisanal crafts and industries which were based on indigenous products such as papyrus, glass and textiles. Alexandria was also known in the eastern Mediterranean for its production of works of art: jewellery, mosaics and sculpture are particularly prominent.

Bibliography: Bernand 1998; Bowman 1996; Fraser 1972; Haas 1997; Sly 1996.

2.1.b Cultural institutions

There was no intellectual and cultural activity in which Alexandria did not play a significant role, and in several spheres her role was paramount. The basis of this eminence was the foundation in the early Ptolemaic period of the Museum and the Great Library in the Royal Quarter (Brucheion) which rapidly became a focus of creative and scholarly literary work and of scientific discovery in almost all fields – mathematics, mechanics, physics, astronomy, geography and many more. The reputation of Alexandria's medical school as the best was established in the third century BC and endured until Late Antiquity; the most famous physician of classical antiquity, Galen of Pergamon, received training there in the second century AD. In the later Ptolemaic period, the foundation of a great philosophical tradition was laid (particularly after the Romans sacked Athens in the mid-80s BC and forced many philosophers to flee), which was to make Alexandria the centre of Platonist and Aristotelian philosophy from the first century AD onwards. This in turn was an important influence on the development of Christianity in the later period, as Christian theology became more heavily intertwined with Platonist thinking. Alexandria's importance in the history of Christianity is by no means confined to intellectual and theological developments, but the early history of the Alexandrian church is obscure and its foundation by St Mark a matter of legend (1.4.b). Alexandria was a centre of Christian speculative thought and of theological controversy throughout Late Antiquity.

2.1.c Physical development

The physical development of the city can be sketched in outline from written sources. The planning and layout of the city in the foundation period are attributed to Deinokrates of Rhodes, the most famous architect of his day. It was based on a rectilinear grid of streets with encircling walls on three sides and to the south the Mahmoudiyeh Canal (Canal of Alexandria), which runs parallel with the shore of Lake

The Library of Alexandria

The early Ptolemies created the largest library the ancient world ever saw with an aggressive book-buying programme during the third century BC. A number of important literary figures headed or worked in the Library, but we know remarkably little about it otherwise. Most of the information transmitted about it by ancient sources comes from a Hellenistic Jewish writer pseudonymously calling himself Aristaeus, who tells a story about the creation of the Greek translation of the Hebrew scriptures under a commission from Ptolemy II. Supposedly, Ptolemy's librarian, Demetrios of Phaleron, was directed to get these scriptures for the Library. The story is apocryphal, and there is no warrant for the enormous figures (500,000 to 700,000 volumes) usually given for the Library's size. It had a branch in the Serapeum (2.2.b). What became of the Great Library is unknown; everyone from Julius Caesar to the Arab conqueror Amr has been blamed for its destruction, but probably it largely disintegrated from neglect over the centuries. The palace quarter, where it was located, suffered severely in 272 (cf. below), and whatever remained may have been destroyed at that time. (Bagnall 2002)

Mareotis. We have almost no information about the construction and early history of the imposing Ptolemaic buildings such as the Museum and the Library in the Royal Palace quarter and the Serapeum. The most detailed and vivid description of the physical appearance of Alexandria comes from the geographer and historian Strabo, who visited Egypt during the 20s BC, in the entourage of Aelius Gallus, one of the first Roman governors of Egypt. He describes the two main arterial streets, the public precincts and the royal palaces covering a quarter or a third of the city, the harbour and the Tomb of Alexander (the Sema or Soma), whose body was hijacked by Ptolemy I and brought to Alexandria when it became his capital. After his description of the harbour and its surrounding buildings – theatre, temple of Poseidon, Caesareum, Emporium, warehouses and ship-houses – he goes on to refer to the Necropolis, the Serapeum, amphitheatre, stadium and gymnasium, which had porticoes over a stade (c. 175 m) in length. He perhaps could not have seen the Caesareum in its completed state, but the Alexandrian Jewish philosopher Philo (*fl.* c. AD 40) describes it as 'decorated on an unparalleled scale . . . surrounded by a girdle of pictures and statues in silver and gold, forming a precinct of enormous breadth, embellished with porticoes, libraries, chambers, groves, gateways, broadwalks and courts'.

Box 2.1

On several occasions in antiquity various of the major buildings in the city suffered severe damage. Caesar's siege of the city in support of Cleopatra VII (48 BC) resulted in the destruction of some of the warehouses or buildings in which books were stored. Violence and the destruction of buildings occurred on the occasion of Caracalla's visit in AD 215, and the Ptolemaic palace complex (Brucheion) was severely damaged or destroyed when Aurelian recovered the city from Palmyrene domination in AD 272. The emperor Diocletian besieged the city in AD 297/8 to recover it from the control of the rebel L. Domitius Domitianus and vowed to slaughter the populace until the rivers of blood reached the knees of his horse; the threat was mitigated by the fact that his horse stumbled as he entered the city, and the grateful Alexandrians are said to have erected a statue of the horse.

The advent of Christianity gradually transformed the appearance of the city. Many of the pagan temples survived and remained in use through most of the fourth century, as did the theatre, amphitheatre, Serapeum and agora. A twelfth-century chronicle, which probably refers to the state of the city in the fourth century AD, describes it as containing 2478 temples, 6152 courts, 24,296 houses (though this may refer to housing units rather than blocks), 1561 baths, 845 taverns and 456 porticoes. It does not mention churches, but the evidence of Athanasius and Epiphanius produces the names of twelve churches in existence by c. AD 375 and there were undoubtedly others as well. Of these, the only one thought to have been built on a former temple site was the Church of St Michael, a new construction within the enclosure of the former Caesareum. During the patriarchate of Theophilus (AD 385–412), the emperor Theodosius I allowed the demolition of pagan temples, and by AD 412 another eight churches had been built.

Alexandria capitulated to the invading Arab army led by the general Amr ibn el-As in the autumn of AD 641, and a treaty was concluded with the Chalcedonian patriarch Cyrus. By the end of September AD 642 the remnants of the Byzantine forces had evacuated the city. The victorious Arabs were stunned by the physical splendour of the city. Amr is said to have written to the Caliph claiming, with obvious exaggeration, to have captured a city containing 4000 palaces, 4000 baths, 400 theatres, 12,000 sellers of green vegetables and 40,000 tributary Jews. They were also impressed by the grandeur of the marble on the pavements, buildings and columns and by the extensive network of underground cisterns for fresh water fed by conduits from the Nile canal. The Pharos lighthouse, built in the third century BC by the architect Sostratos of Knidos, was a particular source of admiration. It consisted of four storeys, the first (ground level) square, the second octagonal, the third circular and the fourth containing a fire and a mirror or reflecting mechanism which projected the image of the flames far out to sea. Within a century of the Arab conquest, the Pharos had been severely damaged, and by the end of the fourteenth century all but the ground level had been demolished. The site on which it stood, at the end of the causeway (Heptastadion) dividing the harbours, is now named after Fort Qait Bey, constructed on what remained of the Pharos in the fifteenth century. Recent underwater explorations by French archaeologists have focussed on this area, which certainly contains fallen building blocks from the lighthouse.

2.1.d Archaeological exploration

There was some modern awareness of the surviving antiquities of Alexandria before the Napoleonic expedition to Egypt. The attention of travellers was largely drawn to the conspicuous monuments such as 'Pompey's Pillar' (at the Serapeum, see 2.2.b, fig. 2.1.2), and the obelisks called Cleopatra's Needles. Other items were added as a result of the expedition and the illustrations produced for the *Description de l'Egypte* (1.7), including the 'Roman Tower' which must have been part of the Caesareum, three granite columns to the south of the mosque named after St Athanasius, an impressive circus or hippodrome situated to the south-west of 'Pompey's Pillar', and the Great Catacomb at Wardian. But proper study of the archaeology of ancient Alexandria only began in 1866 following the publication of a reconstructed ancient street plan, with a descriptive text, by Mahmoud Bey el-Falaki, who was astronomer to the Khedive Ismail. All modern study of the topography of Alexandria is based on this map, plotted on the basis of surviving traces of pavements and colonnades and identifying the two main axial streets along the line of the modern Sharia el-Horreya, the ancient Canopic Street, running from the Moon Gate in the west to the Sun Gate in the east, and the line of the Sharia Nabi Danial, running north to south. The evidence which Mahmoud Bey found was from the Roman period, and later excavations have confirmed the basic layout and revealed small stretches of streets which go back to the Ptolemaic period, proving that the grid plan was in existence then. By the 1870s Tassos D. Néroutsos was aware of the possibilities of further extensive and important archaeological finds under the modern city and also of the fact that the Graeco-Roman city was being ignored by the Egyptian government to the particular detriment of the state of the catacombs in the western necropolis. 'Cleopatra's Needles', the obelisks which stood in front of the Caesareum, left Alexandria soon after that. The one presented to the British Government by Muhammed Ali in 1819 was finally shipped in 1877/8 to its site on the Embankment in London, and the one given to New York to commemorate the building of the Suez Canal was sent in 1879/80 and erected in Central Park.

The acceleration of archaeological investigation and systematization of knowledge began with the foundation of the Graeco-Roman Museum in 1892, followed by the establishment of the Archaeological Society in 1893. The first three directors of the Museum, all Italian scholars, assembled the core of the collection and initiated the most productive period of exploration and publication of the Alexandrian catacombs: G. Botti (1892–1903), E. Breccia (1904–31) and A. Adriani (1932–40 and 1948–52). Adriani's *Repertorio* remains the fullest account of the archaeological sites and artefacts of Alexandria known up to the mid-1960s. Since that time, the most conspicuous systematic archaeo-

Fig. 2.1.2
Diocletian's column
c. 1800 (*Description de l'Egypte* v 34.1).

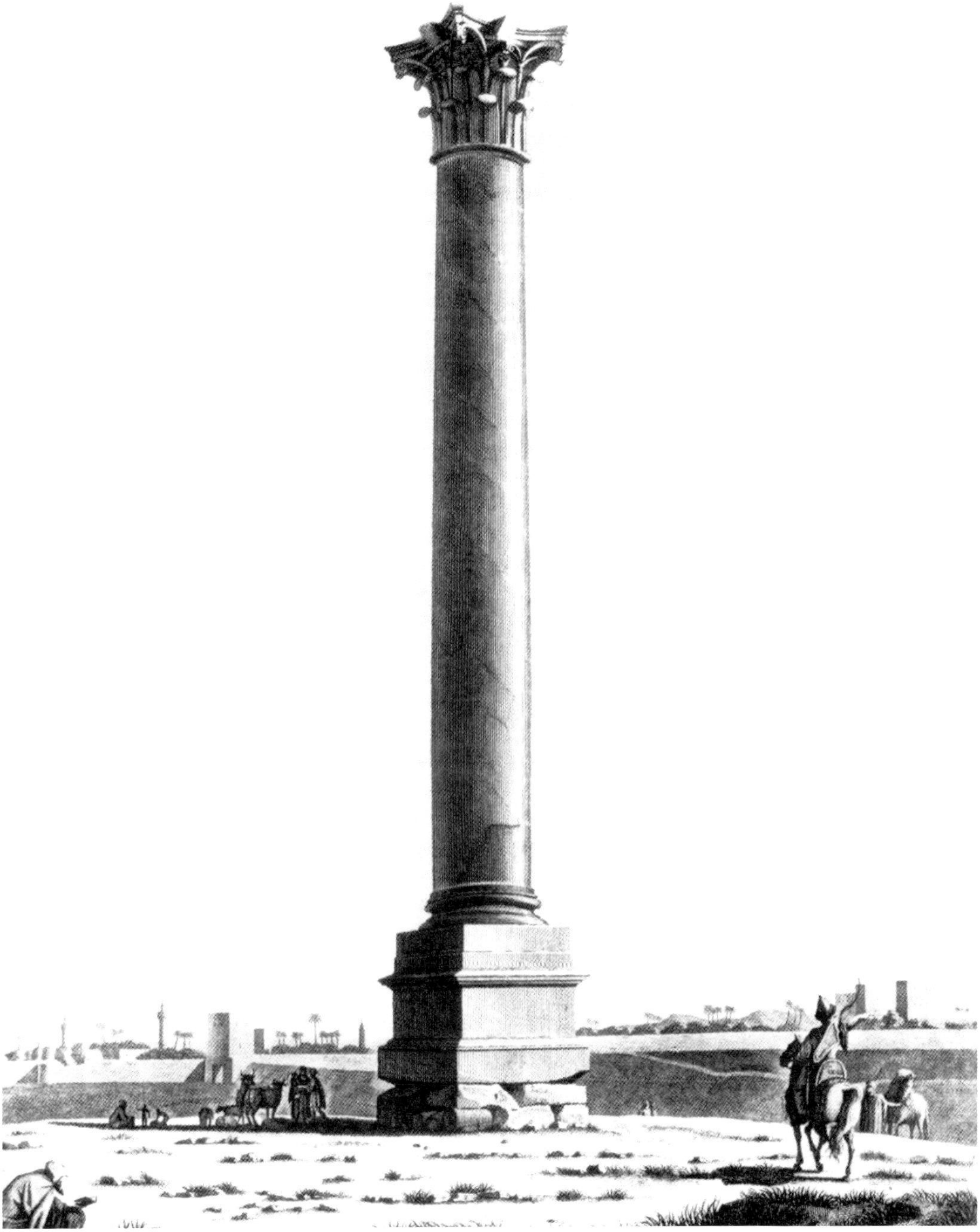

logical excavations undertaken in Alexandria have been those conducted by the successive Polish missions at Kom el-Dikka, beginning in 1960, and the underwater excavations in the Great Harbour by two separate teams of French archaeologists. One of these has also established the Centre d'Études Alexandrines (CEA) which has undertaken a number of rescue excavations in the city.

The archaeological picture as a whole is not very encouraging, as is inevitable when the ancient city lies buried beneath a great modern one. There have been significant changes in the coastline since antiquity and some of the features formerly on land are now submerged. The ancient shoreline of the island on which the lighthouse (Pharos) stood also differs from the present line but has not been accurately established. Extensive submerged harbour works were recorded early in the twentieth century. Recent underwater explorations have revealed remains of a timber jetty dating to before the foundation of Alexandria. The Heptastadion, the artificial dyke which connected the mainland to the island in ancient times, is now completely silted up, but remote sensing by archaeologists at the CEA has shown that the causeway was integrated into the ancient street grid. The recent underwater explorations in this area have also yielded a considerable amount of statuary, including an Isis figure now erected in the Serapeum Gardens (one of a pair; the other stands in front of the new Library of Alexandria), a number of sphinxes and many fragments of architectural columns in the classical style. Another team has explored harbour areas which were originally part of the Royal Quarter and the palaces, although the claim to have specifically identified 'Cleopatra's Palace' is difficult to prove beyond doubt. Of at least equal significance, though less dramatic, are the discoveries in the harbour of about forty wrecks, of which two have been explored in some detail, one Rhodian of the third century BC, one Italian of the first century BC.

Bibliography: Empereur 1998a, 1998b; Frost 1975; Goddio 1998; Hesse 2002; McKenzie 2003; Tkaczow 1993.

2.2 THE VISIBLE SIGHTS

2.2.a Outlines of the city

Of the city walls, only sections of the eastern sector originally identified by Breccia seem relatively secure. The great palaces and monumental buildings of the Royal Quarter lay directly to the south of the Great Harbour and were connected to it. Strabo describes this as having constituted a quarter or a third of the whole area of the ancient city, a district of beautiful palaces and public precincts augmented by successive monarchs, including the Museum and the Tomb of Alexander the Great (the Sema, 'tomb', or in some versions the Soma, 'body'), the exact location of which has proved elusive. The part of the modern city to which it corresponds is the area east of the Cecil Hotel from the Metropole Hotel, opposite Ramleh Station, to the Silsila promontory (ancient Cape Lochias) on which the new Library of Alexandria now stands. No remains of the palaces have been discovered *in situ* on dry land, but there are significant finds of foundations of a monumental building of the third century BC and foundation plaques of a temple dedicated to Harpokrates by Ptolemy IV and Arsinoe III (221–205 BC).

Fig. 2.2.1 Foundation plaque of temple of Harpokrates (Alexandria, Graeco-Roman Museum P8357).

More numerous are the remains of high-quality mosaic floors from banqueting rooms of urban residences, built in classical architectural style, of the third and second centuries BC. Several of these mosaics can be seen in the Graeco-Roman Museum (2.3). A rescue excavation conducted by the CEA at the site of the Diana Cinema discovered a house of the second century BC with a Medusa mosaic in the dining room (now in the National Museum), and glass workshops. Another at the former British Consulate revealed a house with a *triclinium* and pebble mosaics, of which the earliest traces may go back to the first settlers. The remains of the Caesareum described by Philo (see above), in front of which 'Cleopatra's Needles' originally stood, were visible to the Napoleonic scholars but have now disappeared. A CEA rescue excavation beneath the Majestic Cinema at Saphia Zaghloul St revealed probable remains of the Caesareum, and another at the site of the Lux Garage discovered walls said to belong to the Caesareum sanctuary. In the Roman period the legionary camp of Nikopolis was constructed near the coast towards the east; this is now an inaccessible military area.

2.2.b The great **Serapeum** (Temple of Sarapis) was one of the most important monuments of ancient Alexandria, a focus for the cult of the god Sarapis, which eventually became popular all over Egypt and the Mediterranean. The cult had its early Ptolemaic origin in the need to

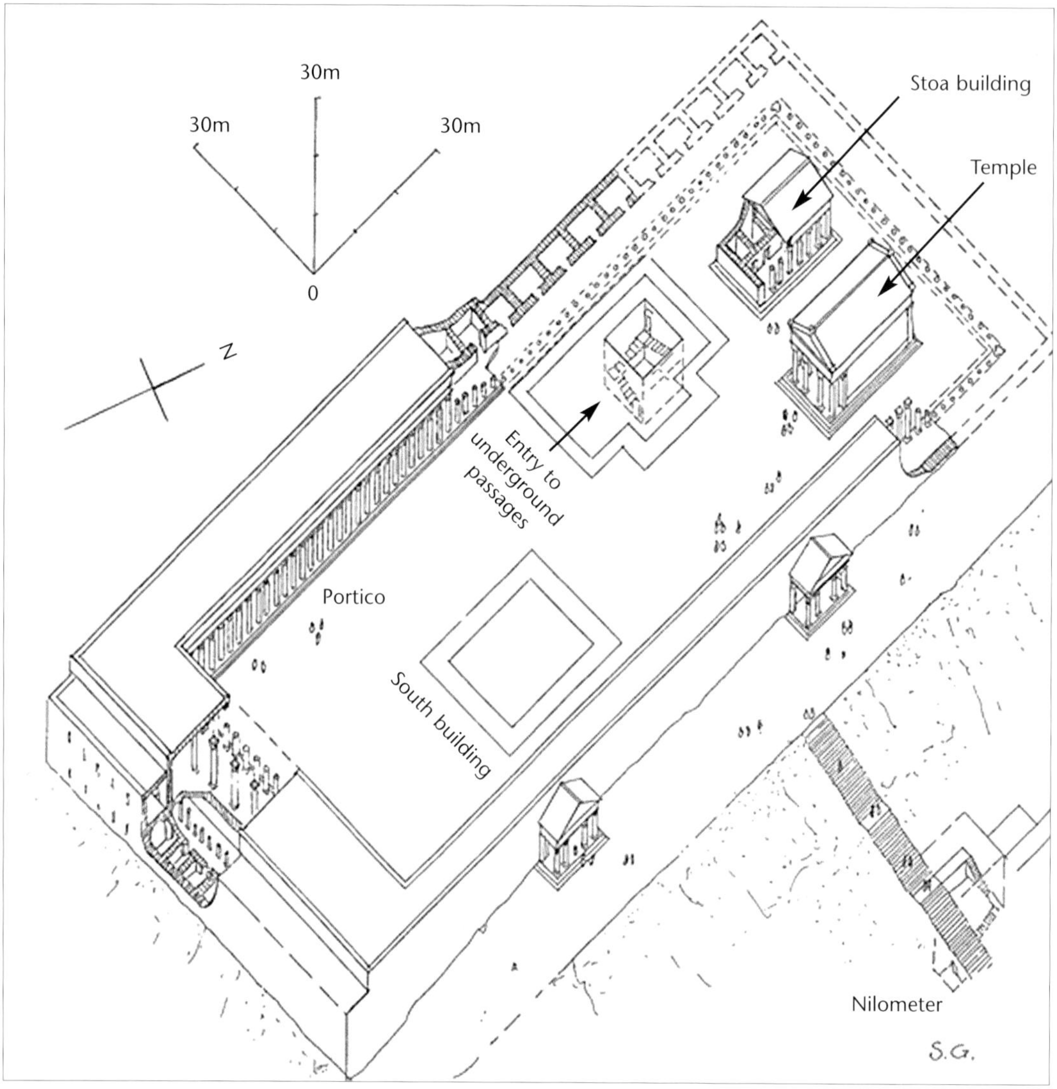

Fig. 2.2.2 The Ptolemaic Serapeum: axonometric reconstruction (McKenzie 2003: 54).

Fig. 2.2.3 The Roman Serapeum: axonometric reconstruction (McKenzie 2003: 55).

put Egyptian religious traditions and characteristics into a form comprehensible to the Greeks. Central to it was the notion that the sacred Apis bull (3.4.b) merged its divine characteristics with those of the god Osiris when it died. The Serapeum itself was a complex of buildings including a library (the 'daughter' of the Great Library), lecture rooms and smaller shrines (fig. 2.2.2). In the huge main temple stood the famous chryselephantine statue of the god by the Athenian sculptor Bryaxis. When a fire destroyed the temple in AD 181, it was rebuilt (by AD 217) on a still larger scale, and the colonnaded court was extended to the north and east (fig. 2.2.3). In AD 391 the Serapeum became the focus for intercommunal violence and street battles between pagans and Christians. Pagans barricaded themselves in the temple. The emperor Theodosius I ordered the cult to be suppressed and the pagans fled.

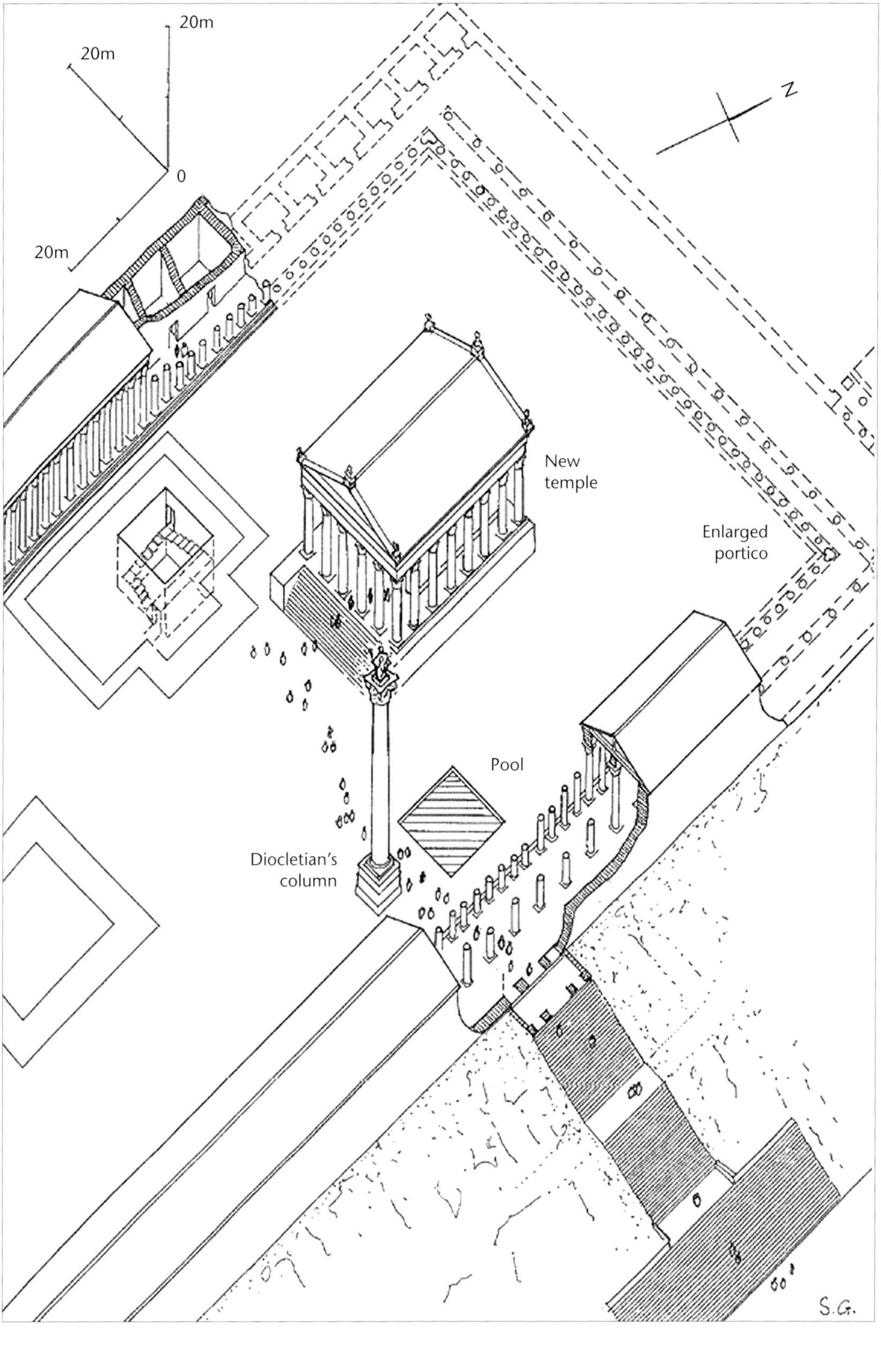
20m
20m
0
20m
N
New
temple
Enlarged
portico
Pool
Diocletian's
column
S.G.

A Christian soldier hacked the famous statue into pieces, which were then symbolically buried in different parts of the city. The temple was located on natural high ground to the south of the palace quarter. What little is known of it is derived from explorations in the 1940s, and only remains of the foundations of the colonnaded court, the temple and some other structures survive, as well as some architectural fragments. But the remains, along with the literary evidence and the inscribed foundation plaques, are sufficient basis for reconstructing the Ptolemaic and Roman phases of construction at the Serapeum, the latter dating to between AD 181 and 217. Conspicuous at the north-western end of the hill is the column popularly mislabelled Pompey's Pillar; its proper designation is Diocletian's Column, and its inscription carries the name of Aelius Publius, the governor of Egypt in the late 290s (figs 2.1.2 and 2.2.3). In 1998 a cistern was discovered, along with a fragment of a mosaic and an inscription with the name of a procurator.

Bibliography: Demougin and Empereur 2002; McKenzie 2003, 2004.

2.2.c The site of the **Lageion** (racecourse or hippodrome) lies to the south-east of the Serapeum and was well known until it was built over by the late nineteenth century. It was the venue for athletic events and processions as well as horseracing and may well have been over 500 m in length. Remains of the dividing barrier (*spina*) and stone seats have been found.

2.2.d On the south side of the main east-west street, directly south of the site of the Caesareum, lies the important site of **Kom el-Dikka**, where excavations by Polish archaeologists began in the 1960s and continue to the present. This is the most coherent and extensive above-ground archaeological site in Alexandria. It affords an excellent impression of the public facilities of the city in the late Roman and Byzantine periods. In the early Roman period this area contained luxurious urban residences of Greek type, which had been damaged or destroyed and abandoned by the mid-fourth century AD, when the whole area was rebuilt with new construction of public buildings. These include a small theatre (or *odeion*), a bath complex and a set of auditoria, probably part of an educational institution. The area may also have included a gymnasium complex. The most important individual buildings are as follows.

An enormous brick-built **bath complex**, covering an area of about 3000 m^2, was probably built in the late fourth century, remaining in use until the seventh. The underground vaulted structure built of limestone blocks is earlier but was adapted as a service area for the baths. Only parts of the ground floor have been preserved. The building was rebuilt twice, first after an earthquake in AD 447, when the *frigidarium* (cold bath) was modified, and again after another earthquake in AD 535, when

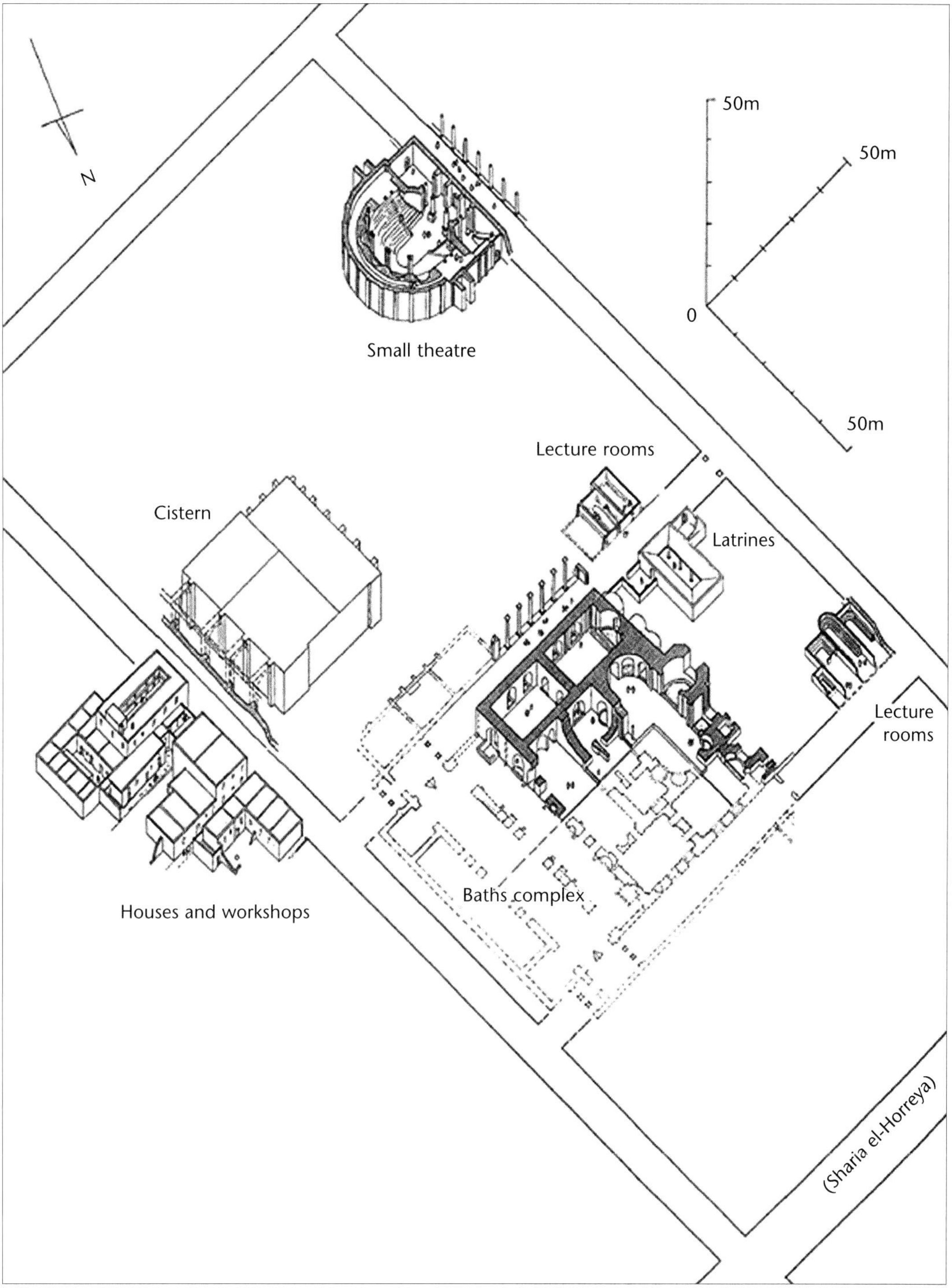

Fig. 2.2.4
Kom el-Dikka: axonometric reconstruction (McKenzie 2003: 60).

the *caldarium* (hot bath) was reconstructed. The entrance consists of a vestibule with a black-and-white mosaic floor, which must have been reached by steps, above street level, leading to the richly decorated cold bath with a small plunge bath (*apodyterium*) on the south side. The *frigidarium* opens onto the bathing rooms and to porticoes on the north and south sides of the building (columns of Aswan granite from the southern portico survive). There is a double sequence of the standard bathing rooms: *tepidarium*, *destrictarium*, *sudatorium* and *caldarium* with a large pool. Beyond the *caldarium* was the service area with the furnaces and storerooms. The bath was supplied with water by a large **cistern,** 36 x 40 m, with several chambers, which lies to the south-east and is notable as the only above-ground water reservoir in the city. There is an earlier brick structure (third-fourth century AD) and a later, larger brick-and-block construction (fifth century), with apartments or shops to the west, remains of an aqueduct to the east and a wall of limestone blocks to the south-west.

At the northern and southern ends of the bath complex two lanes lead to the west. On the south side of the northern lane lies a building, perhaps to be dated to the early sixth century, consisting of three **lecture rooms** or auditoria. The central room is horseshoe-shaped and has a seat at the centre of the short range at the top; the flanking room on the left is square-ended, that on the right horseshoe-shaped. Another ten or more similar rooms are in the immediate vicinity,

Fig. 2.2.5
Kom el-Dikka, later Roman baths.

recently excavated but not yet published. The design of these rooms with stone seating in tiers is unique. They probably are part of an educational establishment. On the north side of this lane is a latrine building constructed in the fourth century. Other significant remains in this area include part of a private house and bath, three rooms of an urban villa under the pavement of the theatre portico and the theatre building, an early Roman villa and later public buildings, and the bath of a private early Roman villa.

The reconstructed **theatre building** excavated in 1964–8 (the 'Small Theatre' or 'Roman Amphitheatre') is a complex and problematic structure in which two main phases can be identified, running from the early fourth to the seventh century. There has been much discussion and no agreement as to its function, especially in the later phase of its existence. It has been suggested that the earliest use might be as a meeting place for the city council (*bouleuterion*), as well as for entertainment. The building was remodelled around AD 500 and remained in use until the second half of the seventh century. Inscriptions carved on the seats in the later period are associated with the circus factions at Alexandria (but the common use of the term 'amphitheatre' is certainly erroneous). The structure is an extended hemicycle with raked auditorium seats built of marble, mainly reused fragments of older structures. The outside wall and the vestibule are limestone. At the top of the auditorium is a row of unmatched reused columns. In its later phase the building

Fig. 2.2.6 Kom el-Dikka, lecture rooms.

had a domed roof. The vestibule was also part of the later addition and is tripartite, divided by columns set on acanthus bases and decorated with black-and-white mosaic floors. The building faced west and opened onto a portico with a granite colonnade and limestone paving.

There is a sizeable complex of **domestic accommodation and workshops**, dating from the early fourth to the mid-seventh centuries, which shows similarities to the archaeological remains at Marea (2.5.b). The latest phase of occupation shows three houses with animal pens. Below this, the best-preserved phase consists of eight houses, formed in a compact block built of limestone and mortar, with a larger house adjoined which had a peristyle court and a pool. The complex was provided with a good sewage system. The largest of the houses in the block consists of workshops lining a corridor, at the end of which is a latrine and staircase. There are remains of a painting on the walls of the corridor, representing the Virgin and Child accompanied by an Archangel, and of monochrome geometric mosaic flooring in some of the rooms. It is assumed that the living accommodation for people using these workshops was on the upper floor(s) which do not survive. Remains of the earlier phases include mosaic floors and traces of walls but are insufficient to recover a plan of the buildings.

Fig. 2.2.7
Kom el-Dikka,
small theatre.

Bibliography: Borkowski 1981; Kiss 2002; Kolotaj 1992; Majcherek 1995; E. Rodziewicz 1993; M. Rodziewicz 1984.

2.3 ALEXANDRIA'S MUSEUMS

The oldest and most important of Alexandria's museums is the **Graeco-Roman Museum.** This was founded in 1892 and contains the largest and most significant collection of artefacts from ancient Alexandria, as well as Graeco-Roman material from other sites in the Fayyum and middle Egypt, and some pharaonic objects. There are plans to close it during 2004 for renovations. The collections were assembled from donations, sporadic finds and excavations by successive directors.

Among the most significant objects from sites outside Alexandria are: a large wooden statue of Sarapis from Theadelphia; the pylons and shrine of the temple of Pnepheros (Sobek) from Theadelphia, which have been reassembled in the garden (the mummified Sobek, door and stelae are in Room 9); the black basalt statue from Soknopaiou Nesos (Room 11); some mummies, funerary masks and mummy portraits (encaustic on wood), from the Fayyum (Room 8); a large collection of terracottas including the small painted statuettes, mainly of the Ptolemaic period, known as Tanagra figurines (Room 18a); and Coptic textiles from Middle Egypt.

Many of the most important artefacts found in the necropoleis are now displayed in the museum, including the Wardian ('Saqiya') Tomb

Fig. 2.2.8
Kom el-Dikka,
houses.

(Room 15, see 2.4.e and col. pl. 2.4.3), various sarcophagi (Room 10), the large and important collection of cinerary urns of Cretan manufacture and known as Hadra hydriae (Room 18), and a large selection of other pottery vessels of various types.

Among the important collection of portrait sculptures and statues, note the heads of Alexander the Great in marble and rose granite, statues of Ptolemaic monarchs including Ptolemy IV and XII, Roman emperors including Caesar, Augustus, Tiberius, Claudius, Vespasian, Hadrian (also a bronze head with glass eyes) and Commodus, and the largest known porphyry statue, probably representing the emperor Diocletian. Other statues include a black basalt Apis bull, a black basalt statue of Isis from Canopus, a marble bust of Sarapis, and marble sculpture from the temple of Ras es-Soda.

Alexandria was particularly renowned as a centre of mosaic artistry, and many examples have been found in the city. Notable exhibits in the Graeco-Roman Museum include the Sophilos mosaic depicting Berenike II with a headdress in the form of a ship's prow (col. pl. 2.3.1) and a Nilotic scene with a banquet and a depiction of Alpheus and Arethusa, both from Thmouis; *erotes* and staghunt from Shatby; centaur and stag, and warrior and mythical beasts, both from the Royal Quarter; and mosaics from the Villa of the Birds at Kom el-Dikka.

There is also an important selection of stelae and inscriptions, including the dedication of a statue of Ptolemy I, the consecration of a synagogue by Jews of Schedia, bilingual foundation plaques in gold and silver of the Serapeum by Ptolemy III, and of temples to Harpokrates, and to Sarapis and Isis, by Ptolemy IV and Arsinoe III (fig. 2.2.1), a list of Ptolemaic mercenaries from Hermopolis and several important military inscriptions of the Roman period.

As well as the major objects of display, there are extensive and important holdings of small artefacts such as terracottas, coins and glassware.

The new **Alexandria National Museum** is at 110 El-Horreya St, opposite the Shallalat Gardens. A grand renovated mansion (1928; formerly the US Consulate), it has a small but well-displayed collection offering a cross section of antiquities from various provenances, ranging from pharaonic times (ground floor) to Coptic. The first floor is devoted to the Graeco-Roman period, including some of the finds from underwater excavations in the Eastern Harbour,

Fig. 2.3.2
Colossal statue of a Ptolemy.

Abu Qir, and Herakleion, with dramatic enlarged photographs. The statuary features a priest of Isis (in black diorite) and Isis herself, a marble head of Berenike, sphinxes and the red granite Caracalla from Kafr Sheikh. The fine Medusa head from the Diana cinema site is the most striking mosaic. A varied display of pottery includes Hadra vases and several amphora types both Egyptian and imported. On the second floor are some Terenouthis stelae (2.6.b) as well as Coptic artefacts – grave stelae, Menas flasks, textiles and metalwork.

Another small museum (**The Antiquities Museum**) is incorporated in the new Bibliotheca Alexandrina, whose entrance is fronted by a colossal statue of a Ptolemy recovered from the underwater excavations in the harbour (fig. 2.3.2). Notable exhibits include a black basalt statue of Isis, a mosaic of a dog with an *askos* (jar) uncovered during the building of the new Library, statuettes of female figures in study and a sleeping child.

There is also a small collection of artefacts at the offices of the **Archaeological Society of Alexandria** (6 Mahmoud Moukhtar St, behind the Graeco-Roman Museum).

Bibliography: Breccia 1914, 1922; Empereur 2000.

2.4 THE NECROPOLEIS

2.4.a Introduction

The underground tombs (catacombs) and cemeteries are the most important and distinctive feature of the surviving archaeological remains of Alexandria. There are a number of sites in the central part of the city, but these underground monumental burial chambers are much more extensively represented in the eastern and western necropoleis. Although their existence was well known early in the nineteenth century, systematic excavation began only after 1892 and continues to the present (most notably at Gabbari in the western necropolis). There is much discussion and little agreement about the precise dates of individual tombs, but it is clear that the date range runs from the earliest phases of the city's existence in the late fourth century BC well into the Roman period, when the Christian community was a significant element in the population.

Both Greek and Egyptian burial traditions of all periods and all population groups, including Jews and Christians, are represented. Evidence for mummification, which was specificially Egyptian, and for cremation and interment, which are predominantly Greek, is clearly present. The physical organization of the tombs reflects a tripartite structure in the organization of the burial ceremony, which was common to both traditions: the preparation of the body for burial and the period of mourning; the journey of the body to the tomb; the deposition of the corpse and the banquet for the relatives and other mourners. Many of these catacombs are very large, containing multiple burials and large numbers of *loculi* (the niches in which the corpses were placed) and the state of preservation is good enough to yield a great deal of architectural detail. It is of great significance that this type of monumental burial complex appears to have developed at Alexandria: there are no direct forerunners or parallels either in Egypt or in the Hellenic world. They are neither completely Greek nor completely Egyptian but contain clearly definable elements of both traditions. The question of direction and chronology of influence has been much discussed, with no universal agreement; the most recent detailed study regards the Greek elements as primary, with Egyptian influence becoming more marked later in the period.

Nor is there complete agreement about the precise classification of types of layout. The traditional distinction identifies two types, though with common elements: an *oikos* or 'house' type on a linear axis, and a peristyle type with rooms distributed around a central court. With two significant exceptions the Ptolemaic tombs are cut vertically into the substrate rock (nummulitic limestone); the rock-cut staircase leads to an open court with an altar and a well, where the burial rites and services took place; situated around the court are burial chambers with rock-cut beds (*klinai*) and niches (*loculi*), cut into the walls and closed with slabs, in which the corpses would be placed; architectural features included brightly decorated columns and capitals. In examples of the Roman period (some of which are reworkings of Ptolemaic catacombs), water is generally provided not by wells but by cisterns at ground level, where there is sometimes also a funerary building and banqueting chamber (*triclinium*). They characteristically have *loculi* as well as freestanding or rock-cut sarcophagi for burials of wealthier individuals.

2.4.b At the north of the city there are two related complexes of tombs on what is now the promontory of Anfushy, formerly the island on which the Pharos stood. The westernmost complex at **Ras el-Tin**, examined by Breccia in 1913 and Adriani in 1939/40, lies in the garden of the royal palace built by Mohammed Ali in the early nineteenth century and is not now accessible. The plan is that of an open court reached by a stair, with rooms leading off in an axial arrangement. Tomb 3 contains a notable classical-style painting of Herakles above a hoopoe bird perched on a plant.

The second complex is near the shore of the bay of **Anfushy**, near the terminus of the no. 15 tram. It contains five tombs of which the earliest is probably mid-second century BC. Tombs 1, 2 and 5 are well preserved, but access to Tomb 5 is restricted. The tombs are of the *oikos* type, with open courts with water facilities and vestibules leading to

Fig. 2.4.1 Kom el-Shoqafa, burial chamber of the great catacomb, first/second century AD.

burial chambers. They are particularly important for the mixture of Egyptian and Hellenizing elements in the decoration. Tomb 2 is the best preserved. The decoration depicts the deceased flanked by the god Horus (left) and male and female figures in the Egyptian style (right). The ceiling of Room 2 is decorated with a trellis-and-tapestry design with a border which has been interpreted either as a Dionysiac scene or as the banqueting tent of Ptolemy II.

2.4.c The catacombs of **Kom el-Shoqafa,** to the south-west of 'Pompey's Pillar' and the Serapeum site, are the most extensive and the best-known complex in Alexandria. The so-called Sieglin Tomb, known from earlier drawings, is no longer extant, nor are any of the Christian catacombs whose presence in this area has been indicated by finds on the surface. The accessible sites are the Great Catacomb and the contiguous Hall of Caracalla (*Nebengrab*), dating to the first/second centuries AD. The Great Catacomb was discovered in 1900 and is probably the best example of Egyptianizing decoration in the catacombs (fig. 2.4.1). The plan is complex and elaborate. There is a funerary chapel at ground level, from which a spiral staircase leads to the the first of three levels undergound, the lowest of which is flooded. On the first level is a vestibule with two double exedrae, a rotunda and a *triclinium* banqueting room. From this a staircase leads to a second level containing the main tomb, whose plan imitates that of the classical temple. The anteroom to the burial chamber has niches at the left and right containing male and female statues in the Egyptian stance but with heads sculpted in the classical style. The *triclinium*-shaped burial chamber is decorated with sculpted reliefs of Egyptian deities. The sarcophagus in the central niche has carvings of a garland, two masks and a reclining female figure; if the latter represents the recipient of the tomb, this will be a rare example of an expensive and luxurious burial of a woman in the Roman period. Below this there is a further level of tombs comprising over 100 *loculi* and many rock-cut sarcophagi. The decoration of the niches includes scenes showing the veneration of the Apis bull by a Roman emperor, possibly Vespasian (AD 69–79). The Hall of Caracalla was originally accessed by a separate staircase, leading to a small court containing an altar. The interior of the tomb consists of two corridors lined with painted niches for rock-cut sarcophagi. At the end of one of the corridors is a room with *loculi*.

2.4.d In the **eastern necropolis** the Alabaster Tomb (in the 'Latin Cemetery' near the junction of the Sharia Anubis and the Sharia el-Horreya) is particularly significant, being uniquely built above ground. There is a single small chamber preserved, constructed of huge blocks of alabaster probably in the third century BC. It has been thought that it might be part of the Sema, or Tomb of Alexander the Great, or of another Ptolemaic royal tomb, although it is not certain whether it lies inside or outside the original city wall. Of the other significant tomb complexes in the eastern necropoleis, those at Hadra, Sidi Gaber and the Antoniadis Gardens (probably the ancient district of Eleusis) are not now accessible, though some of the important artefacts found in them can be seen in the Graeco-Roman Museum (particularly the hydriae from Hadra). Three major sites are accessible. The site of **Chatby** is between the corniche and St Mark's College in the north-east of the ancient city and is the earliest of the complexes, beginning in the late fourth century BC. It contains a variety of types of burials: pit graves, shaft graves, corridor and gallery tombs and hypogea. Hypogeum A is partly preserved, a rock-cut tomb set round an open court. At **Mustapha Kamel** is the most completely preserved cemetery, with eight excavated tombs, of which four are accessible, at Rushdi, a block south of the corniche. Notable features include rooms for the water supply (Tomb 1), a raised (meeting?) room (Tomb 2) and an open court with exedra, raised stage and *scaenae frons* of five doorways (Tomb 3). The **Tigrane Tomb**, of the first or second century AD, is a small one with a painted domed ceiling and Egyptianizing paintings on the walls and in the niches of the *triclinium* (col. pl. 2.4.2). It has now been moved to Kom el-Shoqafa.

2.4.e In the **western necropolis** the Great Catacomb in the Roman-period Wardian complex at the end of Bergouin St is an open peristyle with piers and a circular room with a domed roof which opens onto three rooms of *triclinium* shape. The **Wardian ('Saqiya') Tomb** is a modest hypogeum with unique and remarkable paintings which are preserved not *in situ* but in the Graeco-Roman Museum: those in the *kline* chamber depict a reclining male and those in the court show rural scenes with an ox-driven *saqiya* (waterwheel) (col. pl. 2.4.3), a herm and a shepherd. The Stagni Tomb has been removed and installed on the ground at Kom el-Shoqafa. It consists of a tomb niche holding a rock-cut sarcophagus decorated with Hellenic and Egyptianizing motifs. The most recent extensive excavations were conducted by the CEA in 1998–2000 at **Gabbari** close to the Western Harbour, where there were very extensive tombs, some containing hundreds of *loculi* and large quantities of skeletal remains, terracottas, Hadra vases and other artefacts. There is clear evidence of reuse of the tombs by Christians in the fourth and fifth centuries AD. This site also yielded important evidence of cisterns, and considerable quantities of pottery, some of it stamped or inscribed. Hopes that the area would be preserved as an archaeological site were thwarted by the construction of an elevated section of highway which began in 2000.

Bibliography: Empereur and Nenna 2001, 2003; Venit 2002.

2.5 ENVIRONS OF ALEXANDRIA

2.5.a Canopus (Abu Qir). To the east of Alexandria lies the promontory of Zephyrion (Abu Qir), bisected by the Canopic mouth of the Nile in antiquity. Today much of the eastern part of the promontory lies underwater in the Bay of Abu Qir. The ancient site of Canopus lay on the west side of the promontory, some 15 km to the east of Alexandria. According to Strabo, the town was famous in antiquity for its public religious festivals, marked by music, dancing and licentiousness and for a temple of Sarapis which was credited with great healing powers. An important trilingual inscription of 238 BC records a long decree passed by the Egyptian priests, meeting in a synod at Canopus, in honour of Ptolemy III and his queen Berenike. Many experts believe that the scenes depicted on the famous Palestrina Mosaic are intended to refer to Canopus. Very little of the site has survived to modern times and some of the remains are now submerged. In the 1920s Breccia discovered in the centre of the site at the west side of the promotory remains of Ptolemaic and Roman baths, mosaics and cisterns and of what he believed to be the temple of Sarapis; further to the south on the coast he identified a number of cisterns and basins. Remains of Hellenistic catacombs were found at the village of Abu Qir, and of a Hellenistic building, Roman baths, basins and cisterns at Fort Ramleh and off the coast; this is ancient Menouthis, an important cult centre of Isis and later the site of a healing shrine of Saints Cyrus and John (4.3.b). The most recent important discoveries have been the results of the continuing underwater explorations by Goddio in the bay of Abu Qir. These have located the town of **Herakleion/ Thonis**, which was in use by Greek traders from the fifth century BC, or earlier, and which was the site of an important temple of Herakles, some 5.5 km off the east coast of the peninsula at a depth of 8 m. The submerged town covers an area of 120 hectares and contains harbour basins built of limestone blocks and an Egyptian-style temple in which were found three colossal red-granite statues of a Ptolemaic king and queen and the god Hapy. The explorations have also yielded a 6 m-high stela of Ptolemy VIII and an intact copy of the so-called Naukratis stela, containing a copy of an important decree of Nektanebo I (380–362 BC) which prescribed the levy of a customs tax from Greek traders, to be donated to the temple of the goddess Neith. The majority of artefacts found here date from the fourth to the first centuries BC. Some are now in the new National Museum.

Bibliography: Bernand 1970; Breccia 1926; Goddio 1995.

2.5.b About 45 km to the south-west of Alexandria on the shore of Lake Mareotis lies the important archaeological site of **Marea**, where excavations were conducted in the 1970s and 1980s by the University of Alexandria and Boston University. It is well known that the port of Marea was an important entrepôt before the foundation of Alexandria, but the excavations in the harbour areas have so far revealed no traces earlier than the late Roman/Byzantine period, although further docking

Fig. 2.5.1 Environs of Alexandria.

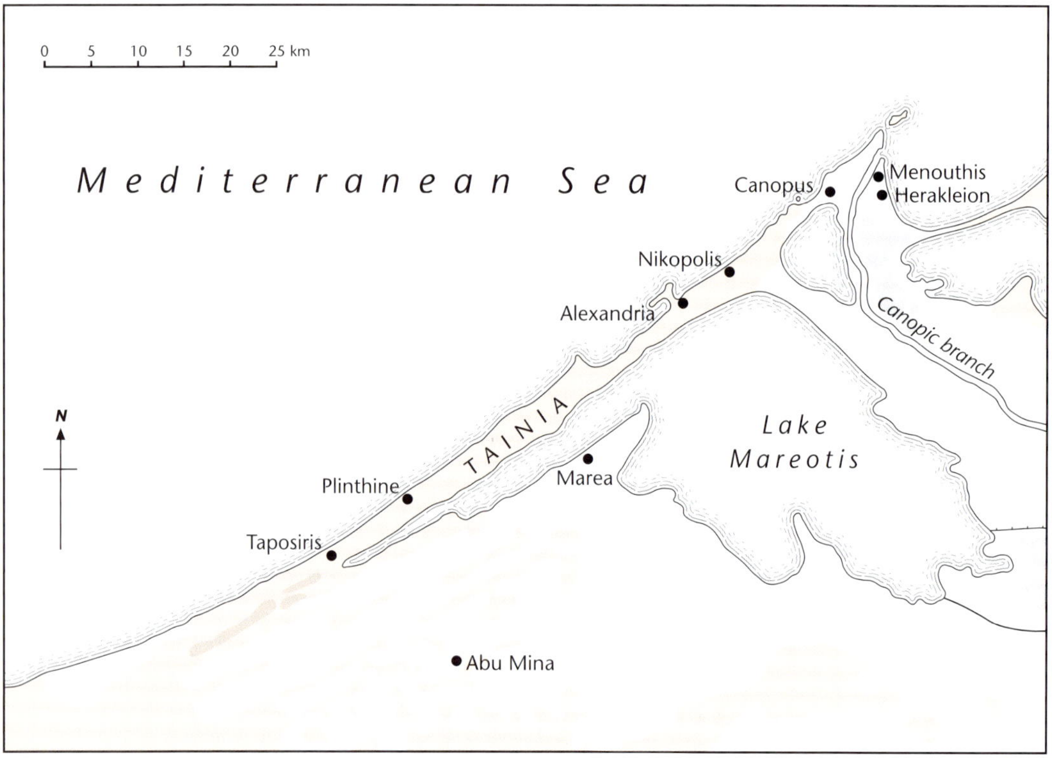

facilities have been observed (but remain unexcavated) about 5 km to the west of the main site. Hence, it has been hypothesized that there may have been two Mareas, an earlier and a later site, or that the main archaeological remains may be those of another port called Philoxenite, rather than Marea itself, a development in late antiquity of a disembarkation point for Christian pilgrims travelling to the important site of Abu Mina (4.3.a). Lake Mareotis was linked by canals to the Nile. It remained an important centre for the export of oil, grain and wine throughout the period, and the whole area was particularly renowned for wine production.

In the cemetery to the west of the town on the limestone ridge are early Ptolemaic *loculi* with gabled roofs (like those at Chatby) and a chamber tomb reached by a descending passage and stairway with a square court and a funerary chamber. There are two cisterns in this area and modest Byzantine-period houses south of the ridge. Further south, 1 km north of the railway line, there is a Christian family tomb of the Byzantine period. In the excavations to the south of the ridge, the easternmost structure is an early Byzantine cistern with a 6 m shaft and a chamber measuring 3 x10 m. South of the ridge, aligned with the centre of the town, is also a Roman well with a 15 m shaft.

The remains of what was evidently a thriving port extend over a kilometre along the lakeshore and consist of three or four visible jetties, the two longer ones about 120 m, providing three separate harbour basins. There is also an artificial dyke connecting to a small natural island. Circular structures at the ends of the jetties may have served as fire beacons to guide ships into the harbour at night. The excavations of the early 1980s in the western port revealed a dry dock of the fifth-sixth century, consisting of a central aisle with two parallel runners extending into the lake.

Fig. 2.5.2 Marea, street of shops.

In the town itself, the main axes of the Byzantine period, the cardo and decumanus, have been identified, the former overlaid by a basilica church. The more important buildings include a large basilica on the eastern promontory, a matching pair of apsidal bath buildings, and a grain mill. The best-preserved building in the town is a complex of Byzantine-period shops on the south side of the decumanus; the building consists of two sections each with five shops or workshops opening onto a covered arcade, with residential accommodation for the merchants to the rear.

Archaeological evidence for wine production has also come to light. South of the limestone ridge are the remains of two wine-producing establishments. The larger and more interesting is aligned with the middle of the town. It contains a large basin lined with four coats of red plaster and two rooms for pressing, the larger with a sloping floor and a lion-head spout in marble, the smaller with the base of a handpress in the centre. From both rooms channels drain the liquid into the basin, which has on one side two funnels on a rectangular podium flanked by a small square podium on either side to hold an amphora, possibly containing liquid flavourings to be infused into the wine. There are also sites of amphora production, including the largest Roman-period kiln known and, 15 km to the east at **Abu Seif Hassan**, a huge unexcavated dump of amphora fragments. It is also notable that 1989 excavations at **Tell el-Shewelhi**, 1.5 km south of Abu Mina, revealed remains of a village with winepresses, houses, shops and water cisterns.

Some 200 m to the north-west of the wine factory is a large, square Byzantine house with two colonnaded peristyles, so far unique in Egypt, and a church-like structure between them; the pottery found suggests a sixth-century date. The house has a winepress at its south-west corner, from which wine was channelled to a round basin outside the south-west façade of the building. In a room at the west side is a podium with some kind of a hypocaust below it. The building has been described as a large country house, but the original construction may later have been adapted to serve as a hostel for pilgrims on their way to Abu Mina.

On the north side of Lake Mareotis is a thin strip of land between the lake and the sea, the Tainia of antiquity, where many orchards and vineyards were located. There are two important town sites in this area, Plinthine and Taposiris.

2.5.c A little to the east of Taposiris (2.5.d) are the remains of **Plinthine**, a sizeable town first examined by Adriani in the 1930s. The best-known aspect of the site is part of the necropolis containing catacombs of the second century BC (four are particularly well preserved), with individual enclosures separated by walls, and remains of monuments on the surface. Like their Alexandrian counterparts, these tombs

Fig. 2.5.3
Taposiris, tomb in form of the Pharos.

are marked by the mixture of Hellenistic and Egyptianizing elements. The town site itself remains unexcavated despite its evident interest.

2.5.d The extensive ruins of **Taposiris (Abusir)**, an important site, extending over more than 1 km^2, have never been systematically excavated, although there have been minor explorations, some recently. The name indicates a tomb of Osiris, and Strabo mentions a great public festival which must have been connected with the cult of Osiris. Remains of a wall running between the coast and the lakeshore to the west of the temple precinct and of a breakwater and wall in the lake suggest measures of traffic control associated with a customs station.

The temple enclosure (100 x 85 m) lies on the ridge between the sea and Lake Mareotis and has remains of two pylons on the east side. The original construction is attributed to Ptolemy II, but the central structures were replaced by a church which has been dated to the fourth century AD. At the foot of the enclosure walls are remains of small rooms and staircases which are perhaps to be associated with a military camp of the later Roman period (using a defunct temple, as at Luxor, 7.2.b). Recent finds from the temple enclosure include a fine head of a statue of Isis.

There are also remains of the necropolis on the ridge, and the most conspicuous building on the site is a funerary monument in the form of a quarter-size replica of the Alexandrian Pharos, with square, octagonal and cylindrical sections rising to 30 m. This stands on top of the main chamber of an underground tomb of the second century BC. Excavations in the 1970s produced three significant discoveries: first, a large fourth-century building constructed of limestone blocks, comprising a main hall flanked by two rooms on each side, a forecourt at the front and courtyard added later at the rear (south); second, a large, richly decorated building of the third century AD and a vaulted stone cistern to the north of it; third, remains of the second century BC disclosed by soundings to the east of the enclosure walls.

2.5.e Marina el-Alamein. Some 100 km west of Alexandria, Polish and Egyptian archaeologists conducted excavations from the 1980s to the present, which revealed remains of a town whose ancient name was either Leucaspis or Antiphrae. There are rock-cut underground tomb complexes dating from the mid-first century BC to the mid-first century AD and remains of houses, port stores, streets, baths, a Christian church and subterranean rock-cut cisterns. The picture which emerges is that of a waterfront harbour with warehouses, the city centre lying further to the south around a bath building. The houses are luxurious complexes with paved central courtyards surrounded by portico wings.

Bibliography: Medeksza and Czerner 2003.

2.6 THE DELTA

2.6.a Two main branches of the Nile, the Canopic to the west and the Pelousiac to the east, defined the ancient Delta; lesser branches, like the Bolbitine and Bousirite, percolated through the central Delta (fig. 2.6.1). The Canopic branch has since silted up, and the Rosetta (Bolbitine) branch is now the westernmost. The number of nomes in the Delta increased in Ptolemaic to Roman times, probably reflecting expansion and intensification of settlement, particularly in the north and on the eastern edge. Much less is known about the Delta than the upper Nile Valley in this period, although it had over half the cultivable

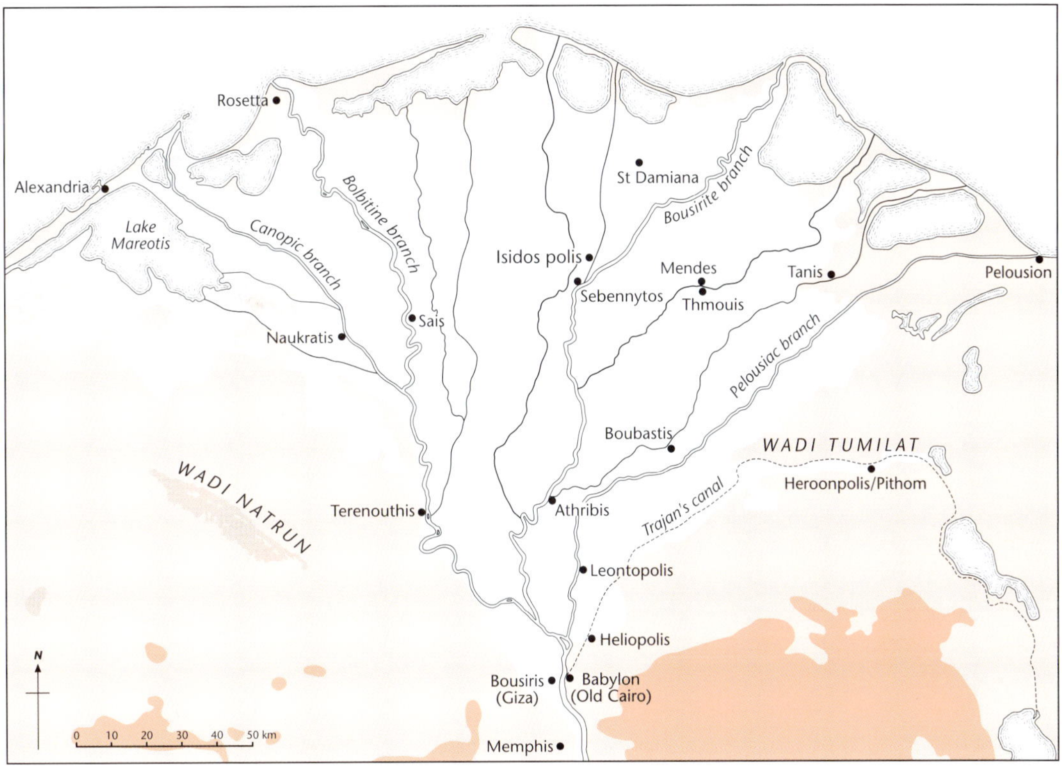

Fig. 2.6.1
The Delta.

land and inhabitants of Egypt, because stone buildings have been reused for later buildings, the high water level damages organic materials like papyrus and impedes excavation, and there has been much less archaeological research. However, in recent years it has been official government policy to redress the balance by focusing new projects here, and archaeological knowledge of the Ptolemaic to Late Antique Delta is beginning to grow considerably. Meanwhile, sites of general interest are sparse.

2.6.b The forlorn traces of **Naukratis** (extending north from the village of **Kom Ge'if**) lie hidden a few kilometres west of the main road to Cairo, some 80 km south-east of Alexandria. In the late seventh and sixth centuries BC the Saite pharaohs made this the designated trading settlement (*emporion*) in Egypt for Greek residents and visitors, and in the fifth or fourth century BC Naukratis became a notionally independent city-state (*polis*), with laws and month names copied from Miletos. The Greek settlers built Greek-style temples to Aphrodite (Naukratis was famed for its courtesans), Zeus, Hera and other deities, as described in the fifth century by Herodotus. Traces of these temples, including inscribed dedications of pottery, and of dense areas of housing, were excavated between 1884 and 1903. The huge enclosure located at the south end of the site was apparently the Ptolemaic *temenos* of

The Rosetta Stone

The Rosetta Stone was found in 1799 at Rosetta by the French, then captured from them and taken to the British Museum (EA 24). It is a dark grey Aswan granite stela, with a pink vein across the top, recording the honours voted to Ptolemy V by the chief priests of the native temples of Egypt at a meeting in Memphis in 196 BC. Their decisions were written up in Greek, then translated into demotic and hieroglyphs. The parallel texts provided the key for the decipherment of hieroglyphs (see box 1.3.1). Fragments of two other copies have been found in the Delta, one at or near Naukratis, in hieroglyphs, and one at Leontopolis, in Greek. Fragments of another trilingual copy have been found at Elephantine, in Upper Egypt.

Box 2.6
Fig. 2.6.2

an earlier Egyptian-style temple to Amun, for there were also Egyptian inhabitants of the city. The robbed-out centre of the site is now a lake ringed with pottery scatters; some column drums are preserved in the village. Naukratis seems to have maintained its Hellenic political and cultural identity, producing writers and rhetors at least to the later third century AD, when annual musical competitions are attested. Pottery found shows that occupation continued into the seventh century; bishops of Naukratis are mentioned into the fourteenth century.

Also west of the Alexandria-Cairo road, some 60 km north-west of Cairo, is the site and cemetery of the ancient town of **Terenouthis (Kom Abu Billo)**. In the town a temple of Hathor, built under Ptolemy I and II, was excavated in 1887–8. The cemetery, which contained around 6000 burials from the Old Kingdom to Late Antiquity, was plundered by *sebakhin*, but excavations in 1935 and 1970/1 found over 420 carved stelae of the late first to early third centuries AD, half of which are in the Kelsey Museum, Ann Arbor (Hooper 1961; Abd el-Hafeez Abd el-Al et al. 1985). These gravestones represent the deceased, male and female, most either with hands raised in worship (as an *orans*) or reclining at a banquet, perhaps their funerary banquet (fig. 2.6.3). The gravestones were brightly painted, and the dead usually identified by an inscription with their name and date of death. Over forty-one people, mostly women and children, died on 8 November of the same year (AD 179?) from some disaster.

Bibliography: Bernand 1970: 575–863; Möller 2000.

2.6.c Some 25 km north of Cairo is the site of **Leontopolis (Tell el-Yahudiyyah,** Mound of the Jews). On the north-east side of the pharaonic military camp and temple complex, late nineteenth-century excavations uncovered traces of the town founded around 160 BC, by permission of Ptolemy VI, for the Jews who had followed Onias IV, son of a high priest, into exile. These settlers, like other Jews in Egypt, loy-

Fig. 2.6.3a–b Terenouthis gravestones (Kelsey Museum, University of Michigan). (a) *[left]* 21114: 'Sisas, loves his children, 70 years.' (b) *[right]* 21073: 'Apia, before her time, 19 years. Year 24, Pharmouthi 8. Keep your spirits up.'

ally provided soldiers for the Ptolemies down to Roman annexation. Onias built a temple to rival the one at Jerusalem, but following Egyptian architectural form. It was closed down by the Romans around AD 73, after the destruction of the temple at Jerusalem. The Jews made their own cemetery among the pharaonic ones on the nearby desert edge, from which some eighty tombstones inscribed in Greek, of the late Ptolemaic to Roman periods, reveal mixed ideas about the possibility and nature of an afterlife.

Further north, in a south-eastern suburb of Benha, around 50 km from Cairo, are the remains of **Athribis** (**Tell Atrib**), where assiduous Polish excavations have revealed, in addition to pharaonic Late Period temples, part of a Graeco-Roman grid plan of streets. To the north are the remains of a public-bath complex of the second century BC, where many erotic terracotta figurines were found, which hints at a link with a fertility cult. To the west is a zone of workshops, mostly of potters producing bowls, lamps and terracotta figurines, but also of gold- and silversmiths, and of sculptors working in both the Greek and Egyptian traditions of statuary. The Roman levels, which survive to the east, include a substantial rich townhouse, which was frequently remodelled over its 200 years of occupation, and brick drains belonging to the civic sewerage system. There are traces of Byzantine settlement too, although the remains of a church, perhaps the church of the Virgin known by the Arab period for its miracles, have now disappeared.

The extensive city of **Boubastis** (**Tell Basta**), a few kilometres south of Zaqaziq, is represented by the remains of several pharaonic temples and one of Roman date. Herodotus enthuses about the beautiful setting of the temple of the local cat deity Bastet and describes the annual pilgrimage to her festival. The huge cemeteries of mummified cats nearby show the continuing popularity of the cult in the Late and Graeco-Roman periods. In the 1960s large numbers of fragments from carbonized rolls of papyrus appeared for sale (they are now mostly at Cologne and Vienna). Parts of almost forty rolls survive, all fiscal records dating between AD 205 and 232, perhaps from a record office which burnt down. This is the single biggest group of documents from the Graeco-Roman Delta found so far.

To the east, the **Wadi Tumilat** forms a natural corridor from this part of the Delta to the lakes at the north end of the Red Sea, which strong rulers from pharaonic times onward tried to protect and develop. A canal linking the Pelousiac branch of the Nile to the Red Sea, begun by Necho II and completed by Darius I (sixth century BC) was refurbished by Ptolemy II, and then again, with other works on the canal system in the Eastern Desert, by Trajan. A hieroglyphic stela from Heroonpolis (biblical Pithom; Tell el-Maskhuta) records the foundation by Ptolemy II in 264 BC of a new port called Arsinoe, probably at the east end of the canal. Under Ptolemy I or II three new nomes were created along

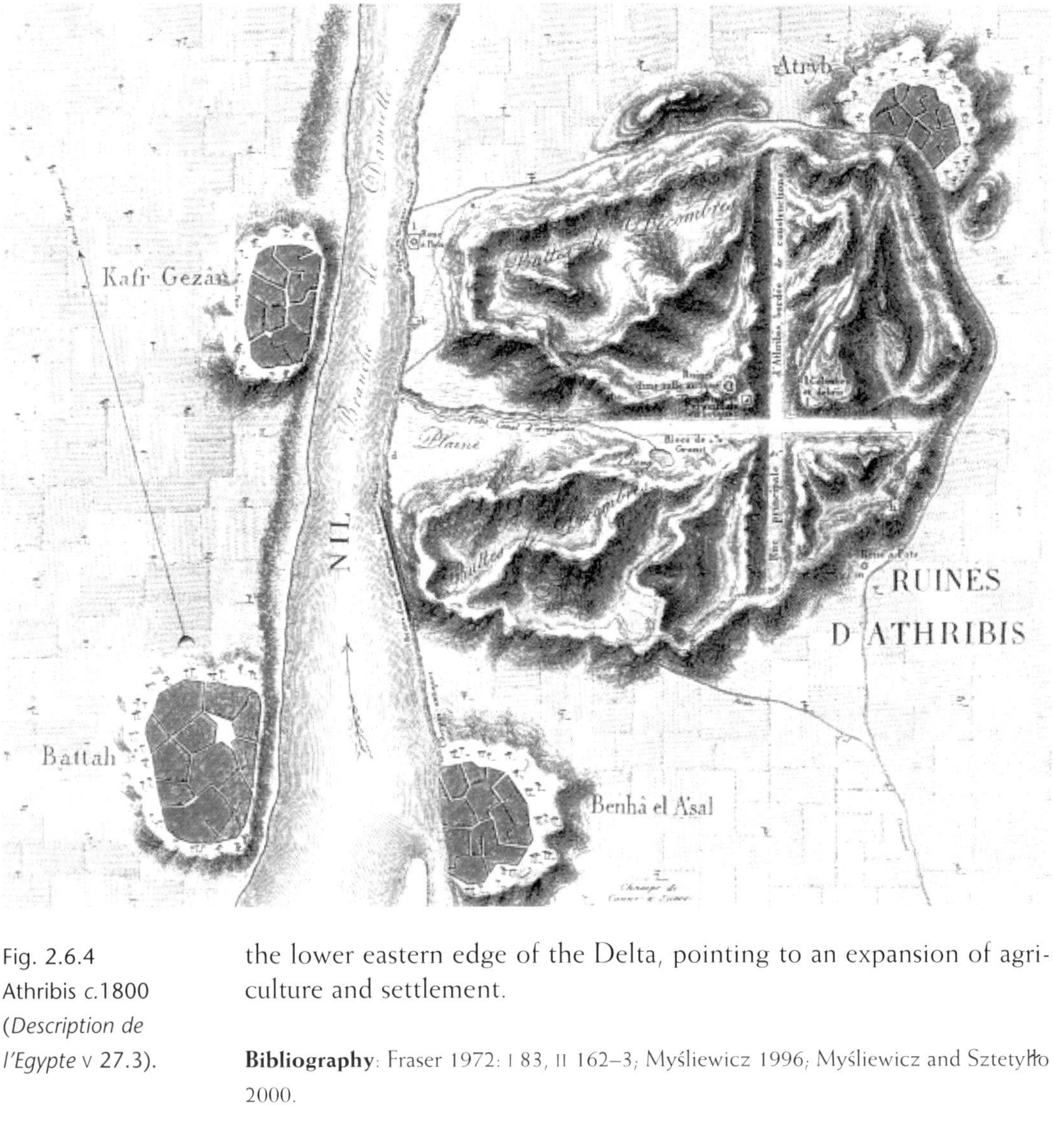

Fig. 2.6.4
Athribis *c.*1800
(*Description de l'Egypte* V 27.3).

the lower eastern edge of the Delta, pointing to an expansion of agriculture and settlement.

Bibliography: Fraser 1972: I 83, II 162–3; Myśliewicz 1996; Myśliewicz and Sztetyłło 2000.

2.6.d The principal trace of **Sebennytos** (**Samannud**), in the central Delta some 10 km west of el-Mansura, is the mound of the temple of the local deity Onuris-Shu. Cartouches on scattered carved blocks suggest that construction of the granite temple was begun under Nektanebo II and continued under Philip III Arrhidaios, Alexander IV, and Ptolemy II. Manetho, who was high priest here, wrote a history, drawing on older traditions, of Egypt down to 342 BC in Greek for Ptolemy II, which provided the basic system of dynasties, dates and names still used today for the pharaohs. A few kilometres to the north lies **Isidos polis** (**Behbeit el-Hagar**) where there was the most important temple of Isis in Lower Egypt. The impressive granite temple, whose blocks litter the site, was begun by Nektanebo I and II, com-

Fig. 2.6.5
Thmouis, the site.

pleted under Ptolemy II and III, and dismantled some time in Late Antiquity. The sculpting of the reliefs is of exceptional quality, and they are judged by many to be the finest of the period.

The ancient city of **Mendes** (**Tell el-Rub'a**), roughly 15 km south-east of el-Mansura, known for its pharaonic temples, especially of the Late Period, lost importance in the Graeco-Roman period to the settlement 700 m to its south called **Thmouis** (**Tell Timai**). At Thmouis there are quite extensive remains of mudbrick structures of Graeco-Roman date, which have been worked over by *sebakhin*. Following excavations in 1892/3 and 1906, numerous carbonized rolls of papyrus were found in a burned-down record office, but most were destroyed by inexpert handling. The few fragments of rolls that survive are fiscal records of the late second to early third centuries.

Further north, near Bilqas, is the **Monastery of St Damiana**, known for its huge pilgrimage and festival (*mulid*) around 20 May. Tradition has it that the Roman governor of the northern Delta under Diocletian founded a retreat there for his Christian daughter and forty virgins, but he was executed and the women martyred, and that Helena, mother of Constantine, had a tomb built for the daughter. The church in the south-west corner dates from the sixth century; the other buildings are modern.

2.7 PELOUSION AND NORTHERN SINAI

In the mid-nineteenth century, construction of the Suez Canal cut off the north-east corner of the Delta, and northern Sinai, from Egypt, and it virtually returned to desert. Resettlement since, and especially construction of the new es-Salaam Canal, pose new threats. Archaeological study, often surface survey, of the numerous archaeological sites began with Clédat in the early twentieth century, was continued by Israeli archaeologists during the occupation of 1967–1982, and since the 1990s has been vigorously pursued by various Egyptian and foreign teams in advance of development. Some of Clédat's finds are in the museums of Ismailia and Cairo; the Israeli finds are in the new museum at Taba, near Eilat, on the Gulf of Aqaba. An archaeological rescue and research centre is being developed at Tell Abu Seifa (see below), near Qantara.

Up into the early Roman period the coastline of the north-eastern Delta had run due west from **Pelousion** (**Tell el-Farama**), but subsequent silting towards the north-west then created the present coastline to Port Said. Thus sites in the triangle to the north-west of Pelousion are all of Roman or later date. Only Pelousion, the major town in the area, whose archaeological remains cover over 6 km^2, is normally accessible. In the fourth century BC Pelousion was the main stronghold on the eastern border of Egypt. In the Roman and Byzantine periods it was the major economic centre of the eastern Delta, the second coastal town of Egypt after Alexandria. On the west side of Pelousion, commercial life is illustrated by traces of large-scale purple dye production, from murex seashells, of the Persian and early Ptolemaic periods. Also

Fig. 2.7.1 Pelousion and northern Sinai.

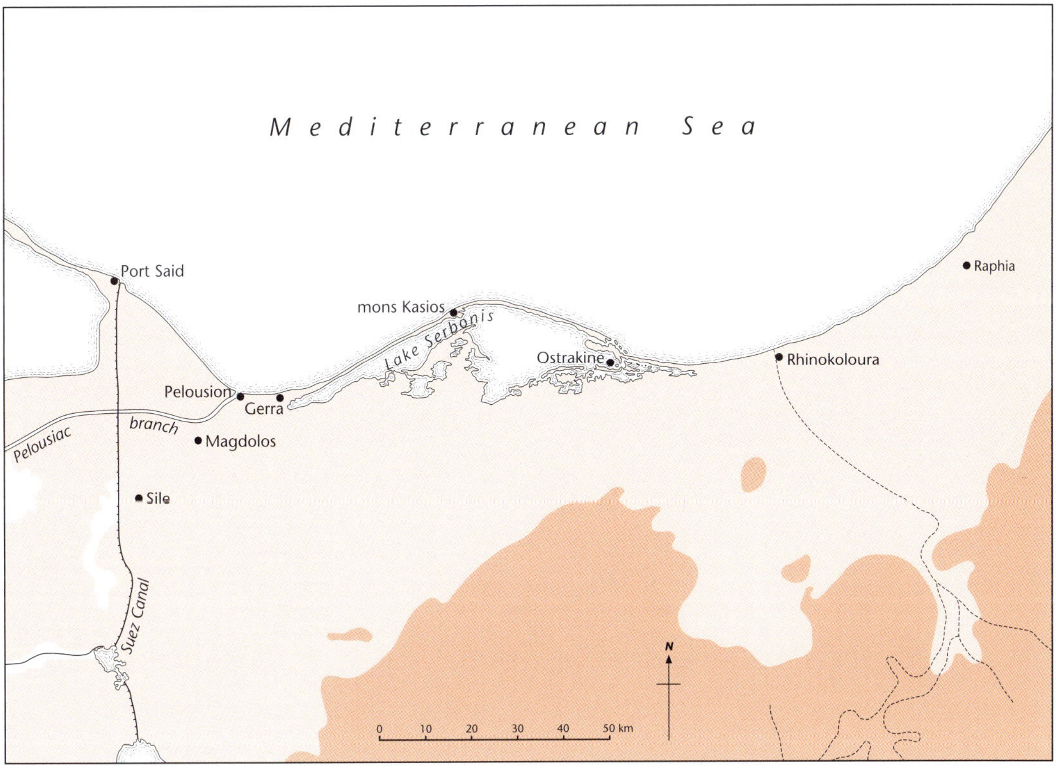

to the west of the site are remains of a large square fort of the late Roman to Byzantine periods. Nearby, excavations have revealed the site of a hippodrome and a huge church complex, including basilica, crypt, baptistery and courtyard, of the fifth to sixth centuries. On the eastern side of the site a third-century bath, with mosaics and water supply, has been found, along with a theatre.

Of the Ptolemaic defence line in the dune area along the old coast-line, south of Pelousion, the forts of **Magdolos** (**Tell el-Herr**) and **Sile** (**Tell Abu Seifa**) are easily accessible. The fortress of Magdolos was founded by the Persians in the sixth century, and rebuilt by them in the fifth century. Ptolemaic settlement is attested by a temple enclosure and a large cemetery. In the third century AD a Roman fortress was built on top of the older ones. The history of Sile is similar: a first fortress from the Persian or Ptolemaic period, a Graeco-Roman settlement, and a mudbrick fortress of the later Roman period. The Roman fort here has been partially rebuilt.

East of Pelousion the military settlement of **Gerra** (**Mahammediya**) guarded the entrance to Egypt from the third century BC onwards, but the site has been partly destroyed by the sea and is difficult to reach. The northern Sinai between Mahammediya and el-Arish is an odd mixture of dunes and marshy pools round Sabkhat Bardawil, ancient Lake Serbonis. Up to the Hellenistic period it was considered a serious risk for invading armies. The coastal road between Pelousion and Rhinokoloura was the main land connection between Egypt and Palestine, but the area remained largely uninhabited until the Roman period. On the narrow strip of land between Lake Serbonis and the sea is **Mount Kasios** (**el-Qels**), where Pompey, the opponent of Julius Caesar, was murdered on 16 August 48 BC. The tomb that his family built there was visited and restored by the emperor Hadrian in AD 130. From the late Hellenistic period onwards the shrinking of the lake made room for agriculture and led to the foundation of **Ostrakine** (**el-Felusiyat**) east of the lake. In the Roman and Byzantine periods the whole region flourished, and new settlements were created, with several bishoprics. In Ostrakine three churches have been excavated. In the early Arabic period the cities along the coast were again abandoned in favour of inland road stations, and after a flood in AD 1169 the lake expanded again. Nowadays most of the area is a military zone and a bird reserve, and access to the archaeological sites is difficult. The expanding city of el-Arish threatens the scanty remains of **Rhinokoloura**, the ancient Egyptian border post.

Bibliography: Carrez–Maratray 1999; Figueras 2000; Valbelle and Bonnet 1998; Valbelle and Carrez-Maratray 2000.

3 THE MEMPHITE REGION

3.1 OLD CAIRO

3.1.a Heliopolis, today the site of Cairo's airport, was the ancient city at the apex of the Delta. Its great temple of Re, despoiled by Alexander, provided many of the pharaonic monuments for his new city of Alexandria. Its port, well to the south, was known as **Babylon**. A fort was built on the Nile quayside under Trajan in AD 98 to control the movement up and down the Nile; this fort was refurbished under Diocletian. (It is no longer on the river, as the Nile has since moved west.) All that remains of Roman Babylon after nineteenth-century demolition are two round towers and two bastions of the western gate, which were preserved because they had been incorporated in the churches of Old Cairo.

3.1.b The Coptic Museum, located in this peaceful and protected area, comprises the old building, with attractive painted ceilings, fountains and screens, and a New Wing which is organized for visits in a counter-clockwise direction. The exhibits are very diverse in date and

Fig. 3.1.1 The Roman fort at Babylon *c.* 1800 (*Description de l'Egypte* v 20.2).

character. It is interesting to note the continuation of older motifs: the Coptic cross is developed from the *ankh*-sign, and names on Coptic tombstones may resemble mummy labels (Room 2). Frescos and niches from Bawit are in Room 3, and Room 6 contains sixth-century objects from the monastery of Apa Jeremias at Saqqara (3.4.c): marble columns with capitals decorated with different designs, some niches (including a Virgin and Child) and the early stone pulpit with a Coptic legend around the decorative shell at its top (fig. 3.1.2). In Room 9 an eleventh-century fresco from a church at Tebtunis shows Adam and Eve

Fig. 3.1.2
Stone pulpit *in situ* at Apa Jeremias monastery, Saqqara (Quibell 1912: pl. XIV).

before and after Eve ate the apple, and a Coptic text tells of their expulsion from the garden. Upstairs in Room 10 a display of Coptic ostraka of clay and limestone and an inscribed camel bone precede a fine collection of textiles. The silver legionary eagle in Room 15 comes from the Roman fort. The Old Wing contains early work from the nearby Coptic churches, a collection of pilgrims' flasks from Abu Mina (fig. 4.3.3), children's toys and even some late mummy portraits. From here there is access to the gate of the Roman fortifications.

3.1.c Coptic churches. The major churches in this area are: the oldest, the fifth-century Church of St Sergius, in whose crypt the Holy Family is said to have sheltered; the attractive ninth-century Hanging Church, dedicated to the Virgin Mary, built on top of the Roman bastions; the tenth-century Monastery and Church of St George which incorporates one of the Roman towers; and the eleventh-century Church of St Barbara. Nearby, the **Ben Ezra Synagogue**, built on the site of a fourth-century church, contained a *geniza*, rediscovered in the nineteenth century, in which all kinds of texts and documents had been carefully discarded and preserved from the eleventh to sixteenth centuries. Beyond here lurks the sadly neglected site of ancient **Fustat**, the original Arab capital of Egypt.

Bibliography: Cannuyer 2001; Gabra 1993.

3.2 CAIRO, THE EGYPTIAN MUSEUM

The Egyptian Museum has the richest collection in the world of Egyptian antiquities, including the art of the Amarna period and the wealth of Tutankhamun's tomb, but the Ptolemaic, Roman and Byzantine periods are also well represented. Since many types of object are displayed together, a room-by-room approach with highlights has been adopted here. Rooms prefixed with G are on the ground floor and U on the upper floor; location plans are available in the museum.

On entering the museum, turn right into corridor G49 where the first and finest mummiform coffin on display is that of Petosiris from Hermopolis (6.3.b). Made of plain wood, it is decorated with five descending columns of hieroglyphs (chapter 42 of the Book of the Dead) inlaid in fine coloured glass. At the end of the corridor stand two colossal statues of red granite of Ptolemaic date: on the left an Egyptian official from Naukratis, and on the right a pharaoh from Karnak, either Ptolemy V or the Roman emperor Augustus. Wearing a *nemes*-headdress, the ruler is portrayed as a traditional Egyptian pharaoh, except for the Greek-style working of his face. In G50 a long-haired Aphrodite in marble together with dolphin and peacock represents the best of Hellenistic Greek art from Alexandria, while in the right alcove a large black granite snake (head restored) curled up on its lid once protected a money chest from the Asklepios temple at Ptolemais. The first-century AD statue of the man with curly hair comes from Herakleopolis Magna; the woman standing opposite is from the same period. On the other side of the stairs in area G57 a group of Roman busts includes the brutal porphyry bust from Athribis of a fourth-century Roman emperor, perhaps Maximinus, wide-eyed with stubbly beard and short-cut hair.

Room G34, the main location for Graeco-Roman antiquities, is down the corridor on the left. Exhibits include numerous representations of Sarapis; in the Roman versions he sometimes wears a *kalathos* (basket) on his head. Two chimaeras from Koptos line the entrance. Turn left past a bearded Roman pharaoh, Egyptian-style, to cabinet C containing a group of inscriptions. The two limestone stelae with triangular tops painted red are the gravestones from the cemetery of Edfu with Greek inscriptions for local notables who were buried with both Greek and Egyptian memorials (8.7.a). A poem of Herodes is recorded on the stone of Euagoras. The second, undistinguished, limestone inscription contains a ruling of Cleopatra and Caesarion in favour of landowners around Alexandria. Continuing clockwise round the room, one reaches three reliefs of Mithras killing the bull. The two above are from Memphis, that with the gilded cloak from Hermopolis Magna (col. pl. 3.2.1).

On the end wall, to the left of cabinet A, stands a black basalt inscription recording a list of victors at the royal festival games (*Basileia*) in honour of Ptolemy II dated 8 March 267 BC. It was erected by a Thracian settler, Amadokos, and various sons of (the same?) Amadokos did well in these games, coming first in the first lap of the torch race, in the boys' sprint, in boxing for both boys and men, and, finally, in dressage. High up is a bust of Antoninus Pius from Hermopolis.

In cabinet A on the end wall is the funerary stela of a young woman, Niko, shown seated and weeping; a child offers her a lyre. This represents good Greek work of the mid-Ptolemaic period. Hanging right of the cabinet are three second-century AD frescos from Hermopolis of traditional Greek literary subjects. The bottom one tells the story of Oedipus in a series of scenes running right to left, with labels to help the viewer. Above, the ostensible subject is the sad tale of Electra; a cock and griffin dominate the scene. Higher still, and hard to see, is a depiction of the Trojan horse.

At either end of the next side wall stand two copies of the decree from Canopus passed in honour of Ptolemy III in 238 BC. Like the later Rosetta decree (box 1.3.1; box 2.6), this is a trilingual priestly decree. One version is headed by a depiction of the royal family and finely inscribed in hieroglyphic, demotic and Greek, all on the front. The other is plainer, with only the hieroglyphic text on the front. Similarly

Foretelling the future (Greek style)

'At the god's command I interpret dreams. Good fortune. The interpreter is a Cretan.' This painted limestone trade sign is composed in Greek verse, and depicts an Apis bull. The role of prophesying god, primarily the province of Imhotep (to the Greeks, Asklepios), seems here to have been transferred to Apis. Records of dreams survive among the papyri.

Box 3.2
Fig. 3.2.2
Cretan dream interpreter (Cairo, Egyptian Museum 27567).

on the Raphia stela of 217 BC, standing free of the wall to the left, the demotic text is relegated to the rear and the Greek to the side. The damaged head of this limestone stela depicts the victorious pharaoh Ptolemy IV on horseback facing a generalized enemy; the mounted depiction of the king is an innovation in an otherwise traditional Egyptian scene. In cabinet B on the end wall is the upper part of a small grey-granite Egyptian statue of a girl with a lotus flower. On the right in this cabinet, note the billboard of the dream interpreter from Saqqara (fig. 3.2.2).

Starting again at the entrance, on the right cabinet D contains a collection of marble statues. Opposite stands another case of small marble heads from Thmouis, from statues probably used in the dynastic cult: Berenike II, with corkscrew curls and diadem is on the left, and her husband Ptolemy III behind her. Alexander (front right), with other queens and goddesses, makes up the group. Further into the room stands a limestone herm with a Herakles statue, and freestanding on the right (with a new nose) is one of the sirens from the Serapeum avenue at Memphis. On the left are four Buchis bull stelae from Hermonthis. The brightly coloured stela records the bull which died, aged almost thirteen, on 14 February 180 BC, and shows Ptolemy V, dressed as pharaoh, making offerings to it.

Upstairs is the **Ancient Egyptian Jewellery Room**. In the first cabinet on the left is a group of mid-Ptolemaic agate vessels from Koptos: a goblet, two round bowls, one small bowl perhaps from a ladle, a shallow dish and a fine calf rhyton perhaps showing Persian influence. Similar influence may be seen in the silver-gilt griffin rhyton, part of the early Ptolemaic treasure from Tukh el-Qaramus (Delta), at the centre of the next display along the wall. The two silver beakers and lotus-flower bowls nearby formed part of this treasure.

Area U13 and Room U14 are where the mummies, shrouds, mummy masks and portraits are displayed. Some of the best examples, including the mummy and portrait of a young boy and painted mummy coffins, are in U13. For most mummies, however, unpersonalized painted and gilded headpieces continued to be used, or painted plaster masks like the striking, brightly painted, first-century AD women's masks from Meir in the last case of U14 on the right.

In corridor U18 is the magic statue of Djed-Hor from Athribis; against his legs a plaque shows Horus standing on crocodiles. The whole monument, including its base, is covered with spells against the bites of snakes and scorpions. A similar 'Horus on crocodiles' stela to the left, inserted into a stone with a simpler basin, comes from Memphis; its inscription is Phoenician. More examples may be found in Room U19, along with many bronzes. On the right hand side are examples of Isis suckling the young Horus, which formed a prototype for images of the Virgin and Child. The large falcon with gold-covered wings in the centre of the room is from Dendera and may have served to cover a falcon mummy.

U24 contains limestone sculptors' models; these sometimes served as dedications. Room U29 displays written material. Some papyri from the Zenon Archive (box 5.2) are in the centre cabinet on the left; on the right a collection of different scripts and writing materials includes ostraka of clay and limestone flakes written in demotic, Greek and Coptic, a lead curse tablet, a camel bone and the inside of a reed used for Coptic messages. At the end of the room a new display shows Latin verses perhaps of Gaius Cornelius Gallus, the first Roman prefect of Egypt, found in the garrison site at Primis (Qasr Ibrim) on the southern border. Books of the Dead are displayed along the right wall.

U39 introduces the minor arts of Graeco-Roman Egypt: lamps, terracottas of both the grotesque kind and the finer, sometimes imported, Tanagra types, mosaics and bronzes. The bronzes on the left wall include Anubis dressed as a Roman soldier. On the end wall to the right is a collection of mummy labels for identification and transport, written in Greek or demotic on wood or, in one case, plastered papyrus, with writing tablets below. On the right wall a display of blue faience includes a 'queen' vase used in the cult of Ptolemaic queens. The collection of glass includes some large dishes in excellent condition.

Room U53 contains a varied display of mummified animals, birds and reptiles, which were popular in the Graeco-Roman period as manifestations of different gods. The Nile *latos*-fish is particularly memorable, as is the striking representation of a young Apis (3.4). White plaster, with the distinctive Apis markings painted in black and red plaster, covers an actual bovid skull. Note the delicate marking of the ears, the red saddle and the lotus between its horns.

The museum garden is a haven of peace in a crowded city. At the library end is the tomb of Mariette, excavator of the Memphite Serapeum and much else. Papyrus grows in the central pool.

Bibliography: Ashton 2001; Bothmer 1960; Doxiadis 1995; Grimm and Johannes 1975; Kyrieleis 1975; Stanwick 2002; Walker and Bierbrier 1997; Walker and Higgs 2001.

3.3 GIZA

The three great pyramids at Giza of Dynasty 4 featured in the standard Graeco-Roman list of the 'seven wonders' of the world. Tourist and religious interest in the site had been revived under the Late Period pharaohs, who had promoted worship of Isis 'mistress of the pyramids', Osiris and the sphinx, now identified as Harmachis, god of the rising and setting sun. A temple to Isis was created by enlarging the chapel of the southernmost small pyramid (of Henoutsen) by the pyramid of Khufu. The sphinx was periodically dug out from drifted sand, repaired and repainted red. Visitors dedicated numerous statues, statuettes, inscriptions and graffiti to Harmachis. The second toe of his left paw was restored with thirteen blocks inscribed with a poem in Greek (the eight surviving blocks are in the Louvre, Paris). In the Roman period two raised paved areas, reached by staircases, and each with a 'viewing' podium, were built in front of the sphinx, over the forgotten remains of the Dynasty 4 temple; they have now been destroyed to reveal the temple. The temple of Osiris lay further south, in the area of modern

Nazlet Batran, as did the local town, called Bousiris, and its cemetery. Little otherwise survives of Graeco-Roman Giza.

Bibliography: Zivie 1980.

3.4 MEMPHIS AND SAQQARA

Memphis lies some 30 km south of Cairo on the west bank of the Nile and can easily be visited in a day trip by car from Cairo. When Alexander of Macedon invaded Egypt in 332 BC, he made for Memphis. Rivalling Thebes in Upper Egypt, Memphis had served as capital for much of Egypt's history. The centre of the administration was located there together with one of Egypt's most impressive temples, the great temple of Ptah which dominated the valley city. At Memphis Alexander sacrificed to Apis and other gods, and held Greek-style games and musical competitions. This was enough to show the Egyptians that the Persians had been replaced and that he was the new ruler of Egypt. In life, as later in death when Ptolemy I brought his embalmed body to

Fig. 3.4.1 Memphis area (after Thompson 1988: 11).

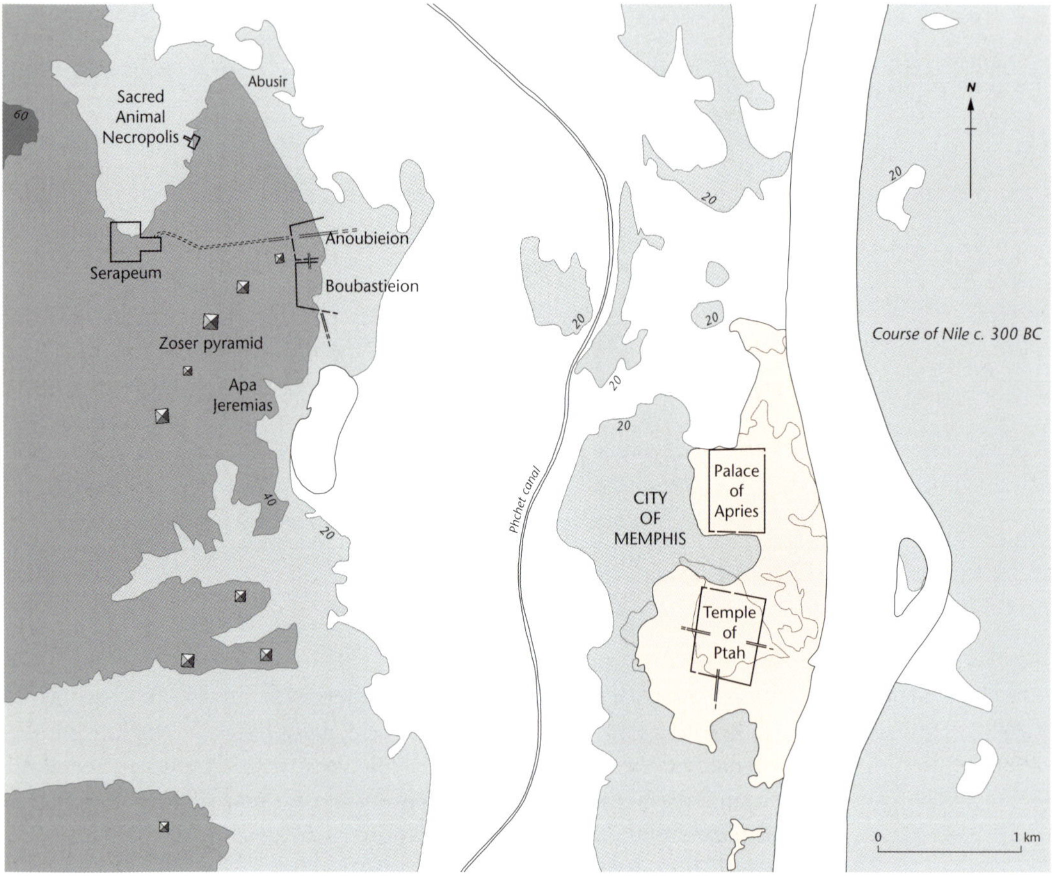

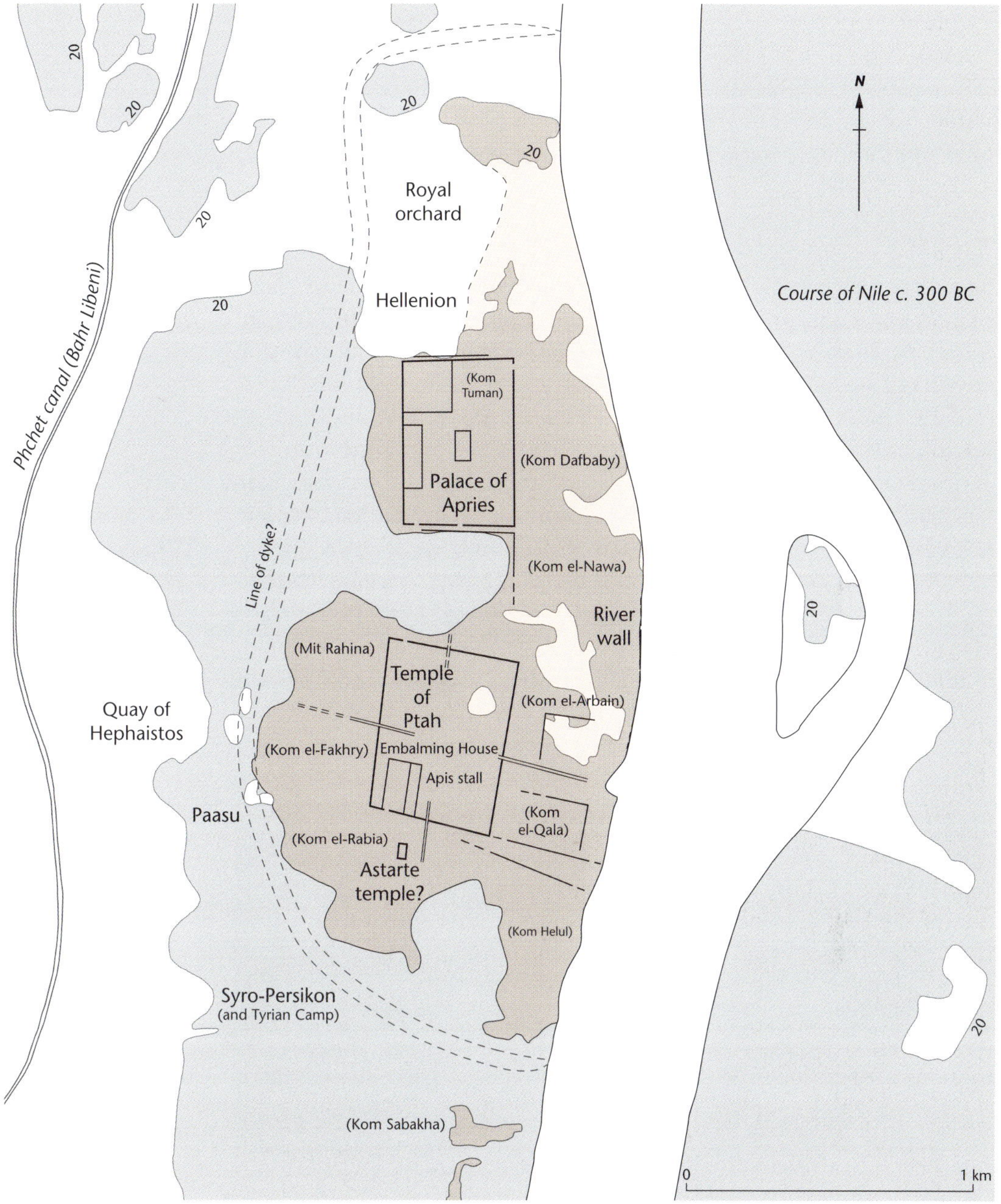

Fig. 3.4.2
The city of Memphis (after Thompson 1988: 14–15).

Memphis, Alexander's presence marked the past importance of the city, which was soon to be eclipsed by his new foundation, Alexandria.

Like other cities in the Nile Valley, Memphis was a settlement with two main centres: the valley city on the banks of the river and the necropolis area of Saqqara, where a series of burial grounds and temple complexes extends for several kilometres along the desert edge, north towards the pyramids of Giza and south towards those of Dahshur. It is not possible to separate out Ptolemaic and Roman Memphis from the earlier Egyptian city. The inhabitants lived and worked among the monuments of earlier times, some ruined but many still standing. Naneferkaptah, a key character of the demotic tale of Setne I from the Ptolemaic period, spent all his hours deciphering earlier inscriptions as he wandered the desert necropolis. Even the great mudbrick walls of later temple enclosures cannot have detracted from the majesty of the early stone pyramid complex of Zoser, which still dominates today. In the valley, however, the present-day landscape is remarkably changed from that of earlier times since here the riverbed has shifted over 3 km to the east. In antiquity it ran alongside the series of *koms* (mounds) that are marked on fig. 3.4.2.

3.4.a The valley city. The best overview of the area of the ancient city is gained from the top of the northern mound of the so-called Palace of Apries (a sixth-century BC pharaoh) excavated by Petrie in 1909. Since this was still known as the palace area in the third century BC, we may assume it continued to serve as the royal residence under the Ptolemies. Already stripped of its superstructure when Petrie started his work, it has little to show now apart from a mound with the mudbrick foundation walls. The valley city has lost its glory, and its site is occupied by the villages, fields and date palms of Mit Rahina, Abusir and Saqqara (fig. 3.4.2). The fine building stones employed in antiquity

Fig. 3.4.3 Apis bull, statue from the Serapeum chapel (Louvre AE N390).

Fig. 1.1.3
Cleopatra VII, blue glass intaglio (British Museum GR 1923.4-1.676).

Fig. 1.6.2
Coptic textiles from Achmim (British Museum EA 20717).

Fig. 2.3.1
Sophilos mosaic, second century BC: Alexandria as deity with ship's prow headdress (Alexandria, Graeco-Roman Museum 21739).

Fig. 2.4.2
Tigrane Tomb, first–second century AD: mummy of the deceased attended by Isis and Nephthys.

Fig. 2.4.3
Wardian Tomb, Alexandria, first century AD: waterwheel scene (Alexandria, Graeco-Roman Museum 27030).

Fig. 3.2.1
Mithras slaying the bull (Cairo, Egyptian Museum 85747).

Fig. 3.4.9
Saqqara, the sacred animal necropolis.

Fig. 4.2.4
Monastery of Macarius, Wadi Natrun, painting of St Onnophrios, eleventh century AD.

Fig. 4.5.1
Monastery of St Catherine.

Fig. 5.2.3
Encaustic mummy portrait, Philadelphia, late second century AD (British Museum EA 65346).

Fig. 5.3.6
Theadelphia, shrine of the temple of Pnepheros.

Fig. 5.4.3
Ptolemaic bodyguards, wall painting at Kom Madi (after Bresciani 2003: 109).

Fig. 5.5.1
Encaustic mummy portrait of a priest of Sarapis, Hawara, mid-second century AD (British Museum EA 74714).

Fig. 6.3.6
Tomb of Petosiris, harvest scenes, Tuna el-Gebel, fourth century BC.

Fig. 6.3.9
Charioteers, papyrus from Antinoopolis, fifth century AD (EES).

Fig. 7.2.5
Luxor military camp, niche in chapel of the imperial cult with traces of the standing figures of the four emperors.

Fig. 7.3.1
The town of Jeme (Medinet Habu).

Fig. 7.3.10
The zodiac on the coffin of Soter (British Museum EA 6705).

Fig. 8.6.1
The village of Elkab
and wall of
Nektanebo II.

Fig. 8.11.2
Kalabsha, temple
pylon (Berlin,
Ägyptisches
Museum), with
cartouche of
Augustus: 'Roman
Caesar the god'.

Fig. 8.7.2
Edfu, temple pylon.

Fig. 9.2.2 (above) Bagawat, a tomb complex.

Fig. 9.2.6 (below) Umm el-Dabadib, the fort.

Fig. 9.3.2 (right) Dakhla, farm building.

Fig. 9.5.1
Siwa, the Oracle Temple.

Fig. 10.3.2
Mons Claudianus.

have mainly disappeared, sometimes reused in later buildings, more often victim of the lime kiln. It is hard to imagine the hustle and bustle of this thriving river city, with its docks, barges and harbour authorities, markets for different goods from many parts of the world, and the different ethnic quarters with their temples and varied cults. A circle of dykes protected the central city from the annual flood of the Nile; cultivated fields, parks and nursery gardens all formed part of the city surrounds. Even after the foundation of Alexandria, Memphis remained 'the second city of Egypt' (Strabo) because of its strategic location in the central Nile Valley south of the Delta. Yet no substantial remains survive to indicate the importance of post-pharaonic Memphis.

In his selective description of Memphis in the late first century BC, Strabo comments on the international aspect of its large population, a feature it shared with Alexandria. There were lakes by the city and its palaces, by Strabo's time in ruins. In the valley, Strabo concentrates on the cult of the Apis bull, which was chosen for certain distinctive features, mainly black with white markings on its forehead and flank. There was only one Apis at a time, and it was known by the name of its mother. It spent a pampered life in its stall within the larger complex of the magnificent temple of Ptah (Hephaistos to the Greeks), with a yard in front where tourists could view the god taking his daily exercise. Of the temple, only the foundations of a large hypostyle hall built by Ramesses II are now to be seen, lying in water close by the village of Mit Rahina. There were other bull cults in Egypt – Mnevis at Heliopolis, for example, or Buchis at Hermonthis – but Apis was the best known.

Before his coronation a pharaoh had to yoke the bull, whose strength and fertility symbolized the power of the king himself. On the death of an Apis, the country mourned for seventy days as the bull was embalmed in the valley prior to burial in the Serapeum of the Saqqara necropolis. We know the procedure from inscriptions put up by those who prepared the vaults and from an Egyptian papyrus which records the embalming ritual. One of the few identifiable remains of the valley city is the collection of Apis embalming beds found in an enclosure south of the Ptah temple near the Ramesside colossus (fig. 3.4.4). These fine alabaster beds, with drainage channels on their upper surfaces, are decorated with elongated lions on their sides. They were used during the early days of embalming when the fluids were drained from the corpse; the corpse was then packed in natron and bound with linen wrappings prior to its burial. The four smaller drainage tables were perhaps used for the separate embalming of the bull's vital organs.

Other animals were also housed within the great temples of the valley city, including the Apis calves and the baboon of Thoth, god of the moon and of writing, which lived in the temple of Ptah-under-his-moringa-tree, together with his troupe. Thoth's bird, the ibis, was tended

Fig. 3.4.4
Apis embalming beds.

along the city's dykes and lakes in special breeding grounds, and the falcon of Horus was presumably bred nearby to meet the demand for mummified and potted birds from tourists and pilgrims. Lions too were bred and buried somewhere in the area.

Under the Ptolemies, Memphis was divided into ethnic quarters, centred on their different temples. Although a number of temple enclosures are known from texts, as are the designations of their inhabitants, their walls can be traced only with difficulty. To the south-west of the Ptah temple lay the Levantine quarter bounded by the 'Syro-Persian section' of the surrounding dyke. The Phoenico-Egyptians from this quarter formed a long-established group in Memphis, who worshipped their goddess Astarte. North of the quay of the Hephaistos temple lay the Carian quarter with its community of Caro-Memphites. Further north was the Hellenion, where the Helleno-Memphites formed a well-established settlement of Greeks. It owed its origin to Greek soldiers from Ionia settled in Egypt in the seventh century BC who, with the Carians, were relocated to Memphis from the Delta in the sixth century in the face of the Persian invasion.

The Romans brought changes in administration, cult and culture. Roman Memphis was divided into fifteen or more smaller administrative units known as *amphoda* (streets). A Mithraeum in the eastern part of the city (somewhere south of Kom Dafbaby) is the source of Mithraic sculpture now in the Egyptian Museum, Cairo. Barracks built for troops on Kom Sabakha to the south of the city shared that area with some brazier-heated baths.

3.4.b To the west of the valley settlement, across the Phchet waterway, lay the other part of the city (fig. 3.4.5). Primarily the domain of the

Fig. 3.4.5
The necropolis-complex of North Saqqara (after Thompson 1988: 22–3).

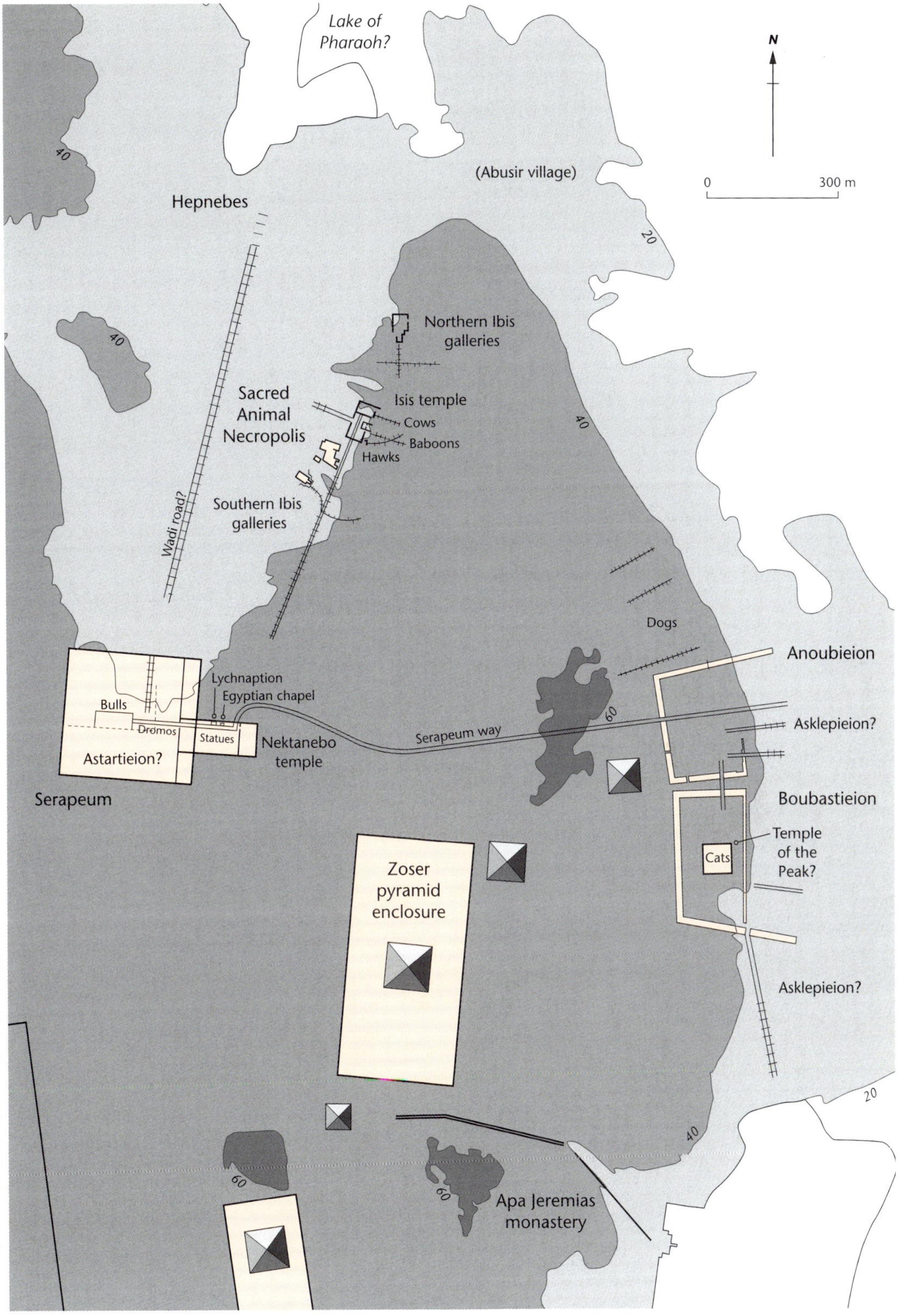
Lake of Pharaoh?
N
0
300 m
(Abusir village)
Hepnebes
40
20
Northern Ibis galleries
Sacred Animal Necropolis
Isis temple
Cows
Baboons
Hawks
Southern Ibis galleries
Wadi road?
Dogs
Anoubieion
Lychnaption
Egyptian chapel
Bulls
Dromos
Statues
Astartieion?
Nektanebo temple
Serapeum way
Asklepieion?
Serapeum
Boubastieion
Temple of the Peak?
Cats
Zoser pyramid enclosure
Asklepieion?
60
Apa Jeremias monastery

dead, **the necropolis area** was also home to many of the living, and not just to those involved in the business of death. In antiquity a number of roads ran up the sandy escarpment to the different temple areas. Today one drives westwards through Mit Rahina, turns north along the main highway to Giza, then west again across low-lying ground and up to the top of the escarpment. Here desert roads lead off southwards to the Step Pyramid, northwards to the Inspectorate of Antiquities and westwards to the Serapeum. The waterway now crossed by the road from the valley is a small trickle compared with the lake that once lay here. When the embalmed Apis had crossed this lake on his special barge in the final stage of his festival, he was carried up the escarpment edge, to the north of the Teti pyramid through the Anoubieion, and across to his temple and burial vaults on the western edge of the necropolis. Here, dug deep into the rock, were the catacombs where the Ptolemaic bulls were buried.

These vaults, discovered in the 1850s by Mariette, are generally known as the **Serapeum**, following the name of the Greek god, Sarapis, derived from Egyptian Osorapis (Osiris-Apis); it was called the 'House of Apis' in demotic and the Sarapieion in Greek. A route of sphinxes led through the older monuments westwards over the escarpment edge (fig. 3.4.6). As Strabo noted, this is an area prone to quick-rising desert

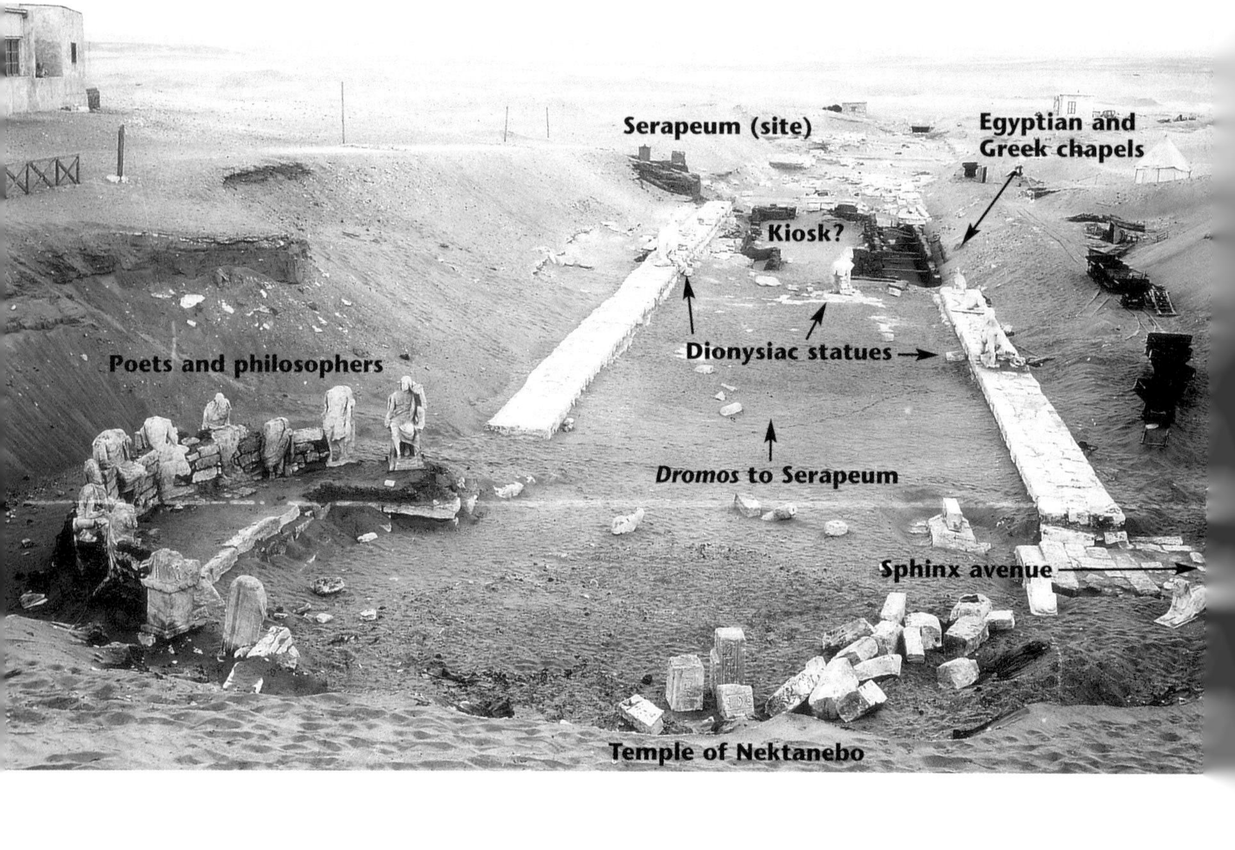

Fig. 3.4.6 Memphite Serapeum, the *dromos* in 1938 (after Lauer and Picard 1955: pl.2a).

Fig. 3.4.7 Memphite Serapeum, the Apis burial vaults (with Mariette to the right).

storms, and the few surviving sphinxes are now often eroded beyond recognition; spotting the sphinx here is a hot and tiring game. Other sphinxes from the Serapeum route were removed even before Mariette made his discoveries; the best surviving examples are in the Louvre.

Going west, the Serapeum route ends at a semicircle of limestone Greek statues, re-erected in Late Antiquity in their original Ptolemaic setting. Although protected by a modern concrete shelter, they are badly weathered and resemble a dejected queue at a bus stop. They are puzzlingly hard to identify and explain: Pindar, Homer (at the centre), Pythagoras and Plato have been identified, among others, but not all scholars accept these names. From here a temple avenue (*dromos*) ran westwards to the Serapeum enclosure. The pylon at its entrance was guarded by two fine lions (in the Louvre) inscribed with the names of Nektanebo II, the last native Egyptian pharaoh. Mariette removed the stone slabs which paved the *dromos* and found several hundred bronze statuettes and amulets underneath. The sand has again covered up the Dionysiac sculpture which once stood on the low walls running either side of the *dromos*. Osiris, god of the dead, was identified by the Greeks as Dionysos. A Cerberus and two Sirens (one now in the Egyptian Museum, Cairo) formed part of this decoration. Some half-way along the *dromos* on the northern side stood two shrines, one Greek, the home of the temple lamp lighters, and one Egyptian, where the statue of the Apis bull (1.28 m high) was housed (in the Louvre; fig. 3.4.3). Side by side Greek and Egyptian statuary, symbolism and even buildings illustrate the mixed culture of the times.

The enclosure wall of the Serapeum was noted by Mariette but can no longer be seen. The entry to the main Apis vaults lies within the Serapeum area, as did shrines and other buildings that we know of only from papyrus texts. A chapel to Phoenician Astarte formed part of the complex, and many smaller chambers served as homes for temple workers, priests, and those known as *katochoi*, 'detainees' of the god.

The burial vaults of the Apis bulls are extensive and impressive. Long galleries underground (the main gallery is over 200 m) are flanked by individual chambers once lined with limestone; monolithic granite sarcophagi, averaging some 65 tons in weight, still lie in many of these. After a bull was laid to rest, the vault was sealed with masonry, but almost all the vaults were found already opened and robbed. The large catacomb was in use from the seventh century BC until the end of the Ptolemaic period. Apis bulls, however, had been buried in individual graves and in the smaller catacomb from the time of Amenophis III. The burial place of the Roman bulls has so far eluded discovery but, as at Hermonthis, the cult went on, and a new Apis bull was conveniently discovered for the pagan emperor Julian. For most Ptolemaic bulls, a hieroglyphic stela on the front of its vault recorded the dates of the god's birth, key events in its life, and its death and burial. Many of these are now in the Louvre, Paris. The years of the relevant Apis were used with those of the king on the numerous devotional dedications fixed to the walls of the entrance by those involved in work for the bull.

From the northern wall of the Serapeum enclosure a gateway opened onto a desert road running northwards down the valley to the Lake of Abusir (fig. 3.4.5; col. pl. 3.4.9). To the east of this valley lay the bluff of North Saqqara, once filled with the funerary establishments of the many workers who formed the community of the necropolis. Some of their private contracts survive, such as family cessions of property, or records of those over whom embalming rights were held, for wealth was reckoned in terms of prospective mummies.

The eastern escarpment of the desert valley is honeycombed with underground galleries for the burial of other sacred animals and birds. The Mother-of-Apis cows, the baboons sacred to Thoth and the Horus falcons shared a temple enclosure, in which each had its separate shrine on a terrace fronting the escarpment. The Mother-of-Apis catacomb resembles a smaller Serapeum and contained the burials of some twenty mummified cows from the early fourth century until the end of the Ptolemaic period. Inscriptions in this catacomb recorded the families of the masons; we learn how they dragged in the heavy sarcophagi and how they built the vaults. A second enclosure was added for the Mother-of-Apis, probably early in the Ptolemaic period, but the resting place of the Children-of-Apis calves is still unlocated. The ibises,

Foretelling the future (Egyptian style)

Hor from Sebennytos in the Delta served as priest in the House of Apis, where he served the ibis cult in troubled times and used the prophesying power of his dreams to his advantage with the rulers. In one dream, as reported on this ostrakon (*O. Hor* 2 verso), he claimed to have learned the actual date (30 Pauni Year 2 – 30 July 168 BC) by which the invading king Antiochus IV of Syria would depart from Egypt following the Roman ultimatum; he announced this date to the Ptolemaic rulers holding audience in the Great Serapeum in Alexandria.

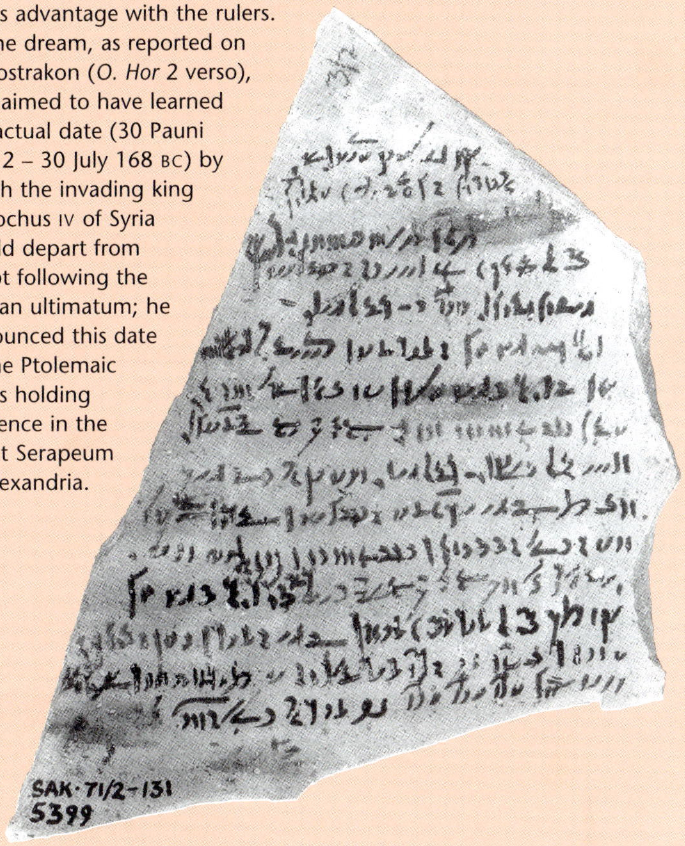

Box 3.4
Fig. 3.4.8

sacred to Thoth, were buried in vast numbers in two catacombs, one further north and one to the south. From the area of the southern catacomb derives the Archive of Hor, a collection of drafts and letters written in demotic in ink on pieces of broken pot (box 3.4). Pilgrims could buy a potted ibis and entrust it to the local priests, who collected them for mass burial in the vaults beneath (fig. 3.4.10). The ibis catacombs comprise main axial galleries over 100 m long, with side galleries of varying lengths, which were stacked high with ibis mummies in pots, generally in orderly fashion. The baboons were much more restricted in number, with a single incarnation animal kept in the temple at Memphis at any one time; a record of their lives was sometimes written on the blocking to their burial niches. Other members of the baboon troupe were also interred in the catacomb, where 21 Barbary macaques were found alongside 146 olive baboons. Their date implies that, when routes to the south were closed in the first half of the troubled second century BC, macaques were obtained from the western Mediterranean as an alternative incarnation for Thoth. The main visible surface trace of these galleries is that the sand above glistens with the bones of the birds and animals ejected from their catacombs.

Near the pyramid of Nyuserra, among the Dynasty 5 pyramids to the north-west at Abusir, lay the burial grounds of the Hellenomemphites, which date back to before Alexander's conquest. The early fourth-century BC text of Timotheus' lyric work *The Persians* comes from a burial here, testifying to the Greek cultural allegiance of this group.

On the western escarpment of the Nile Valley, British excavations have uncovered the outlines of the great temple enclosures of the **Anoubieion** (250 m^2) and the **Boubastieion** (350 x 250 m). The Anoubieion, the precinct of the jackal god Anoubis, lies to the north and the enclosure of the cat goddess Bastet (Boubastis to the Greeks) to the south. Both complexes are well known from papyri, and the identifications are confirmed by associated cat and dog burials, traces of which are still to be found along the desert edge. Imperfectly aligned, the two enclosures were surrounded by mudbrick walls up to 10 m thick, providing protection from wind and attack. The walls are still in part strikingly visible. They may date to the last period of independent Egyptian rule in the mid-fourth century BC (Nektanebo I and II), when animal cults grew in popularity in Egypt as a form of expression of

Fig. 3.4.10 The southern ibis galleries, Saqqara (EES).

Egyptian identity. Taken up also by the Hellenomemphites, the popularity of these cults continued in the Ptolemaic and Roman periods. These temple towns contained limestone shrines and other buildings rising up the escarpment edge on a series of terraces. Besides at least three temples, the Anoubieion housed a registry office, police station, storehouses, mills and housing for the varied population.

The final large enclosure of this area of the necropolis, well known from texts alone and still not located, was the important temple of Imhotep, the deified architect of Zoser's step pyramid, whom the Greeks identified as Asklepios. In the **Asklepieion** supplicants practised incubation, overnighting in the sanctuary to obtain a prophecy or cure through dreams.

Bibliography: Davies and Smith 1997; Jeffreys 1985; Jeffreys and Smith 1988; Lauer 1976; Lichtheim 1980: 125–51; Martin 1981; Petrie 1909; Ray 1976; Smith 1974; Thompson 1988.

3.4.c Coptic Memphis. In the valley city of Memphis a few traces have been found of Coptic settlement and churches. In the necropolis area a Coptic settlement with a monastery of Apa Antinos once overlay the temple terrace of the Sacred Animal Necropolis. However, the main Christian site of the area is the monastery of **Apa Jeremias**, which lies to the south, at the side of the causeway joining the mortuary temple of Unas in the valley to its necropolis pyramid. Excavated twice in the twentieth century, the site yielded paintings, a pulpit and capitals, now in the Coptic Museum in Cairo. The monastery covered almost 2 hectares, with water cisterns and drains, but without any surrounding wall. Probably founded in the late fifth century AD, it finally fell into disuse in the ninth or tenth. The crypts and tombs of a late Roman cemetery were reused by monks as cells fitted with rounded niches for an oratory on the eastern side; some of these were inscribed or decorated with paintings of the Virgin or holy men. The room once identified as a refectory is now believed to have served as a gathering-place for prayer or a workroom for basket-making for the monks. To its east lay a square chapel with four columns; the bluish marble column bases are still to be seen, though the great courtyard with plastered mudbrick walls to its north has been covered by sand. Against its south wall stood an early stone pulpit (fig. 3.1.2). The main church, which lies somewhat further to the south (20 x 40 m), was rebuilt in the seventh century after the Arab conquest. It is a basilica with a rounded apse facing eastwards with two side rooms at a lower level, two lines of eight columns in the nave, a main western entrance with two extra columns, and an ante-chapel. The column capitals are beautifully carved.

Bibliography: Grossmann 2002; Quibell 1912.

Fig. 3.4.11
Apa Jeremias
monastery (after
Quibell 1912: pl.1) .

4 CHRISTIAN MONASTICISM AND PILGRIMAGE IN NORTHERN EGYPT

4.1 INTRODUCTION

Christian monasticism had deep roots in Egyptian culture, and it is not surprising that some of the most important monastic sites of the Christian East are to be found in Egypt. Christian pilgrimage in Egypt likewise owed much to the indigenous Egyptian traditions of religious tourism, but it was also the result of an extensive body of literature about the early years of monasticism in Egypt and its founding figures. Much of this literature concentrated on monastic activity in northern Egypt, where many important sites were located. It was also the part of the country that many of the early writers and pilgrims from outside Egypt, arriving in Alexandria, would have found easiest to visit. Churches and monasteries in northern Egypt increased in importance throughout the later Roman period, while the tourism and activity they engendered spilled over into important sites in the northern parts of the Eastern Desert and the Sinai Peninsula. Many of these sites remained Christian strongholds after the Muslim conquest of Egypt in AD 639–42, and some continue to function as monasteries and pilgrimage sites today.

Many of the important monastic and pilgrimage sites of the later Roman period in northern Egypt survive in some form, usually ruins. The archaeology of these sites has long been a source of interest, but the quality of their excavation has been uneven, and currently occupied sites have often proven inaccessible to archaeologists. Thanks to the efforts of investigators such as White, Guillaumont, Forsyth and Grossmann, among many others, we have an understanding of the basic architectural history of the monasteries and pilgrim centres of northern Egypt. But the artefactual record from the earliest centuries of these sites is still patchy, and we are dependent on the textual sources for much of what we know of these sites in the later Roman period. In some ways these sites are more poorly documented than other Graeco-Roman sites in Egypt: unlike some monastic sites in Upper Egypt, there are no papyri or ostraka surviving that give an insight into their day-to-day functioning. However, monastic and pilgrimage sites of northern Egypt have another dimension of documentation that is lacking for most places in Graeco-Roman Egypt: they were often described in Byzantine pilgrimage itineraries, which sometimes provide a wealth of circumstantial detail of the sort that is not found in the papyri.

Most of the sites described in this section are accessible to the

modern visitor, but with varying degrees of ease. The specific circumstances of each site will be noted separately, but as a general rule it is safe to say that those active monastic sites that still serve as pilgrimage destinations will have well-established access routes and associated accommodation. With these sites in particular, though, the visitor should bear in mind that they remain, first and foremost, centres of worship and devotion. Except as noted, they are today Coptic Orthodox monasteries.

Bibliography: Atiya 1991; Cannuyer 2001; Chitty 1966; Frank 1998; Frankfurter 1998b; Grossmann 2002; Kamil 1987; Külzer 1994; Papaconstantinou 2001.

4.2 NITRIA, KELLIA AND THE MONASTERIES OF THE WADI NATRUN

Although many of the key early figures of Egyptian monasticism in the late third and early fourth centuries came from the south of Egypt, it is in the north that monasticism developed and grew most dramatically. The fourth century AD witnessed an explosion of monastic activity in the desert to the west of the Nile Delta, in a region centred on three major foci: Nitria, Kellia and Scetis. These sites were remote enough to allow the early monks the solitude they required for their spiritual practice, but not so far removed as to be completely cut off from provisions and outside spiritual guidance. Indeed, these northern monastic settlements quickly became popular destinations for both Egyptian and foreign pilgrims. Nitria, Kellia and Scetis all figure prominently in the key texts of early monasticism in Egypt, including the *Apophthegmata Patrum* (Sayings of the Fathers), Palladius's *Historia Lausiaca* and the *Historia Monachorum in Aegypto* (History of the Monks in Egypt). The latter two works served as pilgrimage narratives and itineraries; the later translation into Latin of the three books disseminated the lives and activities of the early Egyptian monks throughout Europe and ultimately had a profound impact on the formation of European monasticism. More immediately, these works led to a surge in religious tourism in northern Egypt. But the popularity of these early monastic settlements came to be a disadvantage to the inhabitants – with so many pilgrims, tourists and would-be followers, it was hard for the resident monks to pursue their lives of solitary devotion. Such settlements either gradually died out or reorganized their practice toward communal monasticism rather than solitary asceticism. Their location in relatively unprotected desert areas made the settlements vulnerable to periodic raids by nomadic desert tribes. Nitria and Kellia were eventually abandoned, but Scetis, home of the famous monasteries of the Wadi Natrun, has continued as an important Egyptian monastic centre to the present.

Fig. 4.2.1 Monasteries in north-west Egypt.

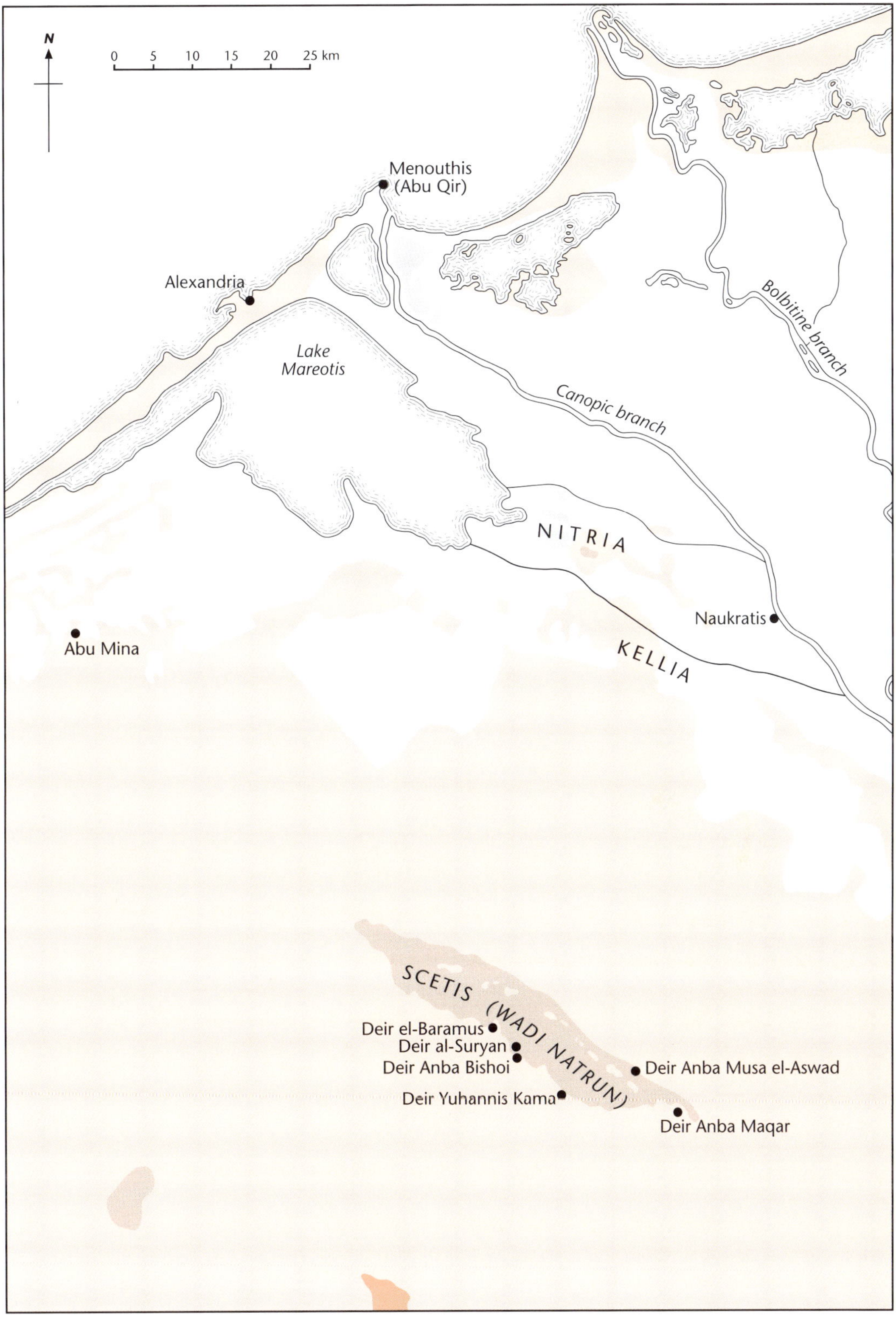
N
0 5 10 15 20 25 km
Menouthis (Abu Qir)
Alexandria
Lake Mareotis
Bolbitine branch
Canopic branch
NITRIA
Naukratis
Abu Mina
KELLIA
SCETIS (WADI NATRUN)
Deir el-Baramus
Deir al-Suryan
Deir Anba Bishoi
Deir Anba Musa el-Aswad
Deir Yuhannis Kama
Deir Anba Maqar

Apophthegmata Patrum

The *Apophthegmata Patrum* (Sayings of the Fathers) is a collection of anecdotes and wisdom attributed to the desert monks of Egypt and Syria, including many based at Scetis, Nitria and Kellia. This anthology exists in a number of versions: an alphabetical series organized by the individual monks involved, with an appendix of anonymous sayings; the 'systematic' collection which was an important influence on Western monasticism; and more miscellaneous collections in a variety of languages – Greek originals, and Coptic, Syriac, Latin, Arabic and Ethiopic translations. The earliest sayings date to the fourth century AD, but the collections were assembled later. The sayings cover a wide range of topics but focus on the monastic life, the daily activities of the monks, and their temptations, hardships and rewards. They were originally collected for use in monastic instruction. Typically the individual sayings consist of a short anecdote culminating in a pithy statement by a revered monk (or 'old man', as they are often referred to), and many graphically illustrate the harsh and dangerous desert environment the monks inhabited. These two examples are translated from the Coptic version of Chaîne 1960 (nos 28, 224; see also Guy 1993; Ward 1975):

(a) One of the brothers inquired of Apa Sarapion, saying: 'Give me a word.' The old man said to him, 'What can I say to you? For you have taken the things of the poor, the widows and the orphans, and put them in your window.' For he saw that the window was filled with books.

(b) There was a man of Egypt who had a lame son. (The man) brought his son and put him by the cell of Apa Macarius, and left him there, crying at the door. Then he went away. The old man glanced out and saw the little boy in tears, and he said to him, 'Who brought you to this place?' And he said, 'My father: he brought me, and left me, and then he went away.' The old man said to him, 'Get up. Go and catch him.' Immediately, he was healed. He stood, and caught up with his father. And so they went back to their home, rejoicing.

4.2.a Nitria (near the modern town of al-Barnuji in the western Nile Delta) is one of the earliest monastic sites in Egypt. The name refers to the local prevalence of natron, the salty mineral compound used in embalming and cleaning in ancient Egypt; the name has also led to the frequent confusion of Nitria with the monasteries of the Wadi Natrun to the south. Nitria was founded around AD 330 by Ammon, an important figure in early Egyptian monasticism. It quickly became a major centre for solitary monks, attracting hundreds, even thousands, of aspiring hermits through the rest of the fourth century. The peak years of monasticism at Nitria in the late fourth century are documented in the letters of Jerome, in the *Historia Monachorum in Aegypto* and especially in the *Historia Lausiaca* of Palladius, who lived in Nitria for a year around AD 390. By the time of Palladius' stay, Nitria had evolved from a collection of isolated monks into a loosely knit community, with bakers, merchants and regular church services. Some of these services had evolved to serve the needs of the monks, but more were on hand for the ever-increasing numbers of pilgrims. As Nitria became a popular tourist destination, however, the monastic population declined through the fifth and sixth centuries, culminating in the abandonment of the site sometime before the middle of the seventh century. In contrast to

Box 4.2

Kellia and the monasteries in the Wadi Natrun, little remains at Nitria today.

4.2.b Kellia, further to the south, was established in the mid-fourth century AD by Ammon as a place for monks who wanted more solitude than Nitria could provide. Palladius records hundreds of monks living at Kellia already in the late fourth century, and at points in the fifth and sixth centuries the population of monks at Kellia numbered in the thousands. Initially a seemingly random collection of cells and small group dwellings, Kellia eventually added churches and other communal structures. Kellia was affected by the doctrinal disputes in Egypt in the sixth and seventh centuries and was also subject to raids by nomadic tribes from the Libyan Desert to the west. Activity at the site tapered off in the seventh and eighth centuries and the site was abandoned by the ninth, its location ultimately forgotten. Before the rediscovery of Kellia in 1964 by French archaeologists, the site appeared to consist of many small hills or *koms* covering an area of approximately 125 km^2. Archaeological survey and excavation have revealed these *koms* to be

Fig. 4.2.2 Kellia, *laurai* at Qasr el-Izeila (*Site monastique* 1984: 14).

the remains of collapsed buildings: over 1500 individual structures have been identified and many more may have existed when the site was inhabited. These structures range from single cells for solitary habitation, to small structures accommodating two or three people, to larger hermitages, some with their own small chapels, separate quarters for elder monks and associated towers. In connection with these various dwelling structures are also found a centre for communal services (Qasr Waheida), a complex of churches (Qasr Isa 1) and what may be an enclosure for commercial functions (Qasr al-Izeila)(fig. 4.2.2). Construction was primarily of sandy mudbrick, structures mostly being roofed with vaulted brick ceilings. Artefactual evidence from the site consists mostly of pottery, while the individual structures often contained Coptic inscriptions, graffiti and paintings. Kellia has been extensively excavated by French, Swiss and Egyptian teams from1964 to the present. Sadly, the site has been heavily damaged by the encroachment of increasing agriculture in the region, which causes flooding, and extension of local railways. The site is relatively remote for the casual visitor but can be reached by car, most conveniently via the monasteries of the Wadi Natrun.

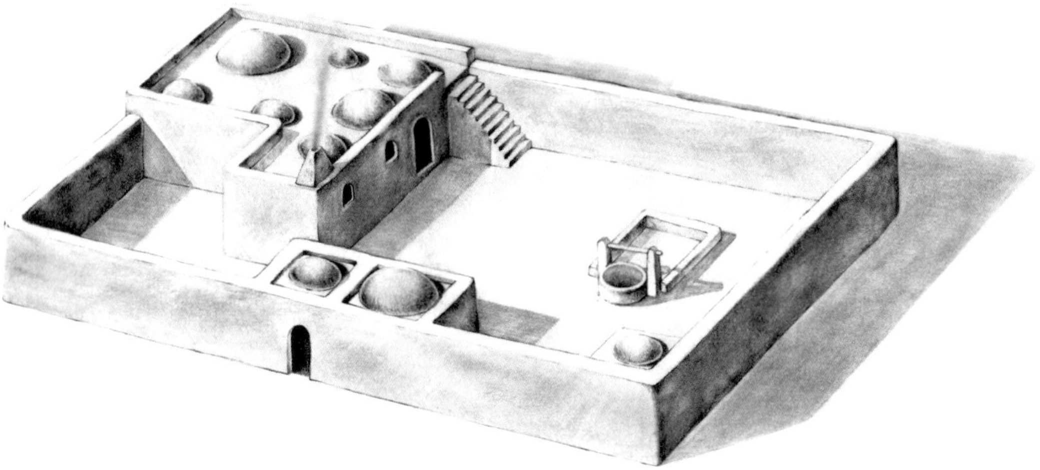

Fig. 4.2.3 Kellia, reconstruction of a monk's cell (after Cannuyer 2001: 35).

4.2.c Beyond Nitria and Kellia lay **Scetis**, a remote assemblage of monastic communities in the **Wadi Natrun** that came to be one of the greatest strongholds of monasticism in Egypt. Scetis was first inhabited as a solitary monastic site by Macarius of Egypt around AD 330. His reputation soon attracted followers, who built cells nearby and thus began a loose confederation of monastic communities. Many of these early settlers had already followed monastic practice in places like Nitria; Scetis was less a place of innovation than a locus of consolidation. By the end of the fourth century, the loose agglomeration of settlers had coalesced into four monastic communities: the monasteries of

Baramus, Macarius, Bishoi and John Kolobos. Initially, these monasteries were simply collections of individual cells and dwellings centred on specific churches and communal facilities, but they gradually developed into enclosures with walls and watchtowers for protection. The monastic communities of Scetis were periodically embroiled in the theological controversies that plagued fifth- and sixth-century Egypt, with additional communities splitting off to accommodate varying doctrinal groups. Like Nitria and Kellia, Scetis was also subject to raids from desert nomads, sometimes resulting in periods of extreme depopulation in the area, for instance at the end of the sixth century. The monasteries at Scetis mostly flourished in the years immediately after the Muslim conquest of Egypt in 639–42, but in the eighth and ninth centuries sporadically came into conflict with the Muslim rulers of Egypt over issues of taxation and administration. Monastic activity at Scetis continued through the medieval period, although some individual monasteries were eventually abandoned, and four of the monasteries continue to be inhabited to the present day; these are described in what follows.

The earliest of the individual monasteries at Scetis in the Wadi Natrun was built around the original cell of Macarius the Egyptian in

Fig. 4.2.5 Deir Anba Bishoi *c.* 1800 (*Description de l'Egypte EM* II 105.4).

Fig. 4.2.6
Deir Anba Bishoi.

the mid-fourth century and has traditionally been identified with the monastery known as the **Monastery of Baramus** (Deir el-Baramus). This monastery, which still functions, is now an extensive walled complex mostly of medieval date, including an extraordinary cycle of murals only recently discovered. Recent excavations and research suggest that this Monastery of Baramus was, in fact, the sixth-century Monastery of the Virgin of Baramus, and that the original mid-fourth-century Monastery of Baramus is what is now known as the Monastery of Moses the Black (Deir Anba Musa el-Aswad), a site that was abandoned by the end of the fourteenth century.

To complicate matters further, there is a second monastery even more closely identified with Macarius the Egyptian: the **Monastery of**

Macarius (Deir Anba Maqar). This monastery was built later in the fourth century around a cell that Macarius is said to have occupied well after his initial move to Scetis. The Monastery of Macarius quickly became one of the more populous settlements in the area, housing hundreds, if not thousands, of monks by the end of the fourth century. The Monastery of Macarius has remained an important institution in the Wadi Natrun ever since, although most of its existing buildings are medieval in date. It is widely known for its mural decorations (col. pl. 4.2.4). It once housed an extensive library containing thousands of volumes, but many of these books have long since been dispersed into European and American collections. Until very recently, the site of the late fourth-century Monastery of John Kolobos (John the Little) was uncertain, but in 1995 an American team located and began excavation of the remains of this monastery, and also identified traces of a number of other early monastic sites in the area.

The **Monastery of Bishoi** (Deir Anba Bishoi; figs 4.2.5–6) was established in the mid-sixth century in a settlement that collected around the cell of the noted monk Bishoi in the late fourth century. Portions of this monastery were destroyed in raids in the mid-sixth and mid-ninth centuries; most of the surviving structures date from the major reconstruction carried out after the middle of the ninth century.

The **Syrian Monastery** (Deir al-Suryan) was founded in the sixth century in reaction to doctrinal disputes as a home for monks from the Monastery of Bishoi who followed Severus of Antioch. In the early eighth century the monastery was sold to a group of Syrian monks, hence its current name. Most of the present structure is medieval in date, and the monastery is especially known for the elaborate carved wood and wall paintings in its churches.

The **Monastery of John the Black** (Deir Yuhannis Kama) was a late addition to the Wadi Natrun area, being founded around AD 840 by John the Black and abandoned in the early fifteenth century.

Visiting the monasteries of the Wadi Natrun is relatively easy from Cairo or Alexandria, but visitors should bear in mind that most are still functioning monasteries, subject to the religious calendar and practices around which they are organized. Each monastery has its own policy on visitors. Some are open to all, while others require advance arrangements or a letter of recommendation.

Bibliography: Atiya 1991; Evelyn White 1932, 1933; Grossmann 2002; Innemée 1999; Kamil 1987; Külzer 1994; Leroy 1982; Papaconstantinou 2001.

4.3 ABU MINA AND MENOUTHIS

Near Alexandria, the capital of Graeco-Roman Egypt and its largest city, were two major Christian pilgrimage centres, Abu Mina and

Menouthis. Both shrines to martyr saints, these pilgrimage destinations were especially popular and active in the fifth to seventh centuries AD. Both had great reputations as centres for healing. Because of their proximity to the great port of Alexandria, both shrines were extremely popular with foreigners as well as Egyptians.

4.3.a Abu Mina, located in the ancient Mareotis district (2.5.a) to the south-west of Alexandria, was a complex of churches with a pilgrim centre dedicated to Menas, an Egyptian martyr who was killed in Asia Minor in the late third century as part of the Diocletianic persecution of Christians (fig. 4.3.1). Menas' cult was primarily restricted to Egypt,

Fig. 4.3.1 Abu Mina, the ecclesiastical centre (after Grossmann 1998).

and his veneration continues to be a major component of Christian worship in Egypt today. Legends about Menas tell that the camel that had brought his remains back to Egypt stopped at the site of Abu Mina and refused to go on, so the martyr was buried there. Stories of miracles attributed to the remains of Menas led to the establishment of a pilgrim church in his honour at the site around AD 363. The cult of Menas initially concentrated on an underground burial chamber where relics of Menas were kept. The facilities at Abu Mina expanded through the fifth and sixth centuries, with churches and buildings being added to house and serve the increasing numbers of pilgrims who visited; a substantial settlement also grew up on the site to house more workers and cater better to the pilgrims' needs. For the most part, the churches at Abu Mina are not particularly Egyptian in architecture, perhaps because they were intended to appeal to foreign pilgrims. The main focus of worship on the site came to be the Martyr Church, which was built above the tomb of Menas. This large structure underwent five phases of construction from the fourth to eighth centuries, resulting in one of the most extensive and elaborate church complexes known from Late Antique Egypt. The Martyr Church was at times lavishly decorated and appointed, but this seems to have made it especially vulnerable to raids and destruction. Directly to the east of the Martyr Church, work was begun on the Great Basilica at the end of the fifth century. Through successive expansions and renovations the Martyr Church and Great Basilica eventually came to be joined and share structural ele-

Fig. 4.3.2
Abu Mina, view south across the site.

ments. Another large church, the Baptistery, was constructed to the west of the Martyr Church and includes baptismal fonts. Around these churches, an administrative residence and pilgrim quarters were built. There was special emphasis on the availability of pilgrim quarters near the remains of Menas – sleeping in close proximity to a martyr's relics was thought to bring cures and blessings. At one point the shrine was partially, although apparently never completely, walled. Another substantial church, the North Basilica, was built beyond this wall. The North Basilica had certain distinctive architectural features (a tripartite sanctuary with western return aisle, specific configuration of the baptistery and related chapel) not found in other Abu Mina churches. These features are, however, characteristic of Egyptian churches identified with Monophysitism, a Christian doctrine widespread in Egypt but at odds with the official doctrines prevalent in the Byzantine world (and at Abu Mina itself). Excavator Peter Grossmann has suggested that these features, along with the North Basilica's location outside the main Abu Mina settlement, show that the church served the needs of a Monophysite population at the site. There were no monastic quarters in the main part of Abu Mina, but some 1.5 km away lay the East Church, built in the sixth century, around which were clustered a number of monks' cells.

Fig. 4.3.3
Menas flask (Kelsey Museum, University of Michigan, 88209).

Pilgrimage to Abu Mina is especially associated with a particular class of artefact, the Menas flask or ampoule, a small pottery flask with two handles, which on one side bears a representation of Menas, often between two camels, sometimes with a pious inscription (fig. 4.3.3). The flasks were used by pilgrims to carry home drops of oil from lamps in the holiest places of the shrine. In addition to the extensive Menas cult at Abu Mina, the site had a cult of Thecla, a martyr from Asia Minor whose worship became popular in Egypt. She sometimes figured on the reverse of the Menas flasks, and her cult at Abu Mina seems to have been specifically aimed at female pilgrims. The shrine of Abu Mina was largely destroyed in the Sassanian Persian invasion of Egypt in AD 619. Although there was considerable rebuilding, especially in connection with the Martyr Church, the site never regained its earlier popularity. Except for limited and sporadic reoccupation, the site was effectively abandoned by the end of the ninth century. Thanks to the efforts of Kaufmann and Grossmann, the site of Abu Mina has been extensively excavated and recorded. The architectural remains from these excavations are still visible, and it is now relatively easy to reach Abu Mina by bus or car from Alexandria. Irrigation in recent years has raised the water table, however, and access beyond the modern monastery complex may be difficult or impossible in the wet season.

4.3.b In contrast to the extensive remains at Abu Mina, practically nothing ancient survives at **Abu Qir** (just to the east of the modern limits of Alexandria). But Abu Qir was once the site, not only of ancient Canopus, but also of **Menouthis**, a temple to the goddess Isis and later a Christian pilgrimage site and shrine that in its heyday might well have rivalled Abu Mina in size. The Roman-period temple of Isis at Menouthis was an important cult site, especially known for oracles and healing, which attracted numerous pilgrims. It seems to have survived the anti-pagan destruction directed at shrines in Alexandria and Canopus and lasted into the fifth century, but ultimately gave way to a parallel Christian cult. By the mid-fifth century, the Christian shrine of Cyrus and John was established at Menouthis and quickly became a popular pilgrim destination. Named after martyrs of the Diocletianic persecution, this shrine developed a complex of churches and buildings dedicated to the housing and activities of pilgrims. The Menouthis shrine included baths for the healing of sick pilgrims, but a more prominent feature was an area for curing by incubation, where as at Abu Mina afflicted pilgrims could sleep near the remains of the martyrs of the shrine and have cures suggested to them in dreams by the martyrs. Many of the pilgrims at the shrine were foreigners; Sophronius of Jerusalem visited the shrine in the seventh century, around its high point, and wrote about his visit. Thereafter, pilgrimage gradually began to die out, and Menouthis was largely abandoned by the end of the ninth century, when the healing cult of Cyrus and John had transferred to Constantinople and Rome. The shrine was gradually dismantled and its stones incorporated into other buildings to the point where little if anything of it survives. Excavations in 1917 yielded a number of artefacts which can be seen in the Graeco-Roman Museum in Alexandria, including some architectural fragments that give some hint of what this magnificent shrine was once like.

Bibliography: Davis 1998; Grossmann 1989, 1998, 2002; Kamil 1987; Külzer 1994; Montserrat 1998; Papaconstantinou 2001.

4.4 THE RED SEA MONASTERIES

The main Christian pilgrimage sites in the Eastern Desert are located in the north inland from the Gulf of Suez (fig. 4.4.2). There is a persistent association of this region with the earliest figures of Egyptian ascetic monasticism, the well-known Antony of Egypt and his more obscure predecessor Paul of Thebes. Although both men came from the Nile Valley and were widely commemorated at monasteries in and around Thebes, the monasteries in the Eastern Desert associated with them were particularly popular as centres for their veneration. These monasteries attracted pilgrims from within Egypt, but they feature in a number of Byzantine pilgrimage itineraries, and even more of their visitors came from elsewhere. The monasteries remain popular tourist destinations to this day and are reasonably accessible, although the best way to reach them is by means of an organized tour.

4.4.a The Monastery of Paul (Deir Anba Bula), about 20 km inland from the Gulf of Suez, was founded in the late fourth or early fifth century AD. It is named in honour of the first Christian hermit, Paul of Thebes, who is said to have fled into the desert in the wake of the Decian persecutions of the mid-third century and to have advised Antony on his ascetic career. The monastery appears in a number of travel accounts but seems not to have been a particularly wealthy or populous institution. Relatively little is known of its early history, and most of its existing structures are medieval or later, the result largely of periodic raids and destruction through the medieval period. The monastery contains four churches. The Church of Paul of Thebes is said to hold Paul's relics and to have been built in and around the cave where Paul lived; it contains decorations that may be of considerable antiquity. Two water sources at the monastery, the Spring of Paul and the Pool of Miriam, have mystical associations. The paintings in the monastery, like those at the Monastery of Antony, have recently been restored by an American-sponsored conservation team.

Fig. 4.4.1 Monastery of Antony.

4.4.b The Monastery of Antony (Deir Anba Antuniya) is about 20 km to the north of the Monastery of Paul and considerably more inland from the Gulf of Suez (fig. 4.4.2). It is named in honour of the man considered the founder of Egyptian ascetic monasticism, celebrated in the *Life of Antony* by Athanasius. The monastery is said to have been established in the mid-fourth century and is first attested at the beginning of the fifth. It began as a relatively simple assemblage of essential structures but soon became popular as a place of pilgrimage and expanded to accommodate its visitors. Eventually, the monastery came to include

Box 4.4

St Antony

The Egyptian figure most strongly associated with early monasticism in the popular mind is St Antony, who was commemorated in a classic biography by Athanasius of Alexandria. Born around AD 251 in Koma (Herakleopolite nome), Antony was inspired by the teachings and example of Jesus to give up his worldly possessions and become an ascetic hermit. Antony soon attracted followers and fled further and further into the desert, eventually settling close to the Red Sea, near the monastery that bears his name. Antony's ascetic adventure was widely known and imitated, and he is often credited with the founding of an ascetic monastic tradition in Egypt. Antony's fame spread greatly after his death in the mid-fourth century, thanks to the wide distribution of his biography by Athanasius. Through this Greek composition and its Latin translation, the *Life of Antony* became a primary text in the development of monasticism in the Mediterranean world and Europe.

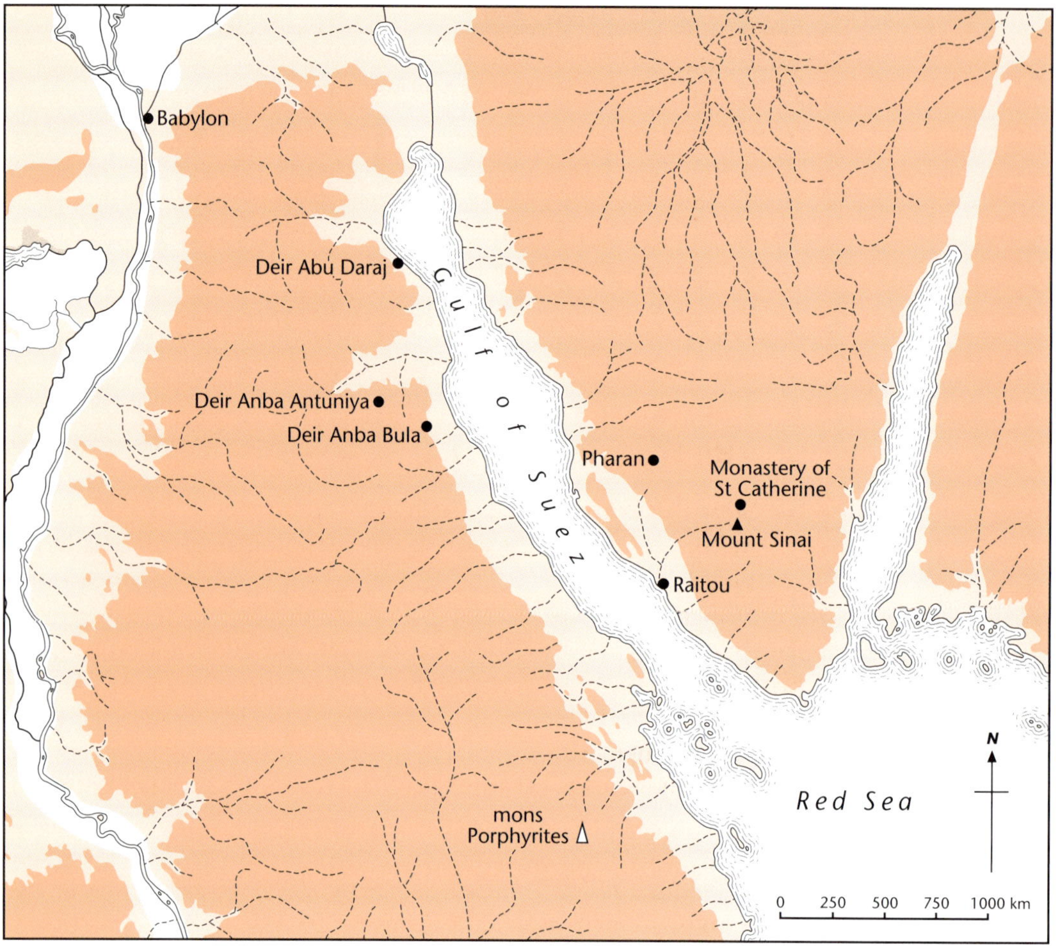

Fig. 4.4.2 Monasteries in the north-east.

four churches in its grounds, as well as quarters for monks and pilgrims. The Monastery of Antony became widely known within and outside Egypt and figures prominently in Byzantine pilgrimage itineraries. In general, the cult of Antony was more popular outside Egypt than within, perhaps reflecting the patterns of circulation of Athanasius' *Life of Antony*. In the seventh and eighth centuries the Monastery of Antony was home to monks following Chalcedonian rather than Coptic doctrines, and in later times the monastery was subject to various thefts and pillaging. It was heavily renovated and rebuilt in the twelfth and thirteenth centuries, this activity including the construction of a fortified wall and the extraordinary programme of wall paintings in the Church of Antony at the monastery. These paintings have recently been the subject of an heroic restoration campaign and are the main reason to see the site today. Although little of the earlier monastery survives, the restoration work has shown Late Antique origins for the oldest parts of the church.

To the north of the monasteries of Paul and Antony are a number of smaller and lesser-known monastic sites that were, in their heydays, important pilgrimage sites as well. The wadis to the north of Antony's monastery contained a number of hermit dwellings, grouped around wells at the monasteries of Deir Bakhit and Ain Bardah, that allowed ascetic monks to live relatively near the larger communities but maintain solitude. Further to the north, towards modern Suez, is the site of Deir Abu Daraj, a ruined monastery known primarily for its Coptic inscriptions and surrounding groups of hermit cells.

Bibliography: Bolman 2002; Grossmann 2002; Jobbins 1989; Kamil 1987; Külzer 1994; Moorsel 2002; Papaconstantinou 2001.

4.5 THE SINAI PENINSULA

The Sinai Peninsula is less accessible to the traveller than the pilgrimage sites on the Egyptian mainland, but this has not prevented pilgrims travelling to this region – indeed it may even have encouraged them. The pilgrim sites cluster in the south of the Sinai, where there are many places that have traditional associations with the biblical wanderings of the Israelites after the Exodus from Egypt (fig. 4.4.2). At present, coastal sites such as Raitou are accessible via the western coastal highways, while there is a well-established route for buses to reach the important sites of Pharan and the Monastery of St Catherine in the interior.

4.5.a The Monastery of St Catherine in the Sinai Peninsula is one of the best-known monastic sites in the world and one of the most frequently visited places in the Sinai (col. pl. 4.5.1). Begun as a fortified monastery by the emperor Justinian I after the death of his empress Theodora in AD 548, the Monastery of St Catherine is situated just below Mount Sinai (Gebel Mousa, Moses' Hill). The entire region is closely connected with biblical tradition: the plain below the monastery is said to have been the location of the camp of the Israelites, the site of the monastery itself where Moses encountered the Burning Bush, and Mount Sinai the place where Moses received the Ten Commandments.

The original sixth-century structure included a fortified wall around the monastery, emphasizing the military character of its architecture (fig. 4.5.2). Just inside the fortified gate was a courtyard, and perhaps quarters for visiting pilgrims and travellers. The monastic quarters, administrative structures and dining area in the original sixth-century monastery must have been extensive but no longer survive. What appears to have been an official residence of the Roman administrators not far from the entrance was converted into a mosque in the Fatimid period. The most extensive building from the original sixth-century

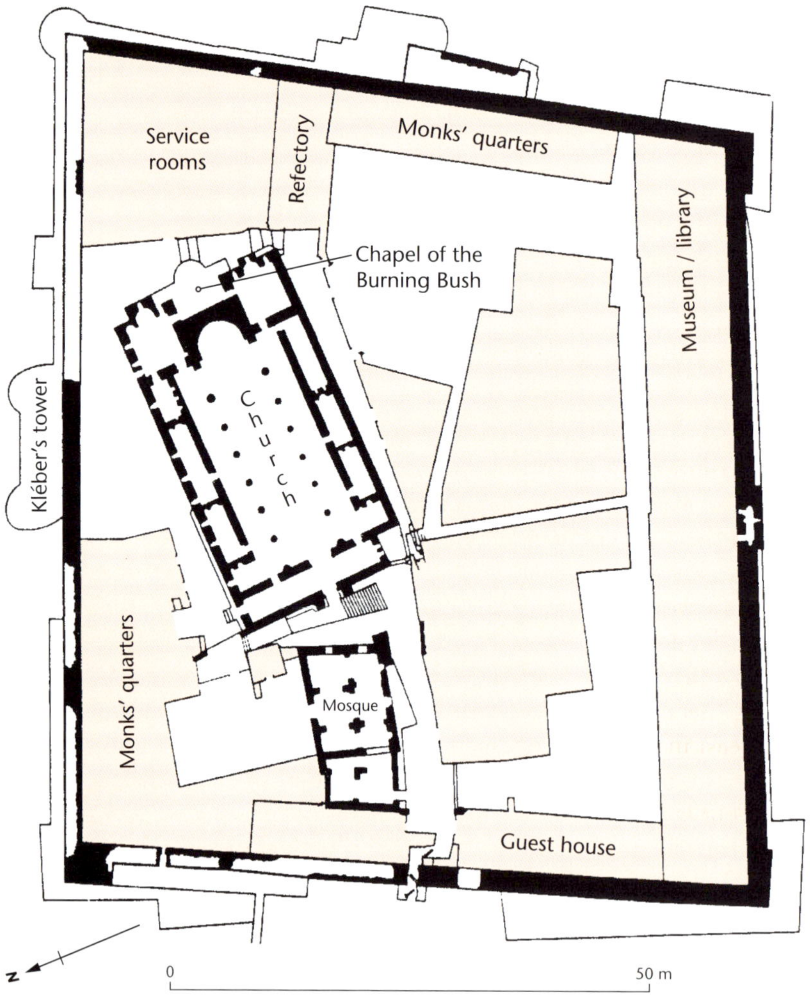

Fig. 4.5.2 St Catherine's Monastery (after Atiya 1991: 1682).

construction, and indeed the focal point of the entire site, is the Church of the Theotokos (Mary the 'God-bearing'). This elaborate and impressive church, some 20 x 50 m in size, originally contained eight chapels to various saints, enhanced in the medieval period by the addition of a chapel to the Burning Bush. Much of the decoration of the church, including an impressive series of mosaics and carved wooden ceiling beams, dates to the original sixth-century construction, although most of the furnishings, and the icons for which the church is renowned, are medieval additions. The church also contains the tomb of St Catherine of Alexandria, after whom the monastery was later named. The remains of St Catherine were transferred here in the fourteenth century from the nearby monastery where they were said to have been found. Given that the monastery is, and has always been, associated with Greek Orthodox rather than the Coptic tradition, it is not surprising that the design and layout of the Church of the

Theotokos and the Monastery of St Catherine in general are closer to Syrian and Palestinian models than Egyptian ones. There is very little here that could be called 'Coptic', and the library contains no Coptic manuscripts except fragments. The Monastery of St Catherine has been the subject of much historical interest over the centuries, but it was not until the University of Michigan–Princeton University expeditions to the site of 1956–65 that the remains of the sixth-century structures were thoroughly recorded. The Monastery of St Catherine was very popular with pilgrims and tourists from its foundation. The site has easy access by bus, and the monastery continues its time-honoured tradition of housing pilgrims, although most tourist accommodation is now outside it.

4.5.b Pharan (Firan) is an extensive site built at an oasis in the Wadi Firan. An already well-established Christian community is attested there in the late fourth/early fifth century, when the appointment of a bishop to Pharan is recorded. Monasteries are known there by the early fifth century, while there are frequent references to ascetic monks living in cells near Pharan, and indeed throughout the Wadi Firan. Later authors attest to the existence of more than 2000 monastic cells in the region. Pharan was a major Christian centre in the Sinai, and its bishop, at least in the sixth century, exerted authority over all monks in the region. The ruins of Pharan show it to have been an extensive walled settlement built on a hill, supporting thousands of inhabitants. In addition to the monasteries there and the many solitary monks, Pharan contained at least five churches, including one that seems to have been of considerable antiquity. Some of these churches were relatively small and unremarkable, but the Bishop's Church and the Church of Saints Cosmas and Damian would have been impressive landmarks. Most of the monasteries and churches of Pharan were ruins by the sixteenth century. The remains of Pharan have been the subject of intensive excavation by Grossmann. Ruins of some of the churches and monasteries at Pharan are still visible to the visitor, and the site is most easily accessible on the way to the Monastery of St Catherine.

4.5.c Raitou (al-Rayah, near modern al-Tur) was an important place in ancient and medieval times on the south-western coast of the Sinai Peninsula, a major centre for travellers headed for the Arabian peninsula. Little is known about its early occupation, but by the later Roman period Raitou was said to have been the resting place of the Israelites on their way out of Egypt after the Exodus and was, as such, a particularly appropriate stopping point for travellers – first Christian pilgrims on their way to the Monastery of St Catherine, and later Muslim pilgrims headed towards Mecca. Raitou was also a pilgrimage destination in itself, and pilgrimage itineraries note the nearby sand dunes and the palm branches available for pious purposes. The earliest records of solitary anchorites at Raitou date to the fifth century; the cells of these monks are mentioned by early travel writers, while the account of the martyrdom of forty Raitou monks at the hands of nomadic tribesmen suggests something of the hazards of this way of life. Indeed, a delegation of monks of the Sinai, presumably including some from Raitou, petitioned the emperor Justinian to build monasteries there to protect against raiders, and by the mid-sixth century there was at least one monastery at Raitou, the monastery of St John the Baptist, as well as a possibly later monastery of St George known from other sources. John, *hegumenos* (leader) of a monastery of Raitou, was the addressee of John Climacus's *Ladder of Divine Ascent* in the late sixth/early seventh century, and there are various references to monks at Raitou in subsequent centuries. By the sixteenth century, the Raitou monasteries seem to have been abandoned and are described as ruins, of which little survives today.

4.5.d Just to the north of Raitou lay a later Roman fort (*castra*) now known as **Qaryat al-Wadi**. This rectangular fort is built on a plan similar to other later Roman frontier forts found in North Africa and southwestern Asia. It was built of stone, approximately 55 x 90 m, and was bounded by an exterior wall incorporating eight towers. Within the fort were a complex of living quarters, a refectory, and administrative and storage structures; in the eastern part of the fort lay a relatively simple church, as had been mandated for all such forts under Theodosius I. This fort was excavated by a Japanese team in the 1990s and its ruins are still visible. Pilgrimage itineraries of Byzantine writers also mention nearby sites such as Busugera, which lay 11 km to the south of Raitou on the Red Sea. Busugera was particularly associated with the Old Testament prophets Elijah and Enoch, and was home to the Church of St Demetrios as well as a monastery to the south. Ancient tourists noted its ascetic cells, its date palms and the excellent hunting and fishing in the area. Also near Raitou, some 8 km to the west, was the church of St John Prodromos, an extensive church complex with numerous monastic cells nearby. Little is visible at, or known about, these sites today.

Bibliography: Forsyth 1968; Forsyth and Weitzmann 1973; Grossmann 1999–2000; Jobbins 1989; Kamil 1987; Külzer 1994.

5 THE FAYYUM

5.1 INTRODUCTION

5.1.a Access

The Fayyum lies to the west of the Nile, some 100 km south of Cairo. It can be reached by car from Cairo via Saqqara, or by the faster desert highway (toll) from Giza. A day trip from Cairo could comfortably take in Karanis, and either Dionysias or Hawara and Lahun. There are hotels and restaurants in Medinet el-Fayyum and along the southern shore of the Birket Qarun. Entrance tickets are required for Karanis and its museum, Dionysias, Hawara and Lahun; there is free access to the Naqlun monastery. This chapter describes those sites and the most important other sites.

Bibliography: Davoli 1998 gives a full gazetteer of sites; see also the Leuven Fayyum Database at fayum.arts.kuleuven.ac.be.

5.1.b Settlement and irrigation history

The Fayyum is a semi-oasis watered, ultimately from the Nile, by the Bahr Yusuf (Joseph's Canal) which flows through the natural gap in the hills at Lahun. From there several main radial canals distribute the water through the Fayyum. Surplus water drains off north into the Birket Qarun, a lake about 45 m below sea level, and now also to the Wadi Rayan to the west. The irrigation history of the Fayyum is still the subject of research and debate. The Fayyum has been inhabited since the fifth millennium BC. By the Old Kingdom it had a settlement called Shedet (Medinet el-Fayyum), which has been the site of the region's capital ever since, and a cult was established of Sobek (Souchos, or Sok-, in Greek), the patron crocodile god of the region. The supply of water from the annual inundation of the Nile was probably irregular and unreliable until Dynasty 12, when a canal was dug through the Lahun gap, and the increased inflow created a high lake (at about 18 m above sea level). The Egyptian name for the area was 'The Lake' – in the New Kingdom *P3-jm*, which is the origin, through the Coptic 'Phiom', of the medieval and modern name 'Fayyum'. An Arab myth attributed the creation of the lake instead to Joseph (hence Joseph's Canal), and explained the name as 'The Work of a Thousand Days' ('alf yom'). The pharaohs of Dynasty 12, especially Amenemhet III, erected several imposing monuments in the Fayyum, including the pyramids and mortuary temples at Lahun and Hawara, and other temples at Shedet, Biahmu, Dja (Medinet Madi) and Qasr es-Sagha. Building activity under later dynasties was relatively little, and confined to the

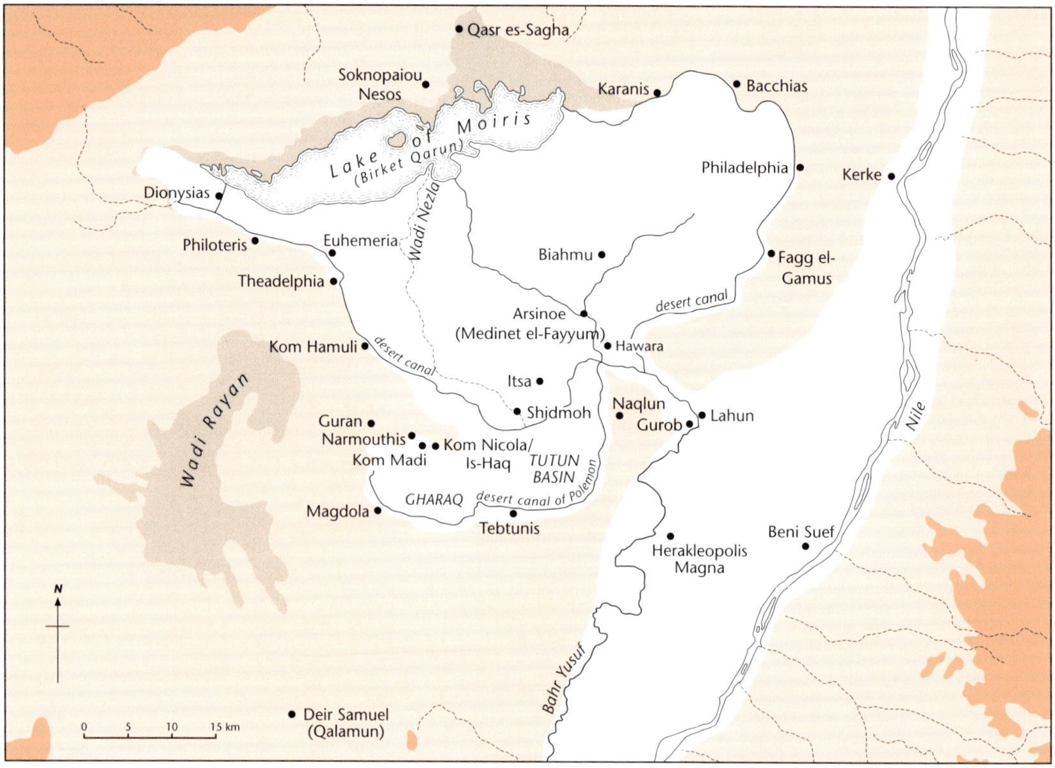

Fig. 5.1.1
The Fayyum.

capital and Lahun gap. Around 430 BC Herodotus claimed to have himself seen the high lake and statues at Biahmu and the temple complex at Hawara (the 'Labyrinth').

Under Ptolemy I and II (*c.* 310–250 BC) Macedonian engineers modified the Lahun dyke to control the inundation of the Fayyum, dug high-level canals running along the desert edges to carry water to the edges of the depression, and reduced the level of the lake (the Lake of Moiris) to approximately the level of the modern Birket Qarun. The cultivable area was tripled to about 1500 km^2, and new villages were founded by settling Greeks and transferring Egyptians from other nomes. Around 267 BC the Lake (in Greek 'Limne') became the Arsinoite nome, a full administrative region of Egypt, named after Arsinoe II, the sister-wife of Ptolemy II. The irrigation system and the prosperity of the Fayyum seem to have been maintained, more or less, through to the late second century AD, when there is evidence for severe depopulation in some villages due to the Antonine plague. Prosperity returned in the third century, when large estates took over vacant land to produce wine. In the early fourth century, for reasons which are not clear, many villages around the edge of the Fayyum ceased to receive adequate water supplies and were partially or wholly abandoned. By the fifth century the Fayyum was predominantly Christian, and numerous churches and monasteries were built. The sixth century saw a spread of small rural settlements, apparently units of large ecclesiastical and secular estates. The Arab conquest of the Fayyum in the 640s, although strongly resisted, did not greatly change the settlement pattern or population. The Fatimid conquest of AD 969, followed by the social and economic shocks of the earlier eleventh century, marked the real break from antiquity to the medieval period. The detailed fiscal description of the Fayyum written in 1245 by en-Nabulsi shows that the population was by then mainly Arab, and that settlement and agriculture were beginning to recover from a long period of contraction. However, although the central plateau of the Fayyum flourished thereafter, the outer zones were dominated by semi-nomadic Beduin to the nineteenth century. Through a gradual process of state investment, which still continues, the Beduin have been settled in villages, and regular irrigation and agriculture extended to near, and sometimes beyond, their Graeco-Roman limits.

Bibliography: Hewison 2001, an engaging introduction to the Fayyum, past and present.

5.1.c Modern research

The Fayyum is renowned for three types of archaeological find from the Ptolemaic to Coptic periods. First, the so-called 'Fayyum' portraits (they were produced elsewhere too), of the early Roman period (first to second centuries AD), which were mostly found in the cemeteries of Hawara, Philadelphia and Fagg el-Gamus (col. pls 5.2.3 and 5.5.1). Second, the Ptolemaic and Roman terracotta figurines (again, made elsewhere too), which populate many museum collections (box 5.1, fig. 5.1.2). Third, the thousands of papyri, mostly in Greek, but also in hieratic, demotic and Coptic Egyptian, Latin, Aramaic, Persian and Arabic, ranging in date from the fourth century BC to the eleventh century AD. Most of these had been dumped as rubbish in and around ancient settlements; some, in the Ptolemaic period, had been reused as 'cartonnage' to wrap mummies. Early Western visitors wanted to locate the fantastic monuments described by Herodotus, but the remains proved disappointing. It was Petrie, while excavating the pharaonic monuments at Lahun and Hawara in the 1880s, who first found and published a number of portraits and realised that the Fayyum was ringed with ancient village sites where papyrus documents might be preserved. Within the next ten years scholars such as Grenfell and Hunt, Jouguet and Rubensohn followed him. They and other entrepreneurs dug holes in numerous sites to find papyri, often with enormous success, but most showed little interest in the archaeology of the sites. Permits were also issued to farmers to demolish the mounds to extract the layers of *sebakh*, decayed organic material, which was used

'Fayyum' terracottas

One of the commonest types of find in excavations of sites of this period is terracotta figurines, called 'Fayyum' terracottas because this is where they were first found in quantity, but now known to have been produced and used throughout Egypt. They were cheaply made in moulds and brightly painted. Many of them represent the deities who were particularly thought to offer personal protection to individuals: Harpokrates was the most popular by far, followed by Isis and Bes, and also some naked female and priapic male demons. Other figurines represent worshippers with their arms raised in prayer (*orantes*), craftsmen and animals, presumably the intended beneficiaries of divine protection. People used the figurines mostly for worship in their homes but sometimes dedicated them in temples. (Dunand 1990)

Fig. 5.1.2 a–b Harpokrates, with wreathed headdress and a corncucopia, on a goose (British Museum EA 22159).

Camel loaded with wine jars (British Museum EA 37628).

as fertilizer; they also reused the ancient stone and mudbrick for their own buildings and sold the archaeological items to dealers. In the 1920s–30s American and Italian teams, while still searching for papyri, carried out more thorough and careful excavations of Karanis, Soknopaiou Nesos, Narmouthis and Tebtunis. From the 1940s onwards there have been excavations at Dionysias, Narmouthis, Tebtunis, Bacchias and Soknopaiou Nesos, on a smaller scale, but with as much care for the archaeology as for finding papyri. Regional surface surveys are trying to record what is left of the other ancient sites before they disappear completely under the re-expansion of settlement and agriculture.

Bibliography: Davoli 1998; Doxiadis 1995; Walker and Bierbrier 1997.

5.2 KARANIS AND THE NORTH-EAST

5.2.a The main modern excavations of the site of **Karanis (Kom Ushim)** were carried out by the University of Michigan in 1925–35, and many of the artefacts and papyri recovered are now in the Kelsey Museum, Ann Arbor. The enormous 60-hectare site, slightly smaller than Pompeii, is one of the best preserved in the Fayyum, although it continues to decay. It was founded in the third century BC, named after Karanos, the mythical Macedonian founder-king, and was occupied through to the sixth century AD or later. Most of the remains visible today are of the early Roman period (first to second century AD), partly because this was an especially prosperous period for Karanis, but also because later layers were largely destroyed before excavations began and earlier layers were often not reached. At its peak Karanis probably had a total population of around 4000, although some scholars think it was up to three times greater.

From the ticket office a path leads to the south temple, which was first excavated in 1895/6. The modern paths on the site have been lined with stones from ancient mills and presses, and pounding jars. The temple was dedicated under Nero to the crocodile-related gods Petesouchos and Pnepheros, as the partly legible inscription above its entrance reveals. It was built in Egyptian style, of limestone blocks, perhaps on the site of an earlier temple. Inside, a long entrance room is followed by two shrine rooms, with small storerooms and niches to each side, and two staircases leading to the roof terrace. The inner shrine has a hollow podium-altar. The temple lies at the west end of its enclosure (*temenos*), which filled a whole block of the street grid. The main gateway (pylon) lay on the east side. The north and south sides of the enclosure were filled by houses and storerooms, for the use of the priests, which were rebuilt several times on different plans. The stone doorway still standing in the south-east corner led into a dining room,
Box 5.1 built under Vespasian according to the inscription, which could be

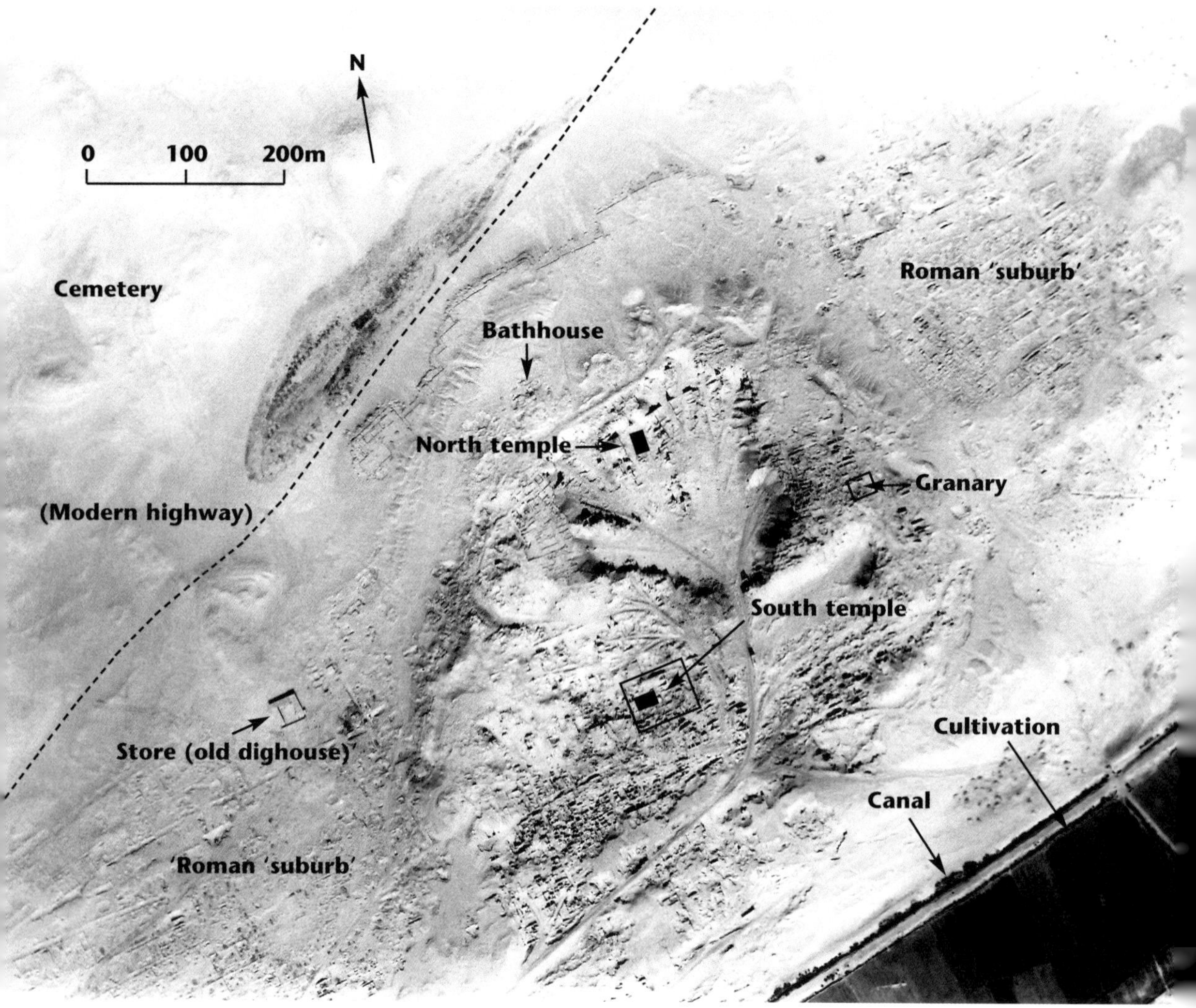

Fig. 5.2.1 Karanis, 1925 aerial view (Kelsey Museum, University of Michigan, neg. 4.1992).

hired for weddings and other ritual banquets. In the late second century a Graeco-Roman-style porticoed courtyard, with eighteen columns resting on a two-course stylobate (still visible), was built in the middle of the enclosure. The courtyard was reached by a staircase from the east gateway and led directly into the temple (the ground between them has been dug out in modern times). Around the same time, the temple doorway was flanked with two statues of crouching lions, and the north gateway of the enclosure, of which a stump survives, was rebuilt.

The modern path leads past the north gateway towards the north temple, passing an open area which may have been a public space. The north temple too is an early Roman construction, in limestone, whose podium overlies the foundations of an earlier building. It is in Egyptian style and undecorated, except for Graeco-Roman-style engaged columns on the outer corners and flanking each internal doorway. It had an inner and outer mudbrick enclosure wall (*peribolos*), each with a stone gateway, which survive in part (the steps up are modern). The god of the temple is unknown. Inside there is a series of three rooms, the last almost filled by a large podium-altar. Among the several side rooms and niches, a staircase on the right leads to the roof terrace, and a recess on the left, which had a slotted cover, gives access to steps to a concealed basement room, probably the temple treasury.

The baths some 50 m north-west of the north temple were excavated in 1975. They were built in the early Roman period, with Roman-style cupola roofing. The sequence of rooms, typical of Roman-style baths, is a changing room (*apodyterium*), a cold bath (*frigidarium*) whose semi-cupola still retains plaster painted with a vine-branch decoration, a warm bath (*tepidarium*), a hot-air room (*laconicum*), and a hot bath (*caldarium*). The heating and drainage systems can also be traced. These small baths probably served a restricted, Romanized, clientele.

Hundreds of houses and other buildings have been excavated at Karanis, but many were destroyed at the time or have crumbled since. The best visible examples are concentrated on the east and west sides of the site. Karanis had an irregular street grid of which little can be seen today. The Ptolemaic village perhaps lay mainly in the centre of the site. In the early Roman period the village expanded into the low-lying areas to the east and west (beyond the ticket office), and in the second century to the north too. There were some groups of finer houses west of the south temple and north of the north temple, but most houses were relatively small and plain, built of mudbrick with timber frame and reinforcements, and flat roofs of laced reeds. Houses were enclosed, with one lockable door off the street leading into a small courtyard, used for cooking (ovens survive) and keeping animals. Rooms were plain and undifferentiated. Floors were usually beaten earth, walls were plastered, then whitewashed; storage areas and corridors were given a black wash. The few windows were slits near ceiling height, more for ventilation than light, and easy to block against sandstorms. Wall niches were common, and served as cupboards, shrines or to hold oil lamps for lighting; some were decorated with coloured and figured paintings. Most houses had at least two storeys, one or two up, or a basement. Because rubbish was dumped everywhere, the ground level rose constantly, and it is difficult to tell how many 'layers' of a house site were occupied contemporaneously. Also, in any block, some houses would be occupied and others not, and unoccupied houses were used for dumping. The rubbish layers produced countless finds illustrating domestic life: furniture, tools, toys, lamps, jars, dishes, textiles, baskets, coins, documents on papyri and ostraka, and foodstuffs.

Other buildings, of which a couple of examples survive along the western ridge, are dovecotes and granaries. The dovecotes, often attached to houses, were hollow mudbrick towers with inward-facing terracotta jars set into the walls to serve as roosts; the rich fertilizer was scraped off the floor at the bottom. Granaries had thick, protective, outer mudbrick walls and rows of identical 'rooms' subdivided into square 'bins', forming a distinctive grid plan (fig. 5.2.2). The bins, in which grains and pulses for consumption and tax payments were stored, were accessed by walkways along the low tops of some internal walls; Roman-period granaries could have two or three stories, each supported by mudbrick vaulting. No definite architectural traces of churches at Karanis are reported, but Grenfell and Hunt found two large rooms with crude paintings of saints, one to the north of the site, the other just south-east of the temple, and there is documentary evidence for a Christian community. The main cemetery of Karanis lay to its north, with another to the north-west. Occasional excavations have revealed modest burials from the late Ptolemaic to Coptic periods.

Fig. 5.2.2 Karanis, granary C123 (Kelsey Museum, University of Michigan, neg. 5.3846).

The **museum** contains a miscellany of objects from pharaonic times to the nineteenth century, some from outside the Fayyum. Local finds include limestone busts of Arsinoe II and Marcus Aurelius from the regional capital Ptolemais Euergetis and of Sarapis from Lahun, and an early Roman mummy with a portrait painted, uniquely, on papyrus, from a cemetery near Naqlun.

Bibliography: Boak 1933, 1935; Boak and Peterson 1931; Husselman 1979.

5.2.b A string of ancient village sites curves round the eastern edge of the Fayyum from Karanis to Hawara, along the routes of the ancient and modern high-level canals. Many buildings are visible at the site of **Bacchias (Umm el-Atl)**, named after Bacchos, that is Dionysos, the patron deity of the Ptolemies, where digging at the turn of the century and recent Italian excavations have produced papyrus documents, many about the running of the temples. The large temple of Soknobkonneus, another form of Souchos, dominates because the ground around it has been dug deeply away. Only its mudbrick core stands, which had a limestone cladding carved with Egyptian-style reliefs and hieroglyphs. Right in front of it are remains of the foundations of another temple, apparently, despite its awkward position, of later date. Bacchias had an orthogonal street plan. The main east-west street ran along the long north side of the two temples. Following it west, there is a mudbrick structure, perhaps a Ptolemaic temple, on the north side, a district of large freestanding houses on the south side, and at the end, a group of recently excavated houses and a possible customs post. A granary is visible on the north-east ridge of the site. Bacchias was founded in the third century BC and was occupied until early Arab times, albeit on a reduced scale from the fourth century. There are no architectural traces of churches.

There was some digging for papyri at the site of **Philadelphia (Kom el-Kharaba el-Kebir)**, but it was farmers who stripped it to the ground to extract *sebakh*. There is virtually nothing to see, but its Roman cemetery (in old accounts said to be at er-Rubbayat) produced many of the 'Fayyum' mummy portraits painted in tempera (col. pl. 5.2.3, though this is an encaustic example), and in the village farmers are said to have found the Zenon Archive (box 5.2). This Ptolemaic foundation proba-

Box 5.2

The Zenon Archive

The Zenon Archive consists of some 2000 documents on papyrus, mostly in Greek, from the period 270–230 BC. Zenon emigrated to Egypt from Kaunos in Caria to work for Apollonios, also from Caria, the *dioiketes* (finance minister) of Ptolemy II. Some of the Zenon documents relate to Apollonios' activities as *dioiketes*, but over half concern the gift-estate of 10,000 *arouras* (2750 hectares) at Philadelphia granted to Apollonios by Ptolemy II, which Zenon managed for him. The archive attests the second phase of development of the estate, after completion of the major irrigation works referred to in other papyri, and illustrates Greek agricultural experimentation, including cultivation of the vine, olive and poppy (for oil), using a predominantly Egyptian labour force, who had been resettled in the Arsinoite from other nomes of Egypt. Other documents relate to Zenon's private affairs: he collected taxes, ran bathhouses, raised sheep and goats, hunted, supported the gymnasium and patronized young athletes. The Zenon Archive is the basis for the traditional view of the economic dynamism and success of the early Ptolemies (the 'royal economy'), but it is also informative on relations between settlers and natives. (Orrieux 1985; Pestman 1981) bly took its name from the 'brother-loving' (*philadelphos*) title of Arsinoe, the sister-wife of Ptolemy II. An aerial photograph of 1925 (fig. 5.2.4) shows that it was laid out on a regular orthogonal plan, parallel to the new high-level canal which had opened up regular irrigation of this area. The grid seems to have been meticulously respected up to the end of occupation in the early sixth century AD. Papyrus documents attest various private and public buildings, including temples to Greek and Egyptian deities, a granary, a record office, a prison, a gymnasium, bathhouses with porticoes and mosaic floors, and perhaps a theatre. Sadly, the site today is almost featureless. The cemetery just east of the village was used from the third century BC to the fourth century AD. In antiquity, as today, a desert road (the Darb Gerza) ran through the site eastwards towards a Nile port called Kerke (ar-Riqqa). Alongside the road ran a north-facing fortified mudbrick wall, probably a customs control and check on the movements of desert nomads.

In the foothills below the step pyramid at **Sila**, built by king Sneferu

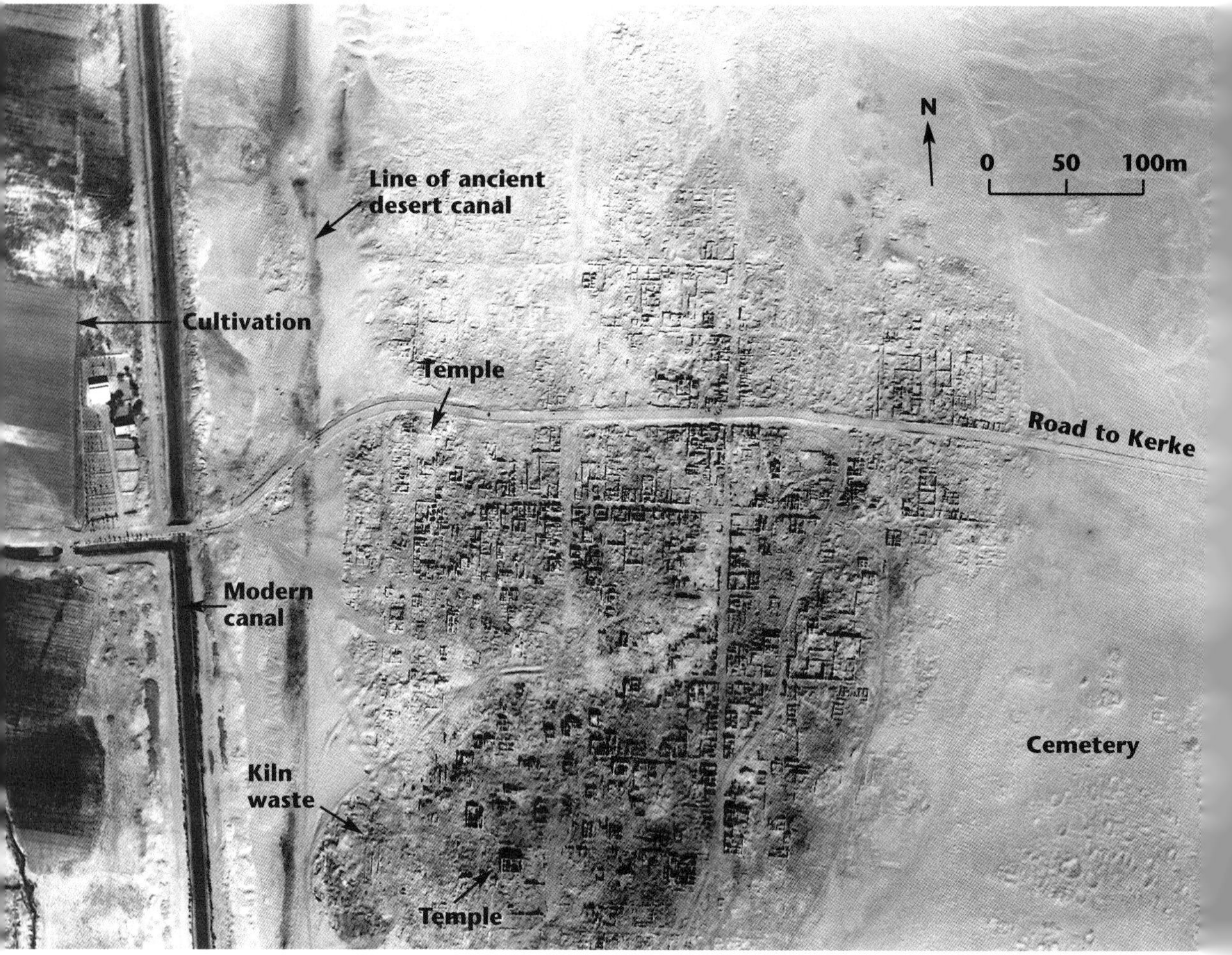

Fig. 5.2.4 Philadelphia, 1925 aerial view (Kelsey Museum, University of Michigan, neg. 4.1994).

of Dynasty 4, in a large area called **Fagg el-Gamus**, more mummy portraits in tempera of the early Roman period were found in the early twentieth century. Recent American excavations have exhumed burials of the late third century BC through to the eighth century AD. The later Roman mummies are often wrapped in layers of fine coloured textiles, and their teeth have been sampled for DNA analysis.

5.2.c On the north side of the Birket Qarun is the site of **Soknopaiou Nesos (Dime)**, which can be reached by boat from Shaksuk and then walking (past the shell of the American mudbrick dig-house of 1931/2). The site, which stands on a north-south ridge about 20 m above sea level, suffered sporadic destructive diggings for papyri, other antiquities, stone and *sebakh*. It is dominated by the temple enclosure (*temenos*) in its north-west corner, whose mudbrick walls were clearly built in sections with a deliberate concave sag for stability, and still stand to a height of 10 m. Inside are the stumps of the dry-stone and mudbrick walls of one temple, which was rebuilt more than once, and, to its north, scattered limestone blocks from another temple, both presumably of forms of Souchos. Several statues of deities and priests, in mixed Egyptian–Hellenistic style, and stelae with Greek inscriptions were found inside the *temenos*, and some survive in the Alexandria and Cairo museums. A long *dromos*, paved in sandstone, leads to the *temenos* from the south end of the village. Its southern gateway was probably the only entrance to the village, which was ringed by walls, incorporating the backs of houses, as a defence against sandstorms. There are residential areas along both sides of the *dromos*, which included freestanding dense blocks of small houses and some fine large houses, mostly built of mudbrick. One of the two well-preserved houses on the east side has cellars with domed ceilings. The houses, and the numerous papyri, are almost all of the first and second centuries AD, but there is evidence of habitation from the third century BC, including Greek and demotic ostraka of the second century BC. The Ptolemaic and Roman cemeteries to the north-west and south-west produced human mummies in cartonnage and crocodile mummies. The village had no permanent agricultural land, and the papyri show that many villagers acted as priests of the temples, donkey- and camel-drivers on the desert routes, and fishermen. The height and name of the site (Island of Sobek), and finds from New Kingdom burials, suggest that the Graeco-Roman temples may overlie a Dynasty 12 temple built to mark the northern edge of the high lake, but proper archaeological investigation of the temples has only just begun. The village was decimated by the Antonine plague and abandoned by the mid-third century, probably because changes in pagan religion had led to a decline of visitors and offerings.

Some 10 km north-east of Soknopaiou Nesos, at **Qasr es-Sagha**, is a Dynasty 12 temple (and workers' town) later occupied by Coptic monks. A few kilometres further north-east are the remains of **Deir Abu Lifa**, a small Coptic monastery of the seventh to ninth centuries. A church and rows of small rooms off two corridors were tunnelled into a striking limestone outcrop, which is now collapsing.

5.3 DIONYSIAS AND THE NORTH-WEST

5.3.a The restored temple at **Dionysias (Qasr Qarun)**, named after Dionysos, the patron deity of the Ptolemies, has been popular since the eighteenth century with visitors, who often carved their names on the jambs of the entrance (fig. 5.3.1). The temple was at first wrongly identified as Herodotus' Labyrinth; locally, the modern village name is taken to mean 'Castle of Karun', a legendary evil ruler (rather than to refer to the adjacent Birket Qarun). The Ptolemaic temple is a limestone construction in a plain Egyptian style, with a simple cornice and decorated doorways. On the ground floor three central rooms lead to the shrine room, where the middle of three niches held a mummified crocodile representing Souchos. On both sides there is a row of storerooms and a staircase to the upper storey; there are also underground and mezzanine rooms. Upstairs, one large room precedes the shrine, where a life-size relief depicts a Ptolemaic king (on the right) making an offering to Souchos, in human form with a crocodile head.

The temple roof offers a panorama over the 40 hectare site. A long *dromos*, flanked by various buildings, including dining rooms and a glassware workshop, leads from an open-air stone kiosk at its east end

Fig. 5.3.1 Dionysias, the temple *c.* 1800 (*Description de l'Egypte* IV 69.2).

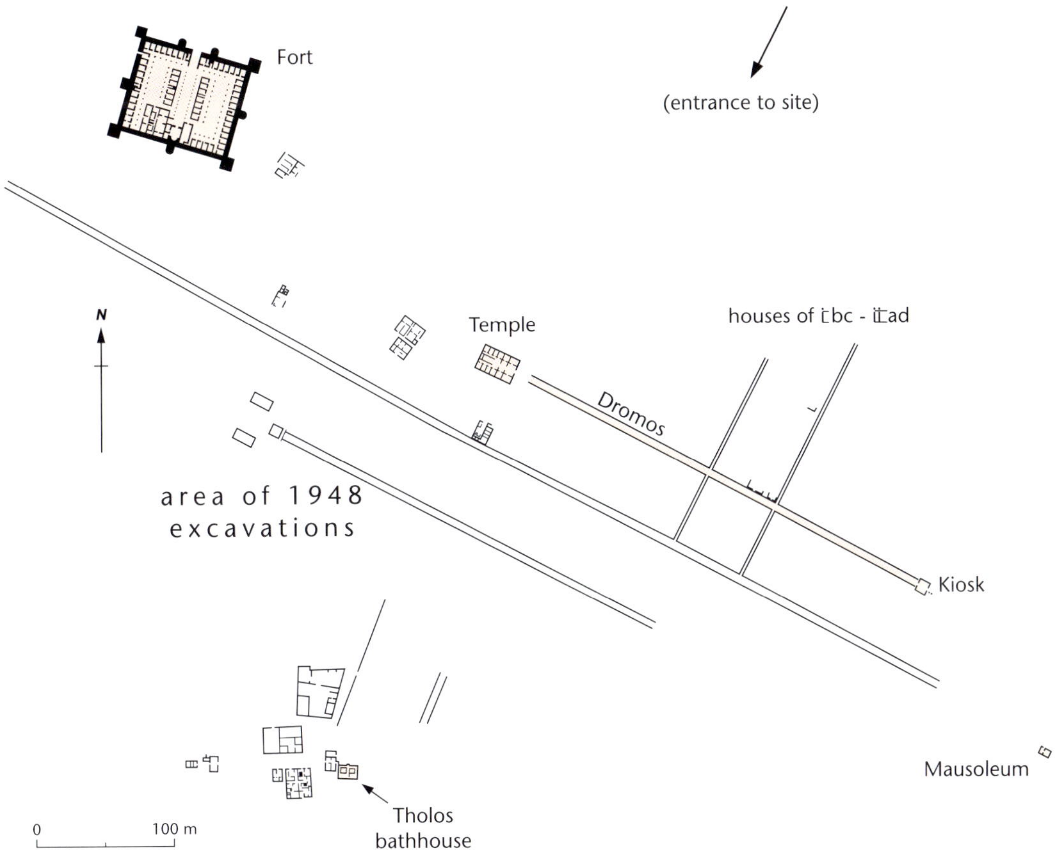

Fig. 5.3.2
The town of Dionysias (after Schwartz and Wild 1950: pl.II).

to the unusual two-storey vestibule building immediately in front of the temple. The village, a new foundation of the third century BC, was sited on a rock platform amid fields irrigated by new canals, of which there are traces along the nearby desert edge. It was centred on the temple and was crossed by several long east-west streets parallel to the *dromos*. Almost nothing is now visible of the houses and other buildings to the west and south of the temple excavated in 1948 and 1950, which included a *tholos* bathhouse (fig. 5.3.3), in which the bathers sat in individual basins around a circular room covered by a vaulted rotunda (*tholos*), while the attendant poured jugs of hot water over them. To the east, however, a large area has been exposed of stone houses built on top of refuse of the late Ptolemaic and early Roman periods. At Dionysias, it seems, most rubbish was cleared away before houses were rebuilt, and so, unusually, no mound was created. South-east of the kiosk stands a mausoleum of the later third century AD. The tombs lie under the stone podium of the octagonal chamber, which had a vaulted roof and was fronted by a four-column portico.

Some 200 m west of the temple is the clear outline of a rectangular fort, built or rebuilt in the early fourth century under Diocletian, to

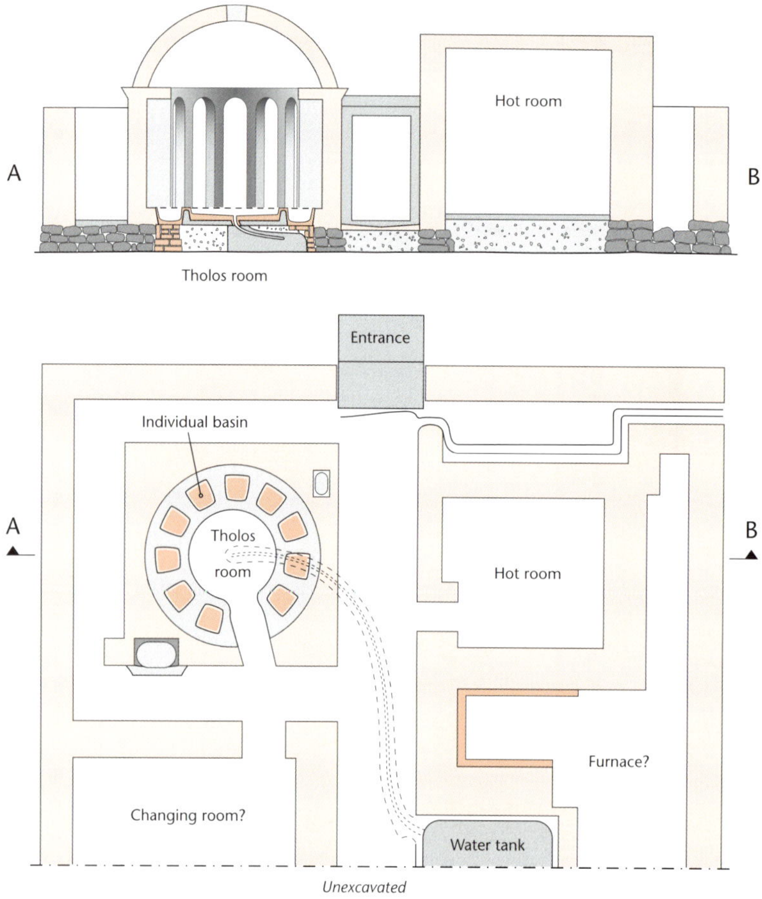

Fig. 5.3.3 Dionysias, *tholos* bathhouse (after Schwartz and Wild 1950: pl.XIV).

control the desert route from the Fayyum to the Oases and the copper mines along it. Each corner has a square tower, three of the walls have an intermediate bastion, and the north wall has the fortified gateway. The gateway opens into a long narrow courtyard, originally lined with columns reused from other buildings, which ends in steps up to an apsidal shrine for the military standards, where fragments of a marble statue of Nemesis (the 'Fortune' of the emperors) were found. On either side of the shrine were headquarters buildings, and the east and west halves of the fort each contained a courtyard surrounded by porticoed rows of small plain rooms, in total just over fifty. Most of the men and horses of the cavalry unit based here were detached to duties elsewhere. In buildings between the fort and the temple, soldiers cast their own bronze coins, and incised images of Sol Invictus (Unconquered Sun), their special deity. Eighty papyri found at Philadelphia relate to Flavius Abinnaeus, who was in charge of this garrison and of policing the area in the mid-fourth century. Dionysias was largely abandoned around the end of the fourth century, but there is some evidence for later occupation.

5.3.b The neighbouring villages of Theadelphia and Euhemeria were both Ptolemaic foundations of the third century BC which were abandoned by the later fourth century AD. In the early twentieth century **Theadelphia (Kharabet Ihrit)** was an imposing undisturbed mound in the desert, and excavations uncovered fine temples and houses. Since then, cultivation has once again surrounded the site, which *sebakhin* have stripped to a flat field of potsherds, except for a dump of waste from a glass-workshop and a few fragments of Roman-period constructions which used hydraulic cement. These include a bathhouse cistern on three brick arches, which were originally underground, the floors of two double-*tholos* bathhouses, and two pairs of vats for collecting the juice from winepresses (fig. 5.3.5). Just north-west of the site the graves of one cemetery are visible. Numerous papyri were found at Theadelphia, notably tax registers of the later second century AD, several certificates of pagan sacrifice from the Decian 'persecution' (c. AD 250), and the Heroninos Archive, around a thousand letters and accounts about the running of a large third-century AD estate (Rathbone 1991). A Ptolemaic temple to Pnepheros (Sobek) was found, from which the stone pylon of the outer wall, with two statues of crouching lions, the pylon of the inner court and the painted shrine were moved to the Graeco-Roman Museum, Alexandria (col. pl. 5.3.6).

Fig. 5.3.4
Theadelphia in 1899
(A.S. Hunt, EES
no.30).

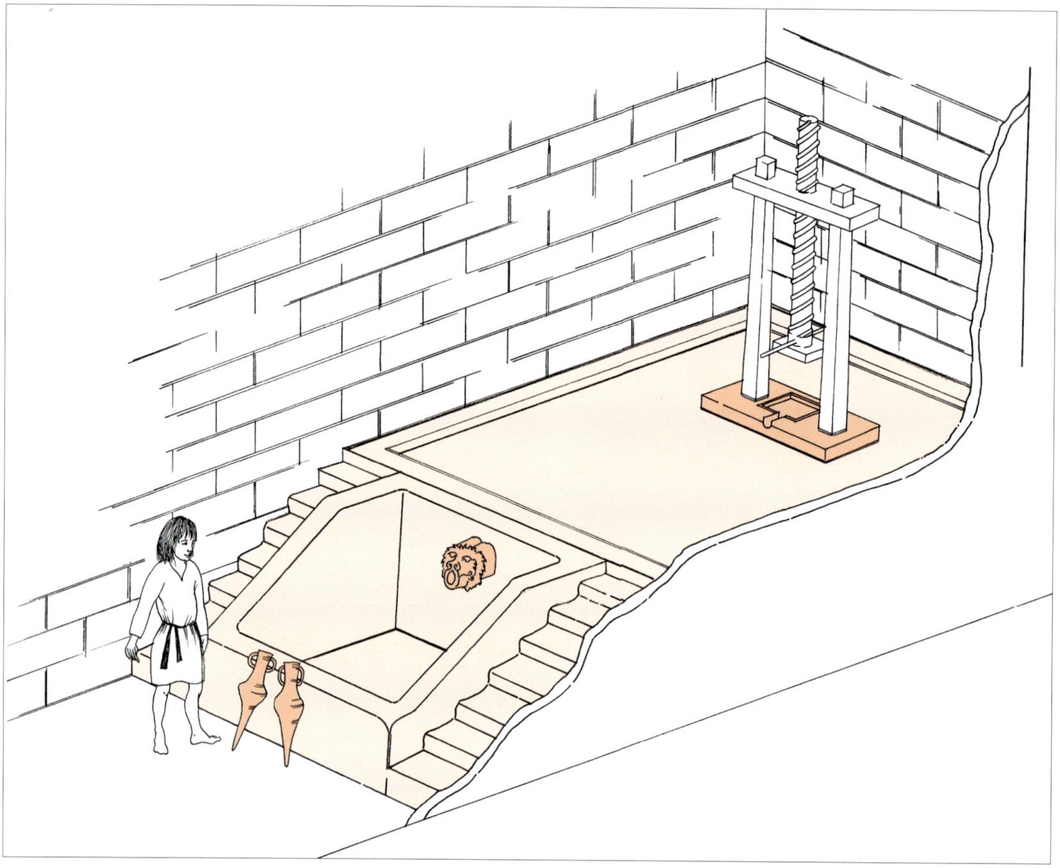

Fig. 5.3.5 Reconstruction of Roman winepress.

Other finds on display there include the wooden gate from the inner pylon, dated to 137 BC, and the mummified crocodile from the shrine's central niche, lying on a bier used for carrying it in processions.

At **Kom Hamuli**, on the desert edge some 10 km south of Theadelphia, a monastery of the Archangel Michael was built on the site of the abandoned Graeco-Roman village of Philagris. *Sebakhin* digging here in 1909 found a rich collection of Coptic codices of the ninth to tenth centuries, most of which are now in the Pierpoint Morgan Library, New York.

5.4 NARMOUTHIS, TEBTUNIS AND THE SOUTH-WEST

5.4.a Tutun basin dyke. Topographically the south-west Fayyum is divided by a rocky ridge into two depressions, the Tutun basin (properly the Hod el-Tuyur) to the east, and the lower-lying Gharaq basin to the west. After the Ptolemaic lowering of the high lake, an enormous dyke was built across the north-west corner of the Tutun basin to hold and control the annual inundation, which otherwise would have drained straight down the natural ravine of the Wadi Nezla into the lake. Substantial sections of the dyke are visible from the road between Itsa and Shidmoh, mostly as repaired or rebuilt in fired brick and cement from the Roman period onwards. The most impressive section is where the dyke, here a huge earth bank retained by brick buttressing, still carries the modern road across the start of the Wadi Nezla. On the south-east side there is a stretch of facing in dressed limestone blocks, perhaps of Ptolemaic date. There is no natural drainage out of the Gharaq ('drowned') basin, which nowadays is drained by pumping. In the Graeco-Roman period it held a small lake of its own, ringed by villages and their irrigated lands which extended far into what is now desert.

Bibliography: Garbrecht and Jaritz 1990.

5.4.b The remains of **Narmouthis (Medinet Madi)**, a settlement of pharaonic origin, occupy a 60 hectare site high on the desert edge. Windblown sand constantly threatens to rebury the buildings cleared by the Italian excavations of 1934–9 and from the 1960s to the present. The site is entered from the north-east, passing the mudbrick dig-house. It consists of two ridges of remains on either side of the north-south temple *dromos*, which slowly spread out and slope away to the south. The *dromos*, which began with a Roman-period kiosk (reburied), was repaved at least twice in Graeco-Roman times. It is lined with stone retaining walls, inset with staircases leading to the priests' houses and other buildings, and pairs of crouching sphinxes, with the face of a Ptolemaic king, at 10 m intervals. A stone wall topped by two crouching lions creates an open-air vestibule to the temple complex. Its original doorway (now in the Graeco-Roman Museum, Alexandria) was inscribed with building dedications of 96 BC, and later with four hymns to Isis-Thermouthis composed in Greek by an Egyptian priest. The mudbrick enclosure wall is entered through a large stone pylon, on whose left inside wall survives the lower part of an unfinished late Ptolemaic relief representing Isis seated and suckling Harpokrates. A break in the enclosure to the right opens to a recently discovered subsidiary Ptolemaic temple oriented to the east. This Egyptian-style complex is of mudbrick, apart from the limestone pylon and doorway to the temple; to one side is a vaulted room with a winepress. The temple has niches for two mummified crocodiles, presumably another Souchos pair. To the south of this temple is a fine house with walls plastered and painted to imitate marble.

The east side of the *temenos* of the main temple is filled with mudbrick storerooms, some vaulted, which were repaired and reused through to Byzantine times. In one room, sealed by a later floor, two storage jars were found which contained over 1500 Greek and demotic ostraka of the second century AD to do with the priests' activities. The second

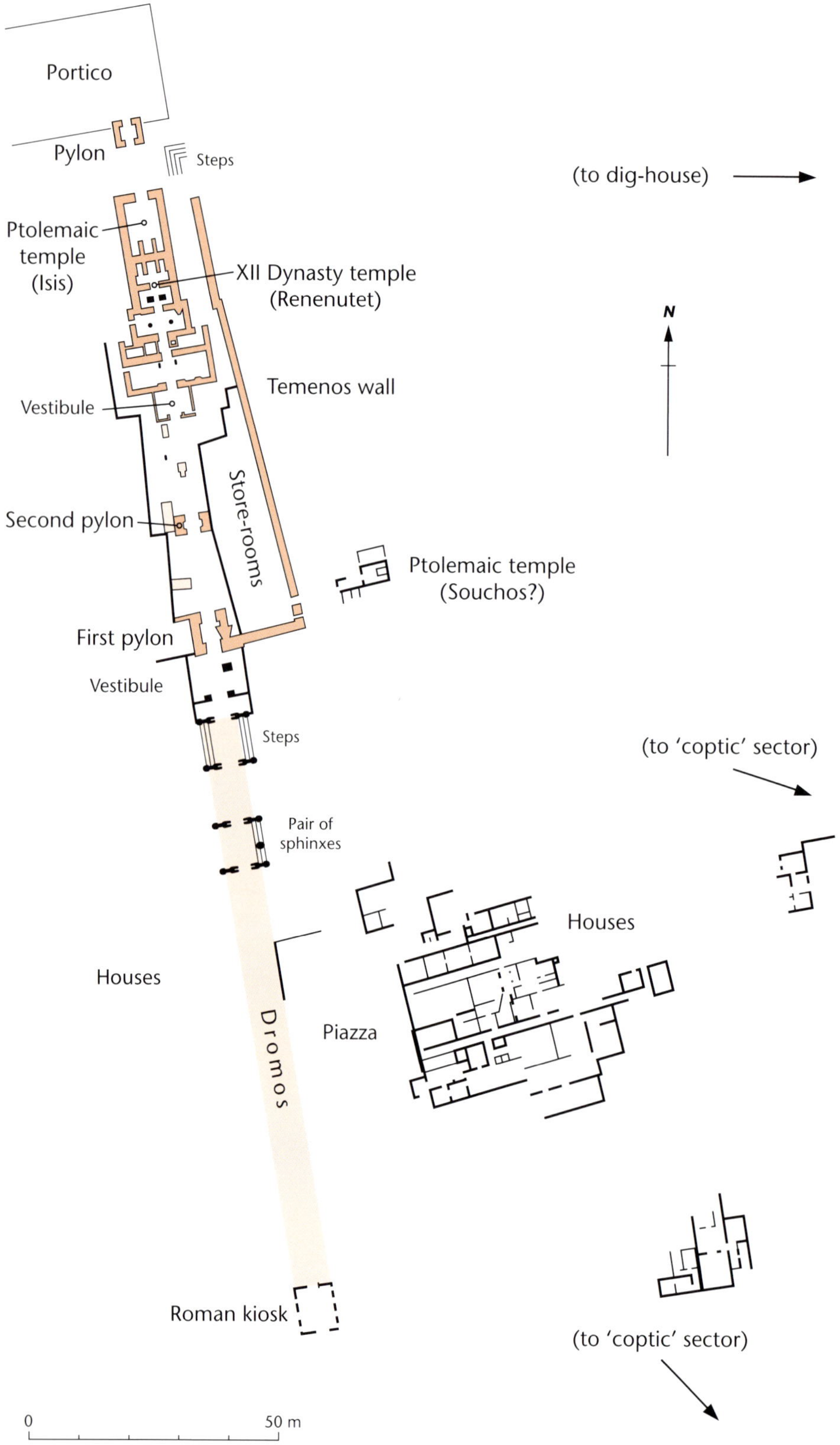
Portico
Pylon
Steps
(to dig-house)
Ptolemaic temple (Isis)
XII Dynasty temple (Renenutet)
N
Temenos wall
Vestibule
Store-rooms
Second pylon
Ptolemaic temple (Souchos?)
First pylon
Vestibule
Steps
(to 'coptic' sector)
Pair of sphinxes
Houses
Houses
Piazza
Dromos
Roman kiosk
(to 'coptic' sector)
0
50 m

pylon between the courtyards leading to the main temple had reliefs representing a Ptolemaic king, whose feet are still visible, on both (south) sides of its doorway. Another open-air vestibule precedes the Ptolemaic façade of the temple, which is embellished with four semi-columns. There follow two anterooms and a courtyard around two columns, all of Ptolemaic date, in which numerous inscriptions and statues were found. The north wall of this inner courtyard made a closed room out of the previously open porch of the original pharaonic temple, whose roof is supported by two massive papyriform columns. The reliefs with hieroglyphic texts on the walls of the porch and the shrine record that the temple was founded by Amenemhet III, and completed by his son Amenemhet IV. It was dedicated to Renenutet, the cobra goddess of harvests, in Dja, the original pharaonic name for the site, and to Sobek. Narmouthis means the town of Thermouthis, which is the Greek form of Renenutet, who, by or in the Ptolemaic period, was being absorbed into the cult of Isis. The shrine has three chapels with platforms for statues of Renenutet and other deities. A Ptolemaic temple was built back-to-back with the pharaonic temple. It has reliefs of a dedicant and of Souchos on the left of the doorways to its two anterooms, and Thermouthis is represented in the middle one of its three chapels. The courtyard in front (north) of this temple has a monumental staircase leading up to an unknown building on the east, and a pylon to the north. A three-sided portico with Corinthian capitals was added outside the pylon in Roman times.

Two areas of housing have been excavated, both with buildings of Roman to Byzantine date overlying Ptolemaic structures. The one just west of the *dromos* has been mostly reburied. The other is a block of eight houses, on stepped levels rising from an open space to the east of the *dromos*, with alleys running west-east between them (fig. 5.4.2). The houses were built of mudbrick with limestone doorways and corners and are large and well appointed. Several big rooms have a wainscoting of stone slates, one has a paved floor, and there are traces of wall plaster painted with coloured rectangles to imitate marble panelling. An aerial photograph (1934) shows that, by the Roman period, the north-east quarter of the site, around the dig-house, was packed with houses on a fairly regular street grid. In the late Roman period the settlement expanded to the south-east, where there are surface traces of eight excavated churches (the northernmost one is about 100 m south of the dig-house). The churches, built from the fourth to sixth centuries AD, were elaborately decorated with reused architectural elements in stone and new woodcarvings and figured wall paintings. But there was still some religious diversity. A box of fourth/fifth-century copies of texts of the Manichaean religion, translated from the Greek and Syriac originals into an Upper Egyptian dialect of Coptic, is said to have been found in the cellar of a house here by *sebakhin*; the texts are now in

Fig. 5.4.1
The centre of Narmouthis (after Ferri 1989).

Berlin and Dublin. Coptic and Arabic texts from the site date through to the early tenth century, after which the village was abandoned. Burial areas of the Ptolemaic to Coptic periods ring the mound.

5.4.c About 1 km south-east of Narmouthis is the small site of **Kom Madi** (or the East Kom), where some buildings were excavated in 1977–8. On the south side of its highest point, where rails and trucks used in the 1939 excavations at Narmouthis are stacked, are the bricked-up remains of a Ptolemaic funerary shrine. Wall paintings of the second century BC in the broad anteroom depict an over life-size ruler, probably a Ptolemy, or possibly Alexander the Great, making a libation and driving a chariot, and a parade of sword-bearing soldiers, perhaps the king's bodyguard (col. pl. 5.4.3). The walls of the central inner shrine depict Osiris flanked by other Egyptian deities and worshippers. The complex was reused in the late Roman period as a bakery. Just north-west lie the remains of a mudbrick shrine to Imhotep, and further north-west the mudbrick façade, with a limestone doorway, of a temple of Anubis, both also of Ptolemaic date. About 1 km further south-east begins an extensive area of ruins, known as **Kom Nicola** and **Kom Is-haq**, where traces of several churches are visible. The ancient names of these sites are unknown.

Fig. 5.4.2 Narmouthis, houses by the *dromos*.

Several kilometres west of Narmouthis in the desert are the compact ruins of **Guran**, another village, the ancient name of which is unknown, excavated by Jouguet in 1901–2. In the Ptolemaic cemetery on the adjacent ridge, he found cartonnage mummies from which numerous Ptolemaic-period documents were extracted. Jouguet also excavated at **Magdola (Medinet en-Nehas)**, on the western edge of the Gharaq basin, where he found more Ptolemaic cartonnage mummies, whose texts include a roll of third-century petitions to the king. Some of Jouguet's finds are at the University of Lille; the papyri are at the Sorbonne. Huge sand dunes are slowly crossing the site of Magdola, whose few visible remains include several Roman-style winepresses and a group of columns reused for a Byzantine church.

Some 25 km south-west of Magdola, at the south end of the Wadi Rayan, lies the **Monastery of St Samuel**. Hermits settled in caves in the hill of **el-Qalamun** in the fourth century. The monastery developed later, and in the seventh century was presided over by Samuel (see Alcock 1983). It was destroyed by Beduin in the ninth century, rebuilt, then abandoned in the sixteenth century; its modern occupation began in 1898. The rectangular stone enclosure wall has been rebuilt frequently, but the stone keep is ancient. The monastic buildings incorporate antique elements, including Corinthian capitals, whether from previous phases or brought here from other sites.

5.4.d The 50 hectare site of **Tebtunis (Umm el-Brigat)** was occupied perhaps from Dynasty 12, certainly from the fourth century BC, to the Fatimid era. Of all the Fayyum sites, it has produced the greatest quantity and variety of documents, mostly in Greek and demotic, on papyrus and ostraka. After the excavations of the early twentieth century (the finds of Grenfell and Hunt are in the Phoebe Hearst Museum and Bancroft Library at Berkeley), *sebakhin* were active across the northern half of the site, but much of it is still relatively intact, and the Italian excavations of 1929–36 (now being studied for proper publication) and the ambitious Franco-Italian project in progress since 1988 are making this the best-excavated village in the Fayyum.

The temple of Soknebtunis, meaning 'Souchos lord of Tynis', lies at the south-west corner of the site. Although Grenfell and Hunt found some Middle and New Kingdom burials, no remains of a temple or houses definitely of pharaonic date have yet been found. The paved *dromos* which leads due south towards the temple is of Augustan date, and was built up over the original early Ptolemaic *dromos*. The bases for a pair of lions mark its start, followed by a kiosk built of rusticated blocks (unusual, so perhaps unfinished) in a walled enclosure. Between them, another *dromos*, also Roman, leads off west into the desert, probably towards a large painted underground chamber (not yet rediscovered), which may have been the funerary temple of Souchos. The pair of crouching lions beyond the kiosk mark where the Ptolemaic

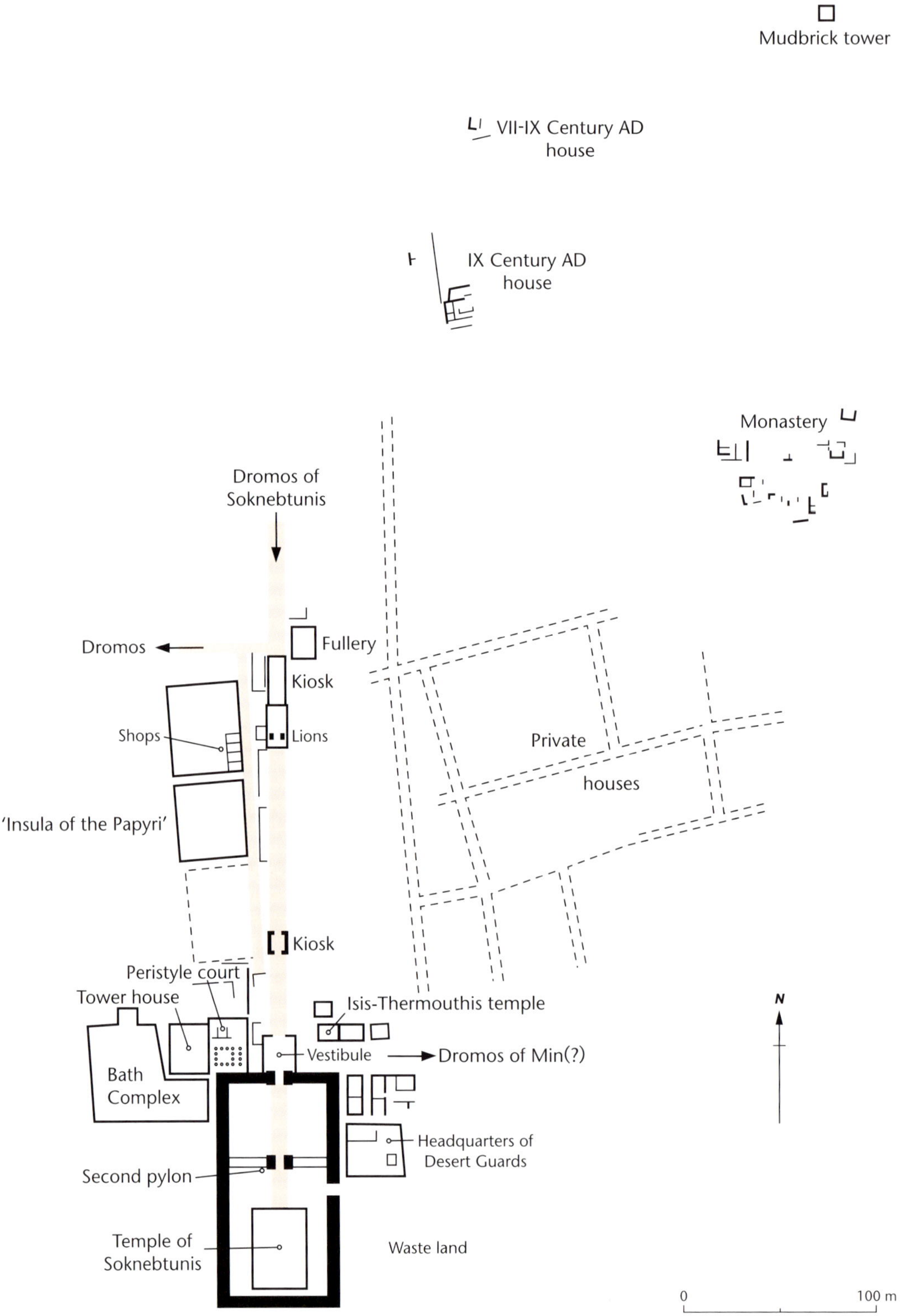
Mudbrick tower
VII-IX Century AD house
IX Century AD house
Monastery
Dromos of Soknebtunis
Dromos
Fullery
Kiosk
Shops
Lions
Private houses
'Insula of the Papyri'
Kiosk
Peristyle court
Tower house
Isis-Thermouthis temple
Bath Complex
Vestibule
Dromos of Min(?)
Headquarters of Desert Guards
Second pylon
Temple of Soknebtunis
Waste land
N
0
100 m

Fig. 5.4.4 The town of Tebtunis (after Gallazzi and Hadji-Minaglou 2000: 39).

dromos began; the next kiosk is early Ptolemaic. The *dromos* ends at an open-air vestibule, built under Ptolemy XII or Augustus, whose stone walls were carved with reliefs representing the elaborate annual procession out of the temple of the mummified crocodile of Soknebtunis. The temple complex of Soknebtunis, along with its enclosure and *dromos*, was a wholly new construction under Ptolemy I. A stone pylon through the massive mudbrick enclosure led into the first courtyard, where various structures were found, including two cellars filled with mostly second-century AD papyri containing religious, scientific, literary, administrative and private texts, in hieratic, demotic and Greek, to do with the temple and its priests. The foot of a relief, probably of a Ptolemy making offerings, is visible on the inside right wall of the second pylon (fig. 5.4.5). In the inner court, surface fragments where the temple once stood showed that it had been built of stone and decorated with painted reliefs, but only the mudbrick foundations survive. Up against the enclosure on both sides are rows of mudbrick cells for the priests or storage. Texts show that the temple prospered through the Roman period, at least into the third century. However, the temple and gateways were dismantled in the Byzantine period to provide stone to build churches.

In the Roman period, dining rooms (*deipneteria*) were built on open ground on both sides of the *dromos* of Soknebtunis and the one leading west from it, and a fullery was established opposite the lateral *dromos*.

Fig. 5.4.5 Tebtunis, Sobek and a Ptolemy on a relief from the temple.

The *deipneteria* were used for club and family feasting. Behind the dining rooms to the west were blocks of Roman housing. The first block down ended with four lock-up shops open to the street, which sold food. The next block, built over a Ptolemaic portico, is called 'the block (*insula*) of the papyri', because it produced almost a thousand administrative and literary texts. Blocks further south contain some tower houses and small granaries. Just before the temple there is a peristyle courtyard of fluted Ionic columns, once plastered and painted to resemble marble, on a stylobate, with a row of Doric columns to their east and a series of rooms to the north, perhaps the base of a club. It was built in the first century BC on the site of earlier buildings, was modified in the first century AD, when the shrine was added, and continued in use to the third century. Immediately to its west is a large mudbrick tower house, built in the first century AD and in use to the third century. Part of it was built over a public bathhouse, of small rooms with individual stone baths, of the third to second century BC. This was replaced by the monumental bath house to its west, of the late second century BC to first century AD, which has separate bathing-rooms for men and women and a massive underground cistern.

On the other side of the main *dromos*, leading off east from the vestibule, is another broad *dromos*, which a document suggests led to a temple (unlocated) of Min or Osiris. Up against the vestibule wall almost a hundred small animals were sacrificed and buried in Roman times. On the corner of these two *dromoi* is a small temple of Isis-Thermouthis, built of mudbrick with limestone doorways, panelling and paving, originally built in the third century BC, then heavily remodelled in Augustan times. Also Augustan is the large adjacent building

The Menches Archive

In January 1900 the workmen of Grenfell and Hunt, who were excavating the desert cemeteries of the site of Tebtunis, found a few mummified crocodiles which, unusually, had been wrapped and stuffed with discarded papyrus documents. Over 130 of these proved to be land surveys and other records of the administration of the village of Kerkeosiris, apparently not far to the north-west of Tebtunis, in the period around 120–110 BC, just after a civil war, when a man called Menches was village scribe of Kerkeosiris. These documents richly illustrate the everyday problems, including uncooperative tenant farmers and corrupt officials, which the Ptolemaic government faced at the local level in controlling state land and raising taxes. They seemed to confirm the traditional view of the decline of the Ptolemaic state, but many of the problems were not new, and serious attempts were being made to maintain agricultural prosperity, including allocating land to soldiers. The archive also gives lively insights into village life. (Crawford 1971; Verhoogt 1998)

Box 5.4

with a columned porch, and the house to its east which had niches with mythological wall paintings. On the south side of the Min/Osiris *dromos* are more blocks of housing, including some second-century BC bakeries, and a large walled complex with a substantial mudbrick tower, built in the first century AD, which texts found there identify as the headquarters of the desert guards. The open area south of this was used from the second century BC to the third century AD to dump rubbish, including thousands of papyri in hieratic, demotic and Greek, hundreds of ostraka, and wine jars with painted labels. Further south and southwest in the desert lie the village cemeteries, of which one contained over 2000 mummified crocodiles. Of these, a few had been wrapped in Ptolemaic administrative documents, including the Menches Archive (box 5.4). The houses in the south-west corner of Tebtunis show various phases of building, abandonment and rebuilding on different plans, from the fourth century BC into the third century AD, when the area, including the temple, was abandoned and covered by sand.

The irregular grid of streets and houses, which is visible in the central area of the site, formed the Roman-period centre of the village, when it reached its greatest extent. Early excavations here produced thousands of private and public documents, mostly of Roman date. Traces of Roman-period buildings extend right to the north edge of the site, but most of what is visible there dates to the Byzantine and Arab phases, in which the occupied area shrank northwards.

By the fifth century AD the village had become a regional capital, called Theodosiopolis, but after the Arab conquest its name reverted to Tutun. Coptic religious texts found elsewhere in Egypt attest a flourishing school of scribes at Tutun in the ninth and tenth centuries. There were at least four large churches, built of reused material from earlier buildings, with fine new wall paintings. The most impressive church belongs to a monastic complex, of which some walls are visible (fig. 5.4.6). It had a columned nave and in the tenth century was decorated

Fig. 5.4.6 Tebtunis, the monastic church in 1933.

with striking paintings of biblical scenes; two, with Adam and Eve before and after the Fall, survive in the Coptic Museum, Cairo. There are two recently excavated houses of the Arab period, one of the ninth century, the other of the seventh to ninth century, and, in the north-east corner of the site, the forlorn remains of a massive mudbrick tower on foundations of reused stone. The site was abandoned by the eleventh century, and the name Tutun later migrated to a new village to the north. The millstones and press parts which litter the northern area represent later use of the abandoned site for processing agricultural products.

5.5 FROM LAHUN TO THE CENTRE OF THE FAYYUM

5.5.a From the modern village of **Lahun**, where the water-control structure originally built around 1260 for Sultan Baibars can be seen from the modern bridge, an enormous earth **dyke**, with modern fired-brick facing and buttresses on its east front, snakes north towards the mortuary pyramid and temple of Sesostris II. Although the dyke, which was used and repaired to the end of the nineteenth century, has received no archaeological study, its relation to the pyramid suggests that it was first constructed under Dynasty 12 to divert the Bahr Yusuf into the Fayyum and create the high lake. Another, less imposing, earth dyke curves west from Lahun towards the ancient site of **Gurob**, where it overlies a New Kingdom cemetery. This was probably an early Ptolemaic construction to control the flow of the Nile inundation into the Fayyum and maintain a low lake. Numerous third-century BC administrative texts were recovered from cartonnage of human mummies from the Graeco-Roman cemetery at Gurob, previously the site of a Dynasty 18 settlement.

At **Hawara**, at the west end of the Lahun gap, lies the unused pyramid of Amenemhet III and the desolate site of his mortuary temple, once a grandiose multi-courtyard building known to Greeks from Herodotus onwards as the **Labyrinth**, and visited by ancient tourists up to the emperor Septimius Severus. North of the temple are remains, mostly Roman, of houses and tombs, and of a fifth(?)-century church, of the ancient village of **Haueris**. Because of the founder-cult of Amenemhet III, the site remained popular for burial with the elite of the Arsinoite nome, and Petrie and others found many late Ptolemaic and Roman mummies, often placed in reused late dynastic graves, with elaborately painted and gilded funerary masks, or with portraits painted in encaustic on oak panels (col. pl. 5.5.1).

5.5.b Ever since the Old Kingdom the regional capital of the Fayyum has been at the site of **Medinet el-Fayyum**, where the Bahr Yusuf ends and branches out into several radial canals. Its pharaonic name was

Shedet. The Greeks first called it **Krokodilonpolis** (Crocodile City) because it was the centre of the regional cult of Sobek. In 116 BC it was renamed **Ptolemais Euergetis** to honour the deceased Ptolemy VIII. In the fourth century AD it was instead called **Arsinoiton polis** (City of the Arsinoites), which had been the second-century Roman name for the civic community; in the Byzantine period this was sometimes shortened to **Arsinoe**, the name commonly used by scholars today. From texts we know that this was a major city of Roman Egypt, with grand residential streets, many fine public buildings, including some of pharaonic origin, a civic water-supply system, and, in Byzantine times, many churches.

An extensive area (3–4 km^2) of pharaonic to Byzantine remains, called **Kiman Faris**, once lay north-west of the modern city centre. Petrie excavated the main temple of Sobek, built in red granite under Dynasty 12, repaired under the Ramesside pharaohs, and surrounded with a massive mudbrick enclosure wall in the late dynastic or early Ptolemaic period. Papyriform columns of red granite were taken from it in the Byzantine period for reuse near a Roman bathhouse to the south (now destroyed), and its entrance was blocked by houses in the fifth or sixth century. Digging by *sebakhin* in 1877/8 produced the first ever big finds of papyrus texts, mostly Byzantine and Arab, while excavations of a fifth-/sixth-century cemetery recovered Coptic textiles now in the Berlin and Vienna museums. Other finds included hundreds of stamped handles from imported Rhodian wine jars of the third to early first centuries BC, and a set of magnificent marble busts of Tiberius, Livia and Augustus, of Tiberian date, now in the Carlsberg Glyptotek, Copenhagen. But very little archaeological work was ever done, and the site has now been erased by the modern city except for a small fenced area (west of the Fire Station), which contains a limestone wall of a theatre with an inscription mentioning Ptolemy III, and remains of a double-*tholos* bathhouse with a coloured mosaic roundel with a star pattern. In the Arab period, settlement shrank south to the banks of the final stretch of the Bahr Yusuf. The mosque of Qaitbey on a two-arch bridge across the Bahr, originally built in 1499 and heavily restored in the twentieth century, was a reconstruction of a much earlier mosque and contains Graeco-Roman columns from Kiman Faris.

5.5.c The monastic complex of **Naqlun**, on the west side of the ridge between the Lahun gap and the Tutun basin, has been explored by a Polish team since 1986. The small valleys at the top of this ridge, with its panoramic views, are riddled with almost a hundred hermitages excavated out of the soft rock, where monks lived in sociable seclusion, no more than a kilometre from the monastery below. The typical hermitage consists of two or more small rooms around a courtyard, often with storage bins, in which papyri have been found with secular and religious texts in Greek, Latin, Coptic and Arabic. The hermitages were privately owned, and some monks ran their business affairs from them. In the seventh century, when Samuel of Qalamun resided there briefly, there are said to have been 120 monks and 200 lay occupants of the complex. The earliest material from a hermitage dates from the fifth century, as do reused architectural elements presumably from the first monastic church. The monastery is claimed to be the oldest in the Fayyum and to have relics of martyrs of the Diocletianic persecution. By the seventh century it comprised several buildings, including three solid mudbrick towers, perhaps reusing mudbricks from a pharaonic site. In the ninth century a church of the Archangel Michael, with rich wall paintings, was erected on the site of earlier buildings, and a completely new church was built to the west, of the Archangel Gabriel, which forms the core of the present-day monastery. Both churches were altered and repainted in the early eleventh century. Surviving paintings in the church of Gabriel include: in the apse, the ascension of Christ; on the west wall, Mary enthroned, one of a pair of mounted martyrs, and Christ on a cosmic cross; on the north wall, an abbot (perhaps Shenoute), and the Archangel Gabriel with three armed riders, including, in the middle, St Mercurius killing the pagan emperor Julian. Some hermitages were still occupied in the twelfth century, but the last few traces are of the fourteenth century, by which time the main complex had been abandoned and was falling into ruin. Rebuilding began in the early twentieth century.

6 MIDDLE EGYPT

6.1. INTRODUCTION

6.1.a Sites

This chapter covers the Nile Valley between Beni Suef and Sohag. The northern part of this area belonged to the administrative district called the Heptanomia (Seven Nomes) in the Roman period, the southern part to the Thebaid, which began immediately south of the Hermopolite nome (around modern Manfalut). Like the Fayyum and the Delta, Middle Egypt was subject to extensive Greek settlement in the Ptolemaic period. It included several towns of 20,000–40,000 inhabitants, which by the Roman period could boast impressive public architecture in the Graeco-Roman style in addition to the older Egyptian temples. Some sites, such as Hermopolis, can still give an impression of this grandeur. Throughout Middle Egypt, the presence of *koms* with pottery or architectural fragments beside modern villages or on the desert edge bears witness to the Graeco-Roman occupation of these sites, but few *koms* have been surveyed, let alone excavated. However, we describe briefly some of the *koms* which have produced valuable information. Several important monasteries were also located in Middle Egypt, of which Bawit and the White Monastery are among the most significant survivors.

6.1.b Access

The northern part of the Heptanomia, including Herakleopolis, is within a convenient day's car trip from Cairo or from Medinet el-Fayyum. Oxyrhynchos could also be visited from Cairo in a longer day, but a round trip of over 500 km from Cairo would leave insufficient time to do justice to the remains at Hermopolis and its necropolis, Tuna el-Gebel. The distance from Luxor is even greater. The most convenient base for visiting the sites of Middle Egypt is Minya, although visitors should first take travel advice from the authorities.

6.2 HERAKLEOPOLIS, OXYRHYNCHOS AND ENVIRONS

6.2.a Adjacent to the modern town lie the extensive, if rather desolate, ruins of **Herakleopolis Magna (Ihnasiya el-Medina)**, a nome capital since the Old Kingdom. Excavations by Naville and Petrie, and more recently by a Spanish team, have focused on the pharaonic remains. Traces of several pharaonic constructions survive, including the foundations of the main temple in a saline hollow. The temple was dedicated to the chief deity of the nome, the ram-headed god Herishef

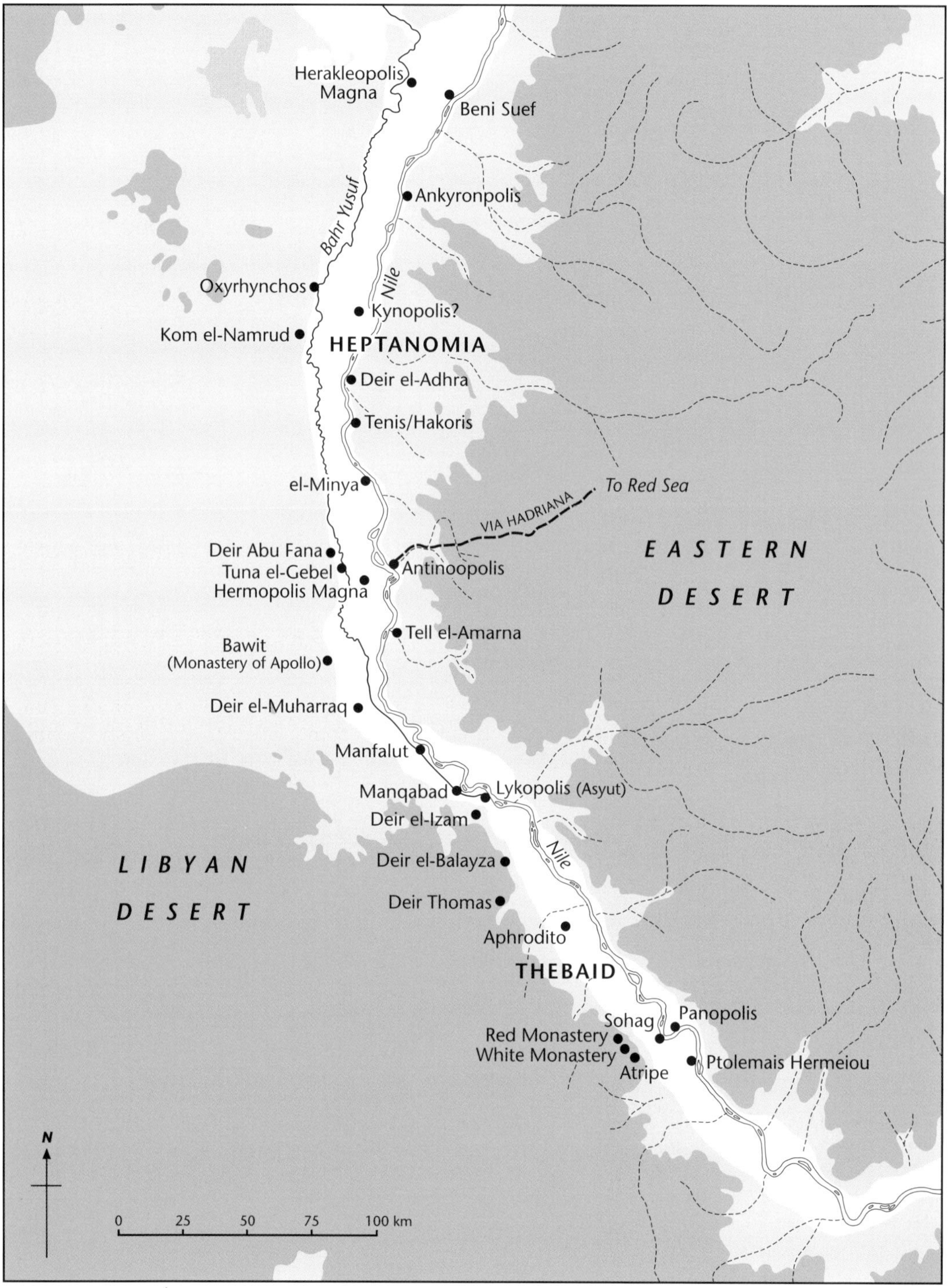

Fig. 6.1.1
Middle Egypt.

(Harsaphis), whom the Greeks equated with Herakles. It was erected under Dynasty 12, reconstructed under Dynasties 18–19, and again rebuilt under Antoninus Pius, but was abandoned and demolished around AD 250. To the north-east, the ancient *kom*, an impressive 20 m or so high, has been preserved by modern settlement on top of it. Excavations by Naville and Petrie of some of the houses and rubbish heaps of the Roman period onwards, which once covered most of the site, produced large amounts of pottery, terracotta figurines and some architectural fragments. Column drums, capitals and bases from Graeco-Roman public buildings are scattered over the site, including four red-granite columns still standing from a once-impressive structure of the second century AD.

Bibliography: Gomaà et al. 1991; Naville and Lewis 1894; Petrie 1905; Porter and Moss 1934.

6.2.b Ankyronpolis (el-Hibeh). Situated on the east bank of the Nile, accessible by ferry from Fashn, on rising ground opposite an island in the river, the Dynasty 21 fortress town of Teudzoi was renamed Ankyronpolis (Anchor City) by the Greeks from the anchor stones cut in the nearby quarries. The quarries and its harbour are also mentioned in the papyri. Finds from the town, with its Dynasty 22 temple, include demotic papyri, some dated to the reign of Darius, and a few Greek papyri of Roman date come from the rubbish mounds. However, the most significant finds come from the New Kingdom to

Fig. 6.2.1 Herakleopolis Magna, the site.

Roman tombs which surround the town on three sides. Alerted by offers of mummy cartonnage by dealers, in 1902–3 Grenfell and Hunt recovered more texts, mostly of the third century BC, which originate from places on the west bank of the Nile. The many burials included two portrait mummies (now in the Egyptian Museum, Cairo and the Fitzwilliam Museum, Cambridge).

Bibliography: Falivene 1998: 39–43; Grenfell and Hunt 1906: 1–12; Kamal 1901.

6.2.c The necropolis of **Kynopolis (el-Sheikh Fadl)**, actually two adjacent necropoleis, lies to the south-east of el-Sheikh Fadl, on the east bank of the Nile opposite Beni Mazar. The site of the town itself, which was a nome capital in the Graeco-Roman period, is a matter of dispute. There is no archaeological support for the suggestion that it too lay on the east bank of the Nile, and a more likely location is one of the substantial koms at el-Qeis on the west bank just south of Beni Mazar.

6.2.d Oxyrhynchos (**el-Behnesa**, called Pemje in Coptic) lies on the western bank of the Bahr Yusuf, some 180 km south of Cairo, at the point where an ancient route from the Bahariya Oasis reaches the Nile Valley. The Greek name derives from its sacred animal, the 'sharp-nosed' elephant-snout fish (fig. 6.2.3). The town is first attested as a

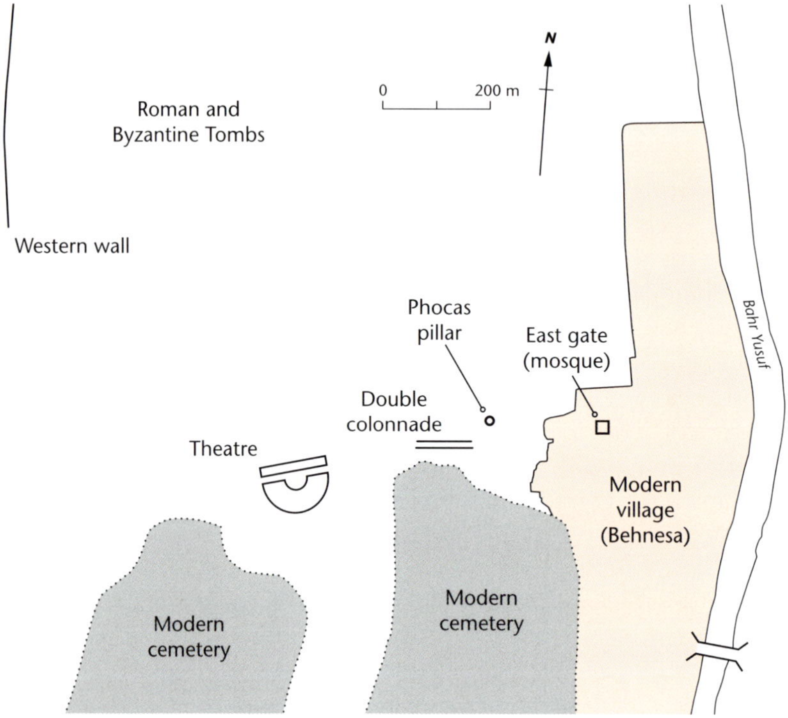

Fig. 6.2.2 The city of Oxyrhynchos.

Fig. 6.2.3
Oxyrhynchos fish, bronze figurine, Late Period (British Museum EA 61953).

nome capital in the seventh century BC, and it continued to grow in importance through to Late Antiquity, when it was the seat of a bishop and the capital of the province of Arcadia (Middle Egypt). Following the Arab conquest, Behnesa remained a significant town, noted for its textile production, until after the Mameluke period when it dwindled to the village that exists today.

The site is chiefly notable for producing the single largest find of papyri of the Roman and Byzantine periods, mainly through the excavations of Grenfell and Hunt from 1897 to 1907, who recognized that papyri were to be found in the rubbish mounds outside the ancient city, and not, as elsewhere, in its buildings or cemeteries. Italian excavations followed between 1910 and 1934. When Petrie visited in 1922 he found the mounds being removed literally by the trainload for use as fertilizer, but he was able to locate and plan the theatre, which he estimated could accommodate some 11,200 spectators, probably the largest theatre in Roman north Africa, and several colonnaded streets. One street led to the 'pillar of Phocas', which bears an inscription to the seventh-century emperor Phocas and is almost the only construction surviving *in situ*. It was drawn by one of Napoleon's officers, Denon, in 1798; it then lost its top and was buried, and so was not seen by Grenfell and Hunt; subsequent clearance uncovered the lower part now visible. Despite its name, the 'Phocas' column dates from the second century AD and was probably part of a *tetrastylon*, a group of four columns, each topped by a statue of the emperor, standing at a major crossroads, a typical piece of Roman imperial architecture. Many great

The Oxyrhynchos Papyri

The Oxford scholars B.P. Grenfell and A.S. Hunt were attracted to the site of Oxyrhynchos by the hope that the site of a city would be particularly productive of literary and biblical texts. This did prove to be the case – for instance, half the published papyrus texts of Herodotus come from Oxyrhynchos – although literary papyri, and 'subliterary' texts, a varied category including magical papyri, horoscopes and music, are vastly outnumbered by documents. The earliest Oxyrhynchos papyri date from the first century BC, but most come from the second and third centuries AD; after relatively few from the fifth century, numbers recover in the sixth, due to the archive of the Apion family, great landowners and imperial officials; a few date from after the Arab conquest. The overwhelming majority of texts are in Greek. Almost no texts in demotic Egyptian from Oxyrhynchos have been found, but Latin, Coptic, Arabic and other languages such as Persian are represented. The first volume of *The Oxyrhynchus Papyri* appeared in 1898, edited by Grenfell and Hunt, and the series is still being published. There are other publications of Oxyrhynchos texts, such as the Italian *Papiri della Società Italiana*. The documents include records of public administration, legal documents (including private sales, leases, loans and so on) and many private letters. They constitute an invaluable historical resource for studying the administration, economy and society of Roman Egypt, the town of Oxyrhynchos itself, and the surrounding countryside.

public buildings at Oxyrhynchos are recorded in papyrus documents, but the stones were removed for reuse or making lime, and little more than lines of limestone chips now remain.

Petrie also investigated the Roman and Byzantine necropolis area, as did the Italian expeditions. Numerous Roman-period grave monuments

Fig. 6.2.4 Excavations of Grenfell and Hunt, site uncertain (EES neg. 746).

Box 6.2.1

from Oxyrhynchos and architectural fragments, mostly from Late Antiquity, are displayed in the Graeco-Roman Museum at Alexandria and in European and North American museums, and more still appear on the antiquities market.

In 1985–7 a Kuwaiti expedition worked on the Islamic remains at the site, and since 1992 Catalan-Egyptian excavations have investigated the north-western necropolis, which has tombs of the Saite and Roman periods. One Roman tomb (no.3) is decorated in Egyptian style and includes representations of the Oxyrhynchos fish. Further east they excavated a Coptic oratory with access to three crypts. They have also made progress in mapping the town itself. The monumental eastern gateway, hidden by the mosque of Zain el-Abidin, has been identified on the same axis as the *tetrastylon* (the 'Phocas pillar'), while a Doric peristyle to the south may have belonged to a gymnasium. This gate, which now adjoins the modern village, must in antiquity have marked the eastern limit of the city, facing the Bahr Yusuf. Even though much of what Petrie recorded is no longer visible, and the site is much destroyed, the combination of additional survey work with the information provided by the papyrus documents offers hope of achieving further clarification of the topography of the ancient city.

Bibliography: Breccia 1932, 1934; Kessler 1983; Krüger 1990; Petrie 1925; Schneider 1982; Turner 1982.

6.2.e The site of **Tenis** also called **Hakoris (Tihneh el-Gebel)** lies on the east side of the river on a picturesque plateau overlooking the valley, 10 km north of the town of Minya, in what was the Hermopolite nome. Human settlement and burial here dates from before the predynastic period. Under the Ptolemies it became a garrison town. The alternative name for the site, Hakoris, is attested only in the Roman period but probably derives from the name of a local Egyptian leader

Box 6.2.2

The Archive of Dionysios son of Kephalas

This bilingual archive of seven demotic and thirty-three Greek papyri is now in the Sorbonne, Paris and the Hermitage Museum, St Petersburg. It dates from 117–103 BC and offers the best historical evidence for the town. Dionysios was a cavalry officer of the Ptolemaic garrison at Tenis. Like Dryton (box 7.4), Dionysios was fully socialized into his Egyptian surroundings and served as a priest in the local Ibis cult. He purchased and leased out land used to maintain the sacred ibises. He also leased some royal land, which he sub-leased, and took advantage of his connections and the status of being a royal tenant. A series of twenty-four loans over twelve years attested in his archive may suggest that he was not a successful farmer and was in a classic debt trap, paying off one loan with another in order to survive. Alternatively, he may have been shrewdly taking advantage of his connections, and mortgaging property to gain liquid assets which he could then re-lend to tenant farmers, to make an overall profit.

who stayed loyal to the Ptolemies during the Theban uprising of the early second century BC. A small Ptolemaic temple was cut into the rock to the north of the town. In the centre there are three smaller chapels built in the reign of Nero. Another temple, perhaps dedicated to Sarapis, was built under Antoninus Pius. Along the western cliffs facing the valley are rock-cut tombs and inscriptions, and, to the south, a chapel, probably Roman. There were, and still are, limestone quarries in the area. The town was still sizeable in Late Antiquity. A number of inscriptions and texts have been found. Some of the Coptic papyri may refer to a local uprising of the late seventh/early eighth century AD.

Bibliography: Clarysse 1991; Lewis 1986: 124–39; Kawanishi 1995; Porter and Moss 1934.

6.3 HERMOPOLIS, ANTINOOPOLIS AND CEMETERIES

6.3.a Hermopolis Magna (el-Ashmunein), a major city of antiquity, lies between el-Minya, the modern regional centre, and Mellawi, which has a museum containing some of the finds from excavations in the region. The Greek name 'City of Hermes' refers to the god Thoth, Hermes in Greek, who invented the art of writing. The Egyptian name of the city, Khemenu (Eight), from which Ashmunein derives, alludes to the eight Egyptian deities who preceded the creation of the world, and Hermopolite cosmology claimed that the world began there, a dry spot in the midst of the water. Indeed Hermopolis does lie in the middle of the floodplain, roughly equidistant from the Nile to the east and the Bahr Yusuf to the west.

Its central location in the Nile Valley made Hermopolis an important stronghold for control of this part of Egypt. In the Late Period Nektanebo I started a major renovation of the city centre, which was finished after the Greeks arrived. The temple of Thoth was rebuilt in the Late Period to the north of the old site. It was one of the largest in Egypt. Each of the sixteen columns of the *pronaos*, the new-style entrance, had a diameter of about 3.5 m. Petosiris, the high priest of Thoth who supervised the renovation, is buried in Tuna el-Gebel (6.3.b). The *pronaos* was finished early in the rule of Ptolemy I. It was still intact when Napoleon invaded, but in 1826 Mohammed Ali allowed it to be burnt for lime to build state factories. Only the foundations survive today, surrounded by rising groundwater.

The site is entered from the north. In the open-air museum stand two huge quartzite baboons, animals sacred to Thoth, which date from the reign of Amenophis III and had been reused, and so covered, in the foundations of the Late Period *pronaos*. The access road approaches the centre of town from the west. To the east the visitor sees the Christian basilica on the south side of the main lateral street. North of the street

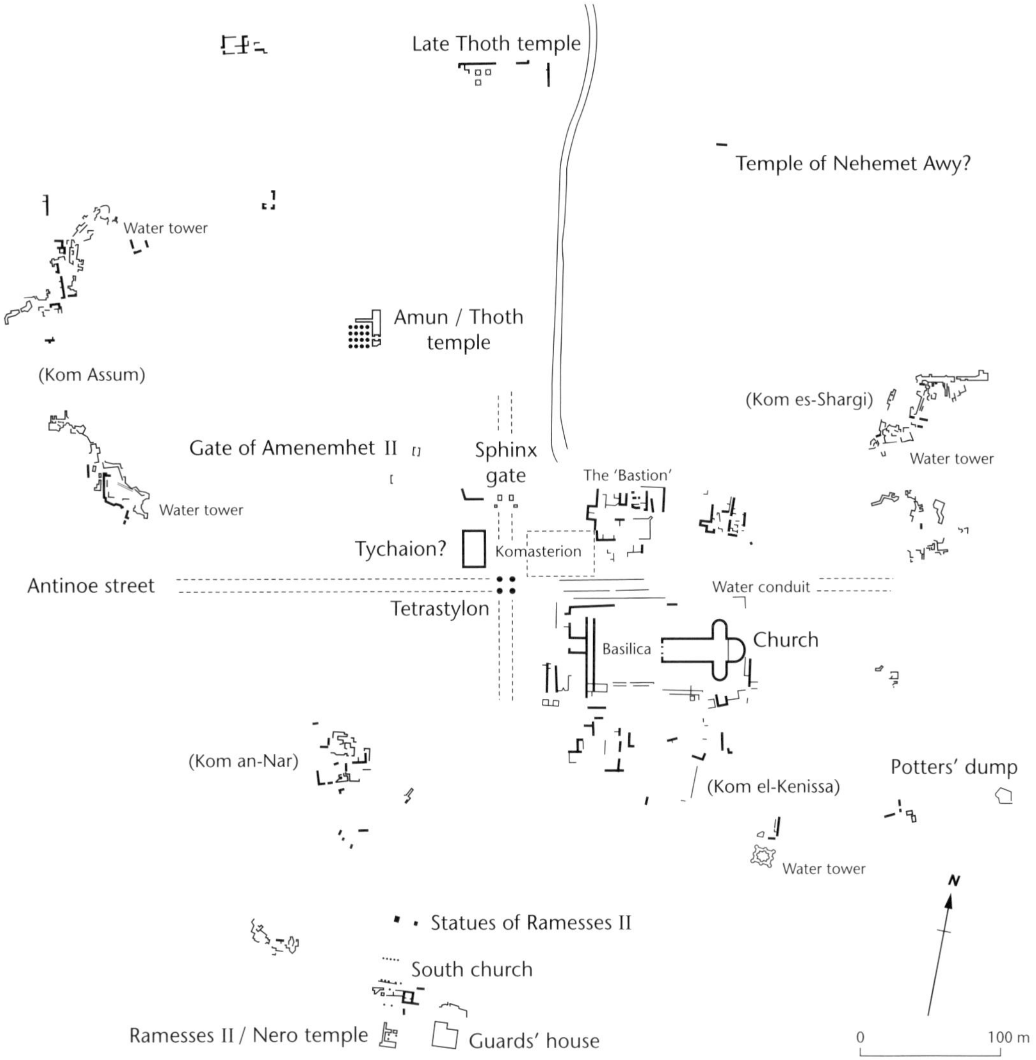

Fig. 6.3.1 The city of Hermopolis Magna (after Bailey 1991: pl.1).

are the remains of the sacred enclosure. Parts of the brick wall of the Late Period are visible in several places. The sacred enclosure was known as the Phrourion or 'fort' in the Graeco-Roman period and was used to garrison troops. The southern part of town was known as the Polis or 'city'. Abutting the sacred enclosure and along the central lateral street are buildings of the Graeco-Roman period.

The first set of columns on the north side of the street belong to the Tychaion, a temple known from a long list of expenses projected for repair of the city centre in AD 264, after political turmoil had led to damage of the city centre. The text, allied to the results of recent excavations by the British Museum, gives us some idea of where buildings were located along the central street. The Tychaion lay next to the central crossing. It was built in the second century AD in the Greek imperial style. To the north-west are the remains of the pylon of the east-facing temple of Amun and Thoth and the hypostyle hall behind it. The pylon was built under Ramesses II and is the oldest structure known on the site. The temple of Amun was in use through to Late Antiquity.

On the central street itself the British Museum expedition identified the location of a set of four columns (*tetrastylon*), marking the central crossing as listed in the papyrus, with a water fountain (*nymphaion*) on either side. A *komasterion* (festival hall) stands immediately to the north-east of the central crossing, and a structure called 'the bastion', apparently a storage facility, adjoins it. The reconstructed view from the north gives some idea of what the centre of town looked like in the Roman period (fig. 6.3.2). The sacred enclosure also contained several structures from the pharaonic period. The Late Period temple of Thoth lies north of the central crossing and faces south. On the right side of the *dromos* (processional way) leading up to the temple was a temple to

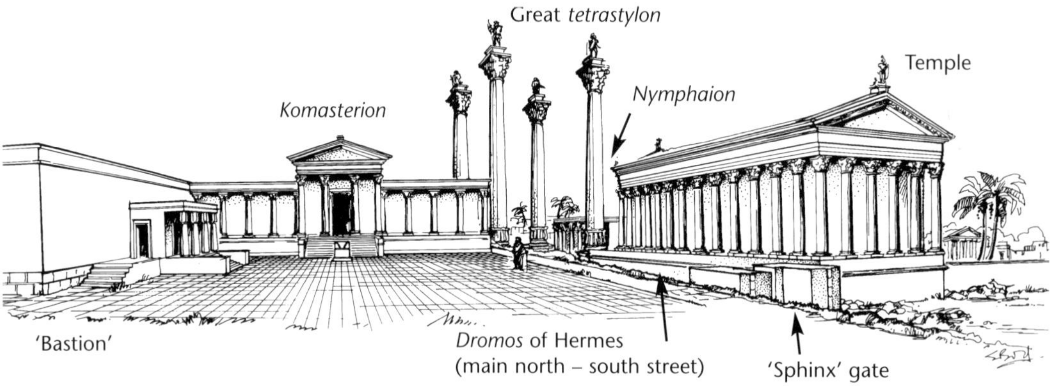

Fig. 6.3.2 Hermopolis Magna, reconstruction of the centre looking south (Bailey 1991: pl. 23).

the consort of Thoth, which was re-dedicated under the Roman emperor Domitian. In the fifth century AD the whole temple complex except the *pronaos* was torn down, and the area was reused for houses.

The buildings on the south side of the central lateral street are dominated by the Christian basilica, dating from the mid-fifth century AD. The basilica was built on the site of a Hellenistic temple complex, which has been excavated by a team from Alexandria University. In the Hellenistic period this was the religious centre of the Greek community, built across the street from the Egyptian temples. The dedicatory inscription of around 240 BC was found: 'To king Ptolemy, son of Ptolemy and Arsinoe, the brother-and-sister gods, and to queen Berenike, his sister and wife, the benefactor gods, and to Ptolemy and Arsinoe, the brother-and-sister gods, the cavalry settlers stationed in the Hermopolite nome (have dedicated) the statues and the temple and the rest inside the sacred precinct and the stoa for the benefactions shown to them.'

Fig. 6.3.3
Hermopolis Magna, the basilica.

The basilica was one of the largest in Egypt. There are a nave and two aisles. In front of the apse runs a transept, not a common feature in Egypt. At the eastern end the circular shape of the apse can be recognized. In the middle was the entrance to a crypt with the tombs of the bishops. The columns and some of the other material used for the construction of the basilica were taken from Roman-period public buildings. At the north-east corner is the baptistery.

South of the basilica is a Roman brick water tower, perched on the steep edge of a mound. This, originally one of several water towers, is the only complete ancient monument on the site. To the east is a potter's dump from Late Antiquity. South of the west end of the central street lies a smaller north-facing temple, which was re-dedicated under Nero. Over its forecourt a large church with a baptistery to the south was initiated in the first half of the fifth century, and often thereafter repaired because of the unstable ground. On all sides of the site are traces of less durable buildings, mainly houses from Late Antiquity,

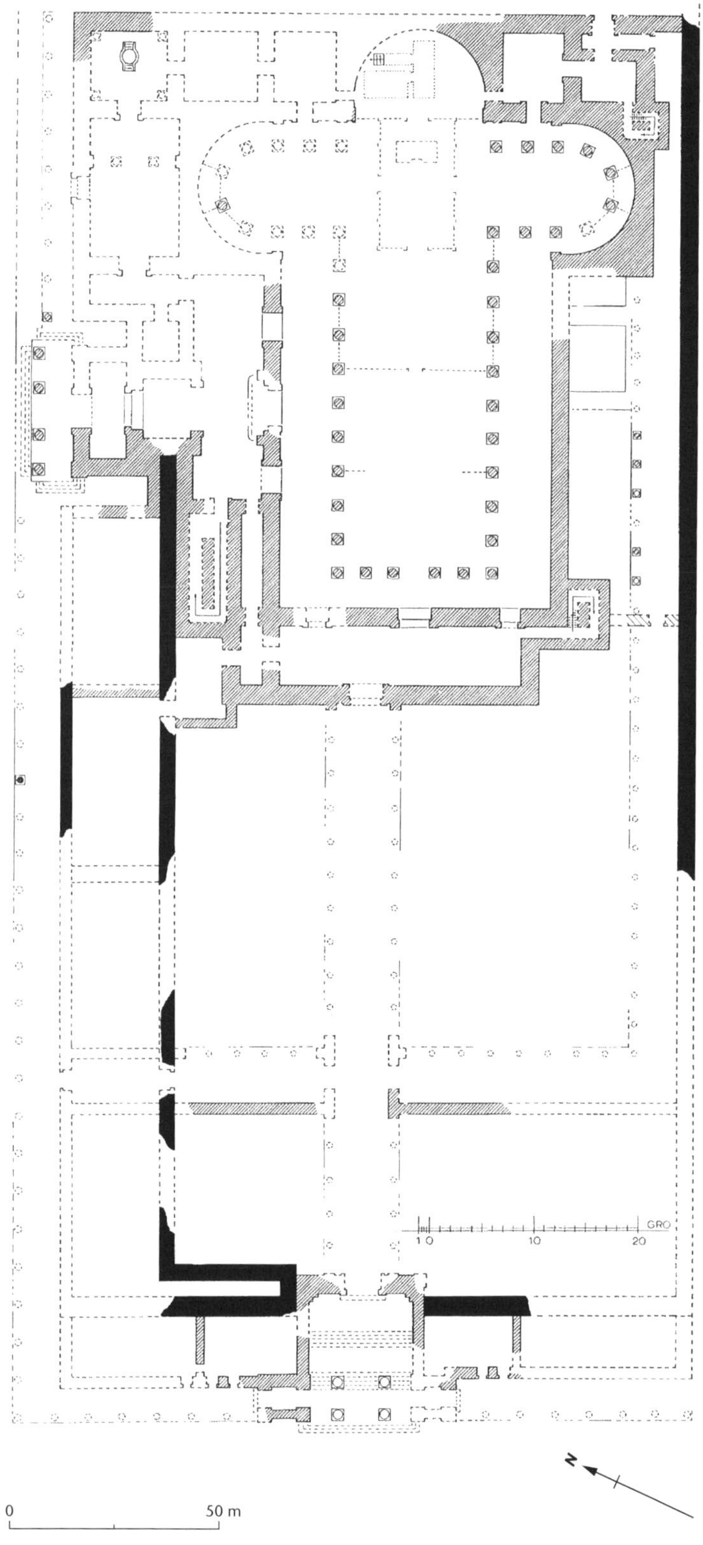

Fig. 6.3.4 Hermopolis Magna, the basilica (after Grossmann 2002: pl. 59).

Athletes from Hermopolis

Part of the archive of the city council of Hermopolis from the reign of Gallienus documents its finances. As well as the programme to repair the city centre mentioned in the text, there are several documents in which 'victors' apply for the pension which the city offered them. Athletes or artists from Hermopolis won victories in competitions organized by other cities in Egypt and the eastern provinces. The athletes of Hermopolis excelled in the 'heavy' disciplines such as boxing, wrestling and the *pankration* ('all-in wrestling'). The most famous pankratiast ever, Marcus Aurelius Asklepiades alias Hermodoros, who figures on several monuments in Rome, came from Hermopolis. The amount of cash the city council expended in pensions for its victors was substantial, but it was apparently worth it in terms of the international prestige they brought the city. And often the victors were themselves members of the council!

Box 6.3.1

which must be the source of many Hermopolite papyri dating to that period.

Bibliography: Arnold 1994; Bailey 1991; Baulig 1984; Drew-Bear 1988; Grossmann 2002; Pensabene 1993; Roeder 1959; Spencer 1983 and 1989; Van Minnen 2002; Wace, Megaw and Skeat 1959.

6.3.b West of Hermopolis across the Bahr Yusuf is **Tuna el-Gebel**, **Thynis** in Greek, the cemetery of Hermopolis, where Egyptian and German teams have worked. The northernmost part had a temple of Sarapis and was dedicated to animal burials. People came from all over Egypt to honour Thoth by dedicating a mummified ibis, the bird sacred to him, slaughtered for the purpose. In the catacombs hundreds of thousands of ibis mummies were buried from the Late Period until the early Roman period. There was a special section for baboons, the animal of Thoth. There is also a Roman *saqiya* (waterwheel) standing over a very deep well.

Further south are the human tombs (fig. 6.3.5). The more elaborate ones, for the elite of Hermopolis, are marked by a superstructure sometimes in stone, more often in brick, usually in the shape of a temple. Some are Hellenistic in date, others Roman. They are decorated inside with reliefs, paintings and inscriptions, many in verse. The most elaborate is the tomb of Petosiris, high priest of Thoth under Ptolemy I. The tomb, which also housed his father and brother, is in the shape of a temple with a *pronaos* in front. The 'temple' is somewhat older. The *pronaos* contains a series of painted reliefs with scenes of daily life (col. pl. 6.3.6). The format of the agricultural scenes is in the ancient Egyptian tradition, but the figures show Greek influence. Biographical inscriptions of Petosiris and others were made inside and outside the tomb. A cult of Petosiris developed in the Roman period. His sarcophagus is in the Egyptian Museum, Cairo. Nearby is the two-storey shrine

Fig. 6.3.5
The necropolis of Tuna el-Gebel (after Pensabene 1993: 259).

of Isidora, of the mid-second century AD, whose death by drowning in the Nile is commemorated in two Greek poems painted on the sides of the doorway to her tomb.

Bibliography: Badawy 1956; Gabra 1941; Gabra and Drioton 1954; Lefebvre 1923–4; Pensabene 1993.

6.3.c The site of **Antinoopolis** is reached by ferry across the Nile to the village of Sheikh Ibada. When Hadrian was touring Egypt in AD 130, his favourite, Antinoos, fell in the Nile here and drowned, thus becoming a god according to Egyptian tradition. To commemorate him, Hadrian founded Antinoopolis on a long-established site, and gave it special privileges as a Greek city. Its population was drawn from communities of 'Greeks' in other parts of Egypt. The brand-new imperial Greek architecture of Antinoopolis was enthusiatically imitated by other cities, causing a short-lived building boom in Egypt. When Diocletian split Egypt into several provinces, Antinoopolis was made the provincial capital of the Lower (Northern) Thebaid.

The pharaonic origins of Antinoopolis are represented by the remains of a temple, from the reign of Ramesses II, to the north of the

Fig. 6.3.7 Antinoopolis, the theatre gateway *c.* 1800 (*Description de l'Egypte* IV 55).

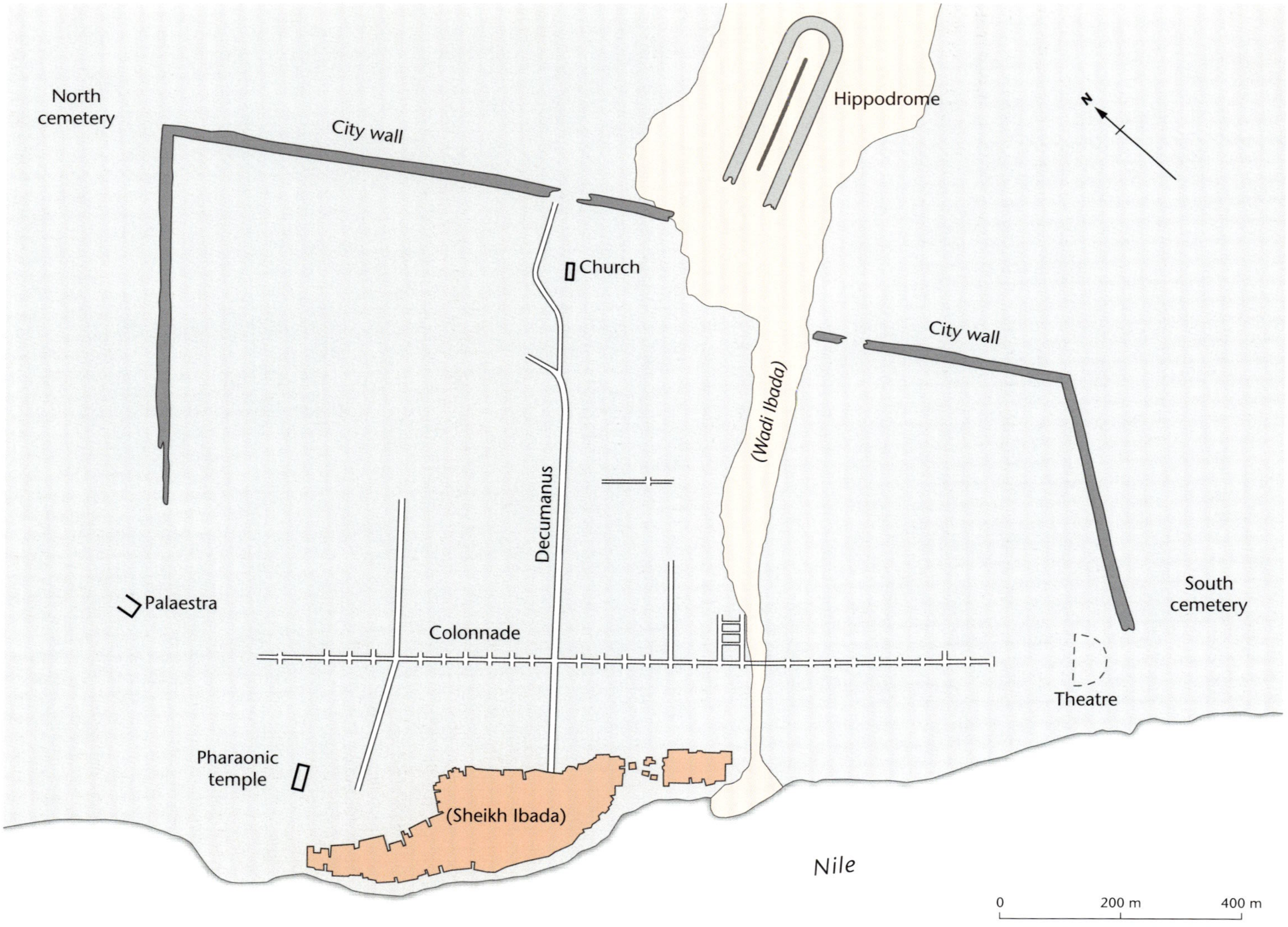
North cemetery
City wall
Hippodrome
N
Church
City wall
(Wadi Ibada)
Decumanus
Palaestra
Colonnade
South cemetery
Theatre
Pharaonic temple
(Sheikh Ibada)
Nile
0
200 m
400 m

Fig. 6.3.8 The city of Antinoopolis (after Pensabene 1993: 274).

site. Hadrian's new city was laid out on a regular grid of streets. The city walls can still be discerned. Several of the imperial buildings were still visible at the time of the Napoleonic expedition but were demolished subsequently. Drawings were made of an arch near the harbour (modern Sheikh Ibada), of two sets of four columns (*tetrastyla*) at the main intersections, and of the entrance to the theatre. Antinoopolis also had a hippodrome just outside the city wall on the east side, north of the wadi that at some point cut the site in two. A papyrus from the site preserves a rare coloured representation of charioteers (col. pl. 6.3.9). Little of the original monuments, which included a bath and several temples, is visible today, but the site is covered with potsherds. Outside the walls to the north-east, Italian excavators have uncovered funerary monuments from Late Antiquity. They also discovered a church near the eastern gate. On the line of the main north-south street to the south some of the spots where columns once stood can be made out, and perhaps some of the pavement. A semicircular area is barely recognizable as the theatre.

Further south is the late ancient cemetery. Little is visible today. Beyond it, near the Nile, lies a monastic settlement known as Upper Ansina. The settlement of the seventh or eighth century combined a group of hermits' cells (*laura*) with a cenobitic monastery. The eastern end of a church with its apse is visible along with a row of dwellings. The village of Deir Abu Hinnes further south was originally a monastic settlement, and parts of the single-nave church go back to the fifth

Box 6.3.2

Gilding the Gymnasium

In AD 263 the council of Antinoopolis solicited bids for the gilding of the ceiling of the portico and the entrances of the circular gymnasium, as part of its large programme of repairs. The two successful bids, each for half the work, survive. The better preserved bid reads as follows:

To the most excellent council of the illustrious Neo-Greek city of Antinoopolis from Aurelius Hermias alias Ammonantinoos of the tribe of Osirantinoos [= Antinoos who became Osiris] and from Aurelius Demetrius alias Alexander of the tribe of Hadrian: We offer of our own free will to undertake the gilding of half of the wood carving that is being done for the roof of the portico and the entrances of the circular gymnasium that is being constructed auspiciously. We are to provide the plaster and the glue and the coating for the gilding and the rest of what is needed and first-class gold leaf of quality gold. We are to receive for the first job, a hexagon, wages included, 9 drachmas and 3 obols, for the second job, a hexagon, wages included, 9 drachmas, for the third job, a hexagon, likewise 7 drachmas and for the fourth job, a tetragon, likewise 4 drachmas and 3 obols and for the fifth job, a tetragon, including wages, likewise 2 drachmas and 6 obols and for each of the so-called lozenges 1 drachma. We understand that we are paid the full amount for whatever job we finish until the project is done. We will do a decent job so that we are not criticized. The supervisors of the project provide one big basket with about a hundred wasted wood chips for the boiling of the glue. If you please, accept us on these conditions. If you do not accept us, we shall not be held liable to this bid. Upon being asked we gave our formal assent. [Date and signatures] (*P.Köln* I 52, col. ii) century. There is a second church located in the rocks above the village, but access to it is limited. It contains frescos of the sixth or seventh century depicting scenes of the life of Christ. The village attracts many Coptic pilgrims and is easily accessible from the south. Further south again is the site of Amarna (6.5.c), the capital of Egypt under Akhenaten. Above the Nile Valley are many ancient stone quarries, which were reused as monastic dwellings in Late Antiquity. There is also a *laura* right above Antinoopolis, called Deir el-Dik. Further south are the ruins of Ansina, the administrative centre of Middle Egypt from the eighth to the thirteenth centuries.

Bibliography: Del Francia Barocas 1998; Donadoni 1974; Grossmann 2002; Pensabene 1993.

6.4 PANOPOLIS, PTOLEMAIS AND ENVIRONS

6.4.a Lykopolis (Asyut). Lykopolis (Wolf city, named after the local jackal god) was an ancient nome capital. It was the birthplace of the neo-Platonist philosopher Plotinus. Although nothing remains of the Graeco-Roman city, there is evidence that the pharaonic cemetery was reused from the Saite to Roman periods. Lykopolis has produced a small number of demotic and Greek papyri. The local museum, in the former American College, has some Coptic artefacts.

6.4.b Panopolis (Achmim) and its cemeteries. The patron deity of Panopolis (Pan's City) was the ithyphallic god Min, whom the Greeks equated with Pan. The Greeks also called it Chemmis, from the Egyptian name; hence the modern Achmim. Ibn Gubayr, around AD 1200, describes the magnificent Ptolemaic temple of Min, comparable in size to the temple of Horus at Edfu, but demolished in 1350. The presence of the modern city has inhibited excavation, although the recent excavation of a limestone Ramesside temple also uncovered traces of Roman brickwork. More discoveries have been made in the cemeteries on the edge of the Eastern Desert, including thousands of 'mummy labels', small wooden tags used when shipping mummified bodies to their place of burial. The cemetery, with three Coptic monasteries, on a low hill east of the village of el-Hawawish, is the source of the many hieroglyphic stelae of the Graeco-Roman period excavated by Maspero in the 1880s and now in the Egyptian Museum, Cairo, and many other museums. To the north, at el-Salamuni, are Graeco-Roman tombs decorated in mixed style, with zodiacs, and figures in Greek or Roman costume facing Egyptian deities.

Literature and philosophy flowered in Panopolis and other cities of Upper Egypt in the fifth century AD. Its most famous poet was Nonnus, who penned an elaborate Greek epic of forty-eight books, the

Dionysiaca, on the life and Indian conquests of the god Dionysos, to rival Homer, and also a hexameter version of St John's gospel.

Bibliography: Egberts 2002; Kanawati 1990; Kuhlmann 1983.

6.4.c Some 6 km west of Sohag is an ancient town and adjoining cemetery, called **Triphion** in Greek and **Atripe** in Coptic; it is commonly, but inaccurately, referred to as Athribis. Petrie's investigations and more recent excavations have revealed a temple of the lioness goddess Triphis, originally dating from Dynasty 26, which underwent major reconstruction in the late Ptolemaic period. Another massive gate was added at the same time to the north-east with a *dromos* running at an angle from it. The sanctuary was enlarged with another limestone temple of unusual shape and dimensions, still in a good state of preservation, begun by Ptolemy XII and added to by various Roman emperors down to Hadrian.

In the cliffs to the south Petrie found the famous 'Zodiac tomb', named after its zodiac ceiling decorations (box 7.3.b). The tomb is dated by two horoscopes in it to the AD 50s. Zodiacs are characteristic of the Panopolis region, and other examples are found in the tombs at el-Salamun. Nearby is the highly decorated and inscribed tomb of Psenosiris, which also has astronomical scenes. Amid these rock-cut tombs, approximately half-way up the cliff, is a temple of Asklepios with an elaborate façade. The two inner chambers contain many graffiti in red and black ink, one in Greek, the rest in demotic, written by people who incubated (slept overnight) there in search of healing.

Bibliography: Arnold 1999; Egberts 2002; el-Farag 1985; Petrie 1908.

6.4.d The mound of **Ptolemais Hermeiou (el-Manshah)** is located about 12 km south of Sohag on the main road, just west of the Nile. Little above ground suggests that underneath lies the southern capital of the Ptolemaic state. The Roman geographer Strabo described it as a large town in the first century BC, 'no smaller than Memphis'. Ptolemy I established Ptolemais Hermeiou ('of Hermias') as a Greek city (*polis*) with a Greek constitution, perhaps to take advantage of the extensive agricultural land in the vicinity. The Ptolemaic cavalry officer Dryton (7.4) was a citizen of Ptolemais. It became the base for regional officials in charge of the administration of the Thebaid, and it may have been captured by the Theban rebels in the second century BC (1.1.c). The town declined in political importance with the fall of the Ptolemies and the rise in the Roman period of Koptos, but occupation continued well beyond the Arab conquest.

Bibliography: Abd el-Ghani 2001; Plaumann 1910.

6.5 MONASTERIES OF MIDDLE EGYPT

6.5.a Introduction

Middle Egypt was in Late Antiquity a hotbed of monastic activity, with numerous monasteries and churches serving a host of regional cults. It was not unusual for eremitical monks to occupy pharaonic tombs, converting them to dwellings and places of worship (for example, the North Tombs at Amarna). Many of the religious institutions recorded by medieval and comparatively modern authors are no longer extant (Coquin 1991 gives an almost comprehensive list of monasteries in the region), but the area can still claim to be the heartland of modern Egyptian Christian communities, with flourishing monasteries such as Deir el-Muharraq.

Much of Middle Egyptian monasticism was in its origins independent of the major monastic groupings known elsewhere in Egypt, both those of Lower Egypt (Chapter 4) and the famous cenobitic traditions associated with Pachomios and Shenoute. The cult of the martyrs was important (Papaconstantinou 2001). The ancient situation is not easy to discern today, partly because few sites have been excavated, scientifically or otherwise (Bawit, Wadi Sarga and Balayza are the main exceptions), partly because many ancient foundations have been rededicated, particularly to the Virgin (e.g. at Gebel el-Teir) and even more have been extensively remodelled and rebuilt. Only the most important monasteries are described here, taking the west and east banks separately and in north to south order.

Bibliography: Cannuyer 2001; Clackson 1999; Coquin 1991.

6.5.b The west bank

At **Kom el-Namrud**, on the western edge of the cultivation near Samalut (north of el-Minya), is a small anchoritic settlement (*laura*). It consists of houses with two churches from the sixth century, one a basilica, recently excavated by the Egyptian authorities. The *laura* may have been affiliated with a religious foundation in Oxyrhynchos mentioned in the *Historia Monachorum*.

Bibliography: Grossmann 2002: 513–15.

North-west of el-Ashmunein, across the Bahr Yusuf and 3 km from Qasr Hur at the edge of the desert, are the remains of **Deir Abu Fana** (the Monastery of Apa Bane), founded in the fourth century. Rediscovered by the Napoleonic mission, a few buildings from the extensive 3 hectare site are visible today. Since 1987 an Austrian mission has excavated the main *kom* preserving part of the basilica church, which is still in use, and, to the north, another church and buildings which have been interpreted as a refectory, several prayer halls and accommodation for monks. According to the Arab historian el-Maqrizi, the monastery once held a thousand monks. Apa Bane's ascetic practices are recorded in the *Apophthegmata Patrum* and *Historia Lausiaca* (see Chapter 4); during the last eighteen years of his life, he is said to have stood upright in a dark cell. A skeleton found at the site is thought to be his.

Bibliography: Atiya 1991: 698–700; *Ägypten Schätze* 1996: 59–68.

At **Bawit,** about 28 km south-west of el-Ashmunein, on the west bank of the Nile, 3 km south-west of Dashlut, the remains of the great **Monastery of Apollo** lie at the foot of the cliffs on the edge of the desert. The site, whose Coptic name, Bawit, means 'The Monastery', was once a major religious centre attracting pilgrims from all over Egypt. The *Historia Monachorum* records that, by the end of the fourth century, five hundred monks were drawn to occupy the monasteries of the charismatic hermit named Apollo. John Moschus recorded feats of asceticism which were possibly performed by the monks of Apollo's monastery at Bawit around the beginning of the seventh century.

Today little is visible above the surface of the 800 m-long *kom* except for masses of broken pottery and glass. At the beginning of the twentieth century, French excavations uncovered a Monastery of Apa Apollo which appears to have been established in the fourth century. Their finds are largely displayed in the Coptic room of the Louvre, Paris. Only a tiny fraction of the site has been excavated to date. The numerous structures uncovered mostly did not survive their excavation and can now only be studied from the photographs and watercolours published in the excavation reports. The function of many of these structures is yet to be fully understood, but they have been interpreted as individual hermitages, with a range of structure types, some of them, it seems, consciously imitating earlier tomb architecture. Typically a hermitage featured a courtyard and a domed oratory with an eastern apse. Two-storey buildings featured stairs leading to an upper floor where monks might live. Many of the mudbrick buildings were plastered and sumptuously decorated with wall paintings, depicting Christian figures and scenes for the edification of the monks, as well as purely ornamental motifs. Many paintings are believed to date to between the sixth and eighth centuries. Often the walls were covered in inscriptions and graffiti, mostly Coptic but some also Greek and Arabic.

Over a period of several centuries, the site accommodated different monastic living options. As well as living communally within an enclosure wall, monks might also choose an isolated existence semi-independently, at a distance from the community, coming together only for religious worship, meals and addresses from the head of the monastery.

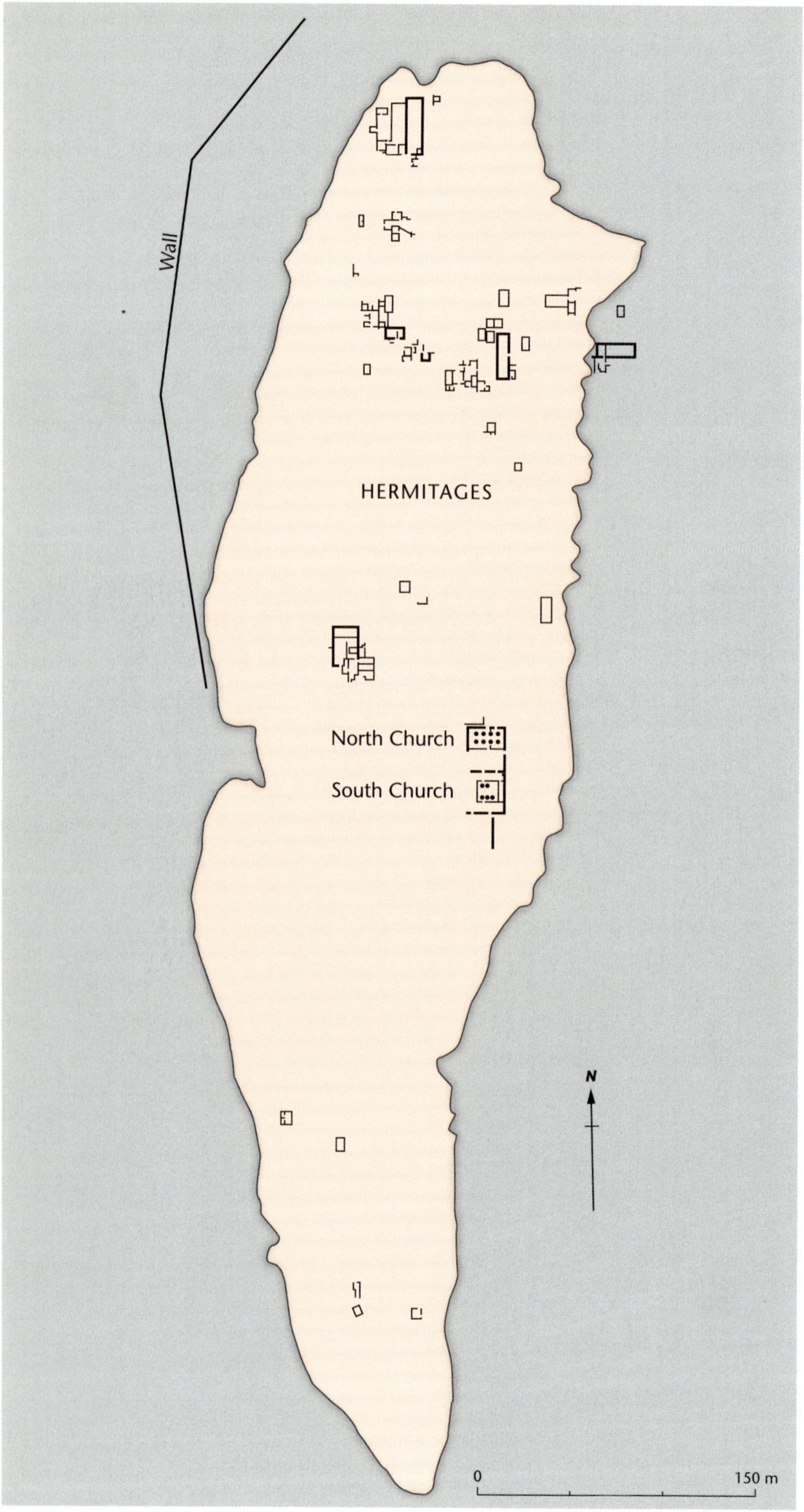

Fig. 6.5.1 Bawit, the Monastery of Apollo (after Clédat 1999: pl.I).

It is believed that separate male and female communities co-existed at Bawit, with the men inhabiting the northern part of the site and the women the south. Coptic and Greek ostraka and papyri excavated (some of them unofficially) at the site illustrate the everyday life of the Monastery of Apollo. Documents drawn up by the monks show that the monastery was a major economic force, producing and distributing commodities such as wine and pickled-fish products, and collecting taxes in the eighth century on behalf of the Arab administration. As at Naqlun, Bawit monks might own their own cells, buying them from the monastery, as well as managing landholdings.

Fig. 6.5.2 Bawit, Mary and the Apostles.

Among the most impressive architectural remains excavated to date were two churches, notably the South Church which contains elements thought to date from the fifth century and shows signs of rebuilding in the late sixth–seventh century (fig. 6.5.1). Numerous artefacts from Bawit are now in museums around the world, most notably the Louvre, where part of the South Church is reconstructed, and the Coptic Museum in Cairo, with some papyri in the Ismailia Museum in the Delta. The monastic buildings, especially the South Church, yielded numerous and varied limestone and wood sculptures of exceptional quality, some similar to those found at the Monastery of Jeremias at Saqqara (3.4.c). Bawit is also the source of what is probably the largest surviving collection of 'Coptic' paintings. In addition to representations of the life of Christ, Mary, the saints and other Christian figures – noteworthy is the depiction of Mary and the Apostles beneath Christ in triumph (fig. 6.5.2) – there were also scenes from the Old and New Testaments, as well as classical representations and motifs.

Bibliography: Clackson 2000; Clédat 1999.

Somewhat further south, on the edge of the desert, 14 km west of el-Qusiya, **Deir el-Muharraq** (the Burnt Monastery), also known as Deir el-Adhra (Monastery of the Virgin), is the largest and wealthiest establishment of its kind in Middle Egypt. Enclosed by a large wall, the monastery occupies a space of 275 x 155 m and houses four churches, both ancient and modern. Chief of these is the Church of the Virgin in the inner court, alleged to be the oldest church in the world. Egyptian tradition proclaims that it was founded on the site of a cave occupied by the Holy Family during its flight from Herod into Egypt. Indeed many other places in Middle Egypt are associated with the Holy Family, including Oxyrhynchos (6.2.d), Gebal el-Teir, el-Ashmunein (6.3.a), Qusqam, and Durunka south-west of Asyut.

Today the medieval church buildings lie a metre below the level of the inner court and contain an ancient altar, dated 11 December AD 747. Every year, from 21 to 28 June, thousands of pilgrims celebrate the consecration of the church. The inner court also houses a nineteenth-century Church of St George and an ancient tower, which is accessed by drawbridge from a small tower and houses a medieval Church of the Archangel Michael. Modern buildings show how the Burnt Monastery has remained active to the present day – the outer court houses a Theological Seminary and a new Church of the Virgin dedicated in 1964. The monastery's foundation is obscure but often attributed to Pachomios – hence the twentieth-century 'Pachomian Castle' which houses the old library and visiting guests.

Bibliography: Atiya 1991: 840–1; Meinardus 1989: 155–67.

The monastic site of **Manqabad**, 12 km north of Asyut, has been excavated by Egyptian archaeologists. It was evidently a reoccupation of an enclosure that may have been a Roman military camp; the remains of several early medieval churches are visible.

Bibliography: Atiya 1991: 1522–3.

Largely destroyed in the 1960s by the military, **Deir el-Izam** (the Monastery of the Bones) is situated on the desert plateau above the necropolis of Asyut. It is associated with John of Lykopolis, a famous ascetic and recluse who acted as adviser to the Emperor Theodosius I. It seems likely that he is the fourth-century Apa John to whom were addressed a number of requests for help written in Greek and Coptic papyri discovered at the monastery in September 1897.

Bibliography: Atiya 1991: 809-10; Zuckerman 1995: 191–2.

Extensive and impressive ruins attest to the existence of the important monastic settlement of **Deir el-Balayza**, located 18 km south of Asyut on the left bank of the Nile. Set into the cliff, the monastery is encompassed by a rectangular enclosing wall with several entrances, and includes numerous mudbrick buildings, some of them at one time multistorey, including dormitories, workshops, refectories and a small church dating to the seventh century. Ancient quarries were reinhabited, one of them used as a church. The site was excavated by Petrie in 1907, when a large number of Coptic (and also some Greek and Arabic) manuscripts were found here. The site seems to have been inhabited until the eighth century.

Bibliography: Grossmann 1993; Timm 1984–92: 686–91; Atiya 1991: 786–7.

About 25 km south of Asyut lie the remains of the Coptic monastic community of **Deir Thomas**, which date from the sixth to eighth centuries and occupy both sides of the Wadi Sarga. The site was excavated in 1913–14 by R.G. Campbell-Thompson. First dedicated to a little-known Thomas, it was later named the Monastery of St Sergius. As well as a cache of manuscripts, several rock-cut churches and cells were found, containing fine paintings, including, in the principal sanctuary cut into rock, a depiction of Christ distributing communion to the Apostles.

Bibliography: Atiya 1991: 2312.

Located on the edge of the Libyan Desert, on the left bank of the Nile, 10 km west of the town of Sohag, is one of the most important Christian monuments surviving in Egypt – the church of the **White Monastery** (Deir el-Abyad) or the **Monastery of Apa Shenoute**. A rectangular structure measuring 75 x 36.85 m, the fortress-like church resembles a pharaonic temple with two rows of windows. Known in Egyptian as Atripe (6.4.c), this area was populated by hermits from the fourth century. Shenoute (AD 350–c. 466), the nephew of the founder, was its abbot for many decades from the late fourth century until after the middle of the fifth. He was, with Antony and Pachomios, a seminal figure in the evolution of Egyptian monasticism. His life is known to us from his own writings and from a biography attributed to his successor

Besa. The outspoken author of a number of letters and sermons, Shenoute adopted a stricter rule than that of Pachomios, governing 2200 men in his own monastery and, in a separate community, 1800 women. He was a stern opponent of pagans and heretics but claimed to champion the oppressed, at one time sheltering a reported 20,000 refugees from invaders within the walls of his monastery.

The layout of Shenoute's monastic complex has yet to be fully determined. In 1908 Petrie identified a mudbrick wall enclosing a series of buildings, including the church (fig. 6.5.4). Erected in the mid-fifth century before Shenoute's death, the church was extensively rebuilt after damage by fire, possibly following the Persian conquest in AD 619. Today it comprises a nave flanked by two aisles, separated by two rows each of nineteen columns. On the north side is a red-granite carved pulpit. Behind the modern screen is a triple apse, each apse decorated

Fig. 6.5.3 The White Monastery.

with two ranges of columns alternating with niches, and the whole topped by an architrave, with a semi-dome overhead. The north sanctuary is dedicated to St George, the central dome contains a painting of the Pantocrator and is dedicated to St Shenoute, and the south sanctuary bears a depiction of the Resurrection and is dedicated to the Virgin Mary.

Later additions include the room placed in front of the sanctuary, possibly in the ninth century, and domed vaulting over the sanctuary executed in the thirteenth century, when major building work was undertaken in the building, from which date paintings and inscriptions. The church had six entrances on all but the east side, including the so-called 'mule gate', named after the legend of a pagan princess who rode in on a mule to desecrate the church and was promptly swallowed up by the earth. Little remains of the original decoration, which included columns with elaborate capitals and other sculptural features executed in limestone, granite and marble. Befitting his hatred of paganism, the

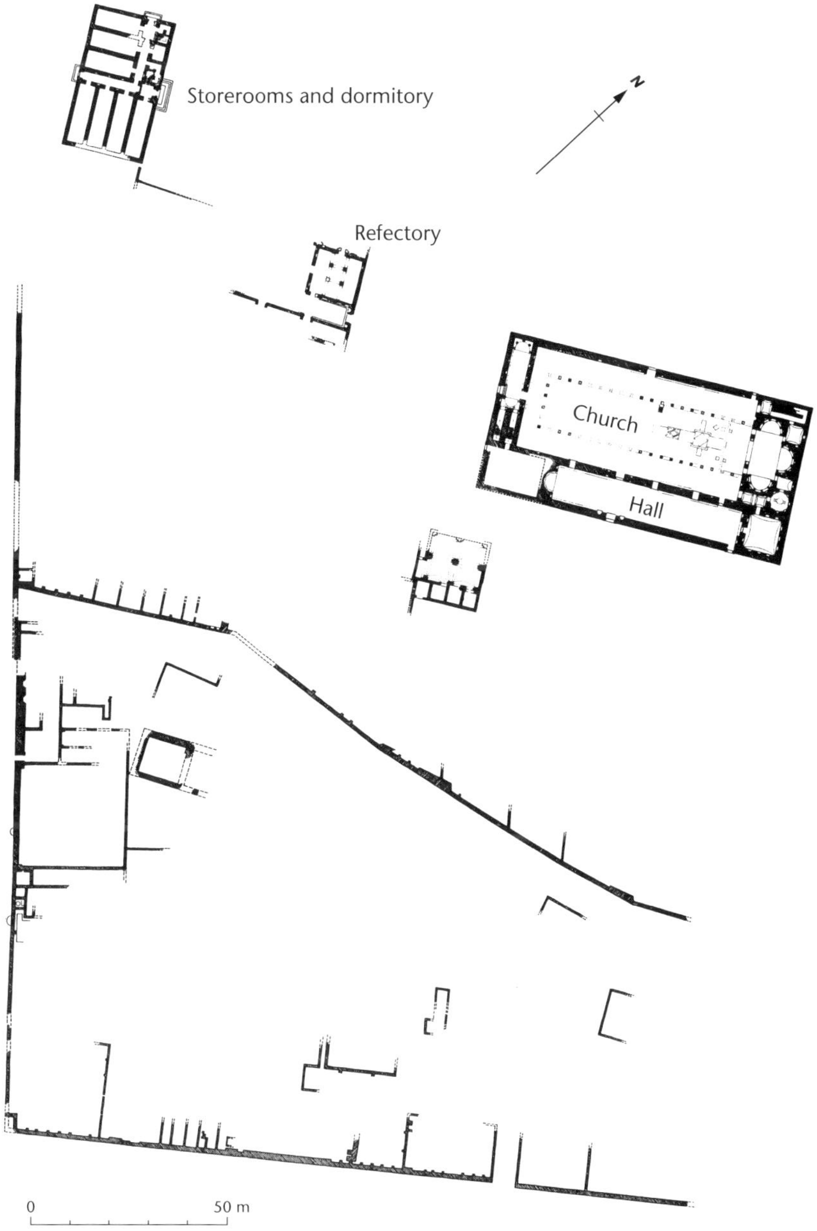

Fig. 6.5.4 The White Monastery (after Atiya 1991: 767).

destruction of pagan structures furnished stone for Shenoute's church: the entrance to the choir had two granite columns reused from a pagan temple, one of them recording the name Heliodoros. The lintel of the west door is a Roman entablature.

Running along most of the south side of the church is the Long Hall. West of the church, excavations carried out between 1985 and 1988 uncovered the remains of a refectory building and of a dormitory, originally with several storeys, providing accommodation for monks and storage rooms. Travellers of the eighteenth and nineteenth centuries, including Napoleon and Curzon, visited the monastery; it was inhabited by villagers and their livestock up until the early twentieth century. The monastery complex is the object of modern-day pilgrimage, especially on Shenoute's feast day, 14 July.

Some 3 km north of the White Monastery is the smaller **Red Monastery** (Deir el-Ahmar), or Monastery of St Bishoi (Deir Anba Bishoi). It no longer houses any resident monks; it is like the White Monastery a popular destination for pilgrims during July. Ongoing restoration work here is recovering well-preserved Late Antique paintings in the church.

Bibliography: Atiya 1991: 736–40; Krawiec 2002.

6.5.c The east bank

The remains of this **Deir el-Adhra** (Monastery of the Virgin) lie 130 m high on a cliff overhanging the east bank of the Nile (accessible by ferry from Samalut, 20 km north of Minya). Also known as Deir el-Bakarah (Monastery of the Pulley) after the method of hoisting goods and visitors up to the top of the cliff, the monastery features a picturesque church with an apse hewn into the rock. This is another site where the Holy Family is alleged to have stayed. Pilgrims visit the site on the Feast of the Assumption of the Virgin (22 August). It was occupied by monks up to the nineteenth century.

Bibliography: Atiya 1991: 715 (no. 6); Meinardus 1977: 362–4.

Recent exploration at **Tell el-Amarna** has found extensive evidence for Christian occupation of this famous New Kingdom site. Most notable is the monastery at **Kom el-Nana**, but some tombs in the northern cemetery were also remodelled, one for use as a church with baptistery.

Bibliography: Clackson 1999; Clédat 1999; Meinardus 1977, 1989.

7 THE THEBAN REGION

7.1 INTRODUCTION

7.1.a Site

In the area of ancient Thebes (around modern Luxor), the Nile Valley broadens and is enclosed by a mountainous area which forms a belt around the Theban plain. The Nile divides Thebes into an East and a West Bank. On the East Bank Amun-Re and other gods were worshipped in the temples of Karnak and, 3 km further south, Luxor. Across the river, on the West Bank, was Egypt's wealthiest necropolis: 'going to the west' meant for the ancient Egyptians 'to die'. Hathor, Greek Aphrodite, was the local goddess of the Theban necropolis and was worshipped there as 'mistress of the West'. Deceased kings as well as private persons were buried here and several pharaohs built mortuary temples.

7.1.b Historical background

At the beginning of the Middle Kingdom a Theban dynasty managed to reunite the country, and Thebes became, for the first time, Egypt's capital. The city rose to prominence and became the political and religious centre of Upper Egypt. Amun-Re, 'King of the gods', was its main god: he had his own temple at Luxor and was worshipped at Karnak together with Montu, the original local god of the Theban area, and the goddess Mut. In economic terms Amun's temple was the most important temple complex in Egypt, and Amun's high priest was a powerful authority, who even competed for authority with the royal power at the end of the New Kingdom. The Ptolemies and Roman emperors supported the cult of Amun of Thebes and of other deities such as Montu. The Greeks identified several Egyptian gods with one of their gods: for instance, Montu was called Apollo by the Greeks, and his temple the Apolloneion. Thus the religious and cultic life of Thebes lived on, but it was no longer the political and administrative centre of the south. Ptolemy I founded a new Greek capital in Upper Egypt, called Ptolemais (6.4.d). Upper Egypt, however, was still named after Thebes; even Greeks spoke of the 'Thebaid'.

Because of its former splendour, Thebes had enough symbolic power to figure as the centre of several insurrections in the south. The fiercest revolt against Ptolemaic rule was that of the rebel king Haronnophris and his successor Chaonnophris in 205–186 BC. They were considered saviour-like figures, who would improve the living conditions of the Egyptians. Control of Thebes alternated between the rebels and the

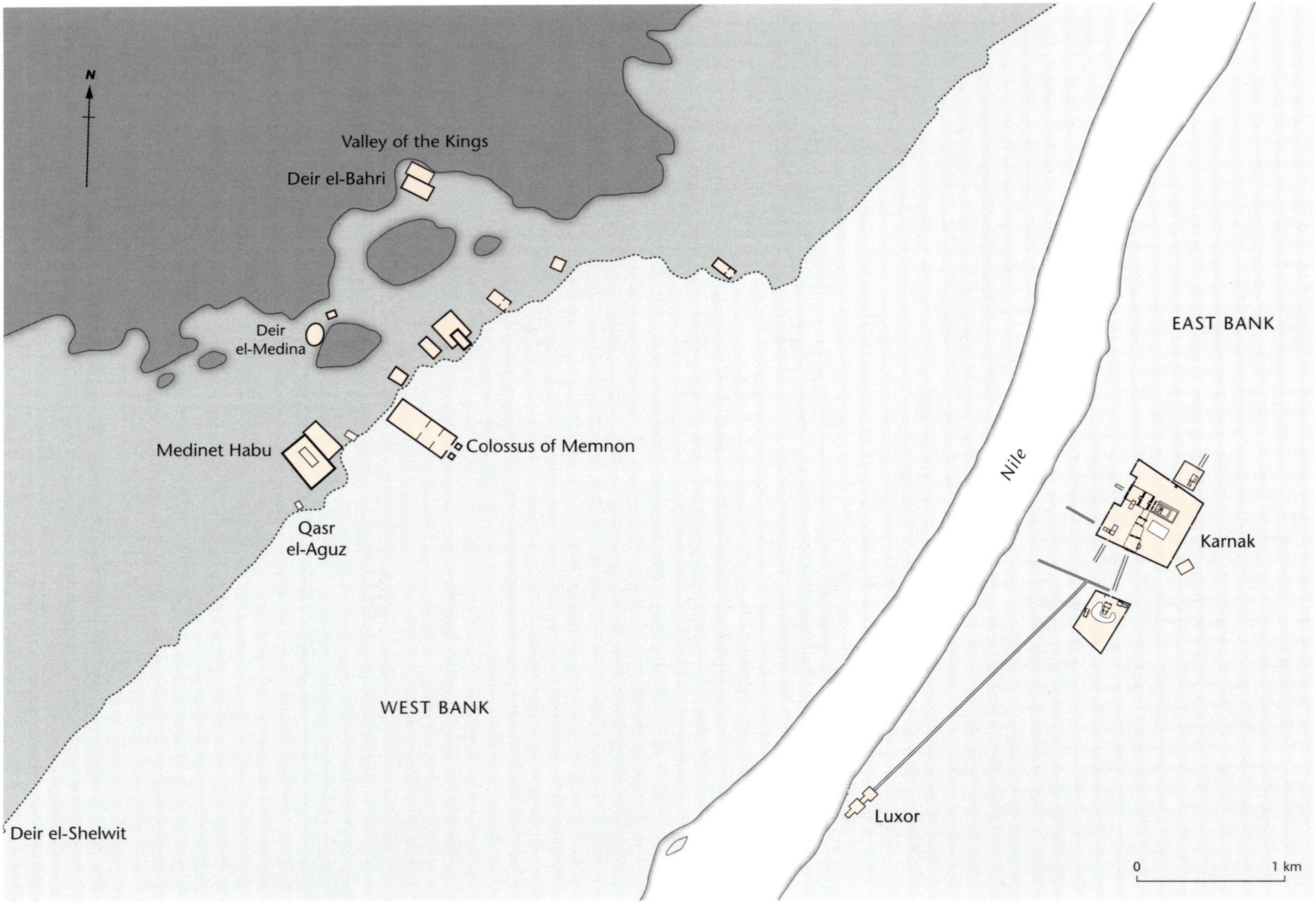
N
Valley of the Kings
Deir el-Bahri
Deir
el-Medina
Medinet Habu
Colossus of Memnon
Qasr
el-Aguz
WEST BANK
Deir el-Shelwit
Nile
EAST BANK
Karnak
Luxor
0
1 km

young king Ptolemy V. It is not clear whether the priests of the Theban temples favoured the rebels in the hope that Upper Egypt would become independent. It seems that they adopted a pragmatic attitude and supported whoever was in power at the moment. In response to this rebellion and some other minor insurrections in the second century BC, the Ptolemaic government tried to establish a firmer grip on Upper Egypt. New garrisons were installed south of Thebes and an extensive Greek administration was introduced to levy taxes. However, the increased Greek presence failed in its purpose, for around 88 BC a new rebellion broke out in the south. Thebes, the stronghold of the rebels, was crushed by Ptolemy IX Soter II, and the Thebans, according to the Greek writer Pausanias, were 'treated so harshly that they lost all memory of their former prosperity'. From then on the importance of the city diminished considerably.

The Romans took the precautions needed in the light of history and stationed a legion at Thebes. Nevertheless, another revolt broke out, apparently in response to excessive Roman taxation. In Philae a trilingual inscription of Cornelius Gallus, the first prefect of Egypt, testifies to his victory over rebels in 29 BC. The Thebaid was finally pacified, and half a century later the legion was withdrawn and replaced with units of auxiliary troops. Thebes had become a quiet provincial town. It had lost much of its charisma and its cultic and religious life was diminished. But it retained attraction as a museum city. Many tourists, among them several emperors, visited Thebes, as is shown by thousands of graffiti in temples and royal tombs and the inscriptions on the legs of the Colossus of Memnon (7.3.a). When Egypt was reorganized under Diocletian, the Thebaid became a separate province, garrisoned by two legions.

Bibliography: Vandorpe 1995; Vleeming 1995; Winnicki 1978.

7.1.c Architectural contributions

Most of the temple complexes on the East Bank were the work of a series of pharaohs, who also constructed impressive rock tombs and built huge mortuary temples on the West Bank. The contributions of the Ptolemaic kings and the Roman emperors are far more modest. Obviously, they did not construct their funerary monuments there. Their new sanctuaries were small: a temple of Sarapis on the East Bank (Luxor) and a few temples on the West Bank, such as those of Hathor (Deir el-Medina), Thoth (Qasr el-Aguz) and Isis (Deir el-Shelwit). Nevertheless the Ptolemies and the first Roman emperor, Augustus, were responsible for several enlargements, alterations, decorations and restorations of the old Theban temples and their enclosure walls. There was also activity under Augustus' successor, Tiberius, at Thebes, espe-

Fig. 7.1.1
The city of Thebes
(after Vleeming
1995: 30).

cially several restoration works after a high inundation. But little was done under later Roman emperors, and their attitude reflects the gradual decline of the pacified city. Interest in Thebes under Diocletian was limited to the construction of the new military camp in Amun's temple at Luxor.

The necropolis on the West Bank was still used by private persons in the Graeco-Roman period. Some new private tombs were constructed, but more often old tombs were simply reused.

Bibliography: Vandorpe 1995; Vleeming 1995.

7.2 THE EAST BANK

7.2.a At **Karnak** there are three temple complexes, each surrounded by a brick wall. The temples were fronted by several imposing gateways called pylons, and the enclosure walls were provided with several gates. No wonder Thebes was called the 'hundred-gated city' in antiquity. The main complex is the central one, the **precinct of Amun-Re.** A long avenue of ram-headed sphinxes leads from the Nile to the entrance of the temple, along which inscriptions from the Graeco-Roman period were found. Many Ptolemaic kings and Roman emperors contributed to Amun's temple. The priests were housed inside the precinct, to the east of the Sacred Lake. Several of their houses date from the Graeco-Roman period and produced numerous Greek and demotic texts on ostraka, including tax receipts and school exercises.

The precinct of Amun encloses some other smaller sanctuaries. One of them was dedicated to the lunar god Khonsu, 'master of lifetime', who was identified with the Greek Herakles. Khonsu-Herakles was worshipped here as judge and healer. On the roof some 300 graffiti can be seen, often accompanied by a footprint. They were inscribed by priests of Khonsu in the late pharaonic and Graeco-Roman times. Ptolemy III built a new propylon for the temple of Khonsu, now called 'Bab el-Amara' (fig. 7.2.2). He is shown on several reliefs on the gateway, but the most conspicuous is the double scene on the front lintel where he, together with his wife Berenike II, makes offerings to Khonsu and other deities. His predecessors are represented on the frieze above, among the deities adoring the moon-disc: Ptolemy II and Arsinoe II at the extreme left, Ptolemy I and Berenike I at the extreme right. This impressive gate was a seat of justice: the priestly judges sat here, oaths were sworn and judgments were pronounced.

To the north of the precinct of Amun lies the **complex of Montu**, the Theban war god, identified with the Greek god Apollo. Ptolemies III and IV were responsible for several constructions in this part of Karnak; for instance, the complex was provided with a new enclosure wall and a monumental gate or propylon, known as the 'Bab el-Abd'.

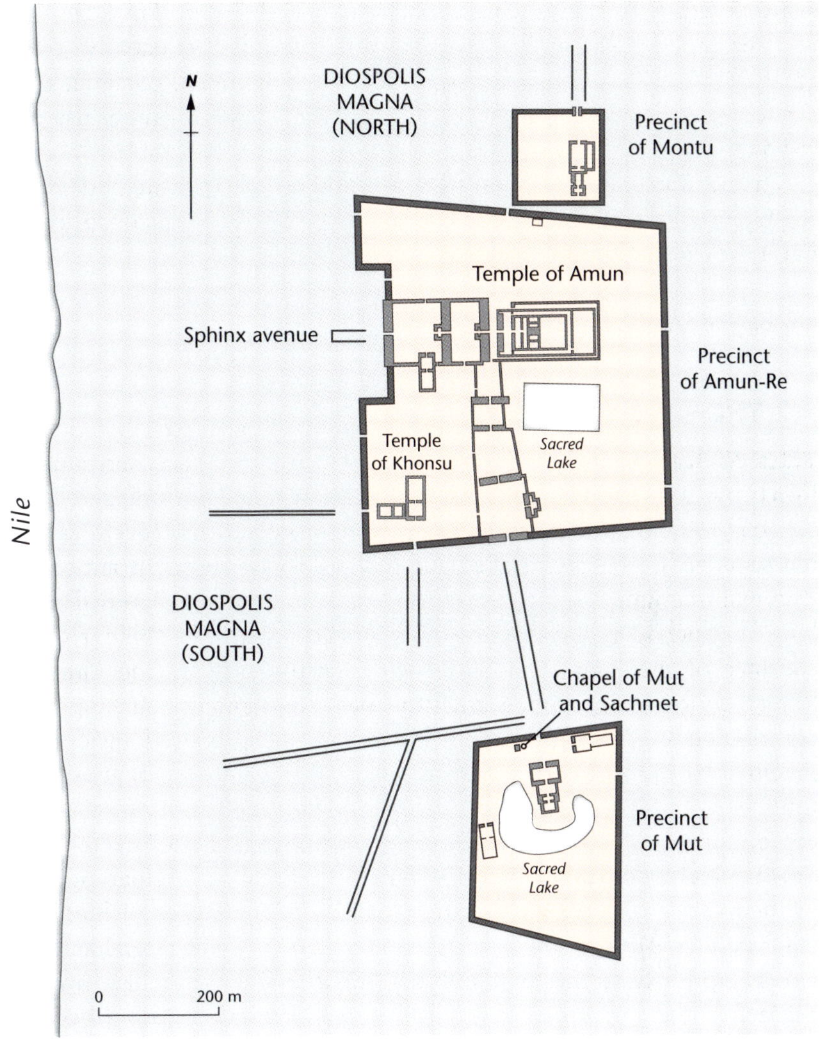

Fig. 7.2.1
The site of Karnak
(after Vleeming
1995: 217).

The two Ramesside colossi in front of the propylon were reused. The propylon was decorated with scenes showing both Ptolemies making offerings.

The third **precinct**, south of Amun's complex, was dedicated to the Egyptian goddess **Mut**, whom the Greeks equated with Hera. The Ptolemies were responsible for the gate in the enclosure wall, additions to her temple and decorations on the second pylon and in the chapel of Mut and Sachmet. Augustus built a new enclosure wall, which was soon damaged by a high inundation and restored by Tiberius.

The main residential area of Graeco-Roman Thebes was called **Diospolis Magna** or 'Diospolis the Great' and lay at present-day Karnak. Diospolis means 'City of Zeus', who was identified with Amun. The Ptolemaic city was located very near the walls of the

Fig. 7.2.2 Karnak, propylon of the temple of Khonsu.

temple enclosures, split up into two zones: the northern quarter, called 'House of the Cow', lay to the north of Amun's enclosure and to the west of Montu's precinct; the southern quarter was located south of Amun's temple. In Roman times the city was divided into more than six districts.

7.2.b The **temple of Amun at Luxor** was a subsidiary of the Karnak temple. Alexander, who probably never visited Thebes, gave instructions to build a sanctuary in the third antechamber of the holy of holies, and cartouches of his brother Philip III Arrhidaios are to be found in the entrance to the colonnade of Amenophis III. The contributions of the Ptolemies to this temple have often been overlooked, such as restorations by Ptolemy IV in the court of Ramesses II. The temple, lying close to the Nile, was damaged by a high inundation before or under the reign of the emperor Tiberius, who ordered repairs, the building of dams and perhaps the digging of canals to protect the temple in the future. Repairs to the enclosure wall, the Nilometer and the quay may date from the same period.

Greek graffiti testify to the worship of Amun by pilgrims in the Graeco-Roman period. They are found in several places: on the base of the west obelisk in front of Ramesses II's pylon (this obelisk is now in Paris); on the pylon of Ramesses II in the entrance, on the western side, to the court of Ramesses II; on the pylon of Amenophis III on the northern side, near the entrance; on the outside wall of the temple. Some graffiti contain only a name, but others explicitly record worship of the god.

In front of Amun's complex a sanctuary probably erected in the first century AD was reconstructed as a small brick **temple of Sarapis** by Gaius Julius Antoninus, a former soldier and *neokoros* (temple attendant) of Sarapis. According to the Greek inscription preserved on the lintel of the entrance gate, the sanctuary was consecrated to the emperor Hadrian on his birthday, 24 January 126. This Serapeum was a *peripteros*-temple, that is surrounded by a portico, unlike most Roman sanctuaries of Sarapis and Isis, which are prostyle, with columns in front. The platform on which the temple is built measures 12 x 8 m. Several niches for statues were cut in the outer temple wall. The back of the *cella* is occupied by a brick bench originally almost a metre high, which supported a series of statues. One is still there: the large well-preserved limestone statue of Isis; her head was still present when it was discovered but has now been removed. In the court before the temple there was an altar and a well. A well was indispensable to the cult of Sarapis and Isis, in which it was used for ritual purifications and libations.

Fig. 7.2.3 Luxor, temple of Sarapis.

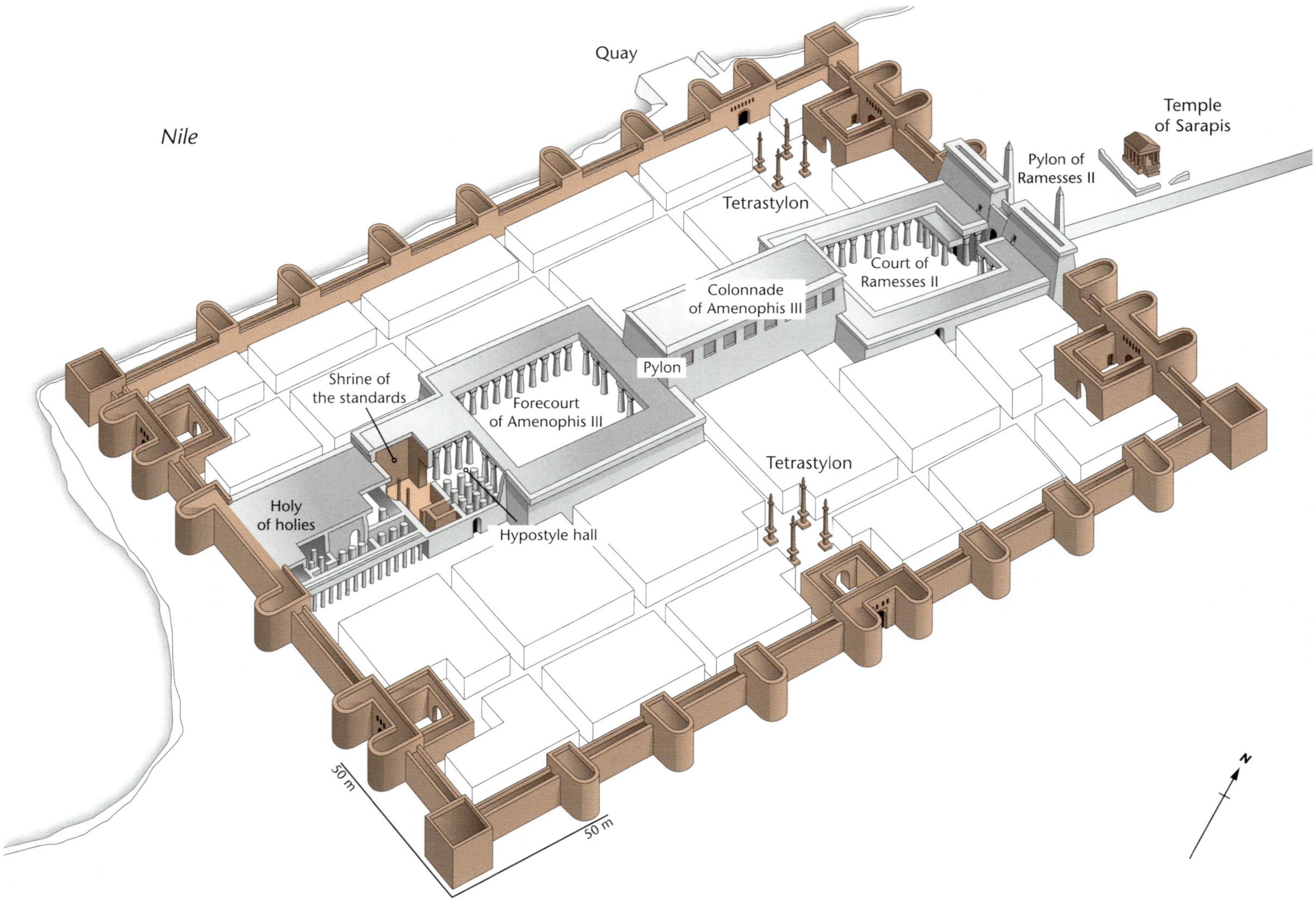
Nile
Quay
Temple
of Sarapis
Pylon of
Ramesses II
Tetrastylon
Court of
Ramesses II
Colonnade
of Amenophis III
Pylon
Shrine of
the standards
Forecourt
of Amenophis III
Tetrastylon
Holy
of holies
Hypostyle hall
50 m
50 m
N

When under Diocletian the Thebaid became a separate province with two legions, Amun's complex became the heart of a new **Roman military camp**. By that time the temple was no longer in use. New excavations and new research at the end of the twentieth century focused on the reconstruction of this camp, but many traces were lost because of the lack of interest by earlier excavators. The camp was enclosed by a huge brick defensive wall. The pylon or gateway of the ancient temple, with two red granite obelisks of Ramesses II in front, was integrated into the defensive wall. Probably six new entrance gates were added. Large parts of the gates are preserved, built of reused pharaonic stone blocks. The gates were provided with trapdoors and were flanked by horseshoe-shaped towers. These towers and the enclosure wall were built of brick and are largely lost. The tower to the left of the pylon is the best preserved and rises 2 m above ground level. Next to this tower, part of the enclosure wall, 4.5 m thick at that point, is visible, with behind it fourteen steps of a staircase leading to the trap door.

The camp was criss-crossed with broad roads. On two intersections a high pillar was erected on each of the four corners to form a *tetrastylon*, or four-pillar monument. The pillars bore statues of the four emperors, the two senior emperors and their two junior colleagues (Caesars). Inscriptions on the pedestals honoured the emperors. Both *tetrastyla* are partly preserved: the bases of the east *tetrastylon* are partly buried and about 2.3 m high; the bases with pillars of the north-west *tetrastylon* are better preserved and are up to 4.2 m high. The barracks of the soldiers were constructed of perishable material and have left no traces.

The pharaonic temple was the centre of the camp. The forecourt of Amenophis III, combined with the hypostyle hall and the sacred rooms behind it, accommodated the headquarters. The court was apparently left unchanged, but the hypostyle hall of thirty-two columns was altered: its central avenue was broadened, which required part of the columns to be cut away. Statues of the emperors were probably set up between the columns. One pedestal of a statue dedicated to the emperor Constantius is still *in situ*. The broadened avenue led directly to the most important room of the camp: the shrine for the legion's standards, decorated with scenes of the imperial cult. To create this chapel, the first of the four antechambers of the former holy of holies was transformed. The eight columns which supported the ceiling were removed; the door which used to lead to the inner sanctum was blocked in stone (the existing opening is modern) and altered into a semicircular niche flanked by four columns of pink granite from Aswan with Corinthian capitals of sandstone (col. pl. 7.2.5). Two columns are still *in situ* and measure about 4.2 m in height; the other two were found to the west of the camp. The four columns formed a kind of canopy for an altar or perhaps a throne for the Roman emperors. The walls of the chapel were redecorated: the ancient reliefs were covered with frescoes, which are

Fig. 7.2.4 Reconstruction of the Roman fortress at Luxor (after el-Saghir 1986: pl.xx).

now badly damaged, but can be partly reconstructed thanks to the watercolours made by J.G. Wilkinson in the nineteenth century. The central niche, for instance, shows the four tetrarchs wearing purple cloaks. Each of them holds a different attribute: the second tetrarch from the left carries a globe and leans on a long staff. In the vault above them is an eagle holding a wreath of laurels in his claws, which symbolizes the protection of Jupiter.

Scholars still debate which legion was stationed here, the III Diocletiana or the II Flavia Constantia, or whether the base was a double camp with room for both legions or detachments of them. In any event, the Roman camp was responsible for the later Arabic name Luxor ('the camps', from Latin *castra* via the Arabic *qasr*). The last attestations of the Luxor camp by name come in Coptic documents from the time of the Persian occupation of Egypt in AD 619–29. The Persians made their headquarters in the camp. Probably when they left it fell into ruin. Around that time the first churches appear to the north of the camp. Later on more churches were built inside it. Since the thirteenth century the courtyard of Ramesses II has been occupied by the small mosque of Abu el-Haggag, which was constructed at what was then ground level but now, after clearance, looks like the second floor. Its sanctity has precluded excavation in this part of the courtyard.

Bibliography: El-Saghir 1986; Golvin 1981; Quaegebeur 1974, 1975–6, 1986; Vandorpe 1995; Vleeming 1995.

7.3 THE WEST BANK

7.3.a Mortuary and other temples

Several New Kingdom pharaohs constructed their mortuary temple, for the cult of the deceased king, in the desert or on the edge of cultivation. A few of these temples were still in use in the Graeco-Roman period, serving for the worship of more popular gods (see below on Medinet Habu, Deir el-Bahri and the Colossus of Memnon). It is doubtful whether the Ramesseum, the mortuary temple of Ramesses II, was still in use in Graeco-Roman times. The Greek historian Diodorus of Sicily, who visited Egypt around 59 BC, gives a description of the temple, calling it 'the tomb of Osymandyas', which is the Greek rendering of one of the first names of Ramesses II – hence Shelley's famous poem on Ozymandias. There may have been a popular cult of Amun-Re with at least two priests, but the evidence is poor. Already in pre-Ptolemaic times some minor temples of the gods were constructed, such as the small Amun temple at Medinet Habu. The Ptolemies and Romans built more of these modest sanctuaries at Qasr el-Aguz, Deir el-Shelwit and Deir el-Medina.

An extensive complex of temples and townsite, **Medinet Habu** centres around the mortuary temple of Ramesses III, an imposing structure surrounded by a substantial enclosure wall. Later structures cluster around the Ramesside temple, including a series of Saite chapels for the Wives of the god Amun. A smaller temple dedicated to Amun became a focus of building activity in the Graeco-Roman period, with a large Ptolemaic pylon and a forecourt built under Antoninus Pius.

The great enclosure wall of the Ramesses III temple at Medinet Habu became home to a town called Memnoneia in Greek and **Jeme** in Egyptian (col. pl. 7.3.1). Jeme was almost continuously occupied from its origin as a small collection of houses around 1000 BC to its abandonment as an extensive Christian town under early Muslim rule around AD 800. Jeme was particularly thriving in the Graeco-Roman period. Demotic texts and artefactual evidence attest to varying degrees of habitation in the Ptolemaic period, while extensive remains of houses, demotic, Greek and later Coptic texts and an wide array of datable artefacts serve as evidence for the complex history of the town under Roman and early Islamic rule. Jeme is best attested after the coming of Christianity. A large church in the ancient temple on which the town was built served the town's population along with three smaller churches, one built on an earlier Roman bathhouse. Documentation and artefactual evidence for the life of the town is most extensive for the seventh and eighth centuries AD, when the town reached its greatest prosperity in the century after the Muslim conquest of Egypt in 639–42. Coptic documentary texts in particular attest the active economic and social life of the town and its relations to nearby monasteries. The town of Jeme, along with much of the western Theban area, was abandoned sometime before AD 800. Today substantial remains of houses and other mudbrick structures of Jeme survive on the enclosure wall to the west and south of the temple of Ramesses III; even in the cleared areas to the west of the temple Late Antique pottery litters the ground. Substantial amounts of stone decorative elements from the houses of Jeme, many decorated with Coptic crosses, can be seen in stacks to the south of the temple, and remains of the Holy Church of Jeme are visible in the large second courtyard of the temple. Many finds from the excavation of the site went to the Oriental Institute Museum, University of Chicago, where a selection of items is on display

Bibliography: Hölscher 1954; Wilfong 2002.

The New Kingdom queen Hatshepsut built an imposing mortuary complex at **Deir el-Bahri** consisting of three terraces. In the Ptolemaic period only two chapels were still in use. The first is located in the south part of the second terrace and was already dedicated to Hathor, mistress of the West, in earlier times. The Greeks equated her with

Aphrodite. This shrine of Aphrodite was surnamed 'on the mountain' to distinguish it from the temple of Aphrodite at Deir el-Medina, called 'in the necropolis'. The second chapel was newly constructed on the third terrace, in the heart of the old mortuary complex. In the back of the central upper court, two rooms were cut in the rock: the sanctuary for Amun's barque (sacred boat), and behind it the chapel for the cult statues of Amun-Re and Hatshepsut. Ptolemy VIII cut a third room in the

Fig. 7.3.2
Deir el-Bahri, the Monastery of Phoibammon in 1894 (H. Carter, EES no.15).

rock for the worship of two healing deities: Imouthes the architect of Zoser, identified by the Greeks with their god of medicine Asklepios, is shown on the left wall together with, among others, his mother and wife; Amenothes son of Hapu, the architect of Amenophis III, is found on the right wall together with Hathor and other deities. Pilgrims left numerous graffiti in Greek and Egyptian.

The Deir el-Bahri temple of Hatshepsut was later reused as the site of the **Monastery of Phoibammon**. Abraham of Hermonthis founded this monastery in the early seventh century to provide a more accessible residence than the earlier monastery, also dedicated to Phoibammon, that he had occupied in the desert towards Hermonthis. The Monastery of Phoibammon at Deir el Bahri quickly became the most important monastery in the western Theban area, as is attested in the extensive corpus of Coptic documents from and concerning the site. The Monastery of Phoibammon had close connections to the nearby town of Jeme. The monastery served as a depository for legal documents from Jeme and there was much interaction and trade between monastery and town. The Monastery of Phoibammon was abandoned sometime before AD 800 along with most of the western Theban area. Graffiti attest visits to the site after its abandonment, suggesting that it may have become a destination for pilgrimage. Documents from the monastery began appearing on the antiquities market in the mid-nineteenth century. The site was first excavated in the early twentieth century by the Egypt Exploration Fund, then by the Metropolitan Museum of Art and the Polish Deir el-Bahri Expedition. The modern presentation of the site of Deir el-Bahri is directed almost entirely towards the architectural and artistic remains of the reign of Hatshepsut, but the determined visitor can find graffiti and other traces of the Monastery of Phoibammon there. Little remains at the site of the original desert monastery, which is difficult for visitors to reach.

Bibliography: Godlewski 1986.

The imposing mortuary temple of Amenophis III was fronted by two monumental seated statues of that New Kingdom pharaoh, each flanked by statuettes of queens by their legs. The temple was destroyed and its materials used for the mortuary complex of Merneptah. Only Amenophis' statues in front of the entrance have survived. The statue on the right earned itself the name **'Colossus of Memnon'** because it began to 'sing' after the earthquake of 27 BC. Often in the morning a sound was produced when the first rays of sun reacted with the dew in the cracks caused by the earthquake. The statue was therefore identified with Memnon, son of Aurora, goddess of dawn. Roman officials and soldiers visiting the colossus inscribed their identities and impressions on the feet and legs in Greek or Latin (fig. 7.3.3); there is only

Fig. 7.3.3 Colossus of Memnon, tourist inscriptions.

one Egyptian text. The inscriptions, about one hundred in total, range from simple texts such as 'I heard Memnon' to long poems. The emperor Hadrian and his empress Sabina were present on 20 and 21 November AD 130. On their first visit Memnon made no sound, according to a poem because Memnon wanted to meet the beautiful empress again. The next day Sabina made another attempt and the colossus raised his voice in the first hour of the day. Hadrian joined his wife at the second hour and again Memnon sang. The poetess Balbilla, who was also present, dedicated four poems to these events, written in Greek reminiscent of Sappho (box 1.7.2). The colossus was repaired under Septimius Severus when he visited Thebes in 199, or, less probably, by Zenobia, queen of Palmyra, some seventy years later. Memnon was thus silenced forever.

Qasr el-Aguz, or the 'Castle of the Elderly' is the Arab name of a small Ptolemaic sanctuary to the south of Medinet Habu. Ptolemy VIII Euergetes II dedicated this well-preserved but unfinished temple to Thoth-the-Ibis about 140–120 BC. Thoth was worshipped here as an oracular god and was surnamed Thotsutmis (Thoth listens) or Teephibis (The face of the ibis has spoken). Undoubtedly the temple was enclosed by a wall, but excavations have yet to find this. Decorations are lacking in the forecourt and first hall. The reliefs in the second hall and in the sanctuary proper mostly show the founder Ptolemy VIII in the offering scenes. He is often accompanied by his first wife and sister Cleopatra II or by his second wife and niece Cleopatra III or by both. The scenes on the upper register of the short walls of the sanctuary deserve particular attention. They show the king offering to

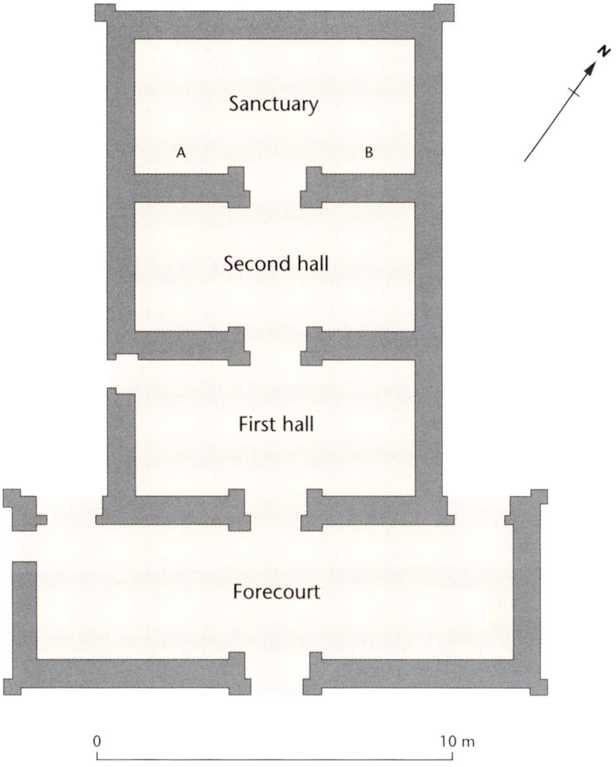

Fig. 7.3.4
Qasr el-Aguz, the Thoth temple (after Porter and Moss 1972: pl.XLIX.2).

four deified royal couples: on wall (a) Ptolemy II and Arsinoe II, and Ptolemy III and Berenike II; on wall (b) Ptolemy V and Cleopatra I, his parents, and Ptolemy IV and Arsinoe III, his grandparents. These scenes may have been an attempt to promote the dynastic cult among Egyptians.

At **Deir el-Shelwit**, in the most southern part of the Theban region, 3.5 km from Medinet Habu, one of the last Egyptian temple complexes was built in the second half of the first century AD; the process of decoration continued until the reign of Antoninus Pius. The temple was dedicated to Isis. The small sanctuary and the court in front of it were enclosed by a brick wall with one monumental gate or propylon. The massive rectangular wall measures 81 x 58 m and is 3–4 m thick. Only the foundations are preserved at certain points. The propylon has suffered severe damage; the lintel and more than half of the northern (right) jamb are lost. The remaining parts show several registers with offering scenes. The visitor walks by four Roman emperors of the first century AD dressed as Egyptian pharaohs: the ephemeral emperors Galba and Otho, then Vespasian and his son Domitian. The base shows two horizontal and several vertical lines containing, among other things, a hymn to Isis. In the courtyard the well, indispensable for an Isis temple (see 7.2.b), has been discovered; it is of elliptical form (about 10 m in diameter) and a staircase was needed to reach the water level.

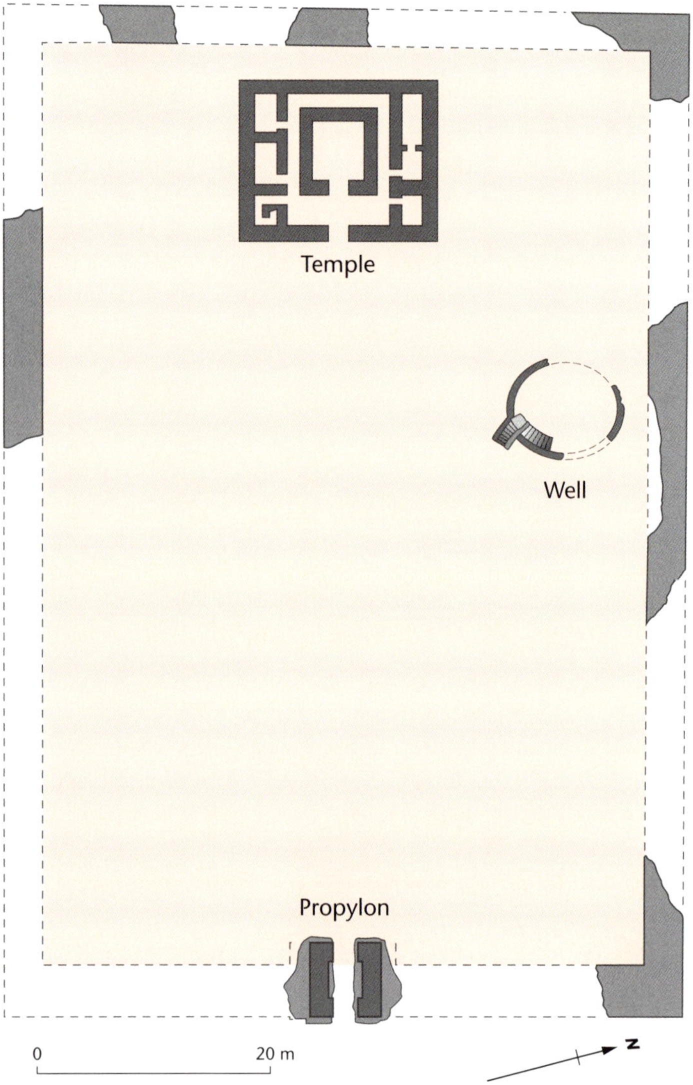

Fig. 7.3.5
Deir el-Shelwit, the Isis temple (after Zivie 1982–92: IV pl.57).

The well-preserved small temple is only partly decorated and has been ignored by Egyptologists because of the mediocre quality of the scenes and their inscriptions. In addition, several scenes and texts are in an unfinished state. The carelessness is typical of late decorations of the second century AD. Under Hadrian the sanctuary proper was decorated with raised relief. The wall in the back has two registers, each with double scenes: the upper register twice shows Hadrian in front of Isis; behind the emperor on the left a vulture appears on a lotus-column, behind the emperor on the right a uraeus on a papyrus-column; the scenes are filled out with several columns of hieroglyphs squeezed closely together. The eastern wall, unfortunately, has been blackened by smoke during the temple's long use as a habitation. Hadrian's successor Antoninus Pius was responsible for decorations in incised relief on the sanctuary's façade in the *pronaos*: some scenes are unfinished, others were never started – for instance, the third of the four registers to the left of the entrance. The four holes in the southern wall are small windows which afforded light to the staircase to the roof. Against the back wall of the temple, in the middle, a niche was constructed for cultic practices outside the temple. There are not only Greek and demotic graffiti in the enclosure of Isis, as expected, but also Coptic graffiti on the roof which show that the temple was reused by the Copts. The architecture, however, shows no sign of alteration into a monastery or church.

At modern **Deir el-Medina** a village was built for the craftsmen of the New Kingdom royal tombs. In the northern part of the village a temple was dedicated to Hathor, the local goddess of the Theban necropolis, as early as Dynasty 18. It was altered and enlarged by the pharaohs Sethos I and Ramesses II. When the sanctuary of Ramesses fell into ruin, a new sandstone temple was built by the architects of Ptolemy IV. Several of his successors added to the decorations. The temple was dedicated to Hathor 'mistress of the West of Jeme', identified with Greek Aphrodite, and to Maat. In addition, the healing gods Imouthes and Amenothes son of Hapu, for whom a chapel was constructed at Deir el-Bahri (see above), were worshipped there. They are represented on the two columns in the façade of the *pronaos* (fig. 7.3.8).

Fig. 7.3.6
Deir el-Medina,
temple and town.

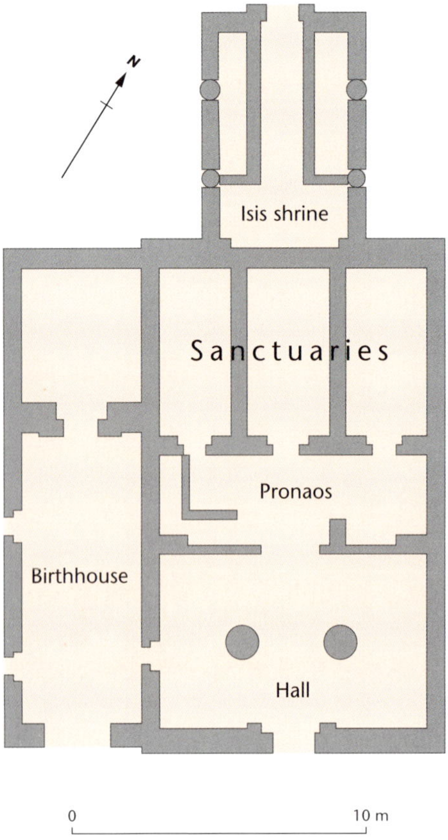

Fig. 7.3.7
Deir el-Medina, the Hathor temple (after Porter and Moss 1972: pl.XXXVIII).

This Hathor temple is one of the most beautiful Ptolemaic temples, surprising the visitor with its well-preserved polychrome reliefs. The inner sanctum contains three chapels, the central one dedicated to Hathor, the south sanctuary (left) to Amun-Sokar-Osiris representing the underworld, and the north sanctuary (right) to the solar god Amun-Re-Osiris. The reliefs of these chapels, which have been cleaned, mostly portray Ptolemies in the offering scenes. The connection of the south sanctuary with the underworld is clear from the judgment scene on the south (left) wall where the heart is being weighed.

Ptolemy XII was the last Ptolemaic king to be active in decorating the temple complex. He decorated the entrance to the columned hall; on the lintel, for instance, he makes offerings to the cow-headed mistress of the temple, Hathor. He also constructed the gate in the well-preserved mudbrick enclosure wall. Against the south wall a mudbrick *mammisi* (birthhouse, see box 8.2.1) was built by Ptolemy IX for the birth of Hathor's son Horus or Harsemtheus. Against the west wall a shrine of Isis was constructed in Roman times, probably under Augustus. In two jars in a house near the precinct of Hathor a private archive was found of a priestly family attached to the temple of Hathor. The modern name Deir el-Medina, 'Monastery of the City' (referring to Jeme),

Fig. 7.3.8
Deir el-Medina, *pronaos* of the Hathor temple.

The archives of the *Choachytai* (second–first century BC)

The *choachytai* (libationers) were funerary priests responsible for the mummies after their embalming. They stored the mummies before burial, interred them in one of their tombs and afterwards presented offerings to the deceased on fixed days as long as a remuneration was paid by the dead person's relatives. As a source of income, these mummies could be inherited by family members of the *choachytai*.

Many of the tombs the *choachytai* possessed were old ones that were ownerless and which they had now occupied, such as the large tomb called Thunabunun, that is 'the tomb of Nabunun', who was a high priest of Amun under Ramesses II, which was capable of holding a large number of mummies. Another tomb was used by the *choachytai* as a store for their equipment and a storage room for mummies awaiting burial. According to a complaint about robbery dated 127/6 BC, thieves stole the tools, plundered the mummies and left the tomb door open so that jackals could enter and devour the mummies. Some *choachytai* kept their family archive in jars or wrapped in linen (see below) in one of the tombs they worked in. Thus several family archives of *choachytai* were discovered in the necropolis in the nineteenth and twentieth centuries, often by illegal excavators, who sold them on the antiquities market. These demotic and Greek papyri are now scattered all over the world.

In order to cement their community, the *choachytai* founded an association under the patronage of Amenophis, a god who was closely connected with the necropolis. Some fifty persons, male, female and children of ten years or older, were members. A list of regulations was drawn up. For instance, a number of 'days of drinking' was introduced on which they had a drink with one another, but with the proviso that no member could have more than two jars of wine. Another sign of solidarity was to be present at each other's embalming and funeral. (Depauw 2000; Pestman 1993)

Box 7.3.1
Fig. 7.3.9

reflects the conversion of the complex into a monastery. The temple was transformed into a church, surrounded by cells and annexes. Some Coptic tombs were found in the court, and there are many Coptic inscriptions of the monastic era on the front of the temple.

A substantial monastic settlement lay near the site of Deir el-Medina at Gurnet Marai, the Monastery of St Mark, which yielded a number of burials and thousands of ostraka in excavations by the French.

Bibliography: Wilfong 1989; Montserrat and Meskell 1997.

7.3.b The Necropolis

The **Valley of the Kings** was already a special tourist attraction in Graeco-Roman Egypt. Most of the tombs had been robbed, or the sarcophagi and tomb furnishings had been hidden in earlier times. The Greeks nicknamed the tombs, which were cut in the cliffs, 'syringes' ('shepherd's pipes'), because of their long tubular shape. In about ten tombs, including those of Ramesses IV and VI, visitors left more than 2000 painted or inscribed graffiti in Greek, Latin or Egyptian.

In Graeco-Roman times new **private tombs** were constructed, but more often old tombs were reused. The Theban rock tomb 157 at Dra Abu el-Naga, which can still be visited, has been identified as the **tomb of Nabunun**, who was high priest of Amun under Ramesses II. It was reused as a collective tomb in the Ptolemaic period by the funerary priests called *choachytai* (box 7.3.1). Another important group burial of the Roman period is the so-called **Soter tomb** (box 7.3.2).

The Dynasty 11 tomb of Daga was much later home to the **Monastery of Epiphanius**, which flourished in the last years of the sixth century and throughout the seventh century AD as part of the larger western Theban community of monasteries and towns. At its most extensive this monastery contained a number of cells and featured two towers. Although it was not particularly large or important, the monastery has acquired great significance for modern scholarship as a result of the wealth of textual and archaeological evidence that its inhabitants left behind, published in the reports from the Metropolitan Museum of Art Egyptian Expedition (1912–14) by Herbert Winlock and Walter Crum. Little survives of the Monastery of Epiphanius *in situ*, but a large number of artefacts from the excavation can be seen at the Metropolitan Museum of Art in New York, and the pottery from the excavation is now mostly at the Oriental Institute Museum, University of Chicago. Many other private tombs in western Thebes were the home to monastic institutions, especially the so-called Monastery of Cyriacus and the substantial monastic remains in tombs at Dra Abu el-Naga.

Bibliography: Bács 2000; Winlock and Crum 1926.

The Soter Tomb and the Rise of the Zodiac

The zodiac originates from the ancient civilization of Mesopotamia (modern Iraq). The Egyptians took over the zodiac at a very late stage. The oldest example dates from around 246–180 BC. It was found near the Upper Egyptian town of Esna, where the Ptolemies had built a temple for the creator god Khnum, which was dismantled in 1843 so its blocks could be used to build a canal. The signs of the zodiac were inserted among the typical Egyptian celestial bodies on the ceiling of the columned hall.

For the best-known representation of the zodiac in Egypt, the visitor must take the staircase to the roof of the temple of Hathor at Dendera. The ceiling in one of the chapels is decorated with the Egyptian celestial bodies, among them the twelve signs of the zodiac. This exquisite piece was discovered during the expedition of Napoleon and was stolen and taken to Paris shortly afterwards. The original can still be admired in the Louvre, but the French made a copy for the temple of Hathor. It is now thought that the zodiac of Dendera dates from 28 December 47 BC, when Cleopatra ruled Egypt.

The zodiac became popular in the Roman period. It seized the limelight, ousting several other celestial bodies, and gradually assumed a life of its own on the ceilings of tombs or on the inner side of the lid of sarcophagi. The coffins of the Soter family have become well known thanks to their representation of the zodiac. Soter was the patriarch of a noble family from second-century AD Thebes. He was married to Cleopatra alias Candake. Their children died young: Cleopatra was eleven, Sensaos sixteen, Petemenophis twenty-one. The tomb was discovered in 1820 in the presence of the Italian treasure-hunter Antonio Lebolo and the English traveller Sir Frederick Hennicker, somewhere in the hills south of Deir el-Bahri, and has tentatively been identified with the Theban tomb no. 32, which originally belonged to Djehutimes, chief steward of Amun and overseer of the granaries of Egypt in the reign of Ramesses II. The fourteen wooden coffins and mummies of Soter and his family were plundered and shipped to Europe, where they were sold to museums in Berlin, Leiden, London, Paris and Turin. The coffin of the daughter Sensaos, to take one example, shows the celestial goddess Nut, surrounded by the signs of the zodiac, all facing the head of Nut, and shows Egyptian influence (col. pl. 7.3.10).

An important innovation in the Roman period is the circular representation of the zodiac, which was to spread to the western part of the Roman empire. In a series of rock tombs in Middle Egyptian Salamini, near Achmim, several ceilings have drawings of circular zodiacs. In the centre the goddess Isis-Sothis may be represented, announcing the beginning of the new year. (Bataille 1952; Bernand and Bernand 1960; Laskowska-Kusztal 1984; Quaegebeur 1974; Vandorpe 1995)

Box 7.3.2

7.4 PATHYRIS (GEBELEIN)

The small town of **Pathyris** is located some 30 km south of Thebes, that is about one day's sailing, and can be reached by a good road. In antiquity **Pathyris** was a strategically important location as it completely commands the Nile Valley, which grows quite narrow there and, on the west bank, is overshadowed and dominated by two rock formations. The first and smaller hill is separated from the Nile by a small strip of land. About 500 m to the west of the first hill, on the edge of the valley, is the second rock formation, much more impressive, higher, longer and with more foothills. A town had existed here from time immemorial. Its religious name was *Inertj*, 'Twin peaks', referring to the two rock formations, and its administrative name *Pathyris*, which means 'The house of (the goddess) Hathor'. The modern name (El-) Gebelein, 'The two mountains', translates the ancient religious name of the village.

After the fierce revolt in the south which ended in 186 BC, the town received a new impulse. The king installed a minor military base in Pathyris and a major one in the neighbouring city of Krokodilopolis. Any future rebels coming from the south had to pass these strategic points if they hoped to conquer Thebes. The family archives of several Greek and Egyptian soldiers serving in the camps have come down to us. The information is copious for almost a century, until 88 BC, when Gebelein was seized by rebels and was destroyed when they were defeated. The village was still unoccupied under the Romans. The topography of the ancient Ptolemaic town is well known, thanks to detailed descriptions in the title deeds which were part of the family archives. It corresponds well with the appearance of the present town.

The greater part of the town lay at the foot of the smaller, eastern hill,

Fig. 7.4.1
Pathyris (Gebelein).

as it still does today. On top of the hill the military base and the temple of the town goddess Hathor were built. Almost nothing remains of the ancient buildings, because some decades back dynamite was used to clear the hill. A police station has now replaced the ancient fortress, and instead of the old temple of Hathor a humble sanctuary for Sheikh Musa can be admired. The town was surrounded by a fertile plain with the same characteristics as today. It extended from the Nile as far as the desert in the west, that is as far as the second, western hill. Between the first hill and the Nile, a small strip of land was planted with palm trees; this palm grove still exists, enriched with some banana trees. The remaining part of the agricultural area was planted with wheat and vines and, apart from the land along the river bank, required artificial irrigation by a system of canals.

Little survives of ancient Pathyris, but many objects from it may be seen in the Museum of Turin, among them impressive tomb paintings. These were acquired in the course of several Italian excavation campaigns. The town is well known to scholars for the hundreds of documents which were discovered in the Ptolemaic houses and often form part of family archives. The best known of these is the archive of a Ptolemaic military officer named Dryton and his Egyptian wife, along with their daughters. A large quantity of the documentation is pre- Box 7.4

Family Archives

A family would keep its archive in the house, for instance under the staircase or in the corner of a room. The documents were written on sheets of papyrus and were rolled one into another. Several packets of papyri might be kept in a jar or wrapped in linen. The husband and wife often preserved important papers of close family members such as their sisters or daughters or mother. The archive was usually inherited by the oldest son or daughter. Three types of texts are found in the archive of Dryton:

(a) Legal documents which could be submitted in case of a trial, the most important group among the family papers. One may glance through a series of title deeds, loans, wills, marriage and divorce contracts, and so on. The following contract records a divorce according to Egyptian custom (100 BC).

He has spoken, the Greek born in Egypt, Pamenos son of Nechouthes, his mother being Senthotis, to the woman Senmonthis the younger, daughter of Kaies, her mother being Senmouthis: 'I have repudiated you as a wife. I am far from you on account of (the) right (to you) as (my) wife. I have nothing in the world to claim of you in the name of the right (to you) as (my) wife. I am the one who says to you: "Take yourself a husband." I will not be able to stand in your way in any place to which you wish to go to take yourself a husband. If I find you together with any man in the world, I will not be able to say to you: "You are my wife", from this day on and afterwards, for ever.'

(b) Literary works, a diversion from the bulk of formulaic contracts. The poem below was copied on the back of an old loan. It is the vividly mimetic song of a woman abandoned by her lover. She sets out for her lover's house, driven through the night by desire, and upon arriving at his locked door, she begs him to let her in.

Our feelings were mutual, we bound ourselves together. And Kypris (Aphrodite) is love's security. It's torture to recall how he kissed me, when he meant to desert me, that inventor of confusion, begetter of my love. Desire gripped me. I don't deny that he's on my mind. O beloved stars and lady Night, companions in my desire, take me even now to him, whom Kypris drives me to as a captive, while potent Eros holds me in his grip. My guide is the potent torch that's ablaze in my soul.

(c) Odd jottings, without any juridical value and kept for sentimental reasons, among them letters. In the following document, the cavalryman Esthladas, who is on campaign, writes to his parents not to worry about rebels in a neighbouring town.

Esthladas to his father and mother, greetings and good health. As I often write you to be of good heart and to look after yourself until things get back to normal, it would be good if you put heart into yourself and our family. For it has come to our ears that in the month of Tybi [the officer] Paos is sailing up the Nile with sufficient forces to suppress the rabble in (the town of) Hermonthis (and) that he will treat them as rebels. Greetings to my sisters and to Pelops, Stachys and Senathyris. Farewell. Year 40, Choiak 23 [that is 15 January 130 BC].

(Vandorpe 2002: texts no. 8, 50 and 36)

served in the Egyptian Museum, Cairo, but an even larger part has reached collections all over the world via the antiquities market.

Bibliography: Pestman 1965.

7.5 HERMONTHIS (ARMANT)

Continuously inhabited since predynastic times, Hermonthis was a significant regional centre, home to important temples and a major animal cult. In the later Roman and early Islamic period, Hermonthis was the seat of the regional governor. It is now the modern village of Armant, a tourist destination from Luxor which is popular not for its scattered ancient remains but for its character as a typical 'unspoiled' Egyptian village.

7.5.1 The **temples** at Hermonthis lay to the north-east of the modern village. The primary temple goes back to the Middle Kingdom or earlier, and its most prominent feature is a pylon from the reign of Tuthmosis III. Most of the temple remains are later, including a secondary temple of Nektanebo II, a gateway of Antoninus Pius and another gateway of the Graeco-Roman period. Perhaps the best-known structure is a *mammisi* built by Cleopatra VII in honour of the birth of her son Ptolemy XV Caesarion. This structure consisted of an outer courtyard, outer and inner halls, and a birth room, partially recorded by European travellers in the early part of the nineteenth century. These records are nearly all that remain of Cleopatra's temple, as it was dismantled in the mid-nineteenth century and the blocks used in the construction of a sugar factory. Parts of the pylon of Tuthmosis III are still visible, as are the two Graeco-Roman gateways. Little survives of the Graeco-Roman habitation at Hermonthis, but remains of Roman baths were found near the modern village of Armant.

Bibliography: Arnold 1999; Mond and Myers 1940.

7.5.2 To the north-west of the temples lay the **Bucheion**, burial place for the Buchis bull, a peripatetic sacred animal, who rotated between Hermonthis and the temples at Tod and Medamud. The cult of the Buchis bull was active by the New Kingdom if not earlier, but the existing Bucheion at Hermonthis was founded under Nektanebo II, and most remains at the site are Ptolemaic and Roman. Excavations at the site in 1929–31 revealed an extensive series of Buchis bull burials. Many had been previously looted, and stelae recording the dates of these burials had made their way to museums, most notably in London and Cairo. Enough survived of the burials to show the elaborate care lavished on the embalming of these animals and provide valuable evidence for animal-mummification techniques. Just to the east of the Bucheion, at Baqaria, lay a related complex of burials of cows who were the mothers of Buchis. Burials at these two sites are attested from the time of Nektanebo II all the way down to AD 340, the date of the last known Buchis burial; this late survival of the Buchis cult is attested in Macrobius' *Saturnalia*. Remains of a Roman-period village were found near Baqaria.

Bibliography: Mond and Myers 1934.

7.5.3 Just to the south of the pylon of Thutmose III lay a large **church**. Hermonthis was the seat of a major bishopric in the Late Antique and early Islamic periods, and this church is likely to have been the 'Holy Church of Hermonthis' known from documents. Constructed partly of stone reused from earlier structures, the church was a substantial basilica with two outer columned porticoes, a complex multi-roomed sanctuary and an elaborate narthex; columns and other fragments of this church are still visible. Also of significance is the later Roman town, dating to the fourth century AD, that was built near the church in the ruins of the Tuthmosis III temple.

Bibliography: Grossmann 2002; Mond and Myers 1940.

8 UPPER EGYPT

8.1 INTRODUCTION

The ancient towns of Upper Egypt that grew up at important nodes connecting the Nile Valley to trade routes from the Eastern Desert and Red Sea were dominated by their temples. Although there was little new building at famous New Kingdom temples like Karnak in Thebes, many temples in the Thebaid were rebuilt under the Ptolemies and the early Roman emperors. Late Period projects were continued and several completely new temples were begun, starting with the temple of Horus at Edfu in 237 BC, a year after the Canopus decree of Ptolemy III and Berenike II. Indeed Ptolemaic temple-building activity was particularly intense in the Thebaid, perhaps in an attempt to gain priestly and divine support.

Bibliography: Kurth 1998.

Fig. 8.2.1 Dendera, Cleopatra VII and Caesarion making offerings to Hathor.

8.2 DENDERA (TENTYRA)

8.2.a Introduction

Dendera is situated 4 km south of the provincial capital at Qena (where there is a railway station), at the great bend in the Nile, some 70 km north of Luxor on the west side of the river. It is frequently visited as a stop on the Nile cruises but can be reached by car from Luxor. The town is of considerable antiquity, for the necropolis dates back to the early dynastic period, but it is most famous for the later Ptolemaic temple dedicated to the goddess Hathor. Unlike Edfu and Thebes, the town of Dendera is poorly documented in our period. As with other important sites in the southern Nile Valley, Dendera was associated with trade coming in through the Eastern Desert. It was the capital of the sixth Upper Egyptian nome, and a temple had been located here since the Old Kingdom. One of the few texts from the Ptolemaic period is a demotic document recording the transfer of property of Horos son of Psemminis, a

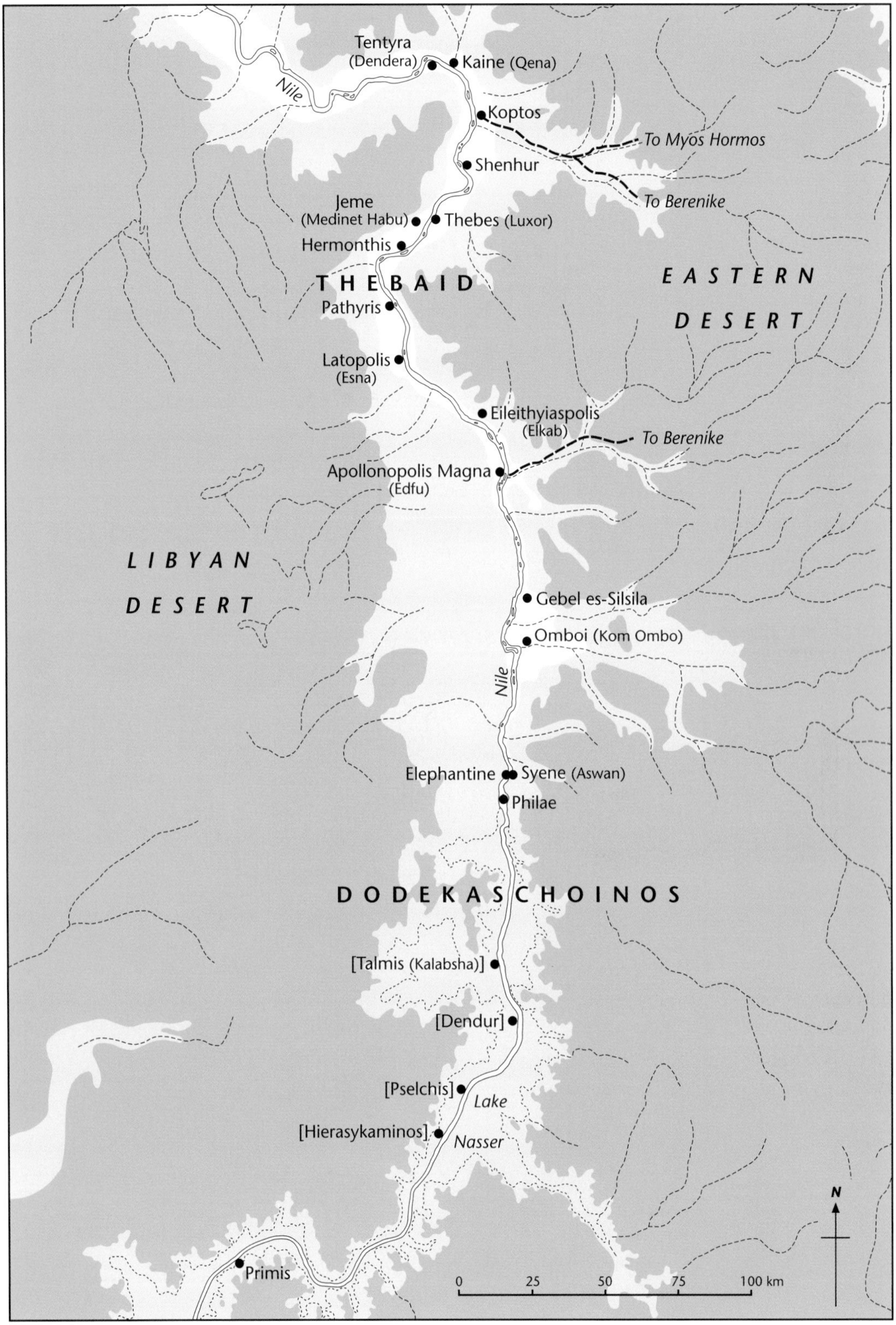
Tentyra
(Dendera)
Kaine (Qena)
Nile
Koptos
To Myos Hormos
Shenhur
To Berenike
Jeme
(Medinet Habu)
Thebes (Luxor)
Hermonthis
THEBAID
EASTERN
DESERT
Pathyris
Latopolis
(Esna)
Eileithyiaspolis
(Elkab)
To Berenike
Apollonopolis Magna
(Edfu)
LIBYAN
DESERT
Gebel es-Silsila
Omboi (Kom Ombo)
Nile
Elephantine
Syene (Aswan)
Philae
DODEKASCHOINOS
[Talmis (Kalabsha)]
[Dendur]
[Pselchis]
Lake
[Hierasykaminos]
Nasser
N
Primis
0
25
50
75
100 km

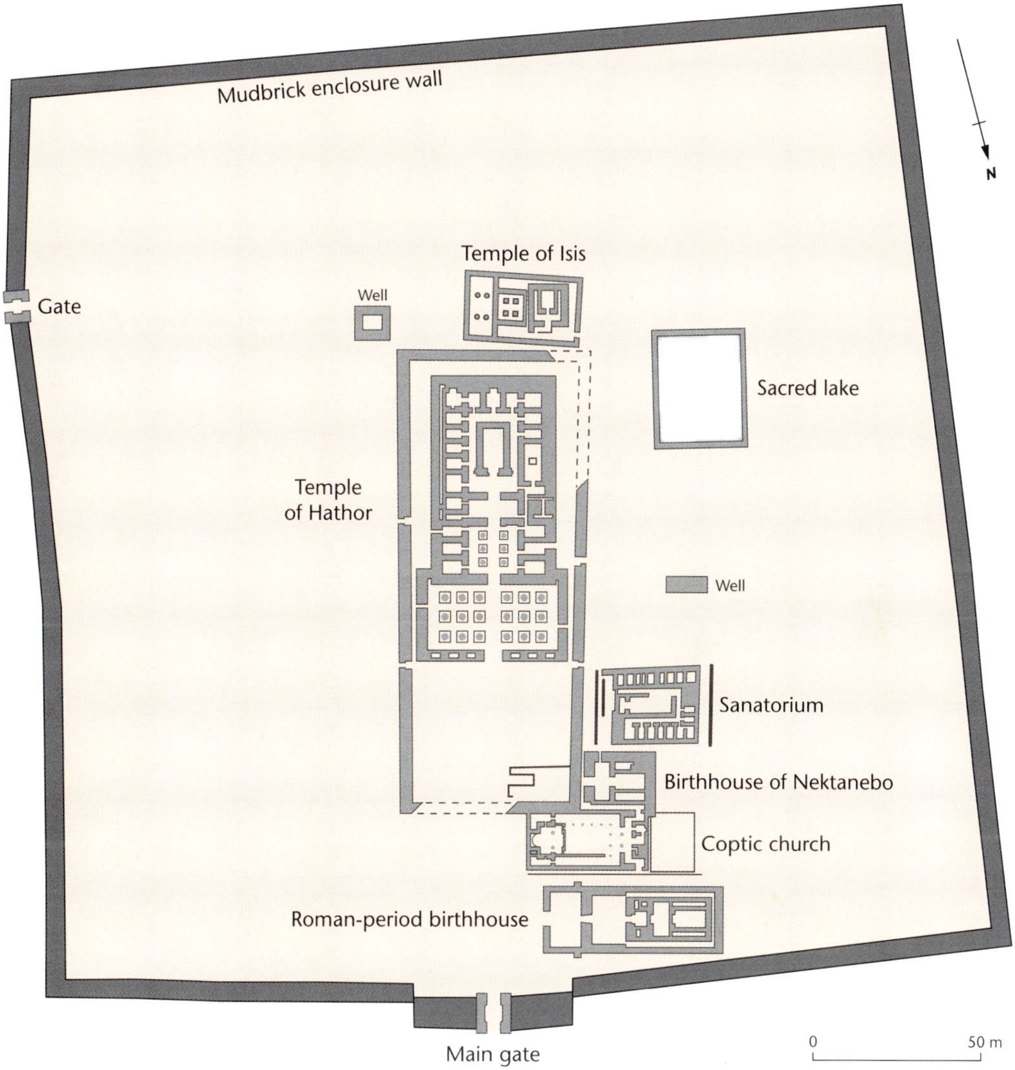

Fig. 8.2.2 Dendera, the temple complex (after Schulz and Seidel 1998: 301).

pastophoros (priest) of Hathor at Dendera, to his son (box 8.2.2). On the south-west corner of the outer wall of the temple, Ptolemy XV Caesarion and Cleopatra VII are depicted (fig. 8.2.1). A hoard of cult objects and inventory lists dating to the late Ptolemaic–early Roman period was discovered near the sacred lake of the temple in the 1910s and 1920s.

8.2.b The Ptolemaic **temple of Hathor**, replacing one built by Nektanebo I, is dedicated to the Egyptian cow goddess Hathor. It is one of the best-preserved temple complexes in Egypt and one of the most important of the later Ptolemaic period. The main temple structure was begun from scratch in 125 BC and was completed in AD 60. The birthhouse (*mammisi*) of Nektanebo was decorated during the reign

Fig. 8.1.1 Upper Egypt.

of Ptolemy II. Many of the Ptolemaic royal cartouches, as elsewhere in Ptolemaic temples, were left blank, probably an indication of the dynastic strife characteristic of the late second and first centuries BC. The earliest king mentioned by name is Ptolemy XII, and most of the building was accomplished in the reign of Cleopatra VII. The columned hall in front was built in the reign of Tiberius. The north-south orientation of the temple is unusual, the result of Dendera's location at the northern end of the Qena bend. The temple had a special cultic relationship with that of Horus at Edfu (8.7), and an architectural one too, since the men who worked on the pylon at Edfu also worked at Dendera, and the plan of the main temple building is very similar to that of the Edfu temple. The temple precinct is surrounded by a mudbrick enclosure wall. After passing through the main gate of the temple precinct built in the reigns of Domitian and Trajan, one encounters several birthhouses (box 8.2.1) to the right of the main temple building. These are a special feature of Late Period and Graeco-Roman Egyptian temples. A Coptic church of the fifth century AD and a mudbrick sanatorium are adjacent. Further south are the well and sacred lake and, behind the temple, another birthhouse dedicated to the goddess Isis.

The roof of the temple is noteworthy for more than the view it provides, for there is a uniquely preserved kiosk used in the New Year's renewal festival, in which the temple's cult statues were renewed by the rays of the sun (fig. 8.2.3). Also on the roof are two pairs of chapels devoted to the god Osiris and his cult. Among the most important architectural features of the first inner chapel is the famous zodiac on the ceiling, dated to 47 BC (see 7.3.b). The original was removed to the Louvre by French collectors in 1820, who left in return conspicuous graffiti on the temple walls and roof, and a copy has been placed in the original location.

Box 8.2.1

Birthhouses

A distinctive feature of Graeco-Roman temples in Egypt are the so-called birthhouses (in Coptic, *ma-n-misi*), an architectural feature that can be traced back to Dynasty 30, but whose conceptual roots extend much further back in Egyptian cult practices. These buildings, separate from the main temple, were the location for the re-enactment of the divine birth of the king, linking the birth of the local child divinity with that of the king, and both of these to the cycle of the sun. The public celebration of the divine/royal births can be traced back to the New Kingdom 'Festival of the Valley' in Thebes. This association, and the need for legitimacy through dramatization expressed in Egyptian cult, had particular importance for the Ptolemies. These birthhouses were always sited in front of the main temple, off the main axis, and typically were surrounded by ambulatory walls with floral capitals, evocative of the swampy marsh where Horus was born.

Fig. 8.2.3
Dendera, kiosk on the temple roof.

As in other temples, the cult at Dendera is devoted to a triad of gods, in this case, Hathor, Horus and their child Ihy. Hathor, one of the most important and oldest deities in Egypt, became associated with Isis in the Late Period. Her cult, centred at Dendera since the First Intermediate period, was based on her attributes as goddess of love, sex and fertility, and focused on her relationship with Horus of Edfu. The

Box 8.2.2

The will of an Egyptian priest

Few texts that document the transmission of property from father to son survive from the Ptolemaic period; in most cases there was probably no need to do this by written deed. One such will, now housed in the Museum of Fine Arts, Boston, was found with a related marriage contract in the north *kom* at Deir el-Ballas, the necropolis of Dendera. The will, dated to 175 BC, lists the landed property of Horos son of Psemminis, a *pastophoros* (priest) of Hathor. Both land and buildings were acquired through inheritance within the family and by purchase. The fact that such a relatively minor priest of Dendera controlled just over 41 *arouras* of land (about 11 hectares) suggests that priests in the Ptolemaic period could be quite well off. Also, it is notable that this land appears to have been private land, not held in virtue of Horos' function in the temple, but held individually and jointly with others. (Parker 1963, 1964)

Hathor cult also celebrated ritual dancing and music. More than twenty-five annual festivals for the goddess are recorded in the temple, the principal one being her annual visit to the Edfu temple (8.7).

Bibliography: Arnold 1999; Murnane 1983; Parker 1963, 1964; Porter and Moss 1939; Vleeming 2001.

8.3 KOPTOS (QIFT)

8.3.a Introduction

Koptos, about 40 km north of Luxor and 500 km south of Cairo, is on the east bank of the Nile halfway between Dendera and Luxor. Because the river makes an eastwards turn in this area, Koptos is the place where the Nile Valley comes closest to the Red Sea, to which it is linked by the Wadi Hammamat, in use since prehistoric times. The economic importance of Koptos in antiquity was due to its location at the end of the caravan roads (Chapter 10). The archaeological zone, surrounded by the modern city, is a desolate group of ruins. The building blocks on the site belong to many different periods, for often older buildings were repaired and redecorated later. Many blocks were taken to Lyons by the French excavators in the early twentieth century.

The cult of the ithyphallic god Min is attested by two colossal statues of about 3000 BC, discovered by Petrie and now in the Ashmolean Museum, Oxford, which represent the god with the typical gesture of his hand, holding a (re)movable penis (now lost). Towards the end of the Old Kingdom (*c.* 2200 BC), eleven decrees granted immunity to some of the temples in Koptos. Some magnificent reliefs from buildings by Sesostris I (*c.* 1950 BC) are now in Oxford and Lyons. Most Ptolemies and several of the first emperors embellished and restored the sacred compound. Horus and Isis were added to the traditional cult of Min in the Late Period. Isis is at the same time the mother of Min and his wife, because the fertility god Min is Ka-moutef, 'bull of his mother'. The most famous relics of the town were the locks of Isis. According to Plutarch Isis cut off (punning on Greek *koptein*, to cut) her beautiful locks at Koptos in mourning for her husband Osiris. In their letters back home travellers duly mention how they venerated the sacred hair and prayed for their relatives in the temple of Isis. The main god of the southern temple complex was Geb, a creator god and dispenser of justice.

8.3.b The archaeological remains

The temple precinct, in the south-east of the archaeological zone, was surrounded by a mudbrick enclosure of about 250 m^2, of which only

Fig. 8.3.1
Temples at Koptos
(after *Coptos* 2000: 93).

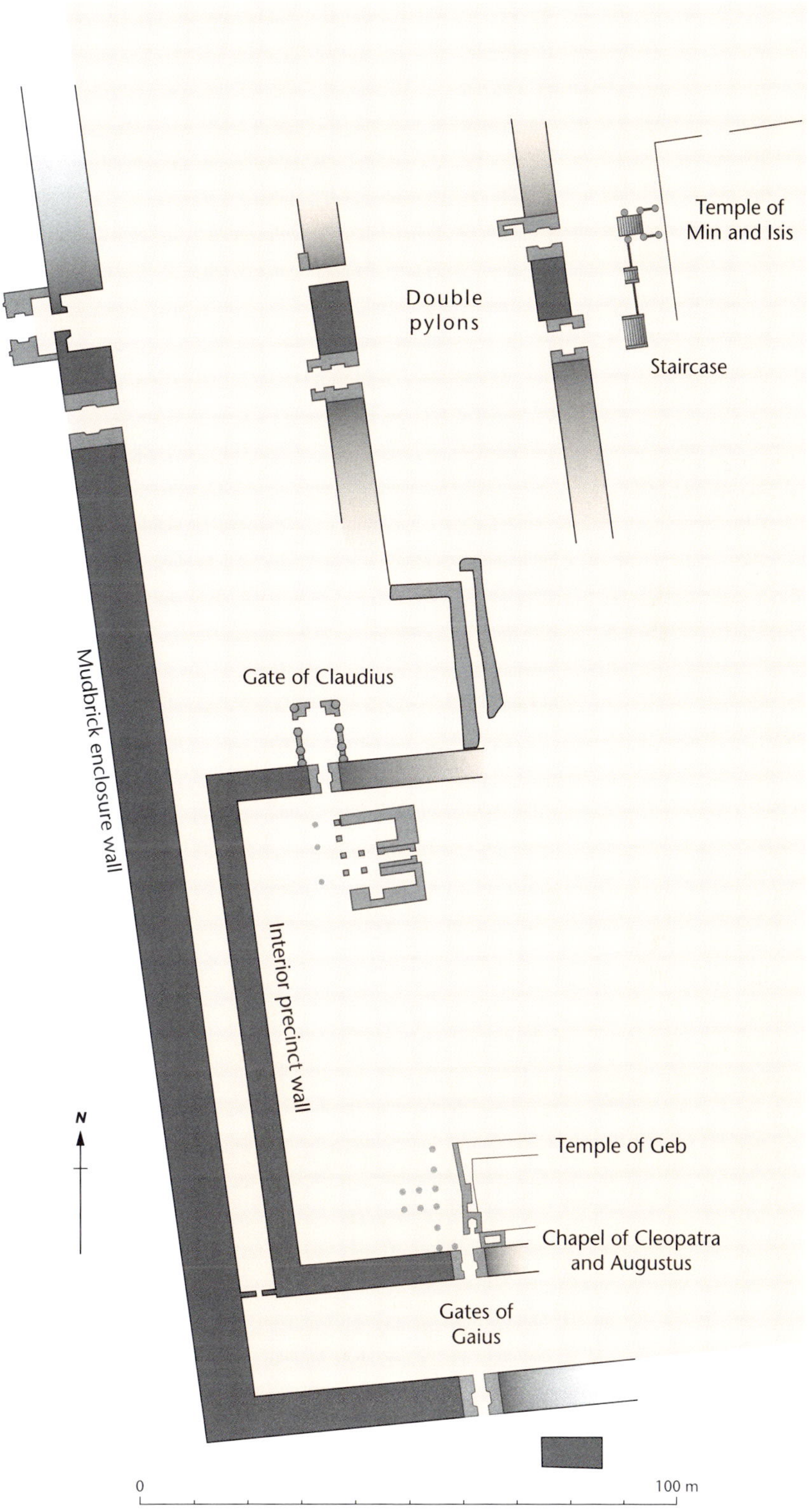

few traces remain. The southern temple complex was once enclosed within a second interior precinct. The northern temple of Min and Isis, built for Ptolemy II by an official called Senuu, replaced a pharaonic sanctuary of the Middle Kingdom and was repaired and redecorated under Ptolemy IV, Gaius and Nero. It has nearly completely disappeared: of the three double pylons, each with a gate for Min and one for Isis, giving access to the temple proper, only the foundations and part of the first row of blocks remain here and there. These are followed by a ruined staircase. Of the temple itself there are only stray blocks, among which was found a Greek inscription of AD 70 by a South Arabian 'trader of the Red Sea'. The immunity decrees of Dynasties 6–7 mentioned above were found by Petrie near the northern gate of the inner precinct. Two stelae of Parthenios (box 8.3) in the same area indicate that the gate was built under Claudius in honour of Isis and Harpokrates.

Though the mudbrick walls have completely disappeared in the south, several gates show where they stood and how large they were. The best-preserved of them, with up to six surviving courses, which bears the name of Gaius, is now part of a farm; originally it stood some 9 m high. The reliefs name Ptolemy XII and Gaius. The interior gate north of it, which leads through the inner precinct, was also decorated under Gaius

A small chapel with the names of both Cleopatra VII and Augustus, orientated north-south, was originally an annex to the larger temple of Geb. The latter had an east-west orientation and was preceded by a gate of Nektanebo II and a portico (now lost). The back wall of the chapel has a block depicting a processional barque on a stand in frontal view, with under it, also represented frontally as small circles, the wooden bars on which the barque was carried in procession (fig. 8.3.2). At the bottom, four royal figures hold up the sky hieroglyph. Above the

Box 8.3

Parthenios

For forty-five years from AD 18 to 63, spanning the reigns of Tiberius, Gaius, Claudius and Nero, Parthenios son of Paminis and Tapchois was 'director' of Isis in Koptos. He never calls himself a priest, but he was the financial head of the temple. Contemporary Greek ostraka found in Koptos by Petrie show that the family was active in the lucrative trade with Myos Hormos and Berenike on the Red Sea coast. More than twenty-five stelae, in Greek, hieroglyphic and demotic, witness his building activities all over the temple precinct. One text explicitly mentions repairs to temples which had fallen into disuse, and another speaks of repairs to the temple precinct. In that same inscription, dated AD 21, an addendum notes that two walls were rebuilt 130 years later by Paniskos son of Ptollis, a successor of Parthenios. The stelae are now scattered over different museums from Koptos to Moscow. They usually represent the reigning emperor offering to the gods, not only Isis and Harpokrates, but also Min-Pan, Geb-Kronos and Osiris.

Fig. 8.3.2 Koptos, barque chapel of Cleopatra (after Traunecker 1992: 294).

picture of the barque is an opening, probably closed with a wooden door, behind which was a second room in which the actual barque was kept. People came to the chapel in order to consult the divine oracle of Geb when the sacred barque left the building for a procession. To the west, outside the ancient enclosure, are the ruins of a Christian church and baptistery built mostly of blocks taken from the nearby temples.

Bibliography: Bernand 1984; Boussac, Gabolde and Galliano 2002; Farid 1988; Traunecker 1992; *Coptos* 2000.

8.3.c El-Qal'a is situated in the north-east of Koptos, less than 1 km from the main sanctuary described above, which is in the southern part of the modern town. The small temple of El-Qal'a (16 x 24 m) is built of hard limestone blocks full of petrified shells, which make it difficult to see the details of the shallow reliefs and hieroglyphs now that the original bright colours have disappeared. The temple stands, unusually, with its back to the Nile. It is well preserved to the north and the east, where even a few blocks of the ceiling are still *in situ*. The main sanctuary in the west is surrounded by an ambulatory, which gives access to two chapels in the north and a New Year chapel (*wabet*) and open court in the south. It is reached from the east through an entrance hall, an offering hall and a *pronaos*. The two small chapels to the north of the entrance hall were store rooms for the divine foods and cloths; a staircase in the south leads to the roof of the temple. The temple has a second north-south axis, with a small entrance hall in the south and a secondary sanctuary, perhaps a birthhouse for the divine child, in the north. The *pronaos* served as a waiting room for both sanctuaries.

The temple was built under Augustus (30 BC–AD 14), whose name appears in the decoration of the two sanctuaries. A single wall in the offering hall mentions Gaius; the other rooms were decorated under Claudius (AD 41–54). The main gods of the temple were those of Koptos in the Graeco-Roman period: Isis, Min and the child god Harpokrates. Isis and Harpokrates appear each under two forms: Isis and Horus son of Osiris in the north, Nephthys and Horus first-born of Amun in the south. Isis is often called 'the great goddess', and this

Fig. 8.3.3 Koptos, temple at El-Qal'a (after Pantalacci and Traunecker 1990: 7).

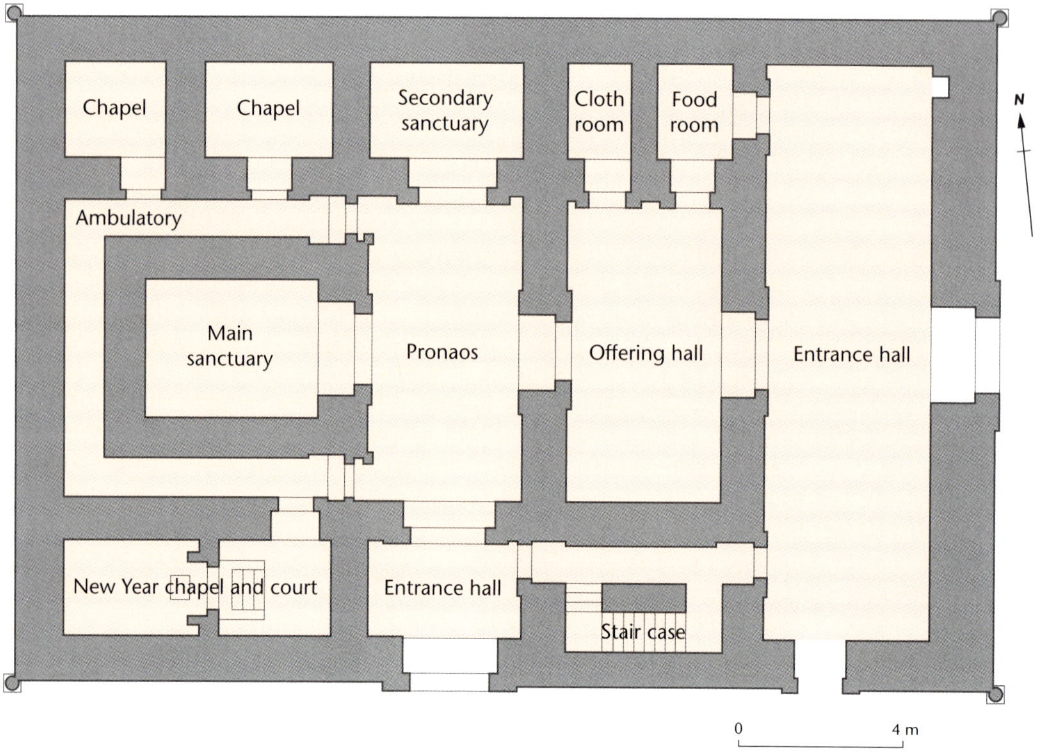

epithet seems to have become a kind of separate goddess, loosely linked with Isis herself. The scenes also allude to the myth of the eye of Re, and the faraway lion goddess returning to Egypt (box 8.6).

Bibliography: Pantalacci and Traunecker 1990, 1998; Traunecker 1997.

8.4 SHENHUR

Shenhur is situated midway between Luxor and Koptos, about 5 km from the main road which leads from Luxor to the Red Sea. The modern name transmits the ancient Egyptian *Sy-n-Hr*, 'lake of Horus', which was transcribed into Greek as Senhyris.

The small temple of Shenhur is built of the same type of stone as that of El-Qal'a. Its sanctuary (13.5 x 19 m) dates from the time of Augustus. Under Tiberius the outside rear wall was decorated and a chapel was built for the child god Horudja. Decoration works continued under Gaius and Claudius. The main temple and the chapel of Horudja were integrated into a single complex by a hypostyle hall, decorated under Nero, and a *pronaos*. The double row of columns surrounding the sanctuary is exceptional in an Egyptian temple. The temple is dedicated to four aspects of Isis: 'Isis the great goddess', often simply called 'the great goddess', Mut, Nephthys and Nebet-ihi. At the same time the divine family of Koptos, that is Min, Isis and Harpokrates, is contrasted with the divine family of Thebes, Amun, Mut and Khonsu. Inside the sanctuary the child gods Harpokrates and Khonsu are accompanied by Tutu and Geb respectively, which shows that the Theban divine family is in fact represented in its Koptite variant, because it is only in Koptos that Geb sometimes takes the place of Khonsu. The two most interesting parts of this temple are the rear wall and the New Year chapel (*wabet*). The scenes on the rear wall show Tiberius making an offering to the main gods and goddesses of the temple on both sides of a false gate, which probably contained a cultic relief as in Dendera; holes in the wall show where wooden beams of a dais were once inserted. Here visitors could come close to the gods in the inner sanctuary. The ceiling of the *wabet* is decorated with a zodiac from leo to capricorn (box 7.3.2). In the open New Year court before the *wabet* an offering block is still *in situ*; here some fragments of stone statues were also found.

Bibliography: Quaegebeur and Traunecker 1994; Traunecker 1998.

8.5 ESNA (LATOPOLIS)

Esna is located on the west bank, 55 km south of Luxor. In the Late Period the town of Esna became a nome capital, which flourished in the Graeco-Roman period. The ancient Egyptian name *Sny* survived into

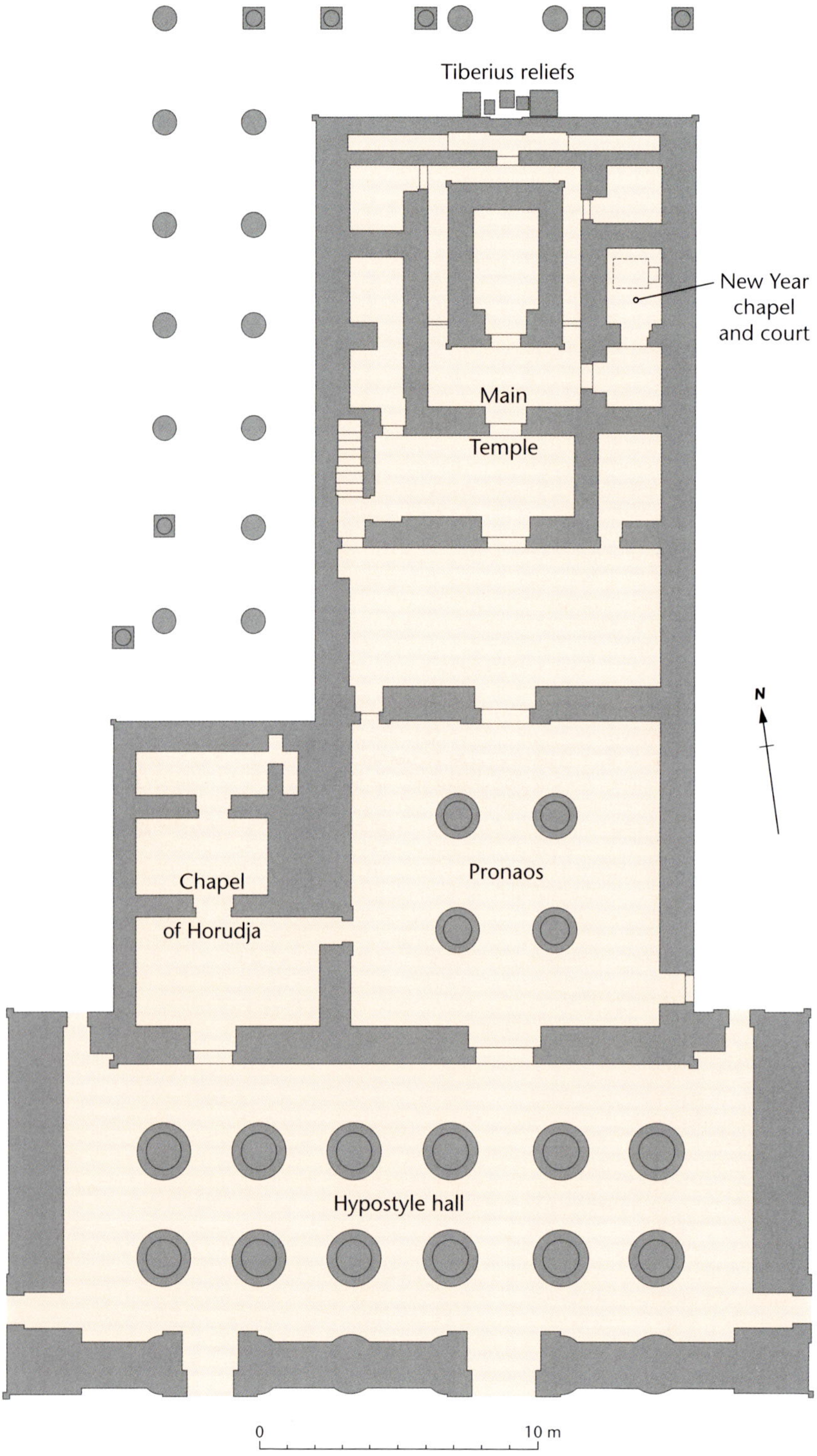

Fig. 8.4.1 Shenhur, temple (after H. Willems).

Coptic as Sne and Esna, whence also the Arabic Esna. Latopolis, the 'city of the *latoi*', was the Greek name, after the great Nile perch (*Lates niloticus*), which was held sacred there in the Late Period. Cemeteries of mummified Nile perches were found at the edge of the desert.

The temple of the creator god Khnum is located in the middle of the modern town in an excavation pit 9 m below ground level. It was probably linked with the quay, which has cartouches of Marcus Aurelius. The temple was begun in the second century BC in the joint reign of Ptolemy VI and Ptolemy VIII but was not continued until the reign of the emperor Claudius, who built a huge hypostyle hall in front of the small temple. The Ptolemaic temple is lost except for its façade, but the hypostyle hall has survived and is one of the most impressive monuments of the Graeco-Roman period. It contains twenty-four columns

Fig. 8.5.1
Esna, temple of Khnum.

each 13.3 m high and with a different capital. The first six columns are connected by low intercolumnar walls at both sides of the main entrance. Two small side doors in these walls were used by the priests. The decoration proceeded slowly. Cartouches with the names of most of the emperors from Claudius (41–54) through to Decius (249–251) are found. For the emperors after Commodus (180–192), Esna is the only Egyptian temple providing these names. The four registers of the south-eastern wall of the hall show family scenes of Septimius Severus, his wife Julia Domna and their two sons Caracalla and Geta, which reflect their visit to Egypt in 199; the image of Geta was mutilated after he was killed by his brother.

Numerous texts decorating the columns, walls and ceiling describe ancient mythological traditions and are among the latest witnesses of pagan Egypt. They show that two aspects of the creator were worshipped at Esna, sometimes even united in one androgyne deity: the male creator Khnum and the female creator Neith. Khnum, the main god at Esna, is represented with the head of a ram; he created the world and moulded all living beings from clay with his potter's wheel. His creating activities were celebrated during the festival of 'the institution of the potter's wheel'. The goddess Neith originated from Sais in the Delta, but her cult spread as far as Esna. She wears the red crown of Lower Egypt and holds a bow and arrow, pointing to her original nature as a goddess of hunting and war. She is worshipped together with her son, the crocodile-headed god Sjema-nefer. Two other goddesses are found at Khnum's side, for instance on the façade of the Ptolemaic temple. Nebetu, mistress of the fields and their products, gave Khnum a son, the child god Heka. The lioness goddess Menhyt was identified

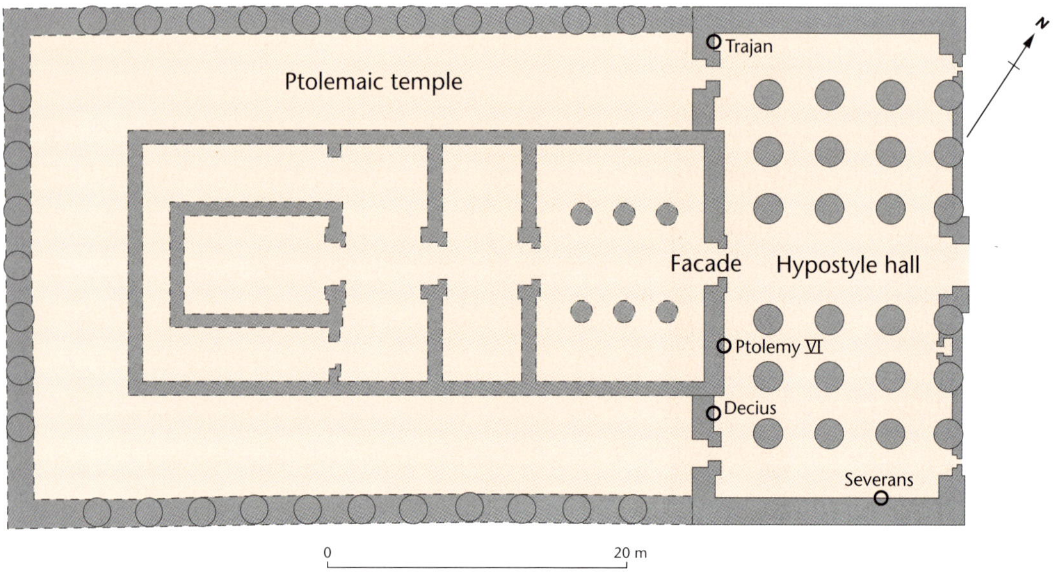

Fig. 8.5.2
Esna, temple of Khnum (after Porter and Moss 1939: 112).

with Tefnut. In some scenes the Roman emperor is represented as dancing before Menhyt-Tefnut.

Several texts refer to the festivals of the sacred year at Esna. A festival calendar enumerates day by day the name and the course of the festivities. The calendar is engraved in the upper part of the hall near the façade, where the light fell. The rituals performed during the festivals are described on the eighteen columns on the inside of the hypostyle hall, and several scenes illustrate general ceremonial rites. The astronomical ceiling of the hall shows, among other things, the signs of the zodiac. The Ptolemaic hieroglyphic system, with its new glyphs and new phonetic values, reached its peak in the hymns engraved in the hypostyle hall of Esna. The system is even carried to extremes in a cryptographic hymn, written almost entirely with glyphs of rams,

Fig. 8.5.3
Esna, hypostyle hall c. 1800 (*Description de l'Egypte* I 83).

without additional determinatives, and in a similar hymn written almost exclusively with a series of crocodiles.

Under the Ptolemaic dynasty (probably between 246–180 BC) another temple for Khnum was erected some 4 km to the north-west of Esna, at Kom Senun, but the building was dismantled in 1843 and is now completely destroyed. Blocks recovered show that the zodiac was again represented on the ceiling of the columned hall. At Komir, 14.5 km south of Esna on the east bank, there is a Graeco-Roman temple dedicated to Nephthys and Anukis. It has been excavated only in part because houses of the modern village are built over it. Under Antoninus Pius hymns for both goddesses were engraved on the outside of the back wall of the temple. Nephthys, sister of Isis and Osiris, was worshipped in the form of a royal falcon with a forked tail. Anukis, the inundation goddess, was venerated in the region of the first cataract and had her main shrine on the Seheil island near Elephantine. As daughter of Khnum and Satet she formed with them the triad of the cataract.

Bibliography: Sauneron 1959–1982.

8.6 ELKAB (EILEITHYIASPOLIS)

8.6.a Introduction

Elkab is situated some 20 km north of Edfu on the east bank of the Nile. It can be reached by taxi from Edfu – the site is close to the main road – or by local train from the station of El-Mahamid. The enormous wall can be spotted from the boat in mid-river (col. pl. 8.6.1). Elkab was an important place at the dawn of Egypt's history. It gave its name to a neolithic period, the Elkabian, around 6400 BC, and there are numerous tombs in the plain and in the rocks from the beginning of the dynastic period up to Graeco-Roman times. The main temple was dedicated to Nekhbet and Sobek, whereas in the wadi west of the temple area several lion goddesses were venerated. The vulture goddess Nekhbet in particular was important from the earliest times. The rock tombs date from the Old Kingdom until the early New Kingdom; the temple near the Nile is predominantly a Dynasty 29–30 reworking of a New Kingdom structure. In the Graeco-Roman period Elkab, called Eileithyiaspolis, was no longer the capital of an independent nome, but was administered from nearby Edfu. Local names, however, point to links with Thebes, which was nearly 100 km away but could be reached both by boat and by caravan along the wadi.

8.6.b Archaeological remains

The temples and the Graeco-Roman village are dwarfed by the immense mudbrick enclosure, 550 m^2 and still more than 10 m high. It was probably built by Nektanebo II as a defence against the Persian invasion. The remains of the temple, surrounded by a second enclosure, are mostly of the Late Period, including a block with the name of king Hakoris. A Graeco-Roman village to the south-west of the temple, and even spilling over inside the enclosure, has been explored by a Belgian expedition. Some houses belonged to potters' families, as is shown by water pipes, levigation pools and mudbrick constructions for pottery wheels. In the early twentieth century the houses were still several metres high, but the mudbrick has been used as fertilizer by the farmers, and at most a few courses of bricks now survive. Ostraka found in the village confirm the importance of natron production, which is well known from ancient texts. A small late-Roman camp to the south was built with stones taken from the temple; it yielded an important coin hoard of the later fourth century AD.

The tombs in the rocks on the other side of the highway are mostly from earlier periods (an enormous Old Kingdom mastaba, which once stood on top of the hill, has been recently excavated), but some were reused later. Numerous *loculi* in the rock and even inside some tombs were used to bury sacred crocodiles in the Graeco-Roman period. One unpublished tomb has a painting in Greek style showing a four-horse chariot. One kilometre into the wadi are two monuments erected by Setaou, viceroy of Nubia under Ramesses II, one of which was completely renovated in the Ptolemaic period. During the reign of Cleopatra III, about 117–107 BC, Setaou's *hemispeos*, or rock-cut temple (as at Abu Simbel), was dedicated to the goddess Smithis. The temple was the place where the ferocious lion goddess was ritually welcomed when she came back to Egypt from the desert. The visitor first ascends a monumental staircase ramp to a platform. The gate between the stair and the platform is now lost, although a few blocks have been reused in the mosque of the nearby village. Texts copied from the gate in 1843 show that it was built in the reign of Ptolemy IX Soter II, and the main actors, that is king and gods, in the liturgy in the temple were represented in relief. Behind it was a sort of kiosk with columns with composite capitals. The entry to the *hemispeos* at the other end of the platform was marked by a portico of alternating round and square columns linked by a wall; the columns had *sistrum* capitals, no doubt carrying a wooden roof. The front wall of the rock is decorated with royal cartouches of Ptolemy IX and Hathor symbols; on both sides of the entrance was a scene with Cleopatra III playing the *sistrum*. Most of this is now seriously damaged. The interior of the chapel was redecorated with offering scenes on stone slabs which have nearly all disappeared. Only a few reliefs carved in the rock itself have survived. The ceiling is

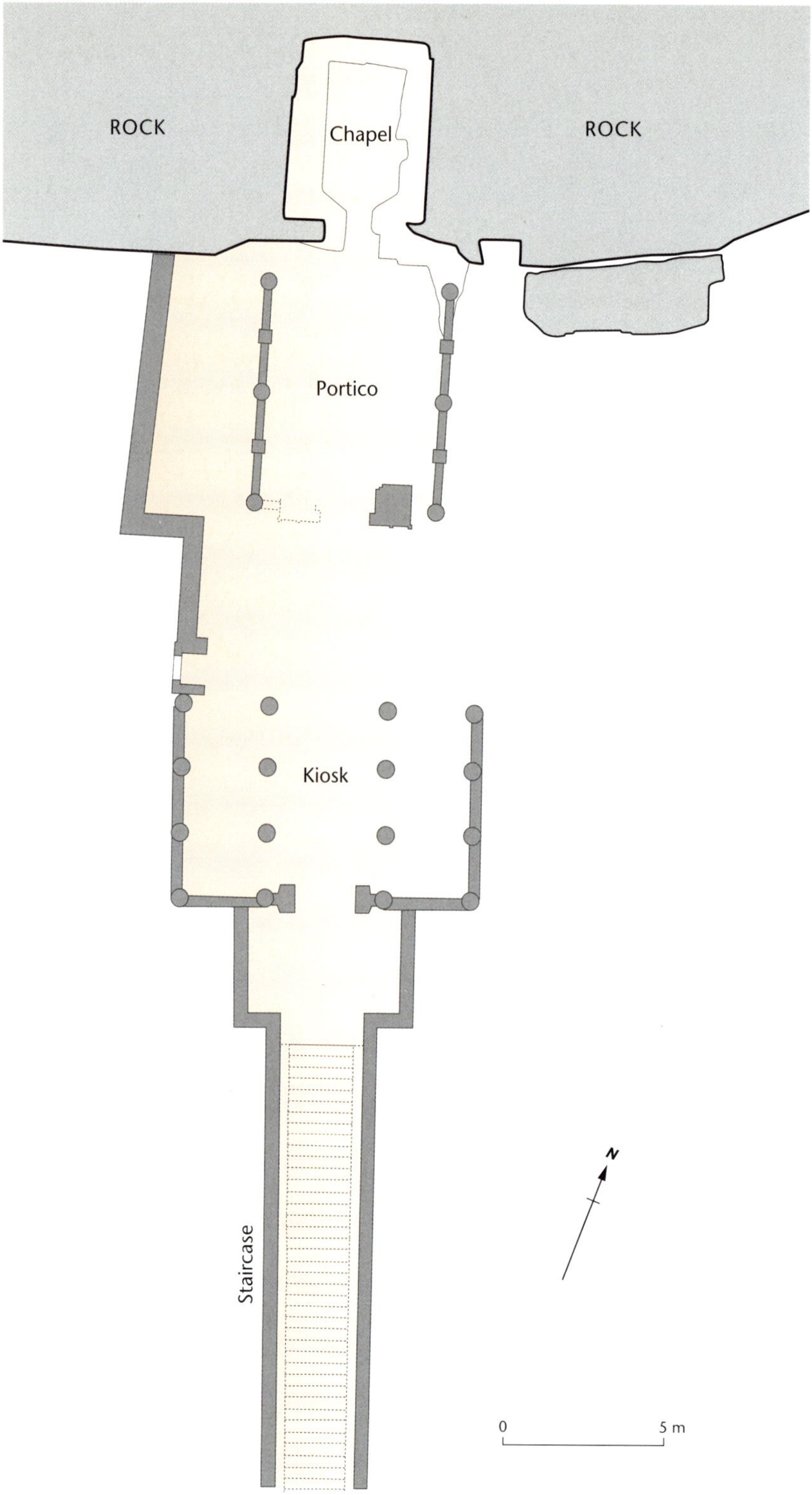

Fig. 8.6.2
Elkab, the *hemispeos* (after Derchain 1971).

The myth of Tefnut

In ancient Egypt, mythology and science were not distinguished as is clear from the numerous creation stories. In one of the myths the two main heavenly bodies, the sun and moon, are portrayed as the two eyes of Re. The moon eye and also the sun eye were personified by the fierce goddess Tefnut, who quarrelled with her father Re and left for Nubia. There she took the form of a lioness and became the terror of the land. Re missed his daughter and sent the gods Shu and Thoth to ask her to return home. By eloquence and magic Thoth, disguised as a baboon (his sacred animal), and Shu her twin brother, convinced her to come back to Egypt, where the game she was chasing in Nubia would be brought to her on altars. She finally gave in, and the return journey became a triumphant progress through the villages and towns of Egypt. The goddess was surrounded by musicians, dancers and baboons, and was acclaimed by the people in carnival-like parades, with lots of wine and beer. When the goddess herself also became drunk, she gradually lost her ferociousness, and the angry lioness became a gentle pussycat. The myth is at the same time a cosmogony, because without sun and moon the dark earth would be uninhabitable, a myth of civilization in which the wild Nubian calms down to become a good citizen, and a New Year's festival celebrating the yearly cycle of the sun. The old Egyptian myth, pieced together from many diverse fragments and allusions, comes in many forms, which are often contradictory. Tefnut is not only a lioness and a cat, but also the uraeus on the front of Re and therefore a cobra. A Greek translation of the myth is known from a papyrus of the Roman period.

Box 8.6

somewhat better preserved and shows the usual vultures with outspread wings, symbols of the goddess Nekhbet, with quite well-preserved colouring, and some fine hieroglyphic inscriptions of hymns in honour of Horus, Temet and Hathor.

Bibliography: Derchain 1971; Hendrickx 1998.

8.7 EDFU (APOLLONOPOLIS MAGNA)

8.7.a Introduction

Edfu is located about 75 km south of Luxor on the west side of the river. The Ptolemaic temple, well worth half a day, is normally all that is visited at Edfu, although the sandstone quarries further south at **Gebel es-Silsila**, with demotic and Greek graffiti, and a few sites in the nearby Eastern Desert (see Chapter 10) are of some interest. Edfu (Idfu; Greek Apollonopolis Magna; Egyptian *Djeba*) had been an important provincial centre since at least the Old Kingdom. It was the capital of the second nome of Upper Egypt and is today dominated by the Ptolemaic temple dedicated to the falcon god Horus. The pylon of the temple may be seen for several kilometres in all directions. The ancient town mound is located to the west of the temple. Excavations were carried out on the site by the French from 1914–33 and by a Polish expedition from 1934–39.

Edfu was well positioned to take advantage of trade coming from the Red Sea through the port at Berenike in the Ptolemaic period (see Chapter 10), although Koptos, 200 km further north, served as the main entrepôt for the Red Sea trade under the Romans and perhaps even under the later Ptolemies. Ptolemy II built a road from Edfu out to the Red Sea port of Berenike. The strategic location of Edfu for controlling the trade, which was mainly in war elephants, and gold and other minerals from the mining regions in the Eastern Desert, prompted the Ptolemies to make the town an important garrison site (box 8.7). A distance marker dated to the mid-third century BC has recently been found in the Eastern Desert at Bir Iayyan (see Chapter 10), which suggests that an official probably based at Edfu was in charge of the Eastern Desert and its trade. The southern boundary of the nome was the important sandstone quarry at Gebel es-Silsila, and there was an ancient route out to the west and south, now known as the Wadi Shatt el-Rigal.

Edfu also derived economic and political importance from its situation in a wide, fertile area, which extended 6 km at its widest, 13 km upstream and 15 km downstream from the town. A minor branch of the Nile ran directly behind the temple. Blemmyes and other tribes of the Eastern Desert were an important local source of labour, as desert guides and scouts, but later they became a source of great distraction to the Roman and Byzantine armies. Large private tombs and a pyramid can be dated to the early Old Kingdom, and the site was continuously occupied from that time through the Byzantine period and beyond. The Ptolemaic cemetery was located south of the town at **Nag el-Hassaya**. The double funerary stelae of the priests at Edfu of the end of the second century BC from that cemetery, written in hieroglyphic and Greek, point to the extent to which some of the local elite had adapted to the larger cultural framework of the Ptolemaic state.

The Ptolemies showed considerable interest in the town. The 'walls' mentioned in Ptolemaic papyri are almost certainly fortifications built during the fourth century BC. Cleruchs were also settled in the area in the third century BC and, in a royal letter, soldiers who were billeted to the region were carefully warned to stay away from a town near Edfu called Arsinoe (exact location unknown), reflecting both the immunity of this village and the number of soldiers in the region. The Jewish 'quarter' mentioned in tax receipts issued to Jews in the Roman period may have had its origins in a military community. The documentary evidence for a Jewish community in the late Ptolemaic period is relatively slight, consisting of names occurring on ostraka. With the shift of caravan trade from Edfu to Koptos, the town probably declined in economic importance. A Roman fort protecting the ancient road out to the Eastern Desert was located on the east side of the river at **Contra Apollonos (El-Ridisiyah Bahari)**. Garrison soldiers are also documented during the Byzantine period.

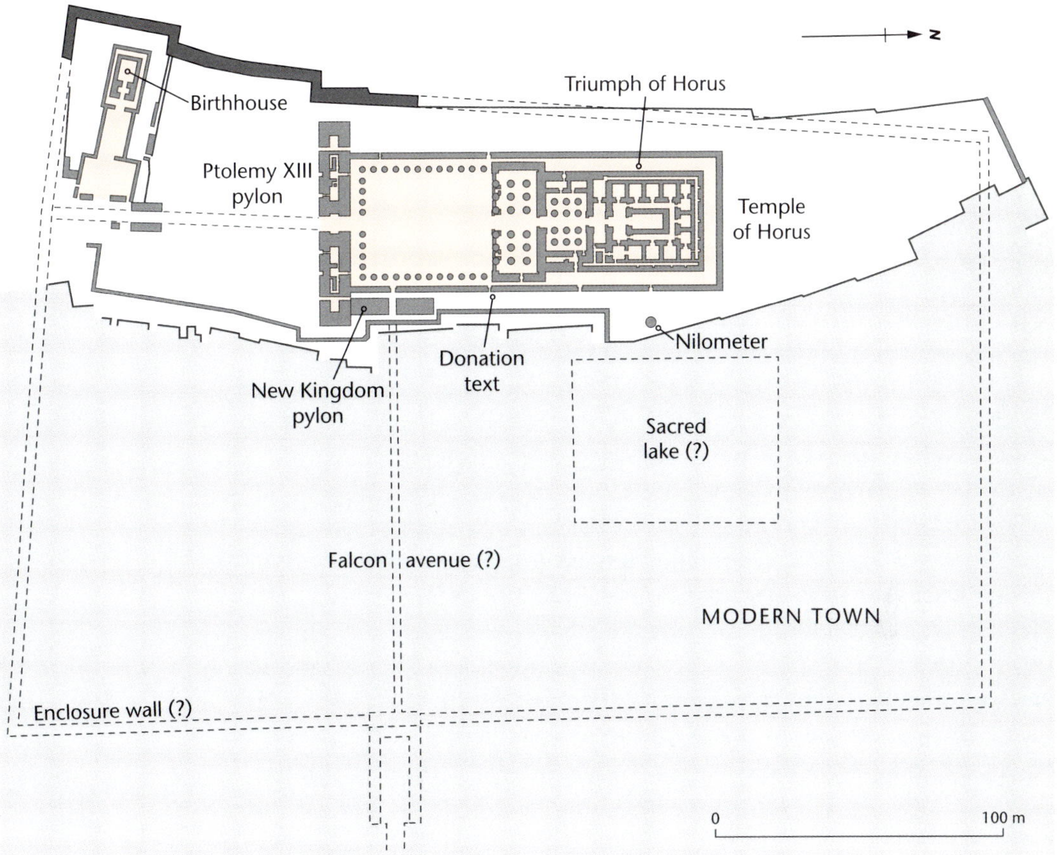

Fig. 8.7.1
Edfu, the temple complex (after Alliot 1954: pl.4).

A major uprising known as the great Theban revolt (206–186 BC), centred at Edfu, represented the most extensive rural upheaval in the Ptolemaic period. It engulfed towns in the Nile Valley from at least Edfu in the south to as far north as Abydos in Middle Egypt. The unrest was characterized in one Greek source as 'the Egyptian revolt', and Chaonnophris, the rebel king, was referred to in an Egyptian text as 'the enemy of the gods who acted as leader of the disorder in Egypt'. Physical violence was reported from Edfu to at least Asyut (Lykopolis), and disruption of the irrigation system was catastrophic in some areas. In Asyut, for example, a text informs us that 'most of the people were destroyed and that the land has gone dry'. The important temple construction project at Edfu and smaller projects in Thebes were halted during the disturbance. The disruption of work is recorded on the Edfu temple itself:

> Then the troubles broke out after which the ignorant rebels in the south have interrupted the work in the throne-of-god. The rebellion raged in the south until year 19 of the King of Upper and Lower Egypt, heir of the god Philopator, son of Re, Ptolemy

> beloved of Ptah, deceased, the god Epiphanes, the strong, the king who chased disorder from the country and whose name is inscribed (in the temple).

Other revolts centred on Upper Egypt occurred during the Ptolemaic and Roman periods, but the unrest recorded in the temple of Edfu was the most violent of the entire period.

8.7.b The Temple of Horus

The most important aspect of the town for the visitor is the beautifully preserved sandstone temple dedicated to the falcon god Horus of Behdet, located more or less in the centre of the ancient town. The temple was the first of the new building projects in Upper Egypt during the Ptolemaic period. Its rebuilding was supported by several of the Ptolemies, who may occasionally have visited the great project in person – Ptolemy III may have attended the inauguration of the project on 23 August 237 BC – but it was not completed until the first century BC. The massive cedar doors, more than 14 m high and covered in copper, were hung in 57 BC. It is the best-preserved temple in Egypt and is renowned, among other things, for having the tallest pylon (36 m) (col. pl. 8.7.2). The temple, focusing on the mythic victory of Horus over his enemy Seth, became a symbol of Ptolemaic rule. It was perhaps this symbolic value, together with the Ptolemies' favour towards the temples, which led to the seizure of the temple in 207 BC by the rebels who instigated the revolt in the Thebaid.

The Ptolemaic temple incorporated part of the New Kingdom pylon, which can still be seen on the eastern side of the first court. Temple inscriptions allow scholars to reconstruct not only the ritual and annual festivals of the cult of Horus but also the universal cosmological concepts of a Late Period temple. The texts form a complete and coherent whole. The hieroglyphic inscriptions on the temple provide a quite detailed building history. Other important texts include the sacred play of the 'Triumph of Horus' over his enemy Seth. One unusual feature of the Edfu corpus is the large text recorded on the outer retaining wall that has come to be known as the Edfu 'donation text' (marked on fig. 8.7.1). It records donations of land to the temple during the fourth century BC, which were renewed by Ptolemy X, and provides useful information about land tenure as well as the socio-economic interconnections between temples in the south. The remains of an ancient Nilometer may be seen on the north-east side of the temple. A separate birthhouse (*mammisi*) is situated to the south of the temple, with reliefs representing the annual rebirth of the god.

8.7.c Cult of Horus

The temple at Edfu was a major cult site of the falcon god Horus, the son of Osiris and Isis. Granite statues of the god stand in front of the main gate. The cult of Horus was linked to that of Hathor at Dendera by the annual 'Festival of the Joyous Union', during which the cult image of Hathor visited the Edfu temple to celebrate her marriage to Horus. It was a great public festival, one of many in the Thebaid, which lasted for two weeks. During the journey from Dendera to Edfu the statue of the goddess stopped to visit Thebes, Elkab, Hierakonpolis, and probably other sacred places along the way. Such ancient religious and economic interconnections – religious ceremonies connecting Dendera to Edfu, land-holding that connected Elephantine to Edfu – reinforced social ones and provided good reason for the Ptolemies to continue to administer the Thebaid as a region.

8.7.d Archives and other texts

Edfu is one of the better-documented town sites in the Nile Valley during the millennium of papyri, and there are several archives and other texts that come from the town. Among the most important published texts are the Hauswaldt Archive and the Milon Archive, both found at

The Milon Archive

An important bilingual archive, found in a jar on Elephantine Island at Aswan, provides a unique view of the relationship of the high priests and *lesonis* (the head of the temple administration) at Edfu to the land and the state. Milon was the *praktor* of the temples in the Edfu nome. Among his papyri are a famous order for the payment of elephant hunters and correspondence with Milon's superiors, apparently resident in Thebes, concerning the finances for the building of the Edfu temple. But the majority of the papers revolve around the dissolution of the landed property of a prominent priestly family who lived in Edfu during the middle years of the third century BC. The following letter of 223 BC, seemingly unconnected to Milon's papers, is suggestive of the importance of the import of war elephants through Edfu in this period:

Mnesarchos to Antipatros, greeting. I have instructed Paniskos to pay from the bank in Arsinoe to Demetrios the secretary of the hunters (hired) through Andronikos for the 231 men who set off with Peitholaos their wages from Artemisios through Panemos, 3 months: 2 talents, 1860 dr., subtracting the advance payment for the month of Artemisios made to the advance guard, 60 dr., a balance of 2 talents, 1800 dr. Carry this out therefore as has been written. Farewell. Year 25, Thouth 21. To Apollonides. Carry this out as has been written. Farewell. Year 25, Thouth 21. (*P. Eleph.* 28, trans. Bagnall and Derow 2004: 201–2; cf. Clarysse 2003)

Box 8.7

Elephantine. Many of the individuals in the Hauswaldt Archive were Blemmyes or Megabarians, well-known natives of the Eastern Desert who were used by the Ptolemies as guards or guides on the routes leading to the gold-mining areas and ports along the Red Sea, and were settled in the area of Edfu by the third century BC. Archaeological work on the town mound in the 1930s yielded many papyri and ostraka ranging in date from the Ptolemaic to the early Islamic periods. Most of the ostraka are tax receipts of various kinds. Archival records extend all the way down to the early eighth-century AD archive of Papas the tax collector.

Bibliography: Alliot 1949, 1954; Bagnall 1976: 24–34; Bietak 1979; Cauville 1984; Cauville and Devauchelle 1984; Fairman 1954; Finnestad 1985; Kornfeld 1973; Meeks 1972; Murnane 1983; Porter and Moss 1939; Rathbone 2002; Schwartz 1983: 61–70; Vandorpe and Clarysse 2003.

8.8 KOM OMBO (OMBOI)

8.8.1 Introduction

The most picturesque approach to the temple of Kom Ombo is by boat, from which one sees the temple, situated on a small hill in a bend of the Nile which has eaten away part of the mudbrick enclosure wall. If one arrives by car, the temple is 3 km from the main road. Building started under Ptolemy VI and continued through to the early third century AD. The early New Kingdom temple, which was seen by Champollion, has disappeared into the Nile.

8.8.2 Archaeological remains

The building was conceived as a double temple with two west-east processional gateways, one leading to the sanctuary of Sobek in the south-east, the other to that of Haroeris ('Horus the great') in the north-west. The crocodile god and falcon god had separate sanctuaries, with large granite pedestals for the sacred barques. Haroeris, identified with Apollo in a Greek inscription, made up a divine family with Hathor and Khonsu; Sobek was linked with Senetnefer ('the good sister') and the child god Panebtawy ('the one of the two lands'). The last two names are artificial and express the function of the goddess as a companion of the god and that of the young god as a king. Three broad rooms and the hypostyle hall, each with a double entry, lead to the two sanctuaries. On the rear wall of the Hall of the Ennead, between the doors of the sanctuaries, a fine relief shows Ptolemy VI Philometor and his queen Cleopatra II standing before the falcon-headed god Khonsu, who is writing the king's name on a palm branch with the symbol of a long reign. Side corridors gave access to ten side chapels, including a New Year chapel (*wabet*) and open-air court, now destroyed. The staircases

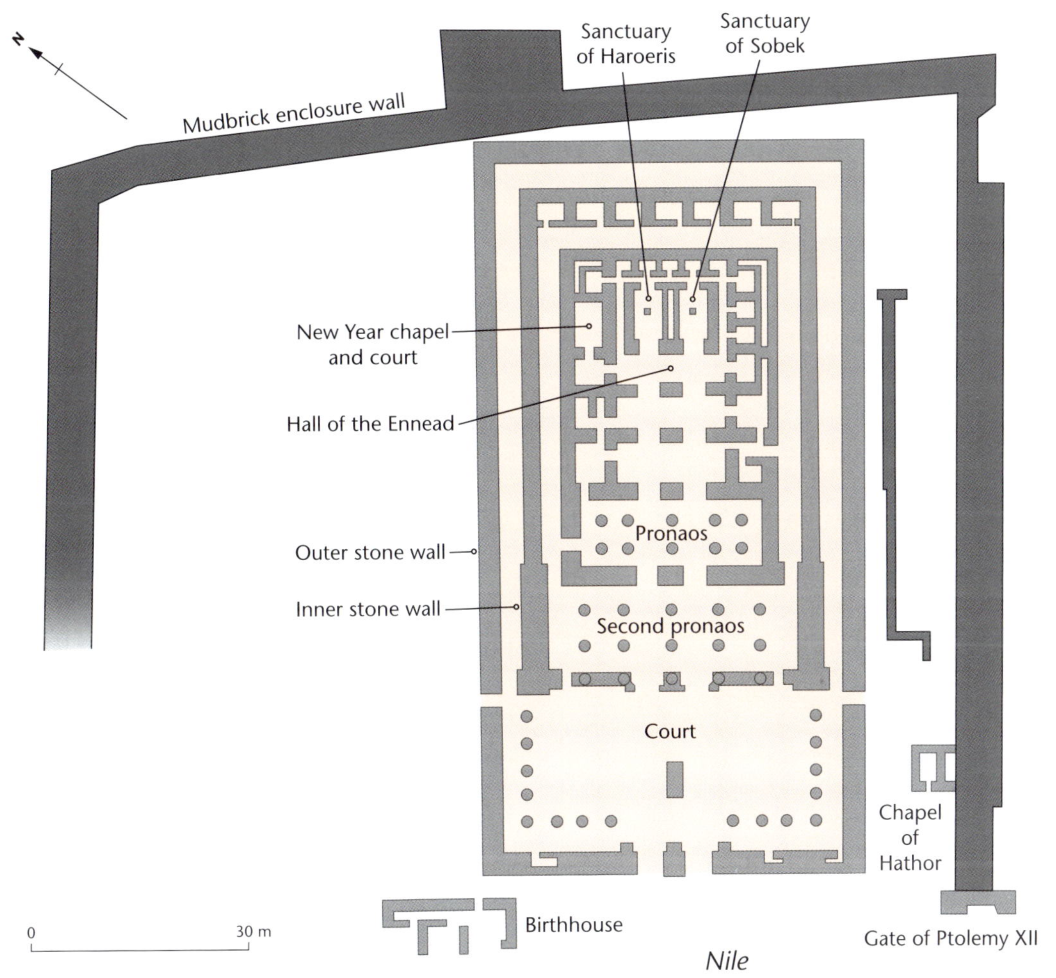

Fig. 8.8.1
Kom Ombo, temple complex (after Baines and Malek 2000: 74).

leading to the roof are located on either side of the second room. In the relief on the north-west wall of the hypostyle *pronaos*, Ptolemy VIII is followed by his two queens, Cleopatra II and III.

Under Ptolemy XII the temple was extended by a second hypostyle *pronaos* with three rows (the first one linked by a wall) of five composite columns. Note the astronomical scenes (star gods in boats) on the underside of the architraves. The colours are still partly preserved. A figure of Haroeris in this room has a hole instead of an eye: for some reason the eye was apparently inlaid with gold. An inner enclosure wall was later added; it continues the walls of the pronaos around the rooms to the north-east. Seven chapels were built against the back of this wall; the central one houses a staircase leading to the roof. The unfinished reliefs in these chambers show different stages of the artist at work; some inscriptions are sketched out, but not completed. In one relief Cleopatra VII is offering to the gods on her own, without an accompanying king. The outside of this wall depicts the two divine triads in full

Fig. 8.8.2
Kom Ombo, temple. A Ptolemy makes offerings.

height in sunk relief on both sides of an interesting cult relief in bas relief, dating from the time of Trajan. The cult relief is situated on the axis of the temple, immediately behind the double sanctuary. Here people who had no priestly function and therefore could not enter the sanctuary proper could come close to the gods to pray. The cult relief contains three registers of which the lowest one is the most important. It figures Sobek and Haroeris looking towards the central scene, showing from top to bottom: the four winds surrounding a winged figure of Maat, the goddess of justice; a shrine with a Maat figure, frontally placed, surrounded by a hieroglyphic text featuring two large *oudjat* eyes and two large ears; a long hieroglyphic hymn, explaining that here the god was present to help the people, 'seeing everything, with many ears, listening to those who invoke him'. In the pavement in front of the relief a balustrade was inserted (the holes for the beams can still be seen); the pavement also bears some graffiti of pilgrims, including a Greek inscription.

Under Augustus a colonnaded court was added with a large altar in the middle. On some of the reliefs which show Tiberius the colours are quite well preserved. The additional buildings all had double gates leading to the two central sanctuaries. The entrance gates in the south-west were 14 m wide and approximately 16 m high. A staircase in the south-east corner of the pylon led to the roof. There are some interesting ancient graffiti on the stone pavement of the courtyard. The whole construction, including the courtyard, was surrounded by a 3 m-thick stone outer enclosure wall, which measures approximately 50 x 100 m. As a result the inner part of the temple is surrounded by a double perambulatory. The inner decoration of the temple was concluded under Ptolemy VIII, but the decoration on the outside walls went on under Nero and Vespasian. The most recent royal titles are those of Commodus, Macrinus (AD 217–18) and his son Diadumenianus on the eastern wall of the outer ambulatory.

The *mammisi* (birthhouse) in front of the temple, which was still standing 9 m high at the time of Napoleon's expedition, with beautiful Hathor columns, is now badly ruined. It was decorated under Ptolemy VIII. A well-preserved relief shows the king standing in a boat in a papyrus swamp surrounded by birds in front of an ithyphallic Min. The building has the plan of an ordinary temple with sanctuary, offering hall and a room for visiting gods. The temple and *mammisi* were surrounded by a mudbrick wall of which the south-west corner has been washed away by the Nile. It was entered by a gate built by Ptolemy XII. Close to this gate is a chapel for Hathor-Aphrodite, with a Greek inscription of AD 88 above the door (note the erasure of the name of the emperor Domitian), in which are stored some mummies of sacred crocodiles from the nearby necropolis.

Fig. 8.8.3
Kom Ombo, temple.

The surgical instruments

One of the most famous scenes of the Kom Ombo temple is found in the north corner of outer ambulatory. It belongs to the time of Marcus Aurelius and depicts, in the centre, a set of surgical instruments laid out on a table, and a shallow basin on a stand beneath a tapered jar bearing a hieroglyphic text. On the left side a kneeling pharaoh, faced by Isis and another goddess on low seats, offers two *oudjat* eyes (now lost) to the god Haroeris, shown on the right side seated on a throne, and the goddess Senetneferet (now lost).

The *oudjat* eyes represent Osiris. The healing of a mythical eye by means of the very real surgical instruments symbolizes the return to life of the murdered god. The tapered jar is a measuring vase; the hieroglyphs on its right side denote fractions going from $\frac{1}{2}$, $\frac{1}{4}$, $\frac{1}{8}$ down to $\frac{1}{128}$, as on a present-day graduated glass. These fractions are numerical representations of the *oudjat* eye: in hieroglyphic script fractions were usually rendered not as figures, but as parts of the eye. All the parts together constitute the healed eye. Water is poured from this vase into the shallow holy water basin on the stand below. The short hieroglyphic text between the vase and the basin explains that 'the sweet water comes out of the interior (of the vase) in order to purify the two *oudjat* eyes'.

The text on the left side of the vase links the water to the places in Lower and Upper Egypt where the chopped-up body of Osiris was buried. The towns are listed from north to south, and the vase represents the shape of Egypt, broader at the top (the Delta) and narrower at the bottom (Elephantine). The water of the Nile from all over Egypt will purify the eye and thus resurrect Osiris, setting in motion a new Nile flood. The temple ritual re-enacts the return of Osiris and helps to recreate the fertility cycle of Egypt. Just as Osiris is restored to life and just as Egypt regains its force with the annual inundation, so illnesses will be cured by both science and magic. This interesting relief offers an exceptional opportunity to link the mythical representations on the temple walls with the ritual which was performed by the priests in the temple.

Box 8.8
Fig. 8.8.4

The remains of the ancient town, buried in the sand at the north-east corner of the plateau, are covered with pottery sherds. About 1 km inland, between the temple and the main road, a large cemetery, where human burials were centred around the tombs of sacred crocodiles, was excavated in the 1970s but never published. The site is now covered with sugar cane.

Bibliography: Arnold 1999: 187–9, 220, 232–5; Sambin 1997.

8.9 ELEPHANTINE (ASWAN)

8.9.a Introduction

Present-day Egypt effectively ends with the great dam, some 12 km upstream from Aswan; south of the dam is the immense Lake Nasser, with important ancient monuments at Philae, Abu Simbel, and so on, but no human settlements. In antiquity Aswan also marked the end of the trip, as boats could not cross the cataracts and goods therefore had to be transported by land over a long stretch of desert. Then as now, Aswan was a frontier town, even though the area to the south was inhabited and was controlled by the Ptolemies and the Roman emperors, who built here several monuments in order to mark their dominance. Whereas Aswan is now one of the major centres of Egypt, a pleasant and modern town on the east bank of the Nile, in antiquity the economic, military and religious centre was on Elephantine, a small island in the Nile (1.5 km north-south, 0.5 km east-west). Aswan (Egyptian *Swn*, Greek Syene) was merely a market place for the city in the Nile.

Elephantine is the Greek translation of Egyptian *ꜣbw*, later written *Yb* 'Elephant island', perhaps named so because of the smooth granite boulders in the river which resemble the backs of elephants, or simply because ivory (Greek *elephas*, after the animal) was bought here. The island was a strategic place, commanding the river traffic on the spot where the Nile became navigable again. The tombs of the princes in the hills of the west bank show that the site was already important at the end of the Old Kingdom. In 591 BC Elephantine was the base for Psammetichos II and his mercenaries on his Nubian campaign (box 1.3.3). In the fifth century there was a fortress occupied by troops from Palestine, Jews and Aramaeans, in the service of the Persian king. The Jews had their temple of Yahweh next to that of the Egyptian god Khnum until it was destroyed by the Egyptian priests in 410 BC, three generations before the arrival of Alexander the Great. More than sixty Aramaic papyri, now in Berlin and Cairo, which belonged to several family archives, offer a vivid glimpse of the daily life of this immigrant community. The temple of Yahweh and some houses have been identi-

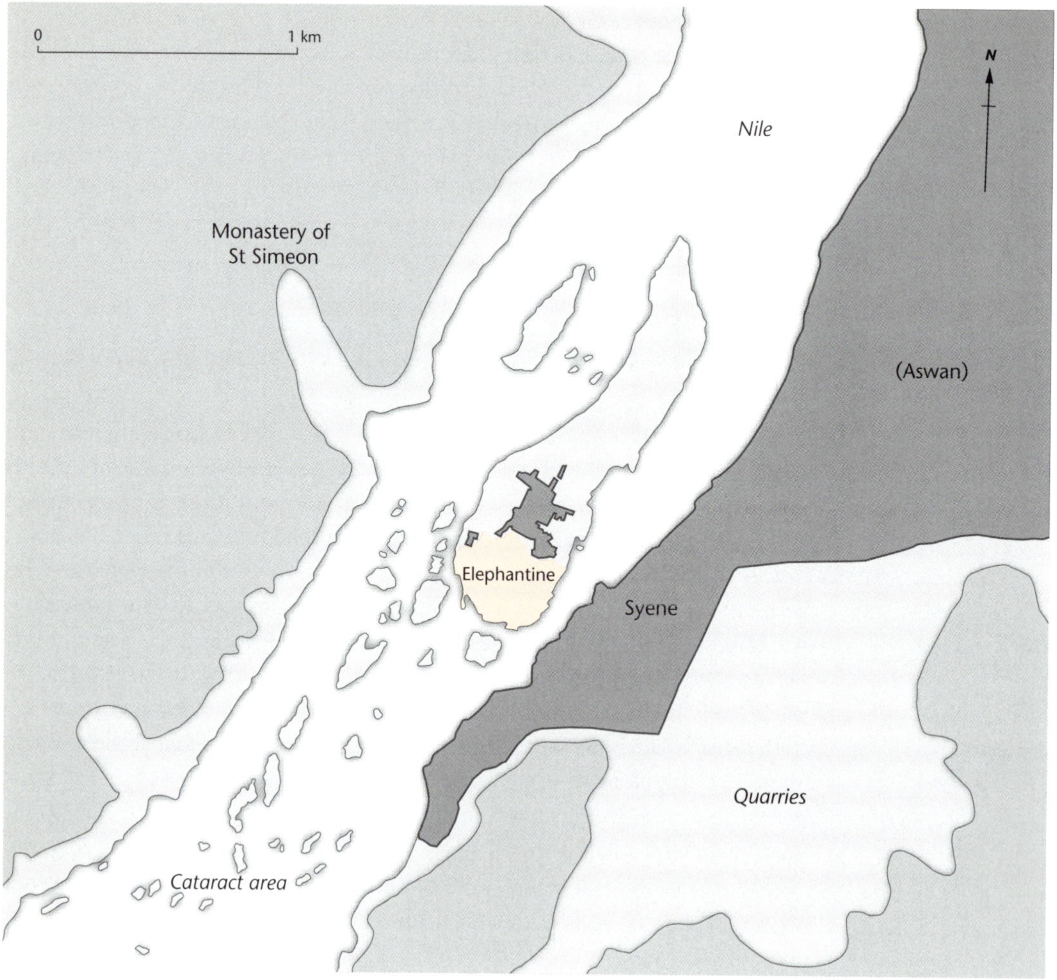

Fig. 8.9.1
Aswan area (after
Ziermann 1993: 13).

Fig. 8.9.2
The Roman quay at
Elephantine.

fied by German archaeologists. The garrison remained important in the Ptolemaic period. When the whole south revolted against the Ptolemies in 206 BC, the insurgents never succeeded in taking the well-defended island. The troops were provisioned by the Ptolemaic Nile fleet until the revolt was finally subdued in 186 BC. In the second century AD the Roman satirical poet Juvenal is said to have been banished to this remote frontier town for his biting attacks on the imperial court.

8.9.b Archaeological remains

The ancient town was on the southern part of the island where the mudbrick ruins, covered with pottery, form a mound nearly 30 m high. The Roman embankment to the south-east, where both ancient and modern visitors arrive, incorporates blocks taken from pharaonic buildings with the names of pharaohs. One element of the quay is the famous Nilometer, as described by the Greek author Strabo, who was in Egypt in the time of Augustus. The first signs of the rising Nile flood were measured here and transmitted by fire signals to the capital in Alexandria, 1000 km away. The marks indicating the lowest and highest points of the flood can still be read on the sides of the well, with inscriptions marking some thirty exceptional floods of 24 and 25 cubits in height from the period of Augustus until Septimius Severus (30 BC–AD 200). Near the Nilometer are the substructures of a small temple of the goddess Satis, the original mistress of Elephantine, surrounded by a brick wall. The building by Ptolemy VI and VIII covers a very old shrine, a niche in the rocks. Because the site was filled in and paved over, this primitive Egyptian temple is exceptionally well preserved. A remarkable demotic graffito, dated shortly after 168 BC, records how the Ptolemaic chapel was re-erected on top of older walls, which the Ptolemaic architects duly excavated.

Further south-west is the great temple (123 m long) of the ram-headed Khnum, the main deity of the island once he became the husband of Satis in the Middle Kingdom. It was rebuilt by Nektanebo II, the last native pharaoh, then works were suspended until Ptolemy VI finished the decoration and added a *pronaos* with two rows of columns, supporting a ceiling with astronomical decoration. Only a few columns of the hypostyle room and a huge granite gate leading to the inner sanctuary remain. The gate shows Alexander, the son of Alexander the Great, sacrificing to Khnum, Satis and Anukis. Only the foundations of the sixth-century church, built in the *pronaos* of the temple, remain. The temple was preceded by a vast stone court of early Roman date. In Late Antiquity this court was built over with mudbrick barracks, which were demolished by the excavators. Between the court and the Nile was a cult terrace with a stone parapet on which were carved hundreds of Greek and demotic graffiti. Close by is the cemetery of the sacred rams,

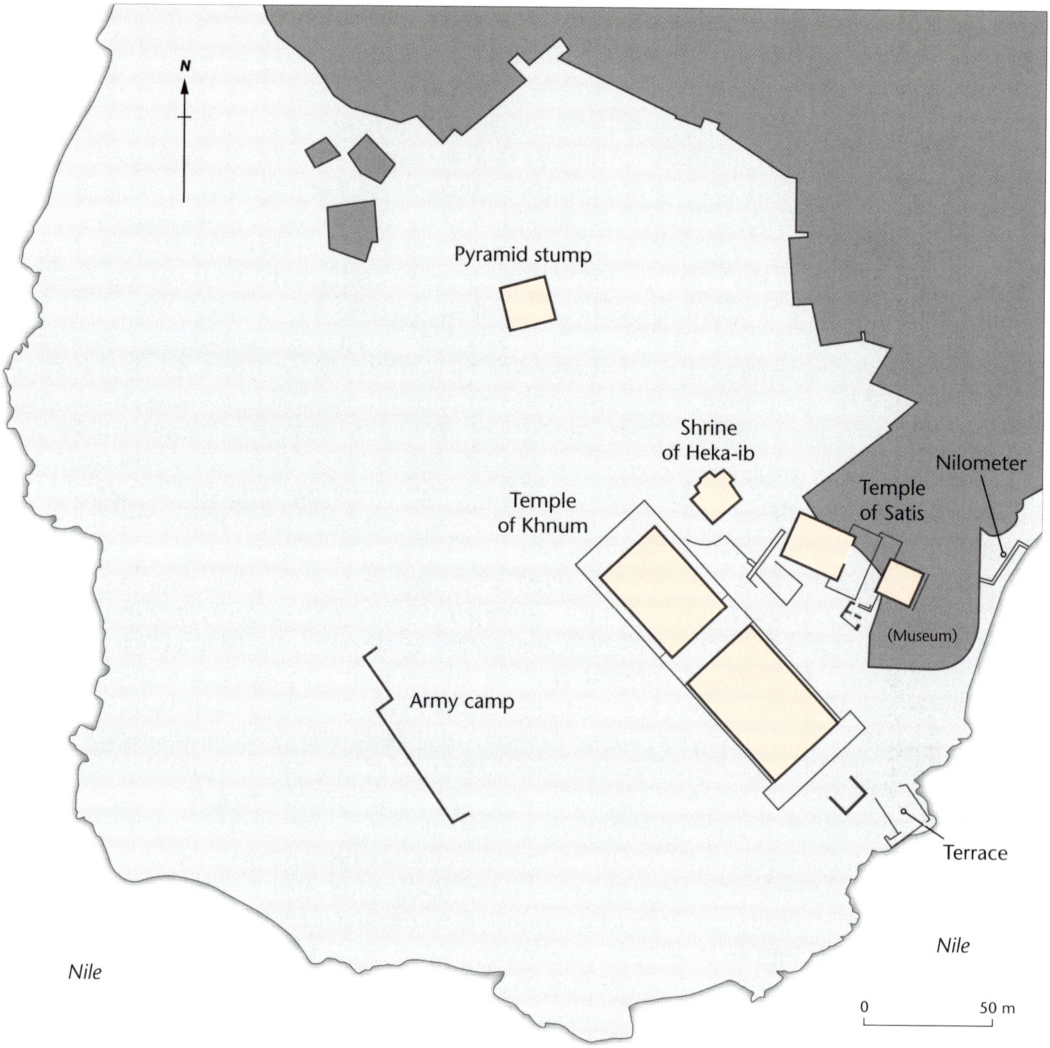

with the sarcophagi still present, surrounded by mudbrick buildings. On the southern point of the island a chapel has been reconstructed from blocks found in the basement of the temple of Kalabsha, which was completely dismantled when the great dam was built in the 1970s. It was decorated by Ptolemy IX and Augustus, but on one door post appears the name of the Meroitic king Arqamani (Ergamenes) of around 200 BC, which shows that construction was earlier.

Fig. 8.9.3 Elephantine, the temple area (after Kaiser 1970: 88).

The ruins of the ancient city of Aswan, on the eastern bank, are largely covered by the southern part of the modern town. Few ancient monuments survive; the most important of them is the temple of Isis, built by Ptolemy III and IV, which stands at the southern edge of the town. A small temple built in the reign of Domitian was found in 1921. It stood with its back to the Nile and was destroyed in the early nine-

Fig. 8.9.4 Aswan, the Monastery of St Simeon.

teenth century. Only the front of the *pronaos* is still visible. The Aswan region was a major source of granite for building and sculpture in all periods. Extensive remains of these quarries, including a famous unfinished obelisk (42 m long), are found south of the town. There is a museum near the landing stage on Elephantine, and the Nubia Museum is located in the city of Aswan on the mainland. The latter houses the famous Piankhi stela and also a beautiful basalt sarcophagus of a sacred ram from Elephantine. It is not yet clear what the function of the Elephantine museum will be. The German excavators have also built a small museum for their finds on the island just north of the Elephantine museum.

Box 8.9
Fig. 8.9.5

The monastery of St Simeon, originally of Anba Hadra, on the west bank of the Nile, can be reached by a footpath in about twenty minutes. It is one of the best preserved Coptic monasteries, founded in the seventh century and abandoned in the thirteenth because of the shortage of water. The buildings, standing in two levels on a rocky hill, are surrounded by a 6 m high wall made of stone and mudbrick. There are many buildings around several courts. The lower level is dominated by the church, a basilica with three aisles. Some of the frescos are well preserved, like that of Christ enthroned between the angels in the central apse. Along the east side of the court in front of the church are bedrooms, perhaps for pilgrims, each with three beds. The upper level, which is reached by a staircase, contains living quarters for the monks, including a refectory with kitchen, a bakery, an oil press and administrative buildings.

Bibliography: Bernand 1989: 169–259; Bresciani 1978; Grossmann 1980; Jaritz 1980.

8.10 PHILAE

8.10.a Introduction

The original island of Philae (Egyptian Pilak), lying between the High Dam to the south (Sadd el-Ali) and the town of Aswan to the north, has been completely submerged as a result of the dam. The Late Period, Ptolemaic and Roman structures were all moved by UNESCO in 1980 to the island of Agilkia and realigned with the original orientation of the buildings; this is the island visited today. The important island of Biggeh, sacred to the god Osiris and believed to be the site of his tomb, where inscriptions and some remains of Ptolemaic and Roman structures survive, stands adjacent.

Philae was dedicated to Isis and her son Harpokrates (Horus the child). It was also, by the fourth century BC, a major cult centre of Osiris. Building on the island seems to begin during Dynasty 26, but the earliest surviving building is that of Nektanebo I. Construction

Famine stela of Seheil

A pleasant journey through the cataracts by felucca brings the visitor to the island of Seheil, some 5 km upstream from Elephantine. On top of a hill, from where one can see a Nubian village, is a famous inscription, the 'famine' stela. The text has the shape of a stela, but is cut in a rock which was apparently already split in antiquity. The upper part represents king Zoser offering incense to Khnum-Re, Satis and Anukis; under it is a royal decree of thirty-two columns, dated to year 18 of Zoser. In it a seven-year famine is described, caused by failed inundations. The learned Imhotep finds in the sacred books that the Nile flood comes from Elephantine and is controlled by Khnum. After Zoser has made offerings, Khnum appears to him in a dream and promises a regular inundation. In return the king promulgates this decree in which the Dodekaschoinos, the region south of Elephantine, is given to Khnum over a distance of 12 *iterou* (*c.* 130 km). His temple at Elephantine has the right to the tithe of all revenues from this land.

The famine stela immediately became famous on its discovery in 1889 because the seven-year famine called to mind the biblical story of Joseph. Perhaps the Egyptian text alludes to this story, which could have been known through the Jewish colony in Elephantine, or the Bible attributed an existing Egyptian tale to the Jewish hero. In any case the stela does not date from Dynasty 3, for the hieroglyphic script is clearly Ptolemaic. It is not a forgery, however, but a recreation of history in later times, no doubt based on some older model, though not necessarily as old as Zoser and his architect Imhotep. The stela functions as a title deed in a long-lasting dispute between the priests of Khnum in Elephantine and those of Isis in Philae. In fact the same area was given by Ptolemy II and several successors to Isis, whose priests were the eventual winners. (Barguet 1953)

Fig. 8.10.1
The island of Philae in 1838, by David Roberts.

continued through the Roman period, although the vast bulk of the building is Ptolemaic. Philae became a major pilgrimage destination during the Roman period, and worship of Isis here continued into the sixth century AD. Evidence of earlier building on Philae used as filler for the Ptolemaic building was discovered during the removal of the buildings to Agilkia. The island was also important for Nubians, who worshipped not only Isis but also Nubian deities; a temple of the Nubian lion god Arsenuphis was unfinished, and little of it survives. The numerous graffiti on the island form an important historical corpus along with historical inscriptions, including one written directly on the *mammisi* (birthhouse) in hieroglyphic and demotic dating to the reign of Ptolemy V, which records the defeat of rebels in the south in the aftermath of the revolt in the Thebaid (205–186 BC). Philae in a sense formed the last bastion of ancient Egypt – the last certainly dated hieroglyphic inscription in Egypt was recorded here on 24 August AD 394.

8.10.b The main building is the **temple dedicated to Isis**, and the many graffiti preserved in and around the temple demonstrate the spread of her cult throughout the Mediterranean world. The temple of Isis and a new temple gate were built by Ptolemy II Philadelphos, perhaps as part of a larger programme to consolidate Ptolemaic power at

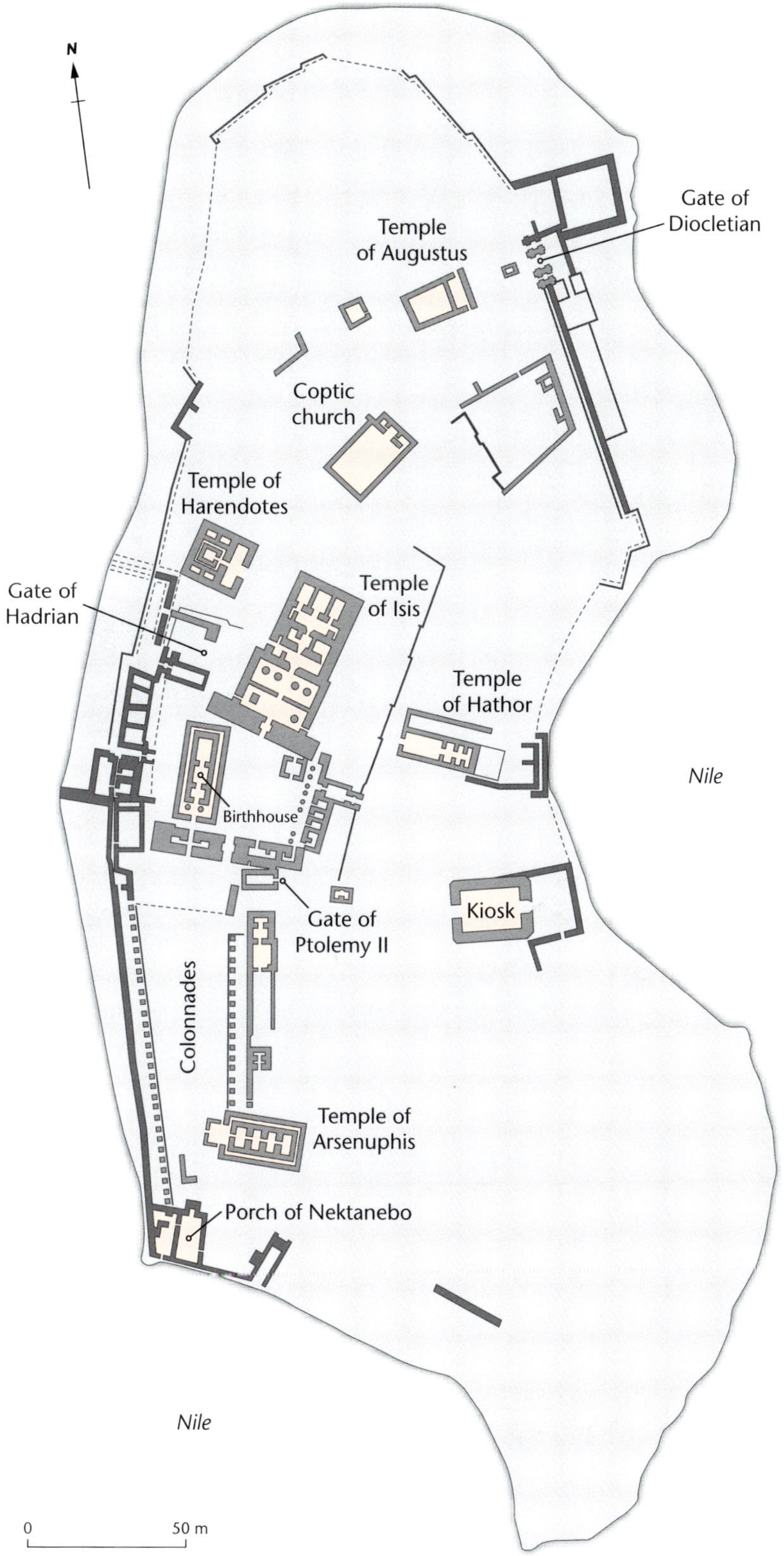

Fig. 8.10.2
Philae, the original island (after Porter and Moss 1939: 202).

the southern border and to control trade from the Eastern Desert and from Nubia. Recent work on the **Kiosk of Trajan**, certainly among the most famous buildings of the period, has suggested that it should be ascribed to the emperor Augustus rather than to Trajan. It probably served as a barque shrine for Isis.

Bibliography: Arnold 1999; Porter and Moss 1939; Simpson 1996; Vassilika 1989.

8.11 KALABSHA (TALMIS)

The temple of Kalabsha, the largest in the Nubian region, was removed in 1970 from its original location in Lower Nubia, 50 km south of Aswan. Along with the kiosk of Qertassi and the Beit el-Wali temple, it was placed in its present position, just above the High Dam at Aswan on the island of New Kalabsha, as part of the large rescue effort led by UNESCO to save ancient monuments from the waters of Lake Nasser. Access to the new site of the temple is by taxi from Aswan, then by boat to the island.

The temple is dedicated to the Nubian sun god Mandulis (Nubian Marul) and Isis. It was built in the late Ptolemaic period on top of a New Kingdom foundation, and then rebuilt, although never completely finished, by Augustus. A small Ptolemaic chapel devoted to the Nubian god Dedwen is located to the south-west of the main building. The large pylon in front is offset from the axis of the temple by 6 degrees. A gateway, probably built in the late Ptolemaic period and partially decorated under Augustus, was reused for the foundations of

Fig. 8.11.1 Kalabsha, the temple (after Arnold 1999: fig. 203).

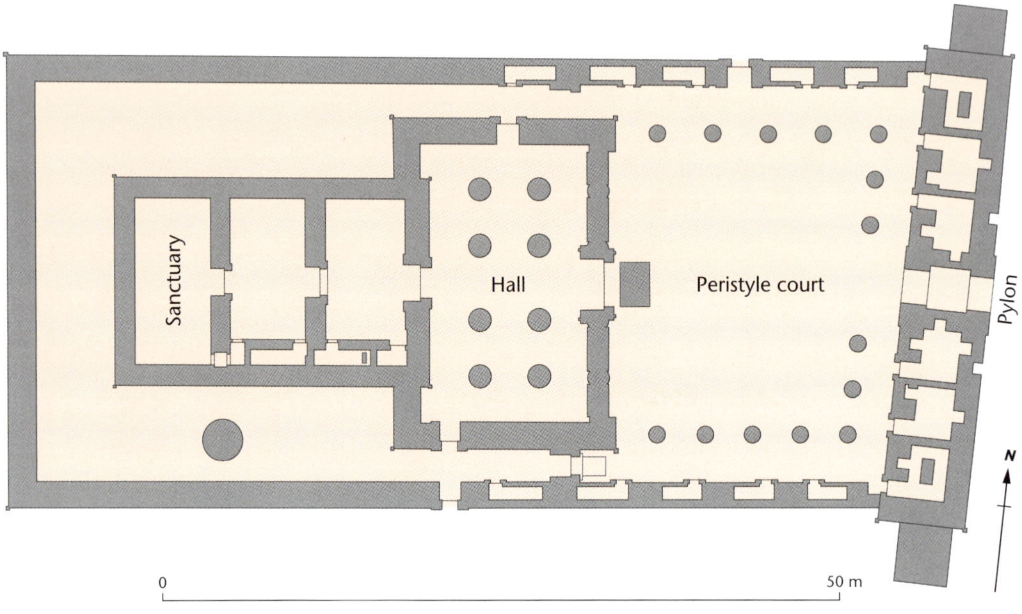

Fig. 8.12.1
The Dendur temple in its original location, 1905/6 (Oriental Institute, University of Chicago).

the Augustan extension to the temple. Its blocks were rediscovered when the temple was dismantled to be moved and have been reassembled in the Egyptian Museum, Berlin; the reliefs depict Augustus supporting the cult of Isis (col. pl. 8.11.2). There are also important inscriptions recorded on the temple, including a decree by the Roman *strategos* (administrator) of the Ombite nome, probably of AD 248/9, ordering the expulsion of pigs from the temple precinct on religious grounds. One of the longest known Meroitic inscriptions, of thirty-four lines, dated to the fifth century AD, is also found here. In so far as the Meroitic can be interpreted, the inscription seems to record the resolution of a dispute between a Blemmyan and a Nubian king over control of the area around Kalabsha.

Bibliography: Arnold 1999; Eide 1998; Winter 2003.

8.12 DENDUR (TUZIS)

The temple at Dendur was originally located about 60 km south of Aswan in what is now the middle of Lake Nasser. As part of the UNESCO Nubian rescue project, the temple was dismantled in 1963, moved to New York City and installed in its own section of the Sackler Wing of the Metropolitan Museum of Art in 1978.

This small but elegant temple, in fact a mortuary chapel, described as an 'exquisite toy' by Amelia Edwards during her visit in 1874, was built in the reign of Augustus around 15 BC. It is dedicated to Isis, Osiris and, unusually, two brothers (Petiese and Pahor), sons of a local Blemmyan king, who had apparently drowned in the Nile. A small tomb of one (or for both) of the brothers was built in the hills behind the temple. It was originally built against a small cliff, with the innermost chamber excavated from the living rock (perhaps intended for the bodies of the two brothers, who became, as it were, cult objects), with a terrace in front typical of the small Nubian temples. The emperor Augustus, depicted as an Egyptian pharaoh, features prominently on the exterior walls making offerings to local deities. A Coptic inscription in the doorway of the *pronaos* indicates that the old temple building was converted to a church in AD 577. It was abandoned in the thirteenth century.

Bibliography: Aldred 1978; Blackman 1911.

9 THE WESTERN OASES

9.1 INTRODUCTION

The oases of Egypt's Western Desert reached a peak of importance and prosperity in the middle to late Roman period, after which all of them declined sharply. Until attempts in the last few decades to develop their agricultural economies as a 'New Valley', they were lightly populated and less extensively cultivated than in antiquity. One result of this history is a wealth of monuments from the Graeco-Roman period hardly matched in the rest of Egypt, coupled with a relative absence of pharaonic remains. With a few exceptions, in fact, there is little to be seen before the Persian period.

Four of the five major oases form a semicircular arc to the west. Because the Nile bends to the east in the latitude of Dakhla and Kharga, all of the oases are located at significant distances from the valley. The fifth oasis, Siwa, is a world apart, for much of its history more closely linked to Libya than to Egypt, and its population has never been predominantly Egyptian; even today much of it speaks a Berber dialect instead of or in addition to Arabic.

There are archaeological remains of the Ptolemaic period in these oases, but they are enormously outweighed by those of the Roman period. Written documentation of the oases is also mainly Roman. Administratively they were divided under the Romans into three parts: the Ammoniake, or Oasis of Ammon (Siwa), the Small Oasis (Bahariya), and the Great Oasis (Kharga and Dakhla). Whether Farafra was considered part of the Small Oasis or is simply never referred to in the documents is hard to say; it has only modest visible archaeological vestiges to indicate that it was occupied in this period. In the later Roman period, the Great Oasis was subdivided into three administrative units, the Hibite (Kharga), Mothite and Trimithite (both Dakhla). From documentary evidence it is clear that Dakhla was substantially more populous and wealthier than Kharga, but Kharga Oasis has more standing monuments visible today, mostly the product of the Roman security network.

The connections of the oases to Egypt in antiquity corresponded to a large degree with those today. Siwa's main lifeline was the route to Paraitonion (Marsa Matruh) on the coast, although it was also linked to the Small Oasis by a caravan route some 400 km long; from there one could reach the valley. The Small Oasis, today reached mainly by a road from Giza (in the ancient Memphite), was connected by roads to the Fayyum and to Oxyrhynchos, neither in use today. The part of the Great Oasis nearest the valley, Kharga, was linked to it by several roads. The most important of these

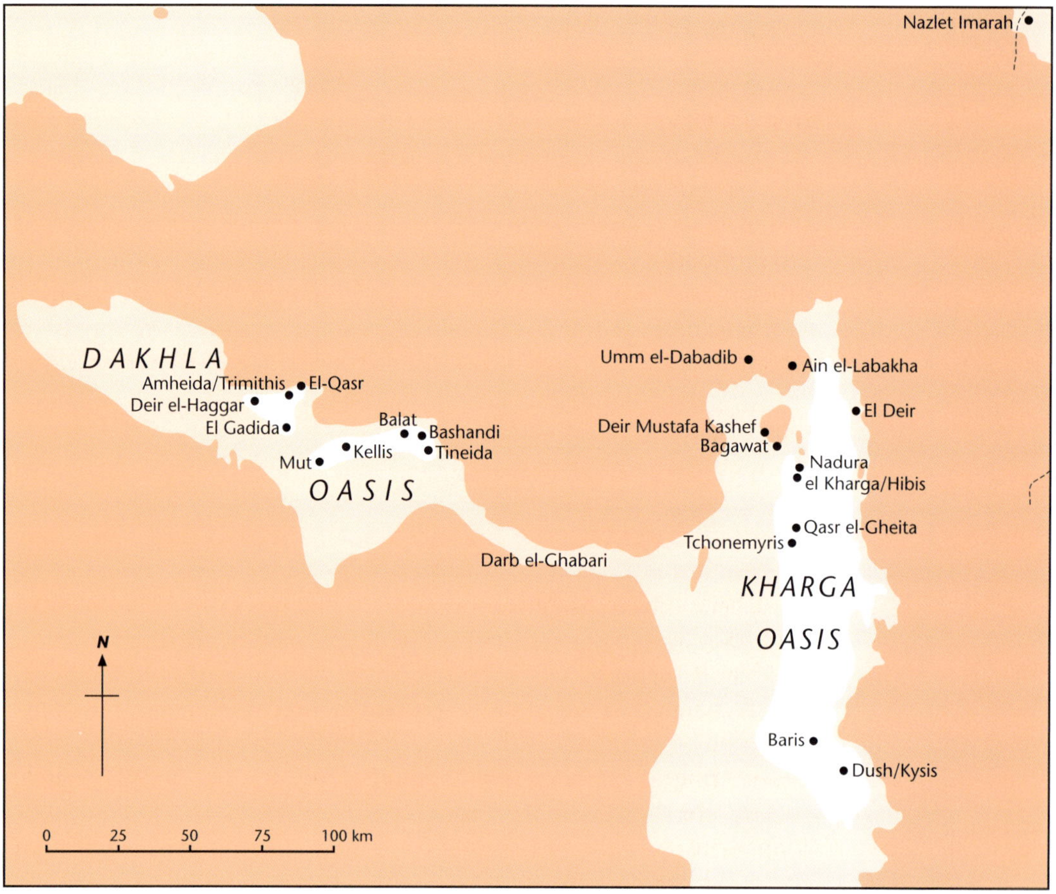

Fig. 9.1.1
Dakhla and Kharga oases.

connected the north of this oasis to Lykopolis (Asyut) and corresponds to the main modern route; almost as important, however, was a road that reached the valley in the northern Panopolite nome, near the Antaiopolite. The oases had close connections with this zone, attested in the papyri from Kellis. Because Kharga is so elongated from north to south, there were also routes connecting the southern part of the oasis, near Kysis, to several valley cities ranging from Hermonthis to Apollonopolis Magna.

Dakhla could be reached from Lykopolis by a direct route, but it is likely that most traffic to Dakhla went via Kharga because the intervals between sources of food and water were shorter. There were two links between the two parts of the Great Oasis, one along roughly the line of the modern road, the other further north, running across the Abu Tartur plateau by way of the spring at Ain Amour. The second of these is shorter and better supplied with water but steeper; the first longer and drier, but more level.

9.1.a Access

Good paved roads to Kharga and on to Dakhla from Asyut; to Bahariya from Giza; to Siwa from Marsa Matruh on the north coast road coming from Alexandria. Good roads connect Bahariya, Farafra, Dakhla and Kharga, but only a difficult four-wheel drive track between Bahariya and Siwa, not always open. Sites off the main modern roads sometimes require four-wheel drive for access. Relatively few sites in the oasis are officially open to visitors. The local inspectorate of the Supreme Council for Antiquities in the chief town of each oasis can advise on which sites may be visited and will provide an escort if necessary.

Bibliography: Jackson 2002; Vivian 2000; Wagner 1987.

9.2 KHARGA

Because little systematic archaeological survey has been carried out in the Kharga Oasis, the distribution of ancient settlement is known only very roughly. Kharga was less well endowed with accessible water than Dakhla. It seems to have been the introduction of *qanat* underground water channels to tap water sources that led to Kharga's first major development under the Persians, but it may have taken Roman water engineering – deep well digging – to produce the growth visible under the empire. Kharga is organized on a north-south axis about 160 km long, with a large area of desert separating the centre of the oasis (around Hibis) from the south (Kysis). The north of the oasis was well equipped with military posts along the road system; some of these had agricultural settlements as well. Many of the sites of Kharga have been known and described since the early nineteenth century but never fully recorded, let alone excavated.

9.2.a Ancient Hibis and its environs

The capital of the Great Oasis lay just on the northern edge of the modern town of Kharga, where the only museum of the Great Oasis is located, the **New Valley Museum**. The varied collection here includes material found in Kharga and Dakhla as well as some pharaonic antiquities transferred from the Egyptian Museum in Cairo. The most striking oasite finds are from the Old Kingdom governors' tombs at Balat (Dakhla), with offering stelae, alabaster and granite vessels and ostrich eggs. There is also a fine display of prehistoric stone tools. From the Graeco-Roman period come most of the remainder of the first-floor displays, including limestone lions from Deir el-Haggar, painted ibis and ram mummies from El-Muzawwaka, sarcophagi, masks, an inscribed stone panel and a painted wood statue of Horus from Ain Labakha, and the wooden codexes of Kellis. Some Late Antique textiles and Coptic gravestones are displayed on the second floor along with a diverse collection of later material.

The most important visible monument of the city is the Temple of Amun-Re, usually called the **Hibis Temple**. The west part, with the essential elements of a temple, was built under Darius I; the large hypostyle hall and the porch came later, under Egyptian kings of the fourth century BC (Nektanebo I and II). Major repairs were already needed at this time because of subsidence of the ground, which caused large cracks. The larger, outer gateway was built under Ptolemy II. There are outer sections built in the late Ptolemaic and Roman periods, when two important edicts of prefects were inscribed. In Late Antiquity a church was built against the north side of the porch. To the south-east of the temple modest remains of the ancient city are visible.

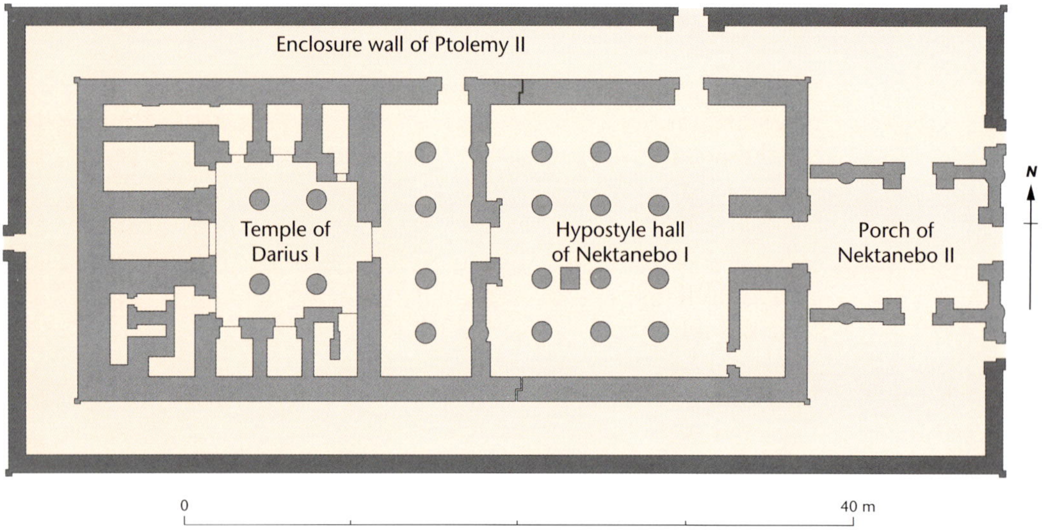

Fig. 9.2.1 Hibis Temple (after Winlock 1941: pl.XXXII).

Another temple, also apparently of Amun-Re, built of sandstone in the second century AD (dated by an inscription of Antoninus), stands on the hill now called **Nadura**, located east of the ancient city centre. It is surrounded by the mudbrick outer wall of the sanctuary, which may like other such temples have been recycled as a late Roman fort. The main entrance to the enclosure is on the east side, but it is not aligned with the temple axis. The north side of this gate preserves a bastion; there is a smaller entrance in the south enclosure wall. Inside the temple, remains of shallow reliefs can be seen. Nadura has views of the entire central part of the oasis, unobstructed to the east; it is a good point from which to see the relative position of other monuments in the area.

The zone north and north-west of Hibis, on and below the foothills of Gebel Teir, offers a rich array of Late Antique funerary, monastic and agricultural structures. The most notable of these is **Bagawat cemetery**, extending over an area some 500 x 200 m (col. pl. 9.2.2). Although it has been claimed that it was in use as early as the second century, its public face is later, fourth to sixth (or even seventh) century, and entirely Christian. The numerous (263) tomb chapels are mostly simple domed or flat-roofed rooms, but there are ten major types, and some multi-room chapels are rather ambitious. Most or all were plastered and painted in antiquity, with considerable architectural ornament; almost all of this is now lost. Plaster and paintings survive inside some chapels; the Chapel of the Exodus and Chapel of Peace are the most noteworthy, both with biblical scenes (largely Old Testament) and with several abstract virtues and scenes of Paul and Thecla in the latter. In a high, central location stand the remains of a large basilica.

If one continues north-west around the foot of the hill beyond the entrance to Bagawat, one comes to further structures, both funerary and monastic. None has been scientifically published. The first, **Deir Mustafa Kashef**, is a high, multi-level mudbrick structure about 21 x 26 m, perched on the side of the hill looking west. Its core was a rock-cut tomb apparently turned into a shrine, perhaps for the monastery's founding father. At the upper level are the remains of a church. Below in the plain is an extensive complex which has been excavated. The ancient visitor entered through a series of passageways and rooms lined with benches, finally arriving in the large central room oriented north-south, of which much still stands. The walls are covered with Coptic graffiti. Off it opens a pair of small rooms oriented east-west, one clearly a chapel. Parts of the second floor survive, and there are extensive remains of domestic facilities.

North of these structures is the area called **Ain Zaaf**, which includes some hillside tombs in the same style as those of Bagawat and a sizable complex at the foot of the hill, larger than the building below Deir Mustafa Kashef. It has been largely re-covered by sand after excavation,

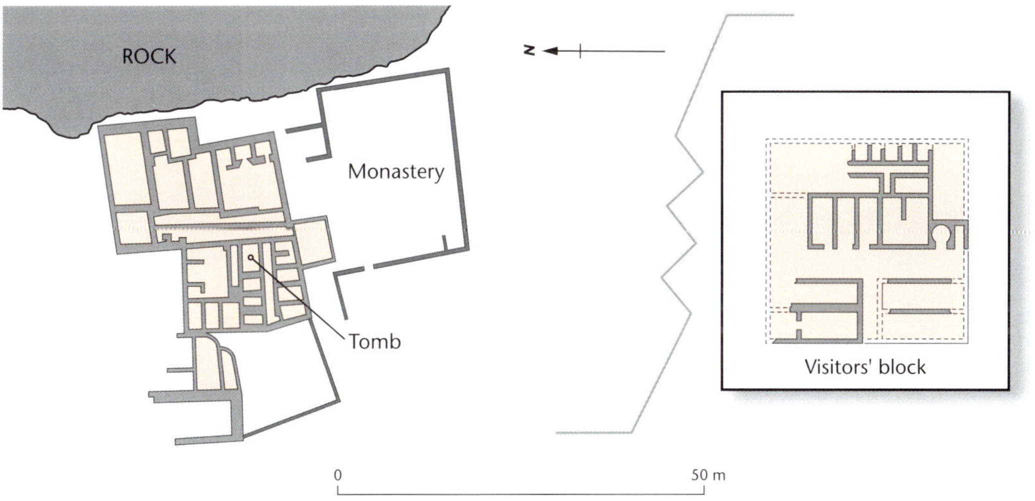

Fig. 9.2.3 Deir Mustafa Kashef (after Müller-Wiener 1963: 124).

but the ground plan is discernible. It has some visible graffiti on the plaster and may well have been another monastic centre.

The plain to the west of this area, now barren, was once under cultivation, and the remains of the irrigation system can be seen, along with a considerable sherd scatter. In it stand two ancient towers. The southern one, **Tahunet el-Hawa**, is 7 x 5 m and is preserved to a height of 11.5 m. The northern, **Borg el-Hammam**, is a bit larger but less well

Fig. 9.2.4
Tahunet el-Hawa.

preserved in height. The latter has pigeon holes preserved on the upper level. Both of these were probably farm towers, providing storage, a pigeon house and perhaps a place of refuge. Similar buildings are known at Beleida and in the Dakhla Oasis.

About 3 km to the north-west of this area, to the south of Gebel Tarif, is a town site called **Beleida**, the visible remains at which, all of mudbrick, date to the Roman period. Excavations by the Egyptian authorities in the late 1980s cleared some of the buildings. They include twin temples side by side, each of three vaulted rooms, 25 m in length and together about 10.5 m in width. To the south-west of the temples is a large rectangular building with vaulted rooms and several stories, which has been identified, perhaps wrongly, as a fort. To the north-east is another, longer temple (33 m), of mudbrick but using sandstone in the sanctuary. About 1 km west of Beleida is a well-preserved pigeon house.

Bibliography: *Hibis*: Winlock 1941; *Nadura*: Naumann 1939: 10–13; *Bagawat*: Fakhry 1951; *Deir Mustafa Kashef*: Müller-Wiener 1963: 123–40; *Tabunet el-Hawa* and *Borg el-Hammam*: Gascou and Wagner 1979; *Beleida*: Wagner 1987: 172–3.

9.2.b North of Hibis

Just to the north of the ancient city, the road forked around the Gebel Teir, the low mountain oriented north-south that divides the northern part of the oasis. The west fork ran through the plain below Deir Mustafa Kashef and arrived eventually at Ain Labakha, where it joined an east-west road for Umm el-Dabadib, Ain Amour and Dakhla. The east fork split again almost immediately into a road headed north-east for El-Deir, the last post before setting out across the desert towards the Panopolite, and a road almost due north headed for Ain Tauleib, Someira, El-Gib, and eventually Lykopolis.

Ain Labakha was a substantial settlement, spread over an area of 1.5 x 2.5 km, standing at the base of the northern escarpment of the oasis. As the junction for the road from Kharga and that connecting to the Asyut road, Ain Labakha was a central node in controlling oasis traffic. French and Egyptian survey and excavations in recent years have made it much better known. Its most visible monument is the late Roman fort, about 17 metres square plus round corner towers and preserved in places to a height of 11.5 m. At least two earlier stages of construction can be identified even without full excavation. There is also one well-preserved mudbrick temple similar to that at Dush, and exploration of the site has uncovered two other temples, one going back to the Ptolemaic period. The most striking is a partly rock-cut **temple of Piyris**, the local god, with graffiti of the second and third centuries. There are also remains of the wells, *qanats* (one now partly cleaned and

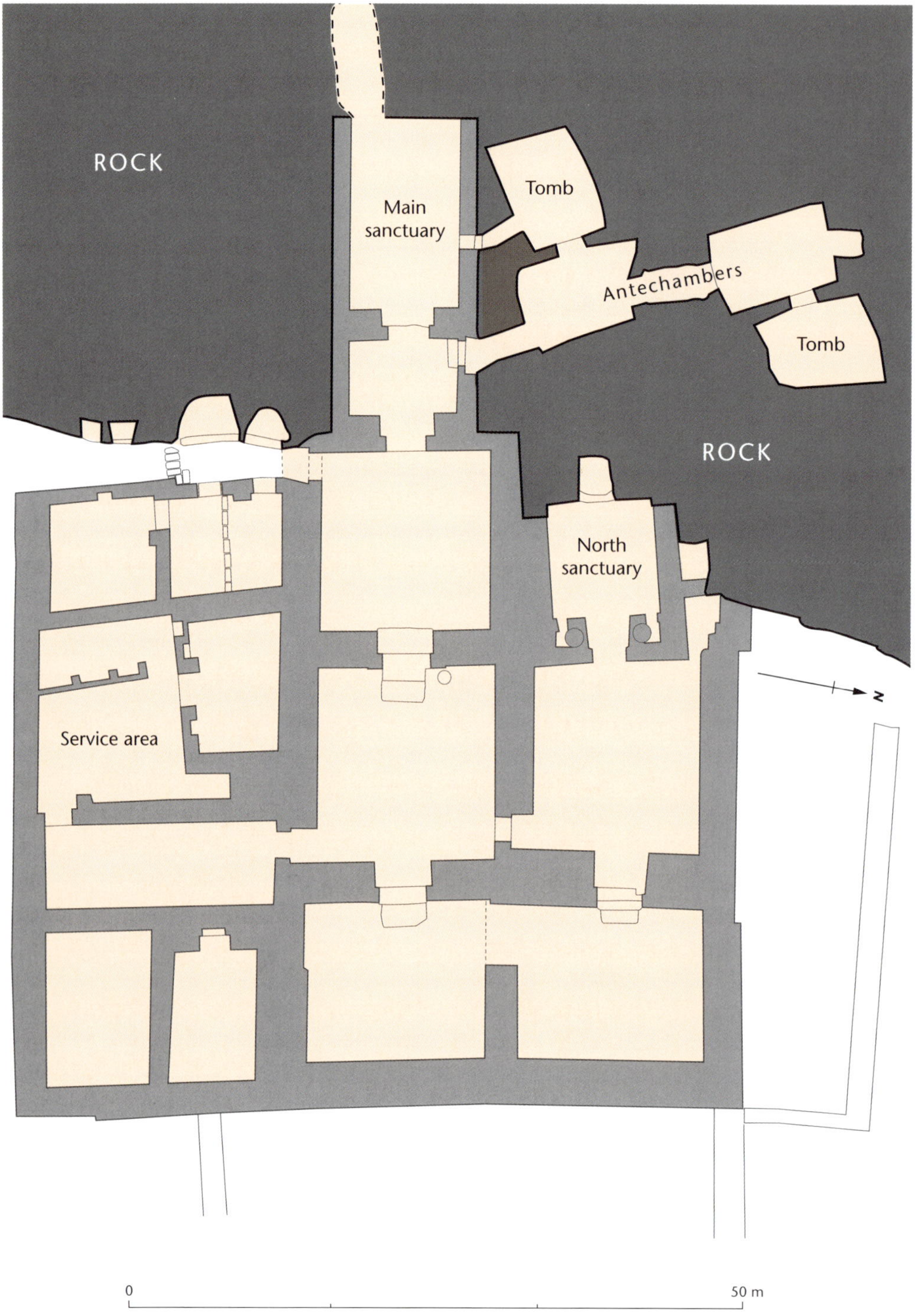
ROCK
Main sanctuary
Tomb
Antechambers
Tomb
ROCK
North sanctuary
Service area
N
0
50 m

Fig. 9.2.5
Piyris sanctuary
(after Hussein 2000).

restored to use), cultivation, and of the ancient village and its cemeteries, finds from which are in the New Valley Museum.

The road to Dakhla ran along the foot of the scarp, passing the north of the Gebel Tarif range and coming after about 12 km (a modern route takes about twice that distance, but this is not the best approach) to the most isolated of Kharga's sites, **Umm el-Dabadib**. Here also there is a late fort (col. pl. 9.2.6) and an extensive area of habitation. The sprawling earlier Roman settlement, with a temple, was located 0.5 km to the north of the fort, but in Late Antiquity the population was settled in a fortified hamlet tightly clustered around the fort. Both settlements are well preserved. The area was supplied with water by a system of at least five *qanats* running into the plain from the escarpment. These are now almost dry – a few trees are still thriving on the remnants of the water – but there was agriculture here as recently as the 1950s. The *qanats* are unusually well preserved. In the eastern hill is a necropolis.

Returning now to the road headed for the Panopolite, in the northeast of the oasis, at the foot of the scarp stands **El-Deir**, the largest military installation known from Roman Kharga, with a square ground

Fig. 9.2.7
El-Deir (after
Naumann 1939: 3).

plan of about 73 m on a side and a dozen towers, mostly still preserved to a height of about 12.5 m but badly damaged to windward (north); the walls were about 3.6 m thick. The ancient structures inside the walls have essentially disappeared; the scanty remains of cells that the visitor sees are modern. Unlike some of the other Roman military installations in the oasis, El-Deir was undoubtedly intended as a major fort, guarding one of the two important entrances to the oasis from the valley. A small mudbrick temple is preserved north of the fort, alongside an extensive field area showing remains of earlier cultivation, most likely an ancient area reused in modern times.

After the road to Umm el-Dabadib and Dakhla has diverged to the left and that to the valley via El-Deir has branched to the right, the ancient and modern road to Lykopolis continues to the north. There are several ancient sites, all of them no doubt part of the security system for the road, along the way. At about 20 km north of Hibis, on a road to Ain Labakha, is **Ain Tauleib**, the remains of a village with ovens and other indications of craft production. In the centre is a rectangular fort about 16 x 22 m, the mudbrick walls of which are preserved to a height of 10 m. On its west side are the remains of a stone gateway. This fort was probably the road junction for the track to Dakhla passing via Ain Labakha.

Further along this road, about 40 km north of Hibis, are two closely spaced small forts. The first is **Someira**, with sides 14 m and the walls preserved up to 7–8 m. The walls are about 50 cm thick at the base and half that at the top, thus considerably thinner than some of the more important forts. The entrance is on the south. Another 2 km to the north is **El Gib**, a more impressive structure although of similar outer dimensions (16.5 x 15 m), built on a rocky eminence that affords good visibility over the plain, with walls about 1.8 m thick at the base; they are well preserved except on the east. The site has little pottery and was probably an isolated defensive post rather than a substantial habitation site. The arched gateway on the south is intact. There is a vaulted underground passage leading from the fort toward the plain in the east. The fort's maximum capacity has been estimated at sixty men, but there is no evidence that it was actually staffed at that level.

Bibliography: *Ain Labakha*: Reddé 1999: 380, 390; Hussein 2000; *Umm el Dabadib*: Rossi 2000; *El-Deir*: Naumann 1939: 2–3; Reddé 1999: 379–80; *Ain Tauleib*: Gascou and Wagner 1979: 26; *Someira*: Gascou and Wagner 1979: 25–6; *El Gib*: Gascou and Wagner 1979: 22–5; Reddé 1999: 378–9.

9.2.c South of Hibis

The road south of Hibis is marked by several ancient sites before entering the long desert stretch that lies between the region of Hibis and that of Kysis. The first of these is **Ain Elwan**, about 5 km south of

Hibis. This was a village site, about 200 m in length, with farmhouses on the usual square plan with sides 7–10 m, pigeon houses and a larger rectangular structure (a small fort?) in ruinous condition. Another 2 km to the south, but largely covered by a dune at present, is **Qasr Baramuni**, with another small walled building and the remains of houses. A further 4 km to the south-east is yet another such site, **Qasr Nessima**, with a 10 x 15 m enclosure and a well-preserved pigeon house and the remains of a church.

At 20 km from Hibis is the most important site of this region, the sanctuary of **Qasr el-Ghueita**, the ancient Egyptian Per-ousekh mentioned in Theban tomb inscriptions as a source of fine wine. The temple was dedicated to Amun; begun under Darius I, it bears inscriptions of Ptolemy III, IV and X. It is thus one of the few oasis sites to have clear documentation of both Persian and Ptolemaic activity. The stone temple, partly reconstructed and offering fine reliefs, is surrounded by a large mudbrick wall and some remains of a small village. Like other such temples, it was apparently used for military purposes in Late Antiquity, and there are mudbrick structures from that period inside the temple.

The last point before the desert is the Ptolemaic temple of Qasr el-Zayyan, ancient **Tchonemyris**, long identified from a Greek inscription erected at the time of renovations under the prefect Avidius Heliodorus (AD 137–42). Its dedication is to Amun of Hibis (Amenebis) and associated gods. Substantial (partly restored) remains of the mudbrick enclosure wall and sandstone temple still stand.

Bibliography: *Ain Elwan*: Wagner 1987: 174; *Qasr Baramuni*: Wagner 1987: 175; *Qasr Nessima*: Wagner 1987: 175; *Qasr el-Ghueita*: Wagner 1987: 165–6; *Tchonemyris*: Wagner 1987: 166–7.

9.2.d The region of Kysis

In the Roman period the southern part of the Hibite nome was known as the toparchy of **Kysis**, after its chief village, today called Dush, located 105 km south of Hibis. Dush has been the object of survey and excavation by the French for more than a quarter of a century and is as a result the best-documented site of the Kharga Oasis. Kysis was set on a hill and was in late antiquity the crucial point controlling the road system at the southern edge of the oasis. To the north and north-east of the village was an extensive necropolis zone, where families of funeral workers plied their trade, and the remains of ancient wells and cultivation occupy considerable parts of the surrounding area.

The centre of the site is occupied by the sandstone temple of the Roman period (inscriptions from Domitian to Antoninus), adjacent to the mudbrick fortress that probably antedates it and remained in use at least until the late fourth century. The inside of the temple was reused

The funeral industry at Kysis

The funeral workers of Kysis are known from an archive of about fifty documents (AD 237–314). In some of them they give or sell parts of their monopoly rights to particular areas.

Aurelius Petosiris son of Petosiris, undertaker from the city of the Hibites, to Aurelius Petchon son of Tmarsis, from the village of Kysis, greetings. I acknowledge that I have granted to you by an inalienable and irrevocable gift, because of the loyalty you have shown to me, a fourth share of the funeral practice belonging to me in Kysis and the villages of Kysis, from now forever, and neither I nor anyone in my family may proceed against you concerning this gift, because I have so decided. This deed of gift, written in a single copy, is to be authoritative and secure as if deposited in a public registry, and on being asked the formal question, I assented.

The date and signatures of the donor, scribe, and witnesses follow (*P.Grenf.* II 68).

Box 9.2

in Late Antiquity. To the west is a second temple, built of mudbrick.

Some 4.5 km west of Kysis lies another hill with a substantial settlement, **Ain Manawir**. French exploration of the area since 1994 has brought to light an extensive system of *qanats*, the largest and best-preserved system of its kind. Thanks to the discovery of dated texts on ostraka it is known that the use of the *qanats* and the agricultural development of the area goes back to the middle of the fifth century BC, under Persian rule. The *qanats*, the water-distribution system and other ancient remains (a temple and houses of the Persian period, limited Ptolemaic traces and more extensive Roman habitation areas) lie on the north and east sides of the hill.

Kysis lay on one fork in the road system; from it a route led to the Nile Valley, connecting with the cities south of Thebes. That fork lay to the north of Kysis, near the modern village of Baris, and perhaps just to its north at the ancient site of **Mounesis** (modern Shams el-Din). This village site, some 200 x 200 m, preserves streets, houses, shops, workshops and a church; it was excavated by the French in 1976.

Bibliography: *Kysis*: Dunand 1992; *Ain Manawir*: Wuttmann 2001; *Mounesis*: Wagner 1987: 182–3.

SELECTED GPS READINGS

Hibis Temple	N 25.28.59	E 30.33.53
Bagawat	N 25.28.96	E 30.33.29
Beleida	N 25.29.43	E 30.30.65
Umm el-Dabadib	N 25.43.80	E 30.25.33
El-Deir turn-off	N 25.36.82	E 30.38.87
Qasr el-Ghueita	N 25.17.28	E 30.33.57
Tchonemyris	N 25.15.05	E 30.34.28
Kysis	N 24.34.94	E 30.42.80

Fig. 9.2.8
Kysis, temple.

9.3 DAKHLA

9.3.a Introduction

Dakhla Oasis was substantially richer than Kharga in the Roman period. A papyrus of AD 368/9 shows the tax quota of Dakhla amounting to 63 per cent of the total for the Great Oasis. It was already richer in the Old Kingdom, it appears, with a major centre around Balat in the eastern part of the oasis and another at Ain el-Gezareen just south of Amheida in the western part. Available water has generally been much more plentiful, and the geology of Dakhla, unlike Kharga, is not suited to and does not require *qanat*s. The survey of the Dakhleh Oasis Project has identified more than fifty sites from the Old Kingdom. But apparently the water available to the technology of that period was soon exhausted here, as in Kharga, for there are hardly any sites from the Middle and New Kingdoms, and even the Ptolemaic period is not richly represented. In the Roman period there is an explosion of settlement: more than 200 sites of all sorts have been registered, and although the density of occupation seems to have slipped in Late Antiquity it remained at a high level by historical standards.

It is therefore all the more noteworthy that Dakhla has much less in the way of visible monuments of interest to the visitor than Kharga. In large part this deficit seems to be the result of a less obvious military presence in the area and a much simpler road system, with little of the complex integration into road networks in all directions – not only the valley but also the Darb el-Arbain desert route to the south – that marks Kharga. The striking, though usually small, forts characteristic of Kharga are absent in Dakhla. The army was, however, present; a Late Antique source reveals that a cavalry unit was stationed at Trimithis and a cohort at Mothis. Despite the superficial appearances, Dakhla is an exceptionally rich area for archaeology, with excellent preservation of organic materials and very large undamaged sites. It has in Kellis a village site of the Roman period that has yielded more exciting finds over the last fifteen years than any other comparable location in Egypt.

As in Kharga, there are areas in Dakhla that today are dry but in antiquity were cultivated. The overall shape of settlement, however, was probably not radically different. The largest extent of cultivation was the north-west, where Amheida became a separate city by Late Antiquity, disposing of a territory about three-quarters the size of that of Mothis (modern Mut); we do not know where their domains divided. Mothis certainly controlled the entire area to the east, including the central zone with the third major settlement of the oasis, Kellis, and the eastern zone around modern Balat, Bashendi and Tineida.

9.3.b North-west Dakhla

The area of **Amheida (Trimithis)** has been one of the major centres of Dakhla in all of the more flourishing periods of the oasis's history. The Old Kingdom site of Ain el-Gezareen, just 2 km south of Amheida, has a very large complex identified by the excavators as a temple. Amheida itself has surface pottery from many periods, although its surface appearance is late Roman. And the medieval to modern town of Qasr is just 4 km to the north, the capital of the oasis until the renewed growth of Mut displaced it in relatively recent times. Qasr's multi-storey houses are built of mudbrick but incorporate sandstone blocks reused from an ancient temple, most likely that of Amheida, along with the intricately carved wooden lintel blocks for which it is famous, some of them with dates (the earliest 1518).

Amheida itself is a large field of mounds, with a dense cover of Roman and late Roman pottery almost throughout. Around its edges, but mostly to the south, are the nearer cemeteries. The relentless north wind has sandblasted most of the above-ground remains, but a fair number of house walls still stand above ground level, and in many areas the plans of the houses can be seen easily from the small amount of wall projecting above the debris and sand. In some cases it is clear that what is visible at ground level is an upper storey, with at least one level entirely buried. Near the road is a curious pyramid, preserved to a considerable height, that serves as a visual marker for the site.

One of the three large Roman-period town sites of Dakhla, Amheida was ancient Trimithis, attested as a city in fourth-century documents found at Kellis; inscriptions on the wall paintings excavated at Amheida help to confirm this identification. No visible remains of any military camp have been found so far, although the *Notitia Dignitatum* identifies Trimithis as the base of the Ala Quadorum. Systematic exploration of the site by an American team began in 2001.

Just under 4 km to the west-northwest of Amheida is the necropolis of **El-Muzawwaka**, with hundreds of tombs cut into the sides of low hills. This cemetery probably served Amheida. There are important wall paintings in the tombs of Petubastis (probably first century) and Petosiris (somewhat later), including ceilings with zodiac designs; these combine Roman identity with traditional Egyptian funerary imagery. The cemetery goes back at least to the Ptolemaic period, as ostraka with Demotic texts from the later Ptolemaic period were found in a brick building about 150 m from the tombs.

About 6 km west of Amheida stands the temple of **Deir el-Haggar**, built in the second half of the first century (Nero to Domitian) of sandstone with mudbrick annexes and enclosure wall. It has been extensively restored (in the 1990s) and is now the most visited antiquity of Dakhla. There are reliefs on the gateways and the sanctuary, occasionally

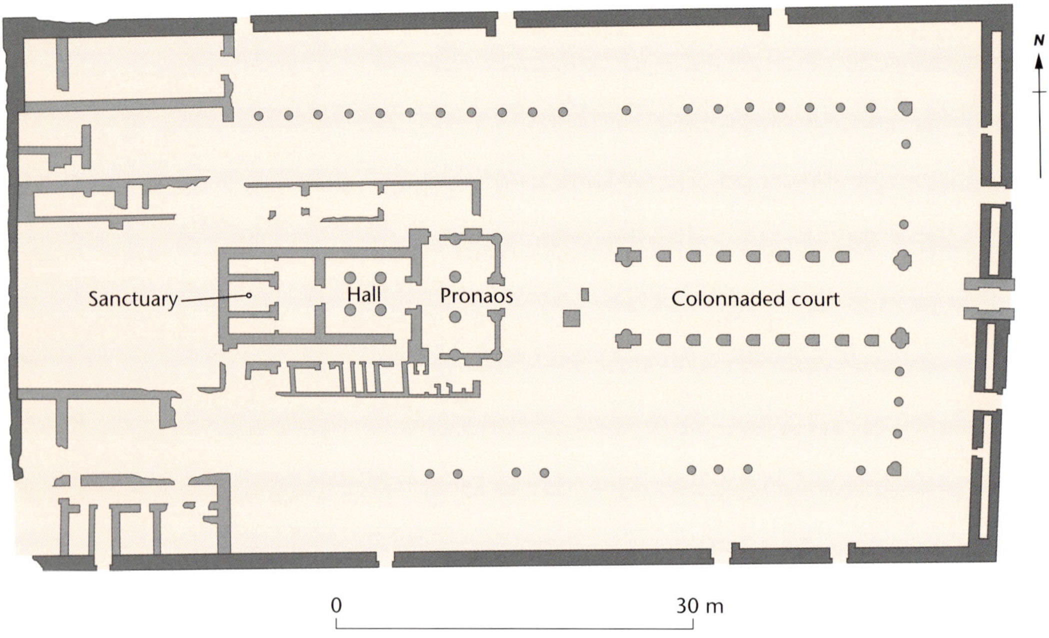

Fig. 9.3.1 Deir el-Haggar (after Mills 1999: 26).

with surviving paint, and interesting graffiti just inside the outer gate. It was dedicated to the Theban triad. In the area north and east of Amheida there are remains of more than a dozen **farmhouses** at several locations, of the Roman period (col. pl. 9.3.2). These typically consist of two levels, the upper one a pigeon house. Some are very well preserved, but none has been fully excavated.

Bibliography: *Deir el-Haggar*: Mills 1999; *El-Muzawwaka*: Whitehouse 1998; Osing 1982: 70–117; *Roman farmhouses*: Mills 1993; *Amheida*: www.learn.columbia.edu/amheida.

9.3.c Central Dakhla

The capital of the oasis today, and its largest city in antiquity, was **Mothis** (modern Mut). The remains of the ancient city are on the south-west side of the modern town and include the (pre-Hellenistic) temple, the remains of a massive wall, and a large ancient well. They had already a century ago suffered greatly both in extent and in condition, but excavations by an Australian team began in 2001.

North-east from Mothis lies the site of **Ain el-Gadida**, excavated by the SCA in 1993–5. This substantial mudbrick complex of buildings, dated by the excavator to the fourth-fifth century on the basis of the similarity of their finds to those from Kellis, contains largely domestic quarters, including cooking facilities. The several adjacent buildings total some 145 rooms. It has been suggested that it may have been a monastic settlement related to Kellis; such establishments are known from the documents. But no specifically Christian material has come to light at this site so far.

Kellis (modern Ismant el-Kharab) was in the Roman period the central village of the portion of Dakhla to the east of Mothis and the third-largest settlement of Dakhla. It was probably the capital of a toparchy in the nome dependent on Mothis. In more than two decades of exploration by an Australian team, it has become the most productive Roman site in Egypt excavated in recent times. With remains covering an area of about 1 km x 650 m, it was a substantial settlement. The areas excavated to date include the main temple, the only standing temple dedicated to Tutu. Substantial remains of wall paintings have been found in this building, which goes back at least to the first century AD.

In the north part of the site is a Roman complex of 216 rooms, including a large peristyle courtyard, of unknown purpose; only part of this has been excavated. The building was reused for domestic purposes,

Fig. 9.3.3
The site of Kellis (after Knudstad and Frey 1999: 194–5).

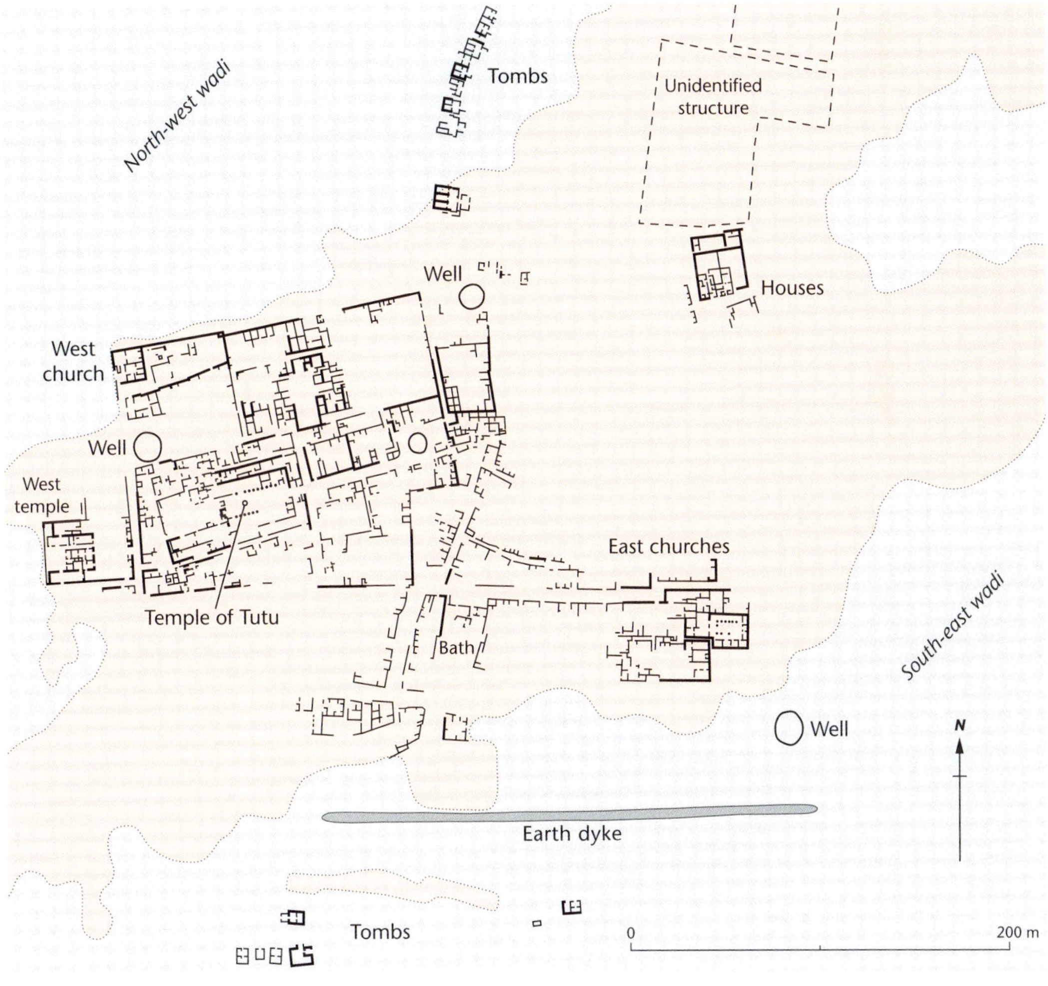

Manichaeans at Kellis

The Coptic letters from Kellis are the largest body of Manichaean correspondence to survive from antiquity, with a mixture of religious feeling, elaborate personal expressions and practical concerns. Here is one letter probably from the 350s:

My brother, my master, the loved one of my soul and my spirit, the child of righteousness, the good limb of the Light Mind, the name which is sweet in my mouth, my beloved brother Hor. It is I, Horion, greetings in the Lord God. There is no measuring the joy that came to me when I received your letter; all the more, for I learned about your health. I brought . . . everything concerning my father. I have hurried writing to you of these two matters; while I greet your gentleness and your immutable, never-changing love. I have received the jar of oil from our son Raz. Look, I left it [with them] for the *agape*, as you said. You also write: 'Buy 6 matia of wheat.' I will buy them at 1200 to the artaba; thus 705 nummi for these 6 matia. I have also received the jlge (a cloth bag?) from our son Pateni (?). Look, I filled it and sent it by way of Raz. When you receive it, write to me. Do not bother (?) yourself about the agape. I will do it gladly. Yes, our brother Pakous is south of the ditch, harvesting. If he does not come by that day, I will send his share south to him. Greet warmly for me those who give you rest, the elect and the catechumens, each one by name. Greet our father Kele. Our son Aetios greets you warmly. Our mother Taese greets you and all who are in the house. Be well and live for a long time, my beloved brother, until we see one another again and my joy is complete.

(*P.Kell.* V Copt. 15)

including animals, in the fourth century. A number of houses to the south of this area have been excavated, yielding most of the written material on papyrus and wood from the site. A considerable body of letters and religious texts in Greek, Coptic and Syriac concern a Manichean community in Kellis; many others document the economic life of Kellis and its surroundings. Box 9.3

Also notable at Kellis are the early fourth-century churches, a pair to the east and one at the west end of the site. The East Churches include a three-aisled basilica, with a raised apse and a row of side rooms, and a smaller adjacent church; these are now partly reburied. The West Church is adjacent to some imposing tombs and a Christian cemetery.

Bibliography: *Ain el-Gadida*: Bayumi 1998; *Kellis*: Hope 1999; Knudstad and Frey 1999.

9.3.d Eastern Dakhla

Relatively little excavation of Roman sites has taken place in the east part of the oasis, which is separated from the area of Kellis by a substantial stretch of desert, estimated by Winlock in the early twentieth century as 10–15 km, and which was probably in the Roman period much less important than the central and western zone. It was, however, the point where the roads both to Kharga and to Lykopolis entered the oasis.

A small site on a hill overlooking the village of Tineida may have been a temple complex. There are a number of Hellenistic-Roman tombs in the village of **Bashendi**, the most famous of them the Tomb of Kitines (probably first–second century), with reliefs and inscriptions on the doorways along the east-west axis and in Room 2. The occupant's name was not Egyptian, unlike his father's, but it has not been securely identified, and it has been suggested that his mother's name was Libyan. This cemetery probably belonged to a village located in the plain to the east of the village, where a small brick temple and remains of domestic or agricultural buildings can be seen; the name of this ancient village is not known, and it has not been excavated.

Bibliography: *Bashendi tombs*: Osing 1982: 57–69; *Settlement near Bashendi*: Winlock 1936: 17–18.

SELECTED GPS READINGS		
Deir el-Haggar	N 25.39.93	E 28.48.75
El-Muzawwaka	N 25.40.84	E 28.50.31
Roman farmhouses	N 25.41.54	E 28.49.87
Amheida	N 25.40.12	E 28.52.50
Mut	N 25.29.69	E 28.58.80
Kellis	N 25.31.08	E 29.05.71
Bashendi	N 25.31.61	E 29.17.74

9.4 BAHARIYA

9.4.a Introduction

The Small Oasis of antiquity, Bahariya is documented in papyri from valley towns to a degree not true of any other oasis. In part this is because it was closely tied – economically, socially, and administratively – to the nome of Oxyrhynchos (6.2.d), where the shortest road (about 190 km) to the valley terminated, and Oxyrhynchos has been one of the richest of all sources of papyri. The Small Oasis also had close ties with the Fayyum villages from which the caravans on the 270 km road between these areas departed, Dionysias and Soknopaiou Nesos, and these too have produced documents.

Because few documents have been found in Bahariya itself, however, our knowledge of the Small Oasis is very uneven. The modern capital, Bawiti-Qasr, is generally and for good reason supposed to occupy the site of the ancient metropolis of the nome, Psobthis, but this is not directly proven by any evidence, and only one other place name attested in the documents can be attached to a known site. The Small Oasis was indeed the smallest of the group; it is hard to judge to what extent the 1954 figures for cultivated land – 1000 hectares (2500 acres) in

Bahariya, 8000 hectares (20,000 acres) in Kharga plus Dakhla – are proportionately in line with ancient realities, but they are suggestive. Bahariya today is divided into two parts separated by about 40 km of desert. Its southern pendant, the El-Heiz area, was certainly well developed in antiquity and must have formed part of the Small Oasis. Whether the intervening area was less barren than now is not clear. Nor is it evident whether Farafra was thought of as another southern dependency of the Small Oasis.

9.4.b Central Bahariya

For the most part, ancient Psobthis presumably lies under modern Qasr, the older part of the oasis capital. There are scattered remains of the ancient town visible, not least the numerous worked-stone blocks built into the walls of houses. Many of these probably come from the **Temple of Ammon and Herakles**, the location of which has been determined from parts of walls remaining in place and from epigraphical evidence. Its construction goes back to the reign of Amasis (Dynasty 26). Not far from it is the curious Roman arch, a multi-level structure that appears to have articulated the juncture between the higher area inside the town and the lower-lying garden zone outside it. Much of its superstructure was visible in the nineteenth century but has now disappeared.

At the other end of town, in Bawiti, part of an ancient **qanat system** (Ain el-Hubaga) can be seen, including the enormous open-spring basin at the head of the line of wells. This is located next to the offices and magazine of the SCA just off the main street.

One indicator of the size and importance of this metropolis is its cemeteries. Best known is the very large and undisturbed cemetery found during the past decade south-west of the city, now famous as the **'Valley of the Golden Mummies'** even though only a small fraction of the bodies found actually fit that description. The tombs excavated by the Egyptian authorities so far belong to the Roman period; these constitute, however, only a tiny sliver of the thousands estimated to have been buried here. The tombs are cut into the rocky plateau, and many of them are complex, multi-chambered structures with a number of bodies in each room, even stacked up like wood. The most interesting funerary monuments of Bahariya, however, go back to Dynasty 26; these include a whole series of large tombs around Bawiti, particularly at Ain el-Muftillah on the north-west side of the town. An underground gallery for the burial of sacred ibis birds at Qaret el-Faragi was in use down at least to the Ptolemaic period and perhaps the Roman. Ahmed Fakhry, the pioneer of oasis archaeology, listed a dozen 'most important' cemeteries around Qasr Bawiti, occupying all of the small hills around the town.

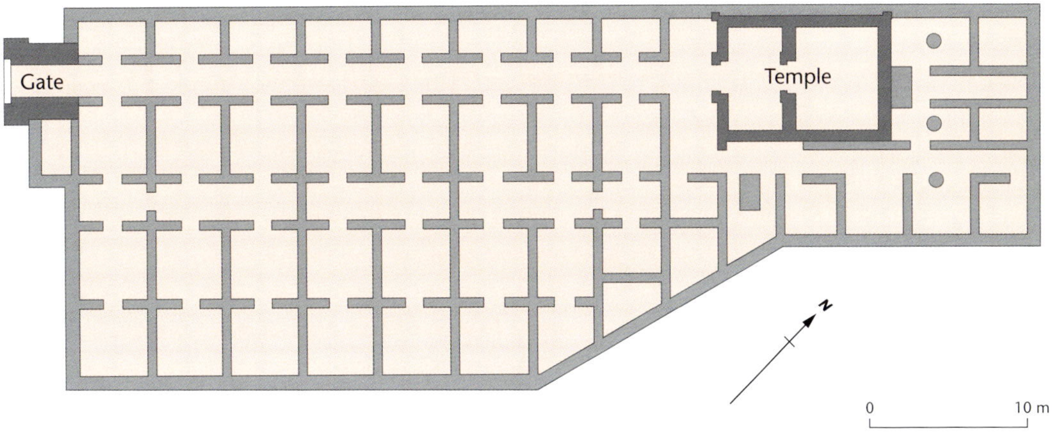

Fig. 9.4.1
The Temple of Alexander (after Fakhry 1974: 102).

Not far north-west of the cemetery, at el-Megysba, is the so-called **Temple of Alexander**, a curious structure with multiple periods of building. The core is a stone temple, the sanctuary of which has shallow reliefs which formerly contained the cartouche of Alexander, now ruined. The reliefs show the king sacrificing before Amun and other divinities. A considerable warren of mudbrick rooms has been built to one side of the main complex, and some of the original rooms have been subdivided. The location of the temple near the point where the track to Siwa leaves Bahariya has led to suggestions that the complex served as a *caravanserai*, but this seems unlikely, given its proximity to the city. Ostraka found here include an order addressed to a monk for him to pay an *artaba* of wheat to a soldier. It is thus possible that the building in its last phase was monastic or ecclesiastical, part of the village named Poka mentioned in an ostrakon.

About 9 km east of Bawiti is one of the more substantial Roman settlements of this oasis, **Qasr Muharib**. The main part of the site, about 110 x 170 m, consists of a number of mudbrick buildings, some preserved to the second storey, and one with some limestone elements (perhaps a temple). One building has been identified as a small fort. To the west a few hundred metres is a second area with sherd scatter and remains of walls, evidently the site described as Dinisah (from Arabic *kinisa*, 'church') by Fakhry.

Bibliography: *Temple of Ammon and Herakles*: Wagner 1974; *'Valley of the Golden Mummies'*: Hawass 2000; *Tombs of Dynasty 26*: Fakhry 1942; *Temple of Alexander*: Fakhry 1974: 99–102; Wagner 1987: 202–3; *Qasr Muharib*: Fakhry 1974: 106, 108.

9.4.c El-Heiz

The most important archaeological zone of the southern part of the Small Oasis is a somewhat dispersed cluster of late Roman remains

Fig. 9.4.2 Church of St George.

some 40 km south of Bawiti-Qasr, in a valley now uncultivated except for a few areas on the edges. There are no pre-Roman remains known so far, and the ancient name of the place is unknown. There is a small mudbrick fort, **Qasr Masuda**, poorly preserved particularly on the inside but probably the home of a modest detachment of Roman auxiliaries. Nearby is a very large and almost entirely unexcavated habitation site. One large building was described by Fakhry (who excavated there in 1945) as a 'mansion or palace'. Like the 'administrative building' at Ain el-Qurayshat in Siwa, it has a colonnaded hall with a raised dais. The site is, however, a large one, and Fakhry suggested that the sherd-covered mounds probably would reveal other such structures. Some 500 m away is the very substantial (about 10 x 20 m) **Church of St George**, so called because of a riding figure in wall paintings still visible to early travellers in the nineteenth century. It is a two-storey basilica in mudbrick, now in more ruinous condition than a half-century ago when Fakhry described it, and undergoing restoration. A staircase in the south-

SELECTED GPS READINGS

Temple of Ammon and Herakles	N 28.21.26	E 28.51.50
Qanat in Bawiti	N 28.20.87	E 28.52.29
'Valley of the Golden Mummies'	N 28.19.79	E 28.49.53
Temple of Alexander	N 28.20.54	E 28.49.34
Qusur Muharib	N 28.20.78	E 28.58.47
Qasr Masuda	N 28.00.46	E 28.41.85
Church of St George	N 28.00.68	E 28.41.92

west corner, across from the entrance to the narthex, led to the balconies, as did a second staircase in the south-east corner. The interior had eight massive columns dividing the space into three aisles.

Bibliography: *Qasr Masuda*: Fakhry 1974: 115–24; *Church of St George*: Fakhry 1974: 114–19.

9.5 SIWA

9.5.a Introduction

The Ammoniac oasis, called Santariya by the early Arab writers, home of the celebrated oracle of Ammon, occupied a place in Egyptian history different from that of the other oases. Its remoteness is extreme. The modern road connection to Cairo via Bahariya is about 750 km, and even air distance to Memphis is about 560 km. Camel caravans took at least twelve days. The other approach, much more common both in antiquity and now, is along the coast from Alexandria to Paraitonion (modern Marsa Matruh) and then across the desert south-south-west to Siwa, each leg about 300 km by modern road and only a little less by ancient routes. The shortest crossing to a watered place was the eight days to Paraitonion, from which a ship could be taken to Alexandria. Siwa has over the centuries had abundant water sources nearer the surface than any of the other oases but generally poor drainage, leading to salinity.

Siwa's early ties were much more with Libya, and the sanctuary developed a close relationship with the archaic Greek settlements in Cyrenaica, from which craftsmen were brought for construction projects. The population was of an indigenous Berber stock, speaking a local language still in use today. Alexander the Great's famous visit to the oracle in early 331 BC is emblematic of its prestige in the classical Greek world, but there is little to suggest that the oasis was securely under the control of any outside power (even the Ptolemies) before the Roman period, and evidence from the Hellenistic period is scanty. With archaeological attention focused on the archaic and classical oracle sanctuary and its immediate surroundings, Roman Siwa was itself very little known until recently. Excavations have now begun to draw out a picture of Roman and late Roman oasis life, indicating that olives and olive oil were a major foundation of prosperity in that period – along with dates and salt, products of the oasis from early times.

9.5.b Around the centre

The famous **Oracle Temple of Aghurmi** (col. pl. 9.5.1), the Ammoneion, is perched high on a rocky hill, partly (and not entirely reassuringly)

Alexander the Great at Siwa

When Alexander had passed through the desert and was come to the place of the oracle, the prophet of Ammon gave him salutation from the god as from a father; whereupon Alexander asked him whether any of the murderers of his father had escaped him. To this the prophet answered by bidding him be more guarded in his speech, since his was not a mortal father. Alexander therefore changed the form of his question, and asked whether the murderers of Philip had all been punished; and then, regarding his own empire, he asked whether it was given to him to become lord and master of all mankind. The god gave him answer that this was given to him, and that Philip was fully avenged. Then Alexander made splendid offerings to the god and gave his priests large gifts of money. This is what most writers state regarding the oracular responses; but Alexander himself, in a letter to his mother, says that he received certain secret responses, which he would tell to her, and to her alone, on his return. And some say that the prophet, wishing to show his friendliness by addressing him with '*O paidion*', or 'O my son', in his foreign pronunciation ended the word with 's' instead of 'n', and said '*O paidios*', and that Alexander was pleased at the slip in pronunciation, and a story became current that the god had addressed him with '*O pai Dios*', or 'O son of Zeus'.

(Plutarch, *Life of Alexander*, 27; transl. B. Perrin, Loeb Classical Library)

supported on ancient and modern substructures. The independent local Libyan princes also had their residence on the hill. Around it is an Islamic-period mudbrick village, no longer inhabited, with a mosque. The temple was built by a Greek workforce, probably from Cyrene, and for the most part goes back to pre-Hellenistic times. Although the god Amun is Egyptian, the cult at Siwa was partly Libyan and the god is referred to in Greek sources by the Cyrenaean form of his name, Ammon. Its great fame belongs to the classical period, when it was ranked with Delphi and Dodona, and to Alexander's visit, on which his claims to divinity were later said to have been founded. There is hardly any evidence for its continued importance in the Hellenistic period, and Strabo reports that in the time of Augustus it was almost abandoned. Box 9.5

The processional way of ancient times led from the front of the Oracle Temple down the south side of the hill and across a plain. Small bits of this *dromos*, used for oracular processions, have been uncovered; it was made of massive stone blocks and was undoubtedly very impressive. It led 400 m south to the contra-temple at **Umm Ubayda**, today a mass of stone blocks lying askew, full of robbed-out areas. Excavators have concluded that unlike the Oracle Temple it was built by Egyptians, with its nucleus going back to Nektanebo II and additions in the Hellenistic and Roman periods. A third temple, only partly excavated, has been found just south-west of the *dromos*; it is also built of large limestone ashlar masonry and is aligned to the *dromos*. Greek mason's marks have been found on some of the blocks. Down a path from Umm Ubayda lies a large circular pool fed by springs, the

Fig. 9.5.2
Siwa, the Oracle Temple (after Kuhlmann 1988: 16).

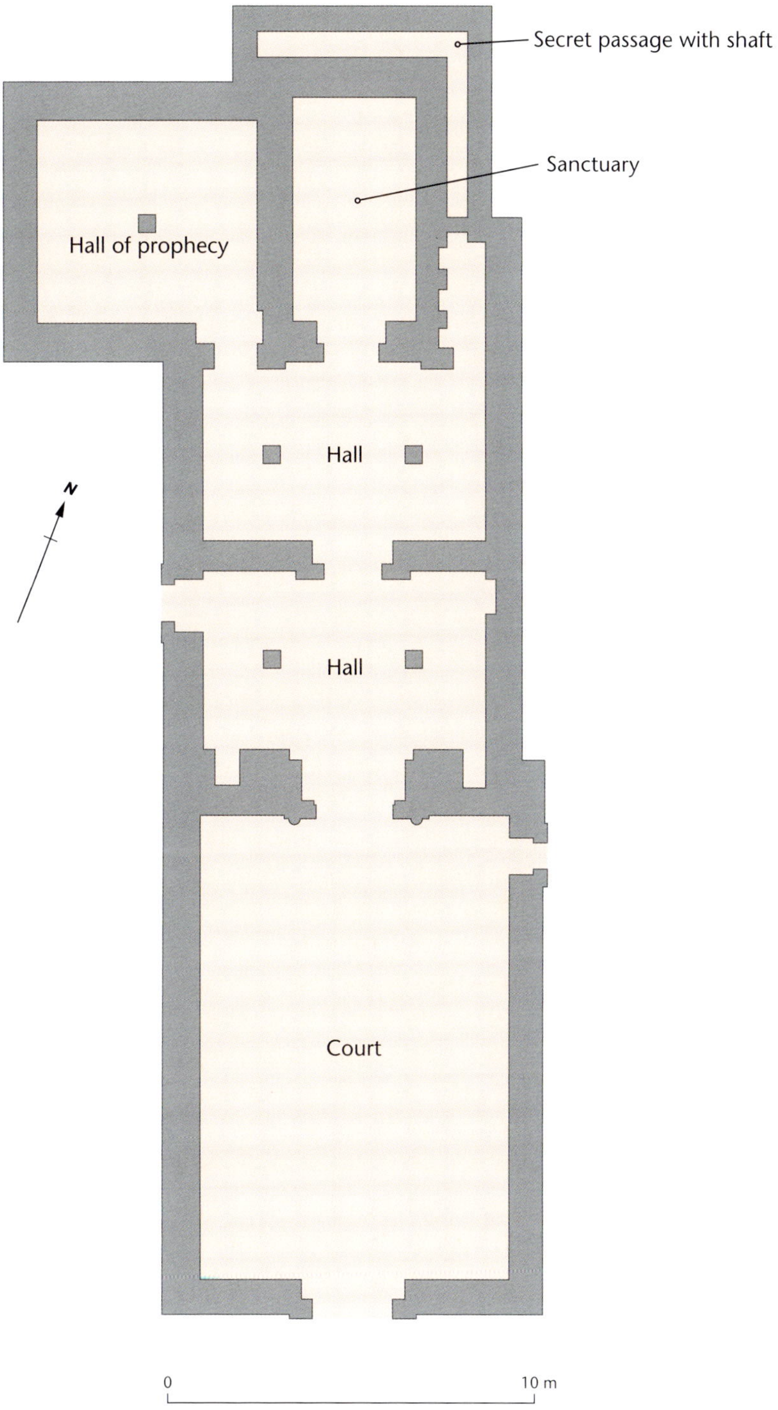

modern descendant of the **Spring of the Sun** (that is, sacred to Ammon) mentioned by ancient authors.

Gebel Mawta, the 'mountain of the dead', was the main necropolis of the oasis capital in antiquity, with hundreds of tombs. (It may also have served an ancient community lying under the medieval remains on the mound at nearby Shali, the modern centre.) Like other such necropolis zones, it is a conical hill with bands of good-quality rock suitable for cutting tombs. There is a combination of multi-room underground complexes, probably shared by multiple families, and smaller tombs cut horizontally into the side of the hill. The most famous of the latter is the painted tomb of Siamun, probably late Hellenistic or early Roman (there are Greek graffiti of the early Roman period), who is depicted both as a clean-shaven Egyptian and a bearded Greek. The tombs more generally range from Dynasty 26 to the Roman period.

Fig. 9.5.3
Siwa, Gebel Mawta.

Bibliography: *Aghurmi, Oracle Temple*: Kuhlmann 1988; *Umm Ubayda, contra-temple*: Kuhlmann 1988; *Gebel Mawta*: Fakhry 1973: 173–206.

9.5.c Eastern Siwa

Although a few monuments to the north-east of the lake now called Birket Zeitun have long been known, it is only recent excavations that have started to give an idea of the scale and character of ancient settlement in this zone. At least six substantial villages with facilities for oil production are known to have stood in this area, only a small fraction of which has been excavated. The remains appear to belong for the most part to the first four centuries AD.

Moving from north-west to south-east, the first major site is **Ain el-Qurayshat**, a village with an enormous 'industrial zone' containing an estimated total of sixty to seventy olive oil presses, some forty-five of which have been excavated. Each of these presses is modest in size, using several stacked millstones on a small gypsum-plastered basin (about 1.6 m^2), but if each produced 10 kg of oil a day the total output would be very considerable. Siwan olive oil was highly valued, as it is today. Adjacent are residential areas, with rubble foundations and mud-brick upper parts, mostly built around large courtyards, as well as a building (*c.* 15.4 x 16.2 m) identified as an administrative centre, with a dais at the centre of a large hall (cf. 9.4.c on Qasr Masuda in Bahariya Oasis). A temple still well preserved a century ago is now a heap of rubble. An ancient spring nearby is still in operation, but the accumulation of salt in the immediate area is impressive and most of the surroundings still wasteland.

Abu Shuruf is similar in character, but much of it is under modern houses. The major monument for which the site is known is its stone temple with plastered walls and vaulted roof, about 9 x 11 m, standing well preserved amid later brick houses. Its entrance is to the north; to the right after entering is a staircase to the roof, to the left a room. Ahead is a complex with a central hall and four side rooms. The cult niche is at the south end of the hall. The date of the temple is probably Roman. At **Abu el-Awwaf** is a major necropolis zone, a few kilometres north-northeast of the agricultural area where the villages are located, with rock-cut chamber tombs in a low ridge and a number of mostly ruined freestanding limestone tomb chapels over tombs cut below the flat surface of the ridge. The high quality of the chapels, with a mixture of Egyptian and Greek architectural features, much better preserved in the nineteenth century than now, suggests that they belonged to wealthy local residents. The cemetery is also probably of Roman date.

El-Zeitoun by its name ('the olives') suggests that it also belongs to the olive-producing zone; the modern village, part of a large estate in the late nineteenth to twentieth century, is abandoned, but the adjacent ancient site has not yet been excavated. There is a small limestone temple here also, more carefully built than that of Abu Shuruf.

Bibliography: *Ain el-Qurayshat*: Kuhlmann 1998: 166–7; *Abu Shuruf*: Fakhry 1973: 130–2; Kuhlmann 1998: 167-8; *Abu el Awwaf*: Fakhry 1973: 132–4; Kuhlmann 1998: 168–70; *El-Zeitoun*: Fakhry 1973: 132–5; Kuhlmann 1998: 168.

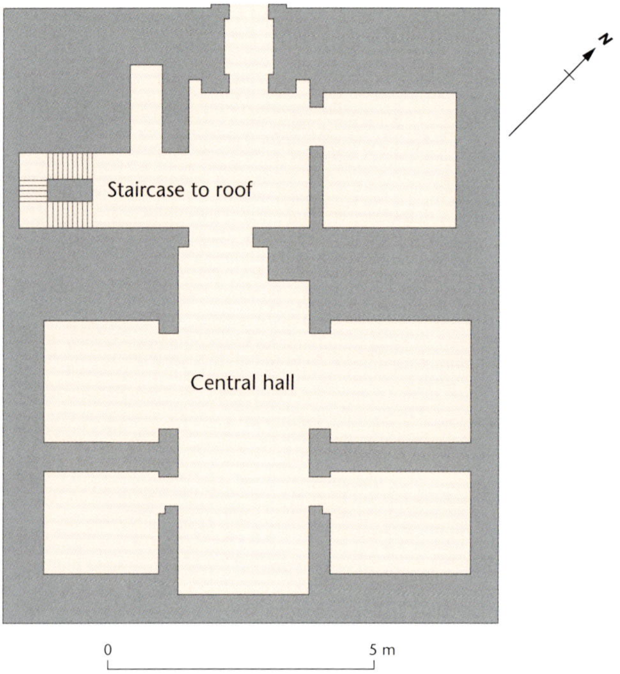

Fig. 9.5.4 Temple of Abu Shuruf (after Fakhry 1973: 131).

9.5.d Western Siwa

There are many rock-cut cemeteries in the western part of the oasis, some with elaborate architectural features. The most important archaeological area west of Aghurmi, however, is **Bilad el-Rum**, the 'village of the Romans'. Coming from the central part of the oasis, one arrives first at the necropolis, with tombs cut into the hillside on several levels. Recent excavations have uncovered extensive freestanding structures in

SELECTED GPS READINGS		
Aghurmi, Oracle Temple	N 29.12.29	E 25.32.64
Umm Ubayda, contra-temple	N 29.12.11	E 25.32.69
Well of the Sun	N 29.11.82	E 25.33.01
Gebel Mawta	N 29.12.67	E 25.31.40
Ain el-Qurayshat	N 29.12.49	E 25.42.73
Abu Shuruf	N 29.10.87	E 25.44.80
Abu el-Awaf turn-off	N 29.10.02	E 25.48.33
Abu el-Awwaf, site	N 29.10.00	E 25.48.37
El-Zeitoun	N 29.09.17	E 25.47.36
Bilad el-Rum, necropolis	N 29.13.65	E 25.24.42
Bilad el-Rum, 'Doric temple'	N 29.13.76	E 25.23.98

front of the rock-cut chambers, again on several levels. The facing of the fronts is in cut stone blocks, the remainder being mudbrick with whitewashed plaster. The latest burials in these tombs are Christian, and some Greek inscriptions have been found. Nearby is a large brick structure that has been variously identified as a fort or church, but which is perhaps in fact a large tomb chapel. The Christian remains are important particularly because the oasis is often regarded as a late bastion of Egyptian religion, and the life of the Coptic monk Samuel of Qalamun (5.4.c) depicts the Berbers as worshipping the sun (Alcock 1983).

The so-called **'Doric temple'** described by nineteenth-century travellers lies nearby. This is the building notoriously claimed to be the tomb of Alexander the Great by the Greek excavators who worked here from 1989–96. (Alexander was actually buried in Alexandria; 2.1.c.) Inside an enclosure wall is a long, narrow temple structure of distinctive plan. The axial entrance leads to a long room, which also has three entrances on each of its long sides. There are also footings for a longitudinal colonnade on both sides of this large room. From this room there is a door, at the end opposite the entrance, into a series of three smaller rooms axially arranged. The entrance to the temple yielded an inscription recording the reconstruction of the temple under the Trajanic prefect Servius Sulpicius Rufus (107–12). The temple plan and much of the decor are Egyptian, but there are many Greek architectural elements responsible for the temple's popular name and for the early traveller Cailliaud's judgement that it was the most beautiful monument of the oasis. The preference for the Doric order in the second century may be another indication of Cyrenaean cultural influence even at this late date.

Bibliography: *Bilad el-Rum, 'Doric temple'*: Fakhry 1973: 126–7.

10.2.1 Desert road network.

10 THE EASTERN DESERT

10.1 INTRODUCTION

The desert between the Nile Valley and the Red Sea is a large area mainly composed of stony terrain, much of it mountainous. In these mountains and the gully systems (wadis) running through them, barren though they look from the air and even from the ground, lay important resources, including gold and desirable building stone. There was also more available water from wells than might seem likely, and in some places run-off from the rare but torrential rains was captured in cisterns. On the Red Sea coast, successive Ptolemaic and Roman governments developed trading ports, particularly Berenike and Myos Hormos, from which and to which most trade between the Mediterranean and India and East Africa sailed, and which also had close connections to the west and south coasts of Arabia. From these exotic sources came pepper and other spices, ivory, pearls and perfumes. Both of these economic spheres – natural resources and trade – were important to the government, and particularly in the first two centuries of the Roman empire tremendous resources were put to work in maintaining a network of roads, wells and small forts through the desert.

The people who maintained this network left behind enough debris that the Eastern Desert has also been a tremendously rich source of textual material, mostly written on potsherds (ostraka) and mostly found in excavations during the last couple of decades. The bulk of these are letters, mostly short and to the point, dealing with needs for supplies, but many other types of texts are also found.

The last two decades have seen not only accelerated archaeological exploration of the Eastern Desert but increased tourism, fuelled in part by the rapid development of resorts along the Red Sea coast and in part by the wider availability of four-wheel drive vehicles, which make many otherwise inaccessible sites reachable. Real-estate development has engulfed sites like Abu Sha'ar, a Late Antique fort and Christian settlement north of Hurghada, and the pressure of tourism has damaged sites like Mons Claudianus and Mons Porphyrites, located near major resorts. Many of the desert stations, mining camps, and sanctuaries, however, are still remote. They are numerous, and only a selection of the most significant is described here.

The modern road system parallels the ancient only in part; details are given in the next section (10.2). The Red Sea resort towns provide abundant hotels to serve as a base for exploration of the area. Many sites are on or near the main roads, but some

(particularly Mons Porphyrites and its area) require four-wheel drive vehicles. The inspectorate for the Eastern Desert of the Supreme Council for Antiquities is based at Qena.

Bibliography: Jackson 2002.

10.2 DESERT ROADS AND STATIONS

Over the hundreds of years of Ptolemaic and Roman exploitation of the desert region, a number of major roads were built (or rebuilt) and equipped with way-stations where water (from wells and cisterns) and shelter were available. Many of these were fully developed and fortified only as late as the period from Vespasian to Hadrian. All of the roads include a network of by-ways to other sites, often mining camps, that will not be described here. The complete Roman system included four points of departure in the Nile Valley. The main terminus for the quarry area was **Kaine** (modern Qena), from which ran a road to the north-northeast, forking at al-Aras 25 km north into a northern route leading past Mons Porphyrites and on to the coast at Abu Sha'ar and a southern route leading to Mons Claudianus and other mining and quarrying areas to its south. The principal road from Qena today runs south of Mons Claudianus to Safaga, the port and transit town for pilgrimage to Mecca.

The major emporium for the caravan routes to the Red Sea ports in the Roman period was **Koptos** (modern Qift). The road from Koptos ran south-east 35 km to a fork at Phoinikon (modern El-Laqeita), from which the road to Myos Hormos (Quseir) ran east through the Wadi Hammamat, as does the modern road (see below) and that to Berenike continued south-east through the stations of Didymoi, Aphrodites and so on via Vetus Hydreuma (Wadi Abu Greiya) to Berenike. Excavations at Didymoi have produced large numbers of ostraka.

From **Apollonopolis Magna** (modern Edfu), still further to the south, another and older road for the caravan traffic ran east to the Pan sanctuary at El-Kanaïs, where it forked into a road running south-east that joined the Koptos-Berenike road at Falakro and a road east to Marsa Nakari. Spurs from these roads also reached some mining operations. The Edfu-Berenike route seems to have been used principally in the Ptolemaic period, with the Koptos-Berenike road supplanting it in the Roman period. Today's road from Edfu to the coast bears somewhat to the north of the ancient road, reaching the coast at Marsa Alam.

The final piece of the road system was the **Via Hadriana**, a road constructed by the orders of the emperor Hadrian, running from Antinoopolis (6.3.c) to the north-east through the mountains, then looping south-east to the coast and running along the coast all the way to Berenike. It was a long and generally well-engineered road, parts of which can still be traced today; the modern coast road follows its traces only in part.

Bibliography: *Kaine-Myos Hormos*: Sidebotham, Zitterkopf and Riley 1991; Cuvigny 2003; *Koptos-Berenike*: Sidebotham 2002; *Edfu-Berenike*: Sidebotham 2002; *Via Hadriana*: Sidebotham, Zitterkopf and Helms 2000.

SELECTED GPS READINGS		
Phoinikon (El-Laqeita)	N 25.53.07	E 33.07.26
Didymoi (Khashm el-Menih)	N 25.45.30	E 33.23.58
Vetus Hydreuma (Wadi Abu Greiya)	N 24.03.68	E 35.17.23

10.2.a Koptos (Egyptian *Kbt*) was located about halfway between the Nile and the edge of the desert. From it departed the caravans of camels and donkeys bound for the ports of Myos Hormos and Berenike. Koptos was not only a caravan hub, however, it was a major religious and administrative centre of considerable antiquity and the home of a cavalry unit in Roman times. Although it is said to have been destroyed under Diocletian for its part in a revolt, it in fact survived into Late Antiquity, its fortunes fluctuating with those of the desert traffic for trade or mining. (For the history and monuments of Koptos, see 8.3.) It became the seat of bishops, from one of whom, Pisenthios (AD 569–632), a considerable cache of correspondence in Coptic has survived. It was fed by a canal from the Nile, which ended in a basin that served as the harbour for shipping coming upriver on the Nile and the terminus for the roads to the Red Sea ports. This was the location of the customs house through which all of this trade passed and where the duty on goods leaving or entering Egypt was collected. Individuals also paid a tax at departure from the country, in amounts varying by their status, as well as a fee for the use of the desert roads.

Box 10.2

Bibliography Boussac 2002; Burkhalter 2002; *Coptos* 2000; Cuvigny 2000a.

The tariff of Koptos

This famous stela (Bernand 1984, no. 67), now in the Graeco-Roman Museum, Alexandria, was found at the beginning of the ancient desert road in 1894. On order of Mettius Rufus, prefect of Egypt at the time of Domitian, the tolls for leaving Egypt and for using the desert road were officially announced on a limestone stela. When they left Egypt by ship, males paid between 5 and 10 drachmas according to their occupation (sailors, shipbuilders 5 dr.; workmen and pilots 8 dr.; guards and officers 10 dr.); women paid double and prostitutes 108 dr. Tickets which gave permission to use the desert road were priced differently for males and females, for camels, donkeys, wagons, ship masts and even dead persons.

10.2.b The Koptos to Myos Hormos Road. The *Hodos Myshormitike*, as it was called in Greek, stretched 174 km from Koptos to Myos Hormos, a journey of five or six days under normal circumstances. Compared to the 392 km to Berenike, requiring twelve days or more, it was short. Given the expense of land transport in antiquity, this comparative proximity was valuable, but it did not always outweigh the difficulty of sailing against the wind up the gulf, particularly as the cargo vessels became larger. As a result of this handicap, Myos Hormos started to lose out to Berenike by the middle of the first century AD. Even so, it retained importance as a link for travellers and the imperial government to Arabia and to the mineral resources of the region.

The road, which runs in part through the flat-bottomed Wadi Hammamat, was in use even in prehistoric times and already in the Old Kingdom led to gold-mining and stone-quarrying operations. Its numerous graffiti testify to visitors across the millennia. The Ptolemaic interest in the India trade led to the development of the old port at the end of the road (see 10.4.c). Little trace remains today of Ptolemaic installations on this road. Its physical face belongs mainly to the first and second centuries, but excavators have noted that the Roman military kept the forts clean, even when they abandoned them; as a result, dating the construction of forts is difficult unless documents from the dump provide information.

The major stations along this road at its peak were, travelling east, **Phoinikon** (El-Laqeita), **Krokodilo** (El-Muwayh), **Persou** (Bir Umm Fawakhir), **Maximianon** (El-Zarqa), the best preserved despite the enormous crater where its cistern was, and **Bir Sayyala**. Other smaller stations used earlier or later have also been identified. Most of these have had some degree of excavation in recent years, including signifi-

Fig. 10.2.2
Maximianon

Fig. 10.2.3
Bir Umm Fawakhir,
the mining village.

cant discoveries of texts; these are for the most part not yet published. What had been unfortified shelters became forts under Vespasian, presumably as a result of increasing threats to travellers' security from desert tribes. The threats were real: an ostrakon from Krokodilo mentions a Bedouin attack on one of these forts, in which prisoners were taken. A quarrying village in the Wadi Hammamat was abandoned around the same time, probably also for security reasons. Apparently Vespasian's administration militarized both caravan roads, most likely in the 70s AD. Successive waves of abandonment and construction under the following emperors kept pace with changing circumstances.

After the early third century, the desert-road infrastructure was allowed to fall out of use, and except for signs of reoccupation in the period of Diocletian and the first tetrarchy, it is not until the fifth century AD that the government again found it worthwhile to support any significant establishment along this road. At that point, the gold- mining activity around **Bir Umm Fawakhir (Persou)** created a sizeable village, perhaps of a thousand inhabitants (about 216 buildings in the main settlement, clustered into larger compounds) 5 km north-east of Wadi Hammamat, which was mapped and surveyed in the 1990s. The house walls are well preserved and have many built-in stone features like niches and benches. The surrounding mountainsides are riddled with mines, both open trenches and tunnels, and there are many signs of crushing and grinding the quartz to extract the gold. Towers placed above and along the road may belong to this period and be connected to the mining in Bir Umm Fawakhir and at Bir al-Nakhil, near Quseir.

Bibliography: Brun 2002; Cuvigny 2003; Zitterkopf and Sidebotham 1989; *Bir Umm Fawakhir mining camp*: Meyer 2000; *Inscriptions*: Bernand 1972a.

SELECTED GPS READINGS		
Phoinikon (El-Laqeita)	N 25.53.07	E 33.07.26
Krokodilo	N 25.56.34	E 33.24.07
Wadi Hammamat graffiti	N 25.59.44	E 33.34.22
Persou	N 26.00.77	E 33.36.49
Maximianon	N 26.00.05	E 33.47.23

10.2.c The Edfu to Marsa Nakari Road. The first third of this route is identical with the first leg of the road from Edfu to Berenike. It includes the important Paneion at **El-Kanaïs**, from which numerous ancient travellers' inscriptions have been recorded. This temple is cut into the rock of the hillside and provided with a pillared façade, a rectangular *pronaos*, and three inner rooms. Originally a sanctuary of Ammon, it was the site of worship of Pan, the god of the desert, in the Hellenistic and Roman periods.

At **Abu Rahal**, a Ptolemaic to early Roman station, the road to Marsa Nakari diverges from the Berenike road. It passes through **Bir 'Iayyan**, an unfortified Ptolemaic station at the foot of a sandstone bluff, where an inscription from 257 BC was found. This records its erection by a toparch (a regional official) and gives the exact distance from the Nile. The road continues on to reach the gold-mining camp of **Barramiya**, no doubt a major reason for the existence of the road; spurs led to other mines as well. From there it continues on a westerly course before dipping south into **Marsa Nakari**, a site on the Red Sea from which only Roman pottery has so far been recovered. It has been speculated that this port was the Nechesia mentioned in the *Geography* of Claudius Ptolemy.

Bibliography: Sidebotham and Wendrich 1999: 364–9; *El-Kanaïs*: Bernand 1972a; *Bir 'Iayyan*: Bagnall 1996.

SELECTED GPS READINGS		
El-Kanaïs	N 25.03.32	E 33.18.56
Abu Rahal West	N 25.00.18	E 33.27.31
Abu Rahal	N 25.00.36	E 33.28.06
Bir 'Iayyan	N 25.02.50	E 33.43.28
Barramiya	N 25.04.14	E 33.47.47
Marsa Nakari	N 24.55.50	E 34.57.74

10.3 QUARRIES

Apart from its importance for the caravan routes to the sea, the desert contained many valuable resources. The earliest of these to have been exploited, in pharaonic times, was gold, which continued to be sought through the Roman period. That era saw an enormous increase in activity in the desert. Some of this was on a relatively small scale, but other ventures were large and can have been possible only with the financial and logistical involvement of the government. The emerald mines at Sikait (the ancient Mons Smaragdus, Emerald Mountain) are currently under excavation, and many more mining camps have been surveyed or excavated.

The most extensive extractive works of the imperial period, however, were for stone, particularly the grey granite of Mons Claudianus and the 'imperial porphyry' of Mons Porphyrites. Both of these have been studied in detail and partially excavated in the last two decades. Supporting the infrastructure of these quarries was enormously difficult and expensive, and the use of these stones thus served as a symbol of imperial wealth and power.

10.3.a The quarry-field of **Mons Claudianus** (col. pl. 10.3.2) is now one of the best known of the Roman world. Its quarries – some 130 small cuttings have been inventoried – produced the columns used for high-prestige imperial projects in Rome like the Temple of the Deified Trajan and the Pantheon. With a central fort and small 'villages' adjacent to the quarries, Mons Claudianus housed a community of as many as 900 individuals at its peak. This venture was expensive to maintain, for it required both regular supply caravans from the valley, a four- to five-day journey (fresh fish deliveries, fortunately, came from the nearby coast) and heavy transport to move the 100-ton columns the 120 km from the quarries to the Nile, a wagon journey that took perhaps twenty days for a hundred camels.

The quarry field lies at an elevation of about 700 m, with the hills rising only modestly above the wadis. The stone was a grey granodiorite. Water is available only at some depth (now 25 m below wadi level), requiring competent well construction; cisterns could hold some of the run-off from occasional rainstorms and supplement the wells. The central complex included the fort (which occupies more than half a hectare), a temple of Sarapis, a bathhouse, provisions for storage and an enormous complex for the care of the numerous animals needed both to supply the quarries and to haul the stone columns. As in general in the Eastern Desert, construction is mainly of dry stone walls, in this case of the local granodiorite; in the bath complex, fired brick is used in places.

Just 1 km to the south-west of the main complex is a smaller settle-

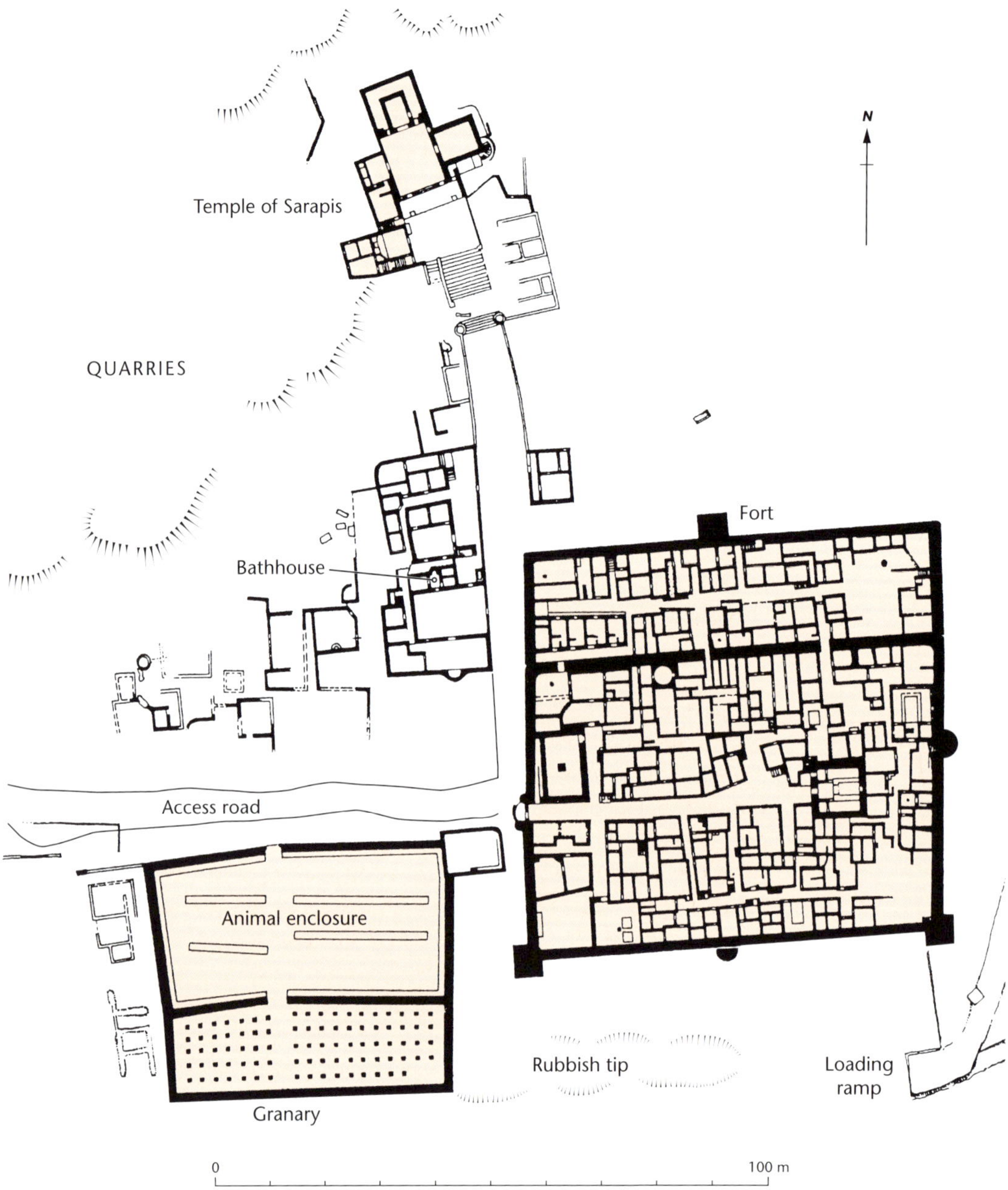

ment now referred to as the Hydreuma (well), although in fact it has no well. It consists of a small fort with a thick outer wall, and adjacent plaster-lined tanks and troughs. Across an erosion gully is a series of irregular buildings (interpreted as workers' housing). To the north-east is a substantial building on a hillside terrace, taken to be the commandant's house. The entire settlement, which existed before the main complex, is probably the original core of the Mons Claudianus quarrying operation.

Fig. 10.3.1
Mons Claudianus (after Peacock and Maxfield 1997: 23).

Food in the Desert

Feeding the large staff, military and civilian, of the quarrying and mining operations in the Eastern Desert posed a challenge to Roman logistics. Many of the letters on ostraka show that food did not always arrive on time: 'Zosimos to Kastor his brother, greetings. Please, brother, send me two loaves of bread. For no grain has come up here for me so far. Farewell' (*O.Claud.* II 284). Other letters ask for fresh produce, fish and other foods to provide variety in the diet. Despite the distance from the valley and the aridity of the desert, however, a remarkable range of foods, some of them very luxurious, made it to Mons Claudianus. Plant remains from the excavations have documented not only garlic, onions and cabbage, but artichoke, cucumber, beets, lettuce, cress, endive, purslane and a number of herbs. Many of these were grown in small gardens where well water was available. Expensive wines and oils, at least for the higher-ranking members of the staff, were also imported.

Box 10.3

Bibliography: Adams 2000; Bingen 1992, 1997; Peacock and Maxfield 1997; Van der Veen 1998.

SELECTED GPS READINGS		
Mons Claudianus, fort	N 26.48.55	E 33.29.20
Mons Claudianus, 'Hydreuma'	N 26.48.31	E 33.28.73

10.3.b The purple stone quarried at **Mons Porphyrites** was highly prized, its colour associated with imperial grandeur; the stone was used in the Temple of Venus and the Basilica of Maxentius at Rome and the imperial palace in Constantinople, among other structures. The quarry area, some 40 km from the modern resort centre of Hurghada, is not far from the coastal plain, but access is difficult even today, with the main route a stony track up a wadi subject to rare but violent deluges that bring down quantities of rock. The site consists of a core settlement ringed by quarry sites with their own encampments. The core includes a fort, a water supply, and two temples (of Sarapis and Isis). The workable stone lies high in the surrounding mountains, at altitudes reaching 1500 m or more, and the quarries are thus more distant and difficult of access than those at Mons Claudianus. The logistical difficulties of removing columns quarried in such locations were formidable, and the travel time (upwards of an hour from the core to some of the quarries) meant that the community lived in a more dispersed fashion than at Claudianus.

An inscription found in the 'Bradford' quarries, 1.7 km north of the fort, claims credit for the discovery of the quarries for Gaius Cominius Leugas. The stone gives an exact date for its erection of 23 July AD 18, or early in the reign of Tiberius. The stela also has a depiction of Pan (Egyptian Min), the ithyphallic god worshipped thoughout the deserts. The core settlement, by contrast, seems to be late first century AD or even later, under Domitian or Trajan. It probably accompanied the

Fig. 10.3.3
Badia, animal lines.

opening of additional quarries. The Lycabettus quarries, with five associated 'villages', were probably among these, and they remained active for a long time, being a major centre of activity in the fourth century, when the slipways and roads were repaired for shipping columns cut for use in Jerusalem.

The first station on the road from the quarries to the valley, Badia, has a well-preserved fort with animal lines. To the south-west is another quarry site, at Umm Balad, that apparently proved unsuccessful as a source of stone because the stone did not split cleanly. Recent excavations in its dump have yielded numerous ostraka, not yet published.

Bibliography: Maxfield and Peacock 1998, 2001a.

SELECTED GPS READINGS		
Mons Porphyrites, fort	N 27.15.03	E 33.18.09
Mons Porphyrites, loading ramp	N 27.18.40	E 33.21.29
Badia	N 27.12.86	E 33.20.69

10.4 PORTS

The Egyptian Red Sea coast is not in general a welcoming one, and ancient ships sailing north against the prevailing winds found few good harbours. The two best were those developed by the Ptolemies and Romans for their naval and trading activities to the south and east, Myos Hormos and Berenike. Both of these have been partly excavated and are discussed in more detail below. Others are known from ancient sources or from archaeological exploration, but it is still uncertain

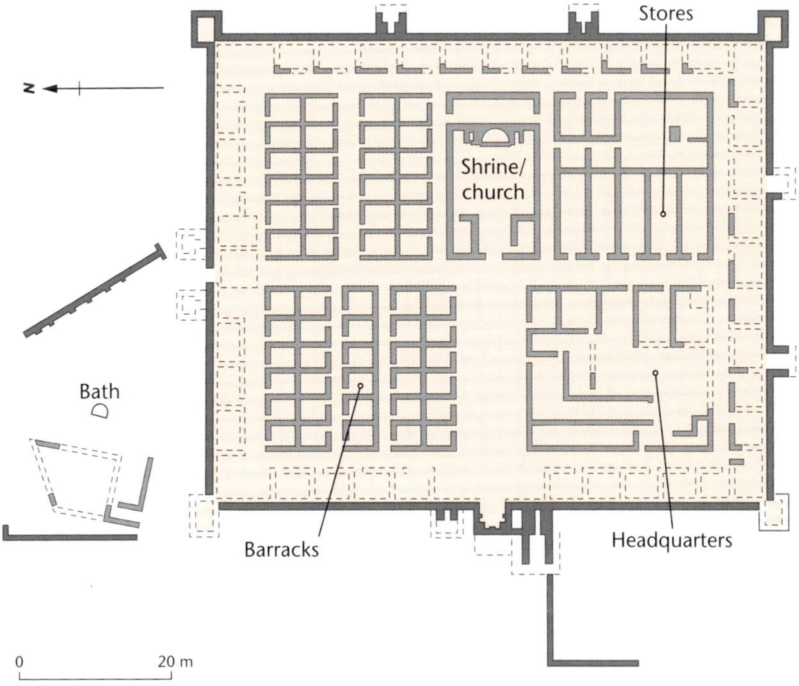

Fig. 10.4.1
Abu Sha'ar, fort
(after Sidebotham
1994: 135).

exactly where some known names like Nechesia and Leukos Limen are to be placed. A Roman fort was built *c.* 309–11 at the end of the road from Kaine to the coast, at **Abu Sha'ar**. After its abandonment by the military, the fort eventually became a Christian settlement, apparently a monastery. Texts found there show connections across the Red Sea, to Sinai or Arabia, and it appears that the headquarters area of the fort became a shrine attracting visitors, who probably came by water. But Abu Sha'ar never became a major port. Other ports have not yet been the subject of systematic exploration.

Bibliography: *Abu Sha'ar*: Bagnall and Sheridan 1994a, 1994b; Sidebotham 1994.

GPS READING		
Abu Sha'ar	N 27.22.13	E 33.40.97

10.4.c Recent archaeological discoveries have demonstrated that **Myos Hormos (Quseir)**, the location of which was long uncertain, was indeed located at or near the modern Quseir. The earliest remains found so far at Quseir el-Qadim ('ancient Quseir'), 10 km to the north of the modern town, are Roman. This was perhaps a new foundation under Augustus to take advantage of the sheltered port, from which Strabo tells us 120 ships sailed to India yearly just a few years after the

Roman conquest. The pharaonic and Ptolemaic port may have been at the modern town.

Quseir el-Qadim was laid out on a regular grid plan. Both stone and brick are found in the buildings, which are spread over a considerable area west of the modern road (the area to the east of the road has been developed). Some of the finds resemble those at Berenike, including teak and wine jars with their plugs. The textual finds, although not as rich as those at Berenike, were of numerous languages, including some from south India.

Bibliography: Bagnall 1986; Peacock 1999–2002; Whitcomb and Johnson 1979, 1982.

GPS READING		
Quseir el-Qadim	N 26.09.42	E 34.14.54

10.4.d Berenike, the most extensively studied of the Red Sea ports, and undoubtedly the most important, was located south of the latitude of Aswan at the head of a bay. Its southerly location – minimizing northward sailing distance – and good harbour were the compensations it offered for its great distance from the Nile Valley and its unpromising hinterland. It is possible that a skeleton population occupied the port during the off-season, supplemented by much larger numbers of service workers during the sailing season. But excavations have found industrial areas, including metalworking shops and brick-firing facilities, that show Berenike was not just a way-station, and the investment in buildings was considerable. However improbable the modern barrenness of the landscape makes it seem, clearly significant quantities of combustibles were found to support industrial activity and water brought in to make life possible. Box 10.4

Goods for India

The dump at Berenike has yielded numerous potsherds used to record permission to pass through the customs gate with goods, mostly wine. The majority give only the minimum information, like this one: 'Sosibios to Andouros, greetings. Let pass for Pakoibis son of Kleitos, 4 half-kadia of oil and 4 *Italika* of wine.' That these were to go on board ships is indicated by slightly fuller texts: 'Rhobaos to those in charge of the customs gate, greetings. Let pass for Petermenis son of Paminis 8 *ladikena* of wine, for outfitting.' (The *ladikenon* is a jar of wine from Laodicaea in Syria.) The ostraka thus confirm the statement of the *Periplus of the Erythraean* Sea (a sailor's manual): "In this port of trade [Barygaza, in India] there is a market for wine, principally Italian but also Laodicaean and Arabian." The Indian courts had a taste for Italian wine, whatever it may have tasted like after traveling from Campania to India.

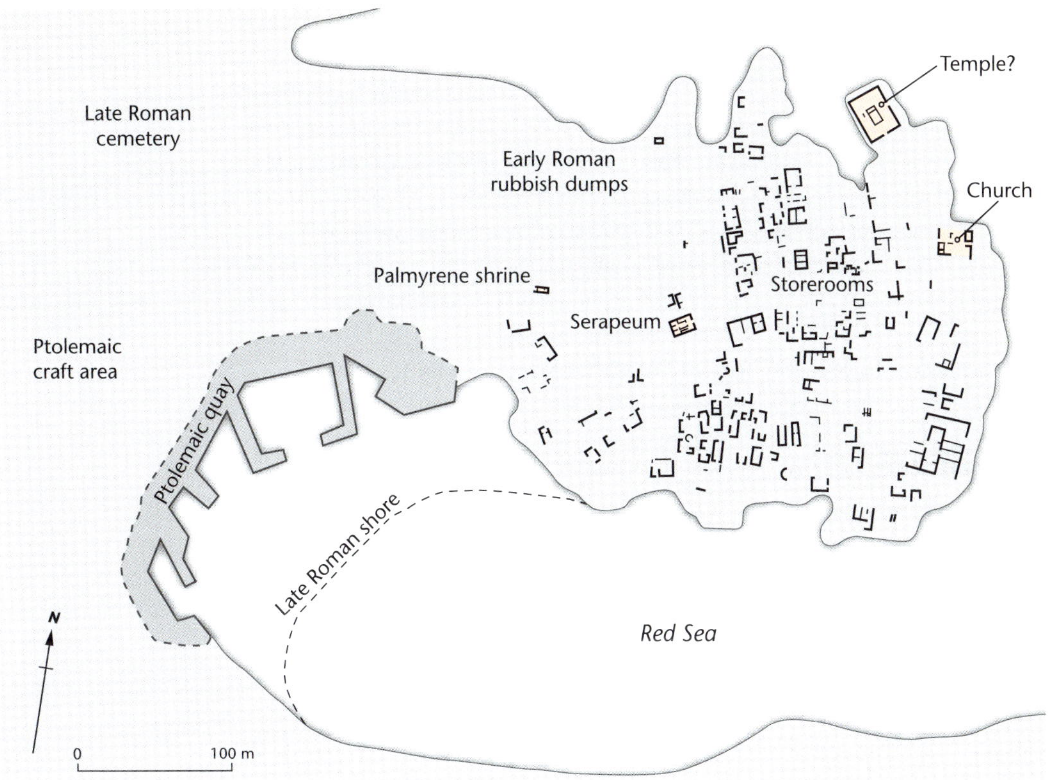

Fig. 10.4.2 Berenike (after Sidebotham).

The early Roman period is particularly well known from the rubbish dump, where conditions of preservation have been favourable to the survival of organic materials and writing. The texts from the dump reveal the existence of Berenike's customs gate, through which passed quantities of wine and oil from around the Mediterranean, headed mainly for India. They also mention the soldiers and tax collectors who controlled the flow of camels and people moving this merchandise and the luxury goods travelling in the return direction.

It is difficult to be certain whether Berenike's existence continued uninterrupted from the third century BC to the end of antiquity (it was abandoned in the first half of the sixth century). Excavations have so far found mainly Roman buildings, and there are no Ptolemaic written documents. There is also a considerable gap from the third century AD until perhaps the late fourth century. Several documents testify to the presence of people from the other side of the Red Sea, Palmyrenes and others. Some eleven languages have appeared in documents from Berenike, including Tamil-Brahmi, reflecting the involvement in the maritime trade of South Asian groups as well as Greeks, Romans, Palmyrenes, Arabs and Egyptians. Considerable finds of south Indian domestic pottery suggest that Indians were residents as well as visitors. There is also evidence for the presence of southern-desert nomadic groups. The religious life of the settlement was correspondingly diverse, ranging from the Greek gods to the Palmyrene, and several pieces of religious sculpture appear to be made from local stone. A temple of Sarapis was a prominent landmark. The largest religious structure, at the east end of a main east-west street, has been identified as a fourth-fifth century Christian church, with adjacent kitchen facilities.

In general, it is striking how much the transient nature of port life did not interfere with a high level of normality in the outfitting of the settlement, even though the coral heads used in most buildings (with gypsum/anhydrite ashlar blocks framing corners and doors) were far from a desirable construction material. The state of building preservation is not outstanding in part for this reason, in part because of the high salinity of the areas nearest the sea. Multi-storey buildings in the areas north and east of the Sarapis temple seem to have served commercial purposes; their heavily worn thresholds show constant traffic, and remains of locks suggest that high-value goods – such as most of the imports from India were – were stored or traded here. The upper floors may have been residential.

Bibliography: Sidebotham and Wendrich 1995–2000, 2001/2.

GPS READING		
Berenike	N 23.54.62	E 35.28.42

CHRONOLOGICAL OUTLINE

	BC
Predynastic Period	3000
Early Dynastic Period	*c.* 3000 – 2686
Old Kingdom	*c.* 2686 – 2181
First Intermediate Period	*c.* 2180 – 2040
Middle Kingdom	*c.* 2040 – 1730
Second Intermediate Period	*c.* 1730 – 1550
New Kingdom	*c.* 1550 – 1080
Third Intermediate Period	*c.* 1080 – 664
Late Period	664 – 332
Dynasty 26 ('Saite')	
Psammetichos I	664 – 610
Foundation of Naukratis	*c.* 630 / 570
Necho II	610 – 595
Psammetichos II	595 – 589
Apries	589 – 570
Amasis	570 – 526
Psammetichos III	526 – 525
Dynasty 27 (1st Persian Occupation)	
Cambyses	525 – 522
Darius I	522 – 486
Xerxes	486 – 465
Dynasty 28	
Amyrtaios	404 – 399
Dynasty 29	
Hakoris	393 – 380
Dynasty 30	
Nektanebo I	380 – 362
Nektanebo II	360 – 343
2nd Persian Occupation	
Artaxerxes III	343 – 338
Darius III	336 – 332
Macedonian dynasty	
Alexander the Great	332 – 323
Foundation of Alexandria	331
Philip III Arrhidaios	323 – 317
Alexander IV (d.310)	323 – 306/5
Ptolemy son of Lagos satrap of Egypt	323 – 306

Ptolemaic dynasty	
Ptolemy I Soter (with Berenike I)	306 – 282
Battle of Ipsos	301
Ptolemy II Philadelphos (with Arsinoe II, d. 270/268)	282 – 246
Ptolemy III Euergetes I (with Berenike II)	246 – 221
Canopus decree	238
Ptolemy IV Philopator (with Arsinoe III)	221 – 204
Battle of Raphia	217
Revolt in the Thebaid under Haronnophris and Chaonnophris	206 – 186
Ptolemy V Epiphanes (with Cleopatra I)	204 – 180
Battle of Panion	200
Memphis decree (Rosetta Stone)	196
Ptolemy VI Philometor and Cleopatra I	180 – 177
Ptolemy VI and Cleopatra II	177 – 170
Ptolemy VI, Ptolemy VIII and Cleopatra II	170 – 164
Antiochus IV invades Egypt	170 – 168
Ptolemy VIII Euergetes II	164 – 163
Ptolemy VI and Cleopatra II	163 – 145
Ptolemy VIII	145 – 116
Cleopatra III and Ptolemy IX Soter II ('Lathyros')	116 – 107
Cleopatra III and Ptolemy X Alexander I	107 – 101
Ptolemy X and Cleopatra Berenike III	101 – 88
Ptolemy IX Soter II	88 – 80
Ptolemy XII Neos Dionysos ('Auletes')	80 – 58
Berenike IV	58 – 55
Ptolemy XII	55 – 51
Cleopatra VII Philopator and Ptolemy XIII	51 – 47
Julius Caesar in Egypt	48 / 7
Cleopatra VII and Ptolemy XIV	47 – 44
Cleopatra VII and Ptolemy XV ('Caesarion')	44 – 30
Mark Antony sometimes in Egypt	41 – 30
Battle of Actium	31

Roman emperors	AD
Augustus (previously Octavian)	27 (BC) – 14
Tiberius	14 – 37
Gaius (Caligula)	37 – 41
Alexandrian Greeks attack the Jews	38
Claudius	41 – 54
Nero	54 – 68
Galba, Otho, Vitellius	68 – 69
Vespasian	69 – 79
Titus	79 – 81
Domitian	81 – 96
Nerva	96 – 98
Trajan	98 – 117
Jewish revolt in Egypt	115 – 117
Hadrian	117 – 138
Hadrian visits Egypt	129 – 130
Antoninus Pius	138 – 161
Marcus Aurelius	161 – 180
and Lucius Verus	161 – 169
Antonine plague in Egypt	167 – c. 179
Revolt of Boukoloi in the Delta	172 – 175
Commodus	180 – 192
Septimius Severus	193 – 211
Septimius Severus visits Egypt	200 – 201
Caracalla	211 – 217
Constitutio Antoniniana (grant of Roman citizenship)	212
Macrinus	217 – 218
Antoninus (Elagabalus)	218 – 222
Severus Alexander	222 – 235
Maximinus the Thracian	235 – 238
Gordian III	238 – 244
Philip the Arab	244 – 249
Decius	249 – 251
Decian 'persecution' of Christians	250
Trebonianus Gallus	251 – 253
Valerian and Gallienus	253 – 260
Gallienus (alone)	260 – 268
Claudius II the Goth	268 – 270
Palmyrenes control Egypt	270 – 272
Aurelian	270 – 275
Tacitus	275 – 276
Probus	276 – 282
Diocletian	284 – 305
Diocletian in Egypt	298
The Great Persecution	303 – 313

Late Antique / Byzantine emperors	
Constantine I	306 – 337
Licinius	308 – 324
Athanasius bishop of Alexandria	328 – 373
Constantine II	337 – 340
Constans II	337 – 350
Constantius II	337 – 361
Julian ('the Apostate')	361 – 363
Jovian	363 – 364
Valens	364 – 378
Theodosius I	379 – 395
Roman Empire divided into eastern and western halves	395
Arcadius	395 – 408
Theodosius II	408 – 450
Marcian	450 – 457
Council of Chalcedon condemns Monophysites	451
Leo	457 – 474
Zeno	474 – 491
Anastasius	491 – 518
Justin I	518 – 527
Justinian	527 – 565
Justin II	565 – 578
Tiberius II	578 – 582
Maurice	582 – 602
Phocas	602 – 610
Heraclius	610 – 641
Sasanian Persians occupy Egypt	619 – 629
Arab conquest	639 – 642
Umayyad khalifate	642 – 750
Abbasid khalifate	750 – 868

BIBLIOGRAPHY

Abd el-Hafeez Abd el-Al et al. (1985), *Stèles funéraires de Kom Abu Bellou*. Paris.

Abd-el-Ghani, M. (2001), 'The role of Ptolemais in Upper Egypt outside its frontiers', in I. Andorlini et al. (eds), *Atti del XXII Congresso Internazionale di Papirologia* (Florence), I: 17–33.

Adams, C. E. P. (2000), 'Who bore the burden?', in D. J. Mattingly and J. Salmon (eds), *Economies Beyond Agriculture in the Classical World* (London), 171–92.

Adriani, A. (1952a), 'Travaux de fouilles et de restauration dans la région d'Abousir', *Annuaire du Musée gréco-romain III, 1940–1950*: 129–39.

— (1952b), 'Nécropole et ville de Plinthine', *Annuaire du Musée gréco-romain III, 1940–1950*: 140–59.

— (1961–6), *Repertorio d'arte dell'Egitto greco-romano*. Rome.

Ägypten Schätze (1996), *Ägypten, Schätze aus dem Wüstenland. Kunst und Kultur der Christen am Nil*. Wiesbaden.

Alcock, A., trans. (1983), *Isaac the Presbyter, The Life of Samuel of Kalamun*. Warminster.

Aldred, C. (1978), 'The temple of Dendur', *The Metropolitan Museum of Art Bulletin* 36/1.

Alliot, M. (1949, 1954), *Le culte d'Horus à Edfou au temps des Ptolémées*. 2 vols. Beirut.

Alston, R. (2002), *The City in Roman and Byzantine Egypt*. London.

Anderson, R. and I. Fawzy (eds) (1987), *Egypt Revealed: Scenes from Napoleon's Description de l'Egypte*. Cairo.

Arnold, D. (1994), 'Zur Rekonstruktion des Pronaos von Hermopolis', *Mitteilungen des Deutschen Archäologischen Instituts (Abt. Kairo)* 50: 13–22.

— (1999), *Temples of the Last Pharaohs*. Oxford and New York.

Ashton, S.-A. (2001), *Ptolemaic Royal Sculpture from Egypt. The Interaction between Greek and Egyptian Traditions*. Oxford.

Atiya, A. S. (ed.) (1991), *The Coptic Encyclopedia*. 8 vols. New York.

Aujac, G. (1993), *Claude Ptolémée astronome, astrologue, géographe*. Paris.

Bács, T. (2000), 'The so-called Monastery of Cyriacus at Thebes', *Egyptian Archaeology* 17: 34–6.

Badawy, A. (1953), *Guide de l'Egypte chrétienne*. Cairo.

— (1956), 'Le grand temple gréco-romain à Hermoupolis-Ouest', *Chronique d'Egypte* 31: 257–66.

— (1978), *Coptic Art and Archaeology: The Art of the Christian Egyptians from the Late Antique to the Middle Ages*. Cambridge.

Bagnall, R. S. (1976), *The Florida Ostraca. Documents from the Roman Army in Upper Egypt*. Durham NC.

— (1986), 'Papyri and Ostraka from Quseir al-Qadim', *Bulletin of the American Society of Papyrologists* 23: 1–60.

— (1993), *Egypt in Late Antiquity*. Princeton.

— (1995), *Reading Papyri, Writing Ancient History*. London.
— (2001a), 'Copts', in D. B. Redford (ed.), *The Oxford Encyclopedia of Ancient Egypt* (Oxford): I: 302–7.
— (2001b), 'Roman Occupation', in D. B. Redford (ed.), *The Oxford Encyclopedia of Ancient Egypt* (Oxford): III: 148–56.
— (2002), 'Alexandria: Library of Dreams', *Proceedings of the American Philosophical Society* 146: 348–62.
Bagnall, R. S. and P. Derow (2004), *The Hellenistic Period*. Oxford.
Bagnall, R. S. and B. W. Frier (eds) (1994), *The Demography of Roman Egypt*. Cambridge.
Bagnall, R. S. et al. (1996), 'A Ptolemaic inscription from Bir 'Iayyan', *Chronique d'Egypte* 71: 317–30.
Bagnall, R. S. and J. A. Sheridan (1994a), 'Greek and Latin documents from 'Abu Sha'ar, 1990–1991', *Journal of the American Research Center in Egypt* 31: 157–66.
— (1994b), 'Greek and Latin documents from 'Abu Sha'ar, 1992–1993', *Bulletin of the American Society of Papyrologists* 31: 109–20.
Bailey, D. M. (1990), 'Classical architecture in Roman Egypt', in M. Henig (ed.), *Architecture and Architectural Sculpture in the Roman Empire* (Oxford): 121–37.
— (1991), *British Museum Expedition to Middle Egypt: Excavations at El-Ashmunein, IV. Hermopolis Magna: Buildings of the Roman Period*. London.
Baines, J. and J. Málek (2000), *Cultural Atlas of Ancient Egypt*. New York.
Ballet, P. et al. (2000), 'La ville de Coptos à l'époque romaine', *Coptos* 2000: 176–87.
Barguet, P. (1953), *La stèle de la famine à Sehel*. Cairo.
Bataille, A. (1951), *Les inscriptions grecques du temple de Hatshepsout à Deir el-Bahari*. Cairo.
— (1952), *Les Memnonia*. Cairo.
Baulig, H. (1984), *Das frühe Christentum in Hermopolis Magna. Beiträge zur Geschichte des christlichen Ägypten*. Trier.
Bayumi, K. (1998), 'Excavations at 'Ain al Gadida in the Dakhleh Oasis', in Kaper 1998: 55–62.
Beaucour, F. et al. (1990), *The Discovery of Egypt*. Paris.
Bell, H. I. (1953), *Cults and Creeds in Graeco-Roman Egypt*. Liverpool (repr. Chicago 1975).
Bernand, A. (1970), *Le Delta égyptien d'après les textes grecs. 1, Les confins libyques*. Cairo.
— (1972a), *De Koptos à Kosseir*. Leiden.
— (1972b), *Le Paneion d'el-Kanaïs: Les inscriptions grecques*. Leiden.
— (1984), *Les portes du desert* (Paris): 151–263.
— (1989), *De Thèbes à Syène* (Paris): 169–259.
— (1998), *Alexandrie la Grande*. Paris.
Bernand, A. and E. Bernand (1960), *Les inscriptions grecques et latines du Colosse de Memnon*. Cairo.
Bietak, M. (1979), 'Urban archeology and the "town problem" in ancient Egypt', in K. Weeks (ed.), *Egyptology and the Social Sciences* (Cairo): 97–144.

Bingen, J. et al. (1992), *Mons Claudianus: Ostraca graeca et latina*, I. Cairo.
— (1997), *Mons Claudianus: Ostraca graeca et latina*, II. Cairo.
Blackman, A. M. (1911), *The Temple of Dendur*. Cairo.
Boak, A. E. R. (ed.) (1933), *Karanis. The Temples, Coin Hoards, Botanical and Zoölogical Reports: Seasons 1924–31*. Ann Arbor.
— (1935), *Soknopaiou Nesos. The University of Michigan Excavations at Dimê in 1931–32*. Ann Arbor.
Boak, A. E. R. and E. E. Peterson (1931), *Karanis. Topographical and Architectural Report of the Excavations during the Seasons 1924–28*. Ann Arbor.
Bolman, E. S. (ed.) (2002), *Monastic Visions: Wall Paintings in the Monastery of St. Antony at the Red Sea*. New Haven.
Borkowski, Z. (1981), *Inscriptions des factions à Alexandrie, Alexandrie II*. Warsaw.
Bothmer, B. V. (1960), *Egyptian Sculpture of the Late Period, 700 B.C. – A.D. 100*. Brooklyn.
Bourguet, P. du (1991), 'Art and architecture', in Atiya (1991): I: 261–78.
Boussac, M.-F. et al. (eds) (2002), *Autour de Coptos. Actes du colloque organisé au Musée des Beaux-Arts de Lyon*. Lyon.
Bowersock, G. W. (1984), 'The miracle of Memnon', *Bulletin of the American Society of Papyrologists* 21: 21–32.
Bowman, A. K. (1986), *Egypt after the Pharaohs*. London.
— (1996), 'Egypt', in A. K. Bowman, E. Champlin and A. Lintott (eds), *The Cambridge Ancient History* X (2nd edn, Cambridge): 676–702.
Bowman, A. K. and E. Rogan (1999), *Agriculture in Egypt: From Pharaonic to Modern Times*. Oxford and New York.
Braun, T. F. R. G. (1982), 'The Greeks in Egypt', in J. Boardman et al. (eds), *The Cambridge Ancient History* III.3 (2nd edn, Cambridge): 132–56.
Braund, D. C. and J. J. Wilkins (eds) (2000), *Athenaeus and His World: Reading Greek Culture in the Roman Empire*. Exeter.
Breccia, E. (1914), *Alexandrea ad Aegyptum. Guide de la ville ancienne et moderne et du Musée Gréco-romain*. Bergamo.
— (1922), *Alexandrea ad Aegyptum. A Guide to the Ancient and Modern Town and to its Graeco-Roman Museum*. Bergamo.
— (1926), *Le rovine e i monumenti di Canopo*. Bergamo.
— (1932), 'Fouilles à Oxyrhynchos et à Tebtunis. 1928–1930', *Le Musée Gréco-Romain d'Alexandrie 1925–1931* (Bergamo): 60–63.
— (1934), 'Fouilles à Oxyrhynchos', *Le Musée Gréco-Romain d'Alexandrie 1931–1932* (Bergamo): 36–47.
Brégeon, J.-J. (1991), *L'Egypte de Bonaparte*. Paris.
Bresciani, E. (1978), *Assuan. Tempio tolemaico di Isi*. Pisa.
— (2003), *Kom Madi 1977 e 1978. Le pitture murali del cenotafio di Alessandro Magno*. Rev. edn. Pisa.
Brun, J.-P. (2002), '*Hodos Myoshormitikè*: L'équipement de la route entre Coptos et la Mer Rouge aux époques ptolémaïque et romaine', in Boussac 2002: 395–414.
Burkhalter, F. (2002), 'Le "Tarif de Coptos". La douane de Coptos, les fermiers de l'*apostolion* et le préfet du désert de Bérénice', in Boussac 2002:

199–233.

Butler, A. J. (1978), *The Arab Conquest of Egypt and the Last Thirty Years of the Roman Dominion*. 2nd edn, rev. P.M. Fraser. Oxford.

Cameron, A. (1965), 'Wandering poets: a literary movement in Byzantine Egypt', *Historia* 14: 470–509.

Cannuyer, C. (2001), *Coptic Egypt: The Christians of the Nile*. London.

Carrez-Maratray, J.-Y. (1999), *Péluse et l'angle oriental du delta égyptien aux époques grecque, romaine et byzantine*. Cairo.

Cauville, S. (1984), *Edfou*. Cairo.

Cauville, S. and D. Devauchelle (1984), 'Le temple d'Edfou: étapes de la construction; nouvelles données historiques', *Revue d'Egyptologie* 35: 31–55.

Chaîne, M. (1960), *Le manuscript de la version copte en dialecte sahidique des 'Apophthegmata Patrum'*. Cairo.

Chauveau, M. (2000), *Egypt in the Age of Cleopatra*, trans. David Lorton. Ithaca NY and London.

— (2002), *Cleopatra: Beyond the Myth*, trans. David Lorton. Ithaca NY and London.

Chitty, D. J. (1966), *The Desert a City: An Introduction to the Study of Egyptian and Palestinian Monasticism under the Christian Empire*. Oxford.

Chugg, A. (2002), 'The tomb of Alexander the Great in Alexandria,' *American Journal of Ancient History* n.s. 1: 75–108.

Clackson, S. J. (1999), 'Ostraca and graffiti excavated at el-Amarna', in S. Emmel et al. (eds), *Akten des 6. Internationalen Koptologenkongresses* (Wiesbaden) 2: 268–78.

— (2000), *Coptic and Greek Texts Relating to the Hermopolite Monastery of Apa Apollo*. Oxford.

— (forthcoming), 'Ostraca from Kom el-Nana', in J. Faiers (ed.), *Excavations at Amarna 1. A Corpus of Late Roman Pottery*. London.

Clarysse, W. (1991), 'Hakoris, an Egyptian nobleman and his family', *Ancient Society* 22: 235–43.

— (2003), 'The archive of the praktor Milon', in Vandorpe and Clarysse 2003: 17–27.

Clédat, J. (1999), *Le Monastère et la nécropole de Baouit*, D. Bénazeth, M.-H. Rutschowscaya et al. (eds). Cairo.

Coquin, R.-G. (1991), 'Monasteries of the Middle Sa'id', in Atiya 1991: V: 1654–5.

Collins, N. L. (2000), *The Library in Alexandria and the Bible in Greek*. Leiden.

Coptos (2000), *Coptos: L'Egypte antique aux portes du désert*. Lyon and Paris.

Crawford, D. J. (1971), *Kerkeosiris: an Egyptian Village in the Ptolemaic Period*. Cambridge.

Cuvigny, H. (2000a), 'Coptos, plaque tournante du commerce érythréen, et les routes transdésertiques', in *Coptos* 2000: 158–75.

— (2000b), *Mons Claudianus: ostraca graeca et Latina*, III: *Les reçus pour avances à la famille*. Cairo.

— (2003) (ed.), *La route de Myos Hormos. L'armée romaine dans le désert Oriental d'Egypte*, 2 vols. Cairo.

Daszewski, W. A. (1985), *Corpus of Mosaics from Egypt I: Hellenistic and Early Roman Period*. Mainz.
Davies, S. and Smith, H. S. (1997), 'Sacred animal temples at Saqqara', in Quirke 1997: 112–31.
Davis, S. J. (1998), 'Pilgrimage and the cult of Saint Thecla in Late Antique Egypt', in Frankfurter 1998a: 303–39.
Davoli, P. (1998), *L'archeologia urbana nel Fayyum di età ellenistica e romana*. Naples.
Dawson, D. (1992), *Allegorical Readers and Cultural Revision in Ancient Alexandria*. Berkeley.
de Cosson, A. (1935), *Mareotis: Being a Short Account of the History and Ancient Monuments of the Northwestern Desert of Egypt and of Lake Mareotis*. London.
Del Francia Barocas, L. (1998), *Antinoe cent'anni dopo. Catalogo della mostra Firenze, Palazzo Medici Riccardi*. Florence.
Demougin, S. and J.-Y. Empereur (2002), 'Inscriptions d'Alexandrie 1: un nouveau procurateur alexandrin', *Alexandrina* 2 (Cairo): 149–58.
Depauw, M. (2000), *The Archive of Teos and Thabis from Early Ptolemaic Thebes. P. Brux. dem. inv. E. 8252–8256*. Turnhout.
Derchain, P. (1971), *Elkab I. Les monuments religieux à l'entrée du wadi Hellal*. Bruxelles.
Donadoni, S. et al. (1974), *Antinoe 1965–1968*. Rome.
Doxiadis, E. C. (1995), *The Mysterious Fayum Portraits: Faces from Ancient Egypt*. London.
Drew-Bear, M. (1988), *Hermoupolis-la-Grande à l'époque de Gallien. Recherches sur l'histoire d'une cité de l'Egypte romaine à la lumière des archives de son conseil*. Diss. Paris.
Dunand, F. (1990), *Musée du Louvre, Département des antiquités grecques et romaines. Catalogue des terres cuites gréco-romaines d'Egypte*. Paris.
— et al. (1992), *Douch I: La nécropole. Exploration archéologique*. Cairo.

Egberts, A., B. P. Muhs and J. van der Vliet (eds) (2002), *Perspectives on Panopolis*. Leiden.
Eide, T. et al. (eds) (1998), *Fontes Historiae Nubiorum. Textual Sources for the History of the Middle Nile Region between the Eighth Century BC and the Sixth Century AD. Vol. III. From the First to the Sixth Century AD*. Bergen.
El-Abbadi, M. A. H. (1990), *The Life and Fate of the Ancient Library of Alexandria*. Paris.
El-Fakharani, F. (1983), 'Recent excavations at Marea in Egypt', in G. Grimm, H. Heinen and E. Winter (eds), *Das römisch-byzantinische Ägypten* (Trier): 175–86.
El-Falaki, Mahmoud-Bey (1872), *Mémoire sur l'antique Alexandrie*. Copenhagen.
El-Farag, R., U. Kaplony-Heckel and K. P. Kuhlmann (1985), 'Recent archaeological explorations at Athribis (*Hw.t Rpjj.t*)', *Mitteilungen des Deutschen Archäologischen Instituts (Abt. Kairo)* 41: 1–8.
El-Saghir, M. et al. (1986), *Le camp romain de Louqsor, avec une étude des graffites*

gréco-romains du temple d'Amon. Cairo.
Empereur, J.-Y. (1995), 'Une fouille récente au coeur d'Alexandrie: le site du cinéma Majestic (1992)', *Alessandria e il mondo ellenistico-romano*: 169–71. Rome.
— (1998a), *Alexandria Rediscovered*. London.
— (1998b), *Le Phare d'Alexandrie, la merveille retrouvée*. Paris.
— (1998c), 'Cinq ans de fouilles et de recherches sur le terrain à Alexandrie', *Alexandrina* 1 (Cairo): 1–6.
— (2000), *A Short Guide to the Graeco-Roman Museum, Alexandria*. Alexandria.
Empereur, J.-Y. and M.-D. Nenna (2001), *Nécropolis* 1. Cairo.
— (2003), *Nécropolis* 2. Cairo.
Evelyn White, H. G. (1932) *Monasteries of the Wadi 'n Natrun II: The History of the Monasteries of Nitria and of Scetis*. New York.
— (1933), *Monasteries of the Wadi 'n Natrun III: The Architecture and Archaeology*. New York.

Fairman, H. W. (1954), 'Worship and festivals in an Egyptian temple', *Bulletin of the John Rylands Library* 37: 165–203.
— (ed.) (1974), *The Triumph of Horus; an Ancient Egyptian Sacred Drama*. London.
Fakhry, A. (1942 and 1950), *Bahria Oasis*, 2 vols. Cairo.
— (1951), *The Necropolis of El-Bagawât in Kharga Oasis*. Cairo.
— (1973), *The Oases of Egypt* 1: *Siwa Oasis*. Cairo.
— (1974), *The Oases of Egypt* 2: *Bahriyah and Farafra Oases*. Cairo.
Falivene, M. R. (1998), *The Herakleopolite Nome*. Atlanta.
Farid, A. (1988), 'Die Denkmäler des Parthenios, Verwalter der Isis von Koptos', *Mitteilungen des Deutschen Archäologischen Instituts (Abt. Kairo)* 44: 13–65.
Faulkner, R. O. (1933), *The Papyrus Bremner-Rhind*. Brussels.
Ferri, W. (1989), 'Rilievo topografico generale di Medinet Madi', *Egitto e Vicino Oriente* 12: 3–19.
Figueras, P. (2000), *From Gaza to Pelusium. Materials for the Historical Geography of North Sinaï and Southwestern Palestine (332 BC – 640 CE)*. Beer-Sheva.
Finnestad, R. B. (1985), *Image of the World and Symbol of the Creator. On the Cosmological and Iconological Values of the Temple of Edfu*. Wiesbaden.
Foertmeyer, V. A. (1989), *Tourism in Graeco-Roman Egypt*. Diss. Princeton.
Foreman, L. (1999), *Cleopatra's Palace. In Search of a Legend*. London.
Forster, E. M. (1961), *Alexandria. A History and a Guide*. New York.
Forsyth, G. H. (1968), 'The Monastery of St. Catherine at Mount Sinai: the church and fortress of Justinian', *Dumbarton Oaks Papers* 22: 1–19.
Forsyth, G. H. and K. Weitzmann (1973), *The Monastery of St. Catherine at Mount Sinai: The Church and Fortress of Justinian: Plates*. Ann Arbor.
Fournet, J.-L. (1999), *Hellénisme dans l'Egypte du VIe siècle. La bibliothèque et l'oeuvre de Dioscore d'Aphrodité*, 2 vols. Cairo.
Fowden, G. (1993), *The Egyptian Hermes: A Historical Approach to the Late Pagan Mind*. 2nd edn. Princeton.
Frank, G. (1998), 'Miracles, monks and monuments: The *Historia Monachorum in Aegypto* as pilgrims' tales', in Frankfurter 1998a: 483–505.
— (2000), *The Memory of the Eyes: Pilgrims to Living Saints in Christian Late Antiquity*. Berkeley.

Frankfurter, D. (ed.) (1998a), *Pilgrimage and Holy Space in Late Antique Egypt*. Leiden.

— (1998b), 'Introduction: approaches to Coptic pilgrimage', in Frankfurter 1998a: 3–48.

— (1998c), *Religion in Roman Egypt*. Princeton.

Fraser, P. M. (1951), 'A Syriac Notitia Urbis Alexandrinae', *Journal of Egyptian Archaeology* 37: 103–8.

— (1972), *Ptolemaic Alexandria*. Oxford.

— (1991), 'The Arab conquest of Alexandria', in Atiya 1991: I: 183–9.

Frost, H. (1975), 'The Pharos site, Alexandria', *International Journal of Nautical Archaeology* 4.1: 126–30.

Gabra, G. with A. Alcock (1993), *Cairo, the Coptic Museum and Old Churches*. Cairo.

Gabra, S. (1941), *Rapport sur les fouilles d'Hermoupolis-Ouest (Touna el-Gebel)*. Cairo.

Gabra, S. and E. Drioton (1954), *Peintures à fresque et scènes peintes à Hermoupolis-Ouest (Touna el-Gebel)*. Cairo.

Gallazzi, C. and G. Hadji-Minaglou (2000), *Tebtynis I. La reprise des fouilles et le quartier de la chapelle d'Isis-Thermouthis*. Cairo.

Garbrecht, G. and H. Jaritz (1990), *Untersuchungen antiker Anlagen zur Wasserspeicherung im Fayum/Ägypten*. Braunschweig.

Gascou, J. and G. Wagner (1979), 'Deux voyages archéologiques dans l'oasis de Khargeh', *Bulletin de l'Institut Français d'Archéologie Orientale* 79: 7–26.

Gazda, E. (ed.) (1983), *Karanis, an Egyptian Town in Roman Times: Discoveries of the University of Michigan Expedition to Egypt (1924–1935)*. Ann Arbor.

Goddio, F. (1995), 'Cartographie des vestiges archéologiques submergés dans le Port Est d'Alexandrie et dans la Rade d'Aboukir', *Alessandria e il mondo ellenistico-romano*: 172–5. Rome.

— (1998), *Alexandria. The Submerged Royal Quarters*. London.

Godlewski, W. (1986), *Deir el-Bahari V. Le monastère de St Phoibammon*. Warsaw.

Golvin, J.-C. et al. (1981), 'Le petit Sarapieion romain de Louqsor', in *Bulletin de l'Institut Français d'Archéologie Orientale* 81: 115–48.

Gomaà, F., R. Müller-Wollermann, W. Schenkel (1991), *Mittelägypten zwischen Samalut und dem Gabal Abu Sir: Beiträge zur historischen Topographie der pharaonischer Zeit*. Wiesbaden.

Grenfell, B. P. and A. S. Hunt (1906), *The Hibeh Papyri* I. London.

Griffith, F. L. (ed.) (1896/7, 1902/3, 1903/4, 1904/5, 1905/6, 1906/7), *Egypt Exploration Fund Archaeological Reports*. London.

Grimm, G. (1998), *Alexandria, Die Erste Königsstadt der hellenistischen Welt*. Mainz.

Grimm, G. and D. Johannes (1975), *Kunst der Ptolemäer- under Römerzeit im Ägyptischen Museum Kairo*. Mainz.

Grossmann, P. (1980), *Elephantine II. Kirche und spätantike Hausanlagen im Chnumtempelhof. Beschreibung und typologische Untersuchung*. Mainz.

— (1989), *Abu Mina I*. Cairo.

— (1993), 'Ruinen des Klosters Dair al-Balaizâ in Oberägypten: eine Surveyaufnahme', *Jahrbuch für Antike und Christentum* 36: 171–205.

— (1998), 'The pilgrimage center of Abu Mina', in Frankfurter 1998a: 281–302.
— (1999–2000), 'Wadi Fayran/Sinai', *Annales du Service des Antiquités d'Egypte* 75: 153–65.
— (2002), *Christliche Architektur in Ägypten* (*Handbuch der Orientalistik* I: 62). Leiden.
Guy, J.-C. (1993), *Les apophthegmes des pères: Collection Systematique, Chapitres I–IX*. Paris.

Haas, C. (1997), *Alexandria in Late Antiquity. Topography and Social Conflict*. Baltimore.
Hairy, I. (2002), 'Une nouvelle cisterne sur le site du Sarapéion', *Alexandrina* 2 (Cairo): 29–38.
Hawass, Z. (2000), *Valley of the Golden Mummies*. New York.
Heinen, H. (1998), 'Das spätantike Ägypten (284–646 n.Chr.)', in M. Krause (ed.), *Ägypten in spätantik-christlicher Zeit. Einführung in die koptische Kultur* (Wiesbaden): 35–79.
Hendrickx, S. (1998), 'Habitations de potiers à Elkab à l'époque romaine', in W. Clarysse et al. (eds), *Egyptian Religion. The Last Thousand Years, Studies Dedicated to the Memory of Jan Quaegebeur* (Leuven): 1353–76.
Hesse, A. et al. (2002), 'L'Heptastade d'Alexandrie (Egypte)', *Alexandrina* 2 (Cairo): 191–273.
Hewison, R. N. (2001), *The Fayoum. History and Guide*. 3rd edn. Cairo and New York.
Hoffmann, F. (2000), *Ägypten. Kultur und Lebenswelt in griechisch-römischer Zeit*. Berlin.
Hölbl, G. (2001a), 'Ptolemaic Egypt', in D. B. Redford (ed.), *The Oxford Encyclopedia of Ancient Egypt* III (Oxford): 76–84.
— (2001b), *A History of the Ptolemaic Empire*, trans. T. Saavedra. London and New York.
Hölscher, U. (1954), *The Excavation of Medinet Habu. Volume 5. Post-Ramessid Remains*. Chicago.
Hooper, F. A. (1961), *Funerary Stelae from Kom Abou Billou*. Ann Arbor.
Hope, C. A. (1999), 'Dakhla Oasis, Ismant el-Kharab', in K. A. Bard (ed.), *Encyclopedia of the Archaeology of Ancient Egypt* (London): 222–6.
Hussein, A. (2000), *Le sanctuaire rupestre de Piyris à Ayn al-Labakha*. Cairo.
Husselman, E. M. (1979), *Karanis Excavations of the University of Michigan in Egypt 1928–1935. Topography and Architecture*. Ann Arbor.
Hutchinson, G. O. (1988), *Hellenistic Poetry*. Oxford.

Innemée, K. (1999), 'The Identity of Deir el-Baramus', *Egyptian Archaeology* 15: 41–3.

Jackson, R. B. (2002), *At Empire's Edge: Exploring Rome's Egyptian Frontier*. New Haven.
James, T. G. H. (1971), 'Egypt: from the expulsion of the Hyksos to Amenophis I', in I. E. S. Edwards et al. (eds), *The Cambridge Ancient History* II.1

(2nd edn, Cambridge): 289–312.
— (1991), 'Egypt: the Twenty-fifth and Twenty-sixth Dynasties', in J. Boardman et al. (eds), *The Cambridge Ancient History* III.2 (2nd edn, Cambridge): 677–738.
Jaritz, H. (1980), *Elephantine III. Die Terrassen vor den Tempeln des Chnum und der Satet. Architektur und Deutung*.
Jeffreys, D. G. (1985), *The Survey of Memphis* I. London.
Jeffreys, D. G. and H. S. Smith (1988), *The Anubieion at Saqqâra. I The Settlement and the Temple Precinct*. London.
Jobbins, J. (1989), *The Red Sea Coasts of Egypt: Sinai and the Mainland*. Cairo.

Kaegi, W. (1998), 'Egypt on the eve of the Muslim Conquest', in Petry 1998: 34–61.
Kaiser, W. et al. (1970), 'Stadt und Tempel von Elephantine. Erster Grabungsbericht', *Mitteilungen des Deutschen Archäologischen Instituts (Abt. Kairo)* 26: 87–139.
Kamal, A. B. (1901), 'Description générale des ruines de Hibé', *Annales du Service des Antiquités d'Egypte* 2: 84–91.
Kamil, J. (1987), *Coptic Egypt: History and Guide*. Cairo.
Kanawati, N. (1990), *Sohag in Upper Egypt: a Glorious History*. Gizeh.
Kaper, O. E. (ed.) (1998), *Life on the Fringe. Living in the Southern Egyptian Deserts during the Roman and early-Byzantine Periods*. Leiden.
Kawanishi, H. et al. (1995), *Akoris. Report of the Excavations at Akoris in Middle Egypt 1981–1992*. Kyoto.
Kayser, F. (1994), *Recueil des inscriptions grecques et latines (non funéraires) d'Alexandrie impériale (Ier – IIIe s. apr. J.-C.)*. Cairo.
Keenan, J. G. (2001), 'Egypt, A.D. 425–600', in A. Cameron, B. Ward-Perkins and M. Whitby (eds), *The Cambridge Ancient History* XIV (2nd edn, Cambridge): 612–37.
Kennedy, H. (1998), 'Egypt as a province in the Islamic caliphate, 641–868', in Petry 1998: 62–85.
Kessler, D. (1983), 'Zwei Grabstelen mit Oxyrhynchosfischen', *Die Welt des Orients* 14: 176–88.
Kienitz, F. K. (1953), *Die politische Geschichte Ägyptens vom 7. bis zum 4. Jahrhundert vor die Zeitwende*. Berlin.
Kiss, Z. et al. (2002), *Alexandrie VII. Fouilles polonaises à Kom el-Dikka (1986–7)*. Warsaw.
Knudstad, J. E. and R. A. Frey (1999), 'Kellis, the architectural survey of the Romano-Byzantine town at Ismant el-Kharab', C. S. Churcher and A. J. Mills (eds), *Reports from the Survey of the Dakhleh Oasis 1977–1987* (Oxford and Oakville CT): 189–214.
Kolotaj, W. (1992), *Alexandrie VI. Imperial Baths at Kom el-Dikka*. Warsaw.
Kornfeld, W. (1973), 'Jüdisch-aramäische Grabinschriften aus Edfu', in *Anzeiger der Österreichischen Akademie der Wissenschaften in Wien* 110: 123–37.
Krawiec, R. (2002), *Shenoute and the Women of the White Monastery: Egyptian Monasticism in Late Antiquity*. Oxford.

Krüger, J. (1990), *Oxyrhynchos in der Kaiserzeit: Studien zur Topographie und Literaturrezeption*. Frankfurt.

Kuhlmann, K. P. (1983), *Materialien zur Archäologie und Geschichte des Raumes von Achmim*. Mainz.

— (1988), *Das Ammoneion. Archäologie, Geschichte und Kultpraxis des Orakels von Siwa*. Mainz.

— (1998), 'Roman and Byzantine Siwa: developing a latent picture', in Kaper 1998: 159–80.

Külzer, A. (1994), *Peregrinatio graeca in Terram Sanctam: Studien su Pilgerführern und Reisebeschreibungen über Syrien, Palästina und den Sinai aus byzantinischer und metabyzantinischer Zeit*. Frankfurt.

Kyrieleis, H. (1975), *Bildnisse der Ptolemäer*. Berlin.

Laskowska-Kusztal, E. (1984), *Deir el-Bahari III. Le sanctuaire ptolémaïque de Deir el-Bahari*. Warsaw.

Lauer, J.-P. (1976), *Saqqara the Royal Cemetery of Memphis. Excavations and Discoveries since 1850*. London.

Lauer, J.-P. and C. Picard (1955), *Les statues ptolémaïques du Sarapieion de Memphis*. Paris.

Lefebvre, G. (1923–4), *Le tombeau de Petosiris*. Cairo.

Leroy, Jules (1975), *Les peintures des couvents du désert d'Esna*. Cairo.

— (1982) *Les peintures des couvents du Ouadi Natroun*. Cairo.

Lewis, N. (1983), *Life in Egypt under Roman Rule*. Oxford.

— (1986), *Greeks in Ptolemaic Egypt*. Oxford (repr. Oakville CT, 2001).

Lichtheim, M. (1980), *Ancient Egyptian Literature: a Book of Readings. Vol. 3: The Late Period*. Berkeley.

Lloyd, A. B. (1975), *Herodotus Book II: Introduction*. Leiden.

— (2000), 'The Late Period', in I. Shaw (ed.), *The Oxford History of Ancient Egypt* (Oxford): 369–94.

Loprieno, A. (1995), *Ancient Egyptian: A Linguistic Introduction*. Cambridge.

MacCoull, L. S. B. (1988), *Dioscorus of Aphrodito, His Work and His World*. Berkeley.

McKenzie, J. S. (2003), 'Glimpsing Alexandria from archaeological evidence', *Journal of Roman Archaeology* 16: 35–61.

McKenzie, J. S. et al. (2004), 'Reconstructing the Serapeum in Alexandria from the archaeological evidence', *Journal of Roman Studies* 94 (forthcoming).

Maehler, H. G. T. (2001), 'Remarks on some sculptures in Alexandria', in *Alexandrian Studies II in Honour of Mostafa el-Abbadi, Bulletin de le Société d'Archéologie d'Alexandrie* 46: 153–66.

Majcherek, G. (1995), 'Notes on Alexandrian habitat. Roman and Byzantine houses from Kom el-Dikka', *Topoi* 5: 133–50.

Martin, G. T. (1981), *The Sacred Animal Necropolis at North Saqqâra*. London.

Martin, M. (1971), *La laure de Deir al-Dîk à Antinoë*. Cairo.

Maxfield, V. and D. P. S. Peacock (1998), 'The archaeology of an industrial landscape', in Kaper 1998: 181–96.

— (2001a), *The Roman Imperial Quarries. Survey and Excavation at Mons Porphyrites 1994–1998*, I: *Topography and Quarries*. London.

— (2001b), *Mons Claudianus, Survey and Excavation 1987–1993*, II: *Excavations: Part 1*. Cairo.

Medeksza, S. and R. Czerner (2003), 'Rescuing Marina el-Alamein: a Graeco-Roman town in Egypt', *Minerva* 14.3: 20–3.

Meeks, D. (1972), *Le grand texte des donations au temple d'Edfou*. Cairo.

Meiggs, R. and D. Lewis (1969), *A Selection of Greek Historical Inscriptions to the End of the Fifth Century* B.C. Oxford.

Meinardus, O. (1977), *Christian Egypt*. Cairo.

— (1989), *Monks and Monasteries of the Egyptian Deserts*. 2nd edn. Cairo.

— (1999), *Two Thousand Years of Coptic Christianity*. Cairo.

Meskell, L. (2002), *Private Life in New Kingdom Egypt*. Princeton.

Metzger, C. (2001), 'Table d'Alexandrie', in *Alexandrian Studies II in Honour of Mostafa el-Abbadi, Bulletin de le Société d'Archéologie d'Alexandrie* 46: 167–76.

Meyer, C. et al. (2000), *Bir Umm Fawakhir Survey Project 1993, a Byzantine Gold-Mining Town*. Chicago.

Mills, A. J. (1993), 'The Dakhleh Oasis columbarium farmhouse', in *Alexandrian Studies in memoriam Daoud Abdu Daoud, Bulletin de le Société d'Archéologie d'Alexandrie* 45: 193–8.

— (1999), 'Deir el-Haggar', in C. A. Hope and A. J. Mills (eds), *Dakhleh Oasis Project: Preliminary Reports on the 1992–1993 and 1993–1994 Field Seasons* (Oxford and Oakville CT): 25–6.

Mirecki, P. and J. BeDuhn (eds) (1997), *Emerging from Darkness: Studies in the Recovery of Manichaean Sources*. Leiden.

Möller, A. (2000), *Naukratis: Trade in Ancient Greece*. Oxford.

Mond, R. and O. H. Myers (1934), *The Bucheum*, 3 vols. London.

— (1940), *Temples of Armant: A Preliminary Survey*, 2 vols. London.

Montserrat, D. (1998), 'Pilgrimage to the shrine of SS Cyrus and John at Menouthis in Late Antiquity', in Frankfurter 1998a: 257–79.

Montserrat, D. and L. Meskell (1997), 'Mortuary landscape and religious landscape at Graeco-Roman Deir el-Medina', *Journal of Egyptian Archaeology* 83: 179–97.

Müller-Wiener, W. (1963), 'Christliche Monumente im Gebiet von Hibis (el-Kharga)', *Mitteilungen des Deutschen Archäologischen Instituts (Abt. Kairo)* 19: 121–40.

Murnane, W. J. (1983), *The Penguin Guide to Ancient Egypt* (London): 308–13.

Myśliwiec, K. (1996), 'Athribis entre Memphis et Alexandrie', in *L'Egypte du delta: les capitales du nord (Les dossiers d'archéologie* 213): 34–43.

— (2000), *The Twilight of Ancient Egypt*, trans. D. Lorton. Ithaca.

Myśliewicz, K. and Z. Sztetyllo (2000), *Tell Atrib 1985–1995. I, Rescue Excavations. II, Pottery Stamps*. Warsaw.

Naumann, R. (1939), 'Bauwerke der Oase Khargeh', *Mitteilungen der Deutschen Archäologischen Instituts (Abt. Kairo)* 8: 1–16.

Naville, E. and T. H. Lewis (1894), *Ahnas el Medineh (Heracleopolis Magna)*. London.
Negm, M. A. A. (1993), 'New ancient village in Mareotis', in *Alexandrian Studies in memoriam Daoud Abdu Daoud, Bulletin de le Société d'Archéologie d'Alexandrie* 45: 217–24.

Ochsenschlager, E. L. (1979), 'Taposiris Magna: 1975 season', *Acts of the First International Congress of Egyptology* (Berlin): 503–6.
Orlandi, T. (1997), 'Letteratura copta e cristianesimo nazionale egiziano', A. Camplani (ed.), *L'Egitto cristiano. Aspetti e problemi in età tardo-antica* (Rome): 39–120.
Orrieux, C. (1985), *Zénon de Caunos, parépidèmos, et le destin grec*. Paris.
Osing, J. et al. (1982), *Denkmäler der Oase Dachla: aus dem Nachlass von Ahmed Fakhry*. Mainz.
— (1999), 'La science sacerdotale', in D. Valbelle and J. Leclant (eds), *Le décret de Memphis* (Paris): 127–40.
Oxford Classical Dictionary, 3rd edn (Oxford, 1996): 511–12 (D. J. T.), 512 (D. W. R.).

Pantalacci, L. and C. Traunecker (1990), *Le Temple d'el-Qal'a. I*. Cairo.
— (1998), *Le Temple d'el-Qal'a. II. Relevé des scènes et des texts*. Cairo.
Papaconstantinou, A. (2001), *Le culte des saints en Egypte des Byzantins aux Abbasides: L'apport des inscriptions et des papyrus grecs et coptes*. Paris.
Parker, R. A. (1963), 'A demotic marriage document from Deir el-Ballas', *Journal of the American Research Center in Egypt* 2: 113–16.
— (1964), 'A property settlement from Deir el-Ballas', *Journal of the American Research Center in Egypt* 3: 89–103, pls 21–3.
Parkinson, R. (1999), *Cracking Codes: The Rosetta Stone and Decipherment*. London.
Peacock, D. P. S. and V. A. Maxfield (1997), *Mons Claudianus. Survey and Excavation 1987–1993, 1: Topography and Quarries*. Cairo.
Peacock, D. et al. (1999–2002), *Myos Hormos – Quseir el-Qadim* [Interim Reports 1999–2002]. Southampton.
Pearson, B. A. and J. E. Goehring (eds) (1986), *The Roots of Egyptian Christianity*. Philadelphia.
Pensabene, P. (1993), *Elementi architettonici di Alessandria e di altri siti egiziani. Repertorio d'Arte dell'Egitto Greco-Romano*. Rome.
Pestman, P. W. (1965), 'Les archives privées de Pathyris à l'époque ptolémaïque. La famille de Pétéharsemtheus, fils de Panebkhounis', in E. Boswinkel et al. (eds), *Studia Papyrologica Varia* (Leiden): 47–105.
— (1981), *A Guide to the Zenon Archive*. Leiden.
— (1993), *The Archive of the Theban Choachytes (Second Century BC). A Survey of the Demotic and Greek Papyri contained in the Archive*. Leuven.
Petrie, W. M. F. (1905), *Ehnasya 1904*. London.
— (1908), *Athribis*. London.
— (1909), *The Palace of Apries (Memphis II)*. London.
— (1925), *Tombs of the Courtiers and Oxyrhynkhos*. London.

Petruso, K. and C. Gabel (1983), 'Marea: a Byzantine port on Egypt's north-west frontier', *Archaeology* 36.5: 62ff.

Petry, C. F. (ed.) (1998), *The Cambridge History of Egypt* I: *Islamic Egypt, 640–1517*. Cambridge.

Pfeiffer, R. (1968), *History of Classical Scholarship from the Beginnings to the End of the Hellenistic Age*. Oxford.

Pfrommer, M. (1999), *Alexandria, in Schatten der Pyramiden*. Mainz.

Plaumann, G. (1910), *Ptolemais in Oberägypten. Ein Beitrag zur Geschichte des Hellenismus in Ägypten*. Leipzig.

Porter, B. and R. L. B. Moss (1934), *Topographical Bibliography of Ancient Egyptian Hieroglyphic Texts, Reliefs and Paintings*, IV. *Lower and Middle Egypt*. Oxford.

— (1939), *Topographical Bibliography of Ancient Egyptian Hieroglyphic Texts, Reliefs and Paintings*, VI. *Upper Egypt: Chief Temples*. Oxford (repr. 1991).

— (1972), *Topographical Bibliography of Ancient Egyptian Hieroglyphic Texts, Reliefs and Paintings*, II. *Theban Temples*. 2nd edn. Oxford.

Quaegebeur, J. (1974), 'Prêtres et cultes thébains à la lumière de documents égyptiens et grecs', *Bulletin de la Société Française d'Egyptologie* 70/71: 44–50.

— (1975–6), 'Les appellations grecques des temples de Karnak', *Orientalia Lovaniensia Periodica* 6/7: 463–77.

— (1986), 'Louqsor sous les Ptolemées', *Dossiers d'histoire et archéologie* 101: 63.

— (1988), 'Cleopatra VII and the cults of the Ptolemaic queens', in *Cleopatra's Egypt: Age of the Ptolemies* (Brooklyn): 41–54.

Quaegebeur, J. and C. Traunecker (1994), 'Chenhour 1839–1993', *Cahiers de Recherche de l'Institut de Papyrologie et d'Egyptologie de Lille* 16: 167–209.

Quasten, J. (1953–2000), *Patrology* 2–3 and *Patrologia* 5. Westminster MD and Genova. (Note that *Patrologia* 3 was translated as *Patrology* 4; it and *Patrologia* 4 cover Latin Church fathers only; vols 3–5 (ed.) A. Di Berardino.)

Quibell, J. E. (1912), *Excavations at Saqqara (1908–9, 1909–10). The Monastery of Apa Jeremias*. Cairo.

Quirke, S. (ed.) (1997), *The Temple in Ancient Egypt: New Discoveries and Recent Research*. London.

Quirke, S. and C. Andrews (1988), *The Rosetta Stone*. London.

Rathbone, D. W. (1991), *Economic Rationalism and Rural Society in Third-Century A.D. Egypt. The Heroninos Archive and the Appianus Estate*. Cambridge.

— (2002), 'Koptos the emporion. Economy and society, I–III AD', in Boussac 2002: 179–98.

Ray, J. D. (1976), *The Archive of Hor*. London.

Raymond, A. (2000), *Cairo*. Cambridge MA.

Reddé, M. (1999), 'Sites militaires romains de l'oasis de Kharga', *Bulletin de l'Institut Français d'Archéologie Orientale* 99: 377–96.

Rice, E. E. (1983), *The Grand Procession of Ptolemy Philadelphus*. Oxford.

Ritner, R. K. (1998), 'Egypt under Roman rule: the legacy of ancient Egypt', in Petry 1998: 1–33.

Rodziewicz, E. (1993), 'The late Roman auditoria in Alexandria in the light of ivory carvings', in *Alexandrian Studies in memoriam Daoud Abdu Daoud, Bulletin de le Société d'Archéologie d'Alexandrie* 45: 269–79.

Rodziewicz, M. (1984), *Les habitations romaines tardives d'Alexandrie à la lumière des fouilles polonaises à Kom el-Dikka, Alexandrie III*. Warsaw.

— (1988), 'Remarks to the peristyle house in Alexandria and Mareotis', *12. Congrès international d'archéologie classique 1983* IV: 175–8.

Roeder, G. (1959), *Hermopolis 1929–1939. Ausgrabungen der deutschen Hermopolis-Expedition in Hermopolis, Ober-Ägypten*. Hildesheim.

Rossi, C. (2000), 'Umm el-Dabadib, Roman settlement in the Kharga Oasis', *Mitteilungen des Deutschen Archäologischen Instituts (Abt. Kairo)* 56: 335–52.

Rousseau, P. (1985), *Pachomius: The Making of a Community in Fourth-Century Egypt*. Berkeley and Los Angeles (repr. with suppl. Princeton 1999).

Rowe, A. (1946), *Discovery of the Famous Temple and Enclosure of Serapis at Alexandria*. Cairo.

Rowlandson, J. (ed.) (1998), *Woman and Society in Greek and Roman Egypt. A Sourcebook*. Cambridge.

Rutherford, I. (1990), 'Island of extremity: space, language and power in the pilgrimage traditions of Philae', in Frankfurter 1998a: 229–79.

Sadek, M. (1992), 'The baths at the ancient harbour of Marea', *Sesto Congresso Internazionale di Egittologia, Atti* I: 549–53. Turin.

Sambin, C. (1997), 'La purification de l'oeil divin ou les deux vases de Kom Ombo', *Revue d'Egyptologie* 48: 179–200.

Sandmel, S. (1979), *Philo of Alexandria*. Oxford.

Sauneron, S. (1959–1982), *Esna* I–X. Cairo.

Schneider, H. D. (1982), *Beelden van Behnasa: Egyptische kunst uit de Romeinse Keizertijd 1e-3e eeuw na Chr.* Zutphen.

Schulz, R. and M. Seidel (eds) (1998), *Egypt. The World of the Pharaohs*. Cologne.

Schwartz, J. (1983), 'La communauté d'Edfou (Haute-Egypte) jusqu'à la fin du règne de Trajan', in R. Kuntzmann and J. Schlosser (eds), *Etudes sur le judaïsme hellénistique* (Paris): 61–70.

Schwartz, J. and H. Wild (1950), *Qasr-Qarun / Dionysias 1948*. Cairo.

Shaw, I. (2003), *Exploring Ancient Egypt*. Oxford.

Sidebotham, S. E. (1994), 'Preliminary report on the 1990–1991 seasons of fieldwork at 'Abu Sha'ar (Red Sea coast)', *Journal of the American Research Center in Egypt* 31: 133–58.

— (2002), 'From Berenike to Koptos: recent results of the desert route survey', in Boussac 2002: 415–38.

Sidebotham, S. E., R. E. Zitterkopf and C. C. Helms (2000), 'Survey of the Via Hadriana: the 1998 season', *Journal of the American Research Center in Egypt* 37: 115–26.

Sidebotham, S. E., R. E. Zitterkopf and J. A. Riley (1991), 'Survey of the 'Abu Sha'ar-Nile Road', *American Journal of Archaeology* 95: 571–622.

Sidebotham, S. E. and W. Z. Wendrich (eds) (1995), *Berenike 1994: Preliminary Report of the 1994 Excavations at Berenike (Egyptian Red Sea Coast) and the Survey of the Eastern Desert*. Leiden.

— (1996), *Berenike 1995. Preliminary Report of the 1995 Excavations at Berenike (Egyptian Red Sea Coast) and the Survey of the Eastern Desert.* Leiden.
— (1998), *Berenike 1996. Report of the 1996 Excavations at Berenike (Egyptian Red Sea Coast) and the Survey of the Eastern Desert.* Leiden.
— (1999), *Berenike 1997. Report of the 1997 Excavations at Berenike and the Survey of the Egyptian Eastern Desert, including Excavations at Shenshef.* Leiden.
— (2000), *Berenike 1998. Report of the 1998 Excavations at Berenike and the Survey of the Egyptian Eastern Desert, including Excavations in Wadi Kalalat.* Leiden.
— (2001/2), 'Berenike: archaeological fieldwork at a Ptolemaic-Roman port on the Red Sea coast of Egypt 1999–2001', *Sahara* 13: 23–50.
Simpson, R. S. (1996), *Demotic Grammar in the Ptolemaic Sacerdotal Decrees.* Oxford.
Site monastique (1984), *Le site monastique des Kellia (Basse-Egypte). Recherches des années 1981–1983.* Louvain.
Sly, D. (1996), *Philo's Alexandria.* London.
Smith, H. S. (1974), *A Visit to Ancient Egypt. Life at Memphis and Saqqara* (c.500–30 BC). Warminster.
Spencer, A. J. (1983), *British Museum Expedition to Middle Egypt: Excavations at El-Ashmunein*, I. London.
— (1989), *British Museum Expedition to Middle Egypt: Excavations at El-Ashmunein*, II. London.
Stanwick, P. E. (2002), *Portraits of the Ptolemies. Greek Kings as Egyptian Pharaohs.* Austin TX.

Thomas, T. K. (2000), *Late Antique Egyptian Funerary Sculpture.* Princeton.
Thompson, D. J. (1988), *Memphis under the Ptolemies.* Princeton.
— (2000), 'Philadelphus' procession: dynastic power in a Mediterranean context', in L. Mooren (ed.), *Politics, Administration and Society in the Hellenistic World. Proceedings of the International Colloquium, Bertinoro 19–24 July 1997* (Leiden): 365–88.
Thomson, G. (1960), *The Greek Language.* Cambridge.
Timm, S. (1984–92), *Das christlich-koptisch Ägypten in arabischer Zeit*, 6 vols. Wiesbaden.
Tkaczow, B. (1993), *Topography of Ancient Alexandria (An Archaeological Map).* Warsaw.
Traunecker, C. (1992), *Coptos. Hommes et dieux sur le parvis de Geb.* Leuven.
— (1997), 'Lessons from the Upper Egyptian Temple of el-Qal'a', in Quirke 1997: 168–78.
Traunecker, C. et al. (1998), 'Chenhour. Rapport des travaux en 1998 et 1997', *Cahiers de Recherche de l'Institut de Papyrologie et d'Egyptologie de Lille* 19: 111–46.
Turner, E. G. (1982), 'The Graeco-Roman Branch', in T. G. H. James (ed.), *Excavating in Egypt: The Egypt Exploration Society 1882–1982* (London): 161–78.
— (1984), 'Ptolemaic Egypt', in F. W. Walbank et al. (eds), *The Cambridge Ancient History* VII.1 (2nd edn, Cambridge): 118–74.
Turner, J. D. and A. McGuire (1997), *The Nag Hammadi Library after Fifty Years.* Leiden.

Usick, P. (2002), *Adventures in Egypt and Nubia: the Travels of William John Bankes.* London.

Valbelle, D. and C. Bonnet (eds) (1998), *Le Sinaï durant l'Antiquité et le Moyen Age. 4000 ans d'histoire pour un désert.* Paris.

Valbelle, D. and J.-Y. Carrez-Maratray (2000), *Le camp romain du Bas-Empire à Tell el-Herr.* Paris.

Van der Veen, M. (1998), 'Gardens in the desert', in Kaper 1998: 221–42.

Van Minnen, P. (1998), 'Boorish or bookish? Literature in Egyptian villages in the Fayum in the Graeco-Roman period', *Journal of Juristic Papyrology* 30: 99–184.

— (2002), 'Hermopolis in the crisis of the Roman Empire', in W. Jongman and M. Kleijwegt (eds), *After the Past: Essays in Ancient History in Honour of H. W. Pleket* (Leiden): 285–304.

Van Moorsel, P. (1995–97), *Les peintures du monastère de Saint-Antoine près de la mer Rouge.* Cairo.

— (2002), *Les peintures du monastère de Saint-Paul près de la mer rouge.* Cairo.

Vandorpe, K. (1995), 'City of many a gate, harbour for many a rebel. Historical and topographical outline of Greco-Roman Thebes', in Vleeming 1995: 203–39.

— (2002), *The Bilingual Family Archive of Dryton, his Wife Apollonia and their Daughter Senmouthis.* Brussels.

Vandorpe, K. and W. Clarysse (eds) (2003), *Edfu. An Egyptian Provincial Capital in the Ptolemaic Period.* Brussels.

Vassilika, E. (1989), *Ptolemaic Philae.* Leuven.

Venit, M. S. (2002), *Monumental Tombs of Ancient Alexandria. The Theatre of the Dead.* Cambridge.

Verhoeven, U. (2001), *Untersuchungen zur späthieratischen Buchschrift.* Leuven.

Verhoogt, A. M. F. W. (1998), *Menches, Komogrammateus of Kerkeosiris.* Leiden.

Verreth, H. (1998), *Historical Topography of the Northern Sinai from the 7th Century BC till the 7th Century AD. A Guide to the Sources.* Diss. Leuven.

Vivian, C. (2000), *The Western Desert of Egypt.* Cairo.

Vleeming, S. P. (ed.) (1995), *Hundred-Gated Thebes. Acts of a Colloquium on Thebes and the Theban Area in the Graeco-Roman Period.* Leiden.

Vleeming, S. P. (2001), *Some Coins of Artaxerxes and Other Short Texts in the Demotic Script Found on Various Objects and Gathered from Many Publications.* Leuven.

Vörös, G. (2001), *Taposiris Magna. Port of Isis: Hungarian Excavations at Alexandria (1998–2001).* Budapest.

Wace, A. J. B., A. H. S. Megaw and T. C. Skeat (1959), *Hermopolis Magna, Ashmunein: The Ptolemaic Sanctuary and the Basilica.* Alexandria.

Wagner, G. (1974), 'Le temple d'Herakles Kallinikos et d'Ammon à Psôbthis-Qasr, métropole de la Petite Oasis', *Bulletin de l'Institut Français d'Archéologie Orientale* 74: 23–7.

— (1987), *Les oasis d'Egypte.* Cairo.

Walker, S. and M. Bierbrier (eds) (1997), *Ancient Faces: Mummy Portraits from*

Roman Egypt. London.
Walker, S. and P. Higgs (2001), *Cleopatra of Egypt: From History to Myth*. London.
Ward, B. (1975), *The Sayings of the Desert Fathers: The Alphabetical Collection*. Kalamazoo.
Watterson, B. (1988), *Coptic Egypt*. Edinburgh.
— (1997), *The Egyptians*. Oxford.
Whitcomb, D. S. and J. H. Johnson (1979), *Quseir al-Qadim 1978: Preliminary Report*. Princeton.
— (1982), *Quseir al-Qadim 1980: Preliminary Report*. Malibu.
Whitehouse, H. (1998), 'Roman in life, Egyptian in death: the painted tomb of Petosiris in the Dakhleh Oasis', in Kaper 1998: 253–70.
Wilfong, T. G. (1989), 'Western Thebes in the seventh and eighth centuries: a bibliographic survey of Jême and its surroundings', *Bulletin of the American Society of Papyrologists* 26: 89–145.
— (1997), *Women and Gender in Ancient Egypt from Prehistory to Late Antiquity. An Exhibition at the Kelsey Museum of Archaeology 14 March–15 June 1997*. Ann Arbor.
— (1998), 'The non-Muslim communities: Christian communities', in Petry 1998: 175–97.
— (2002), *Women of Jeme. Lives in a Coptic Town in Late Antique Egypt*. Ann Arbor.
Wilkinson, R. (2000), *The Complete Temples of Ancient Egypt*. New York.
Willems, H. and W. Clarysse (2000), *Les empereurs du Nil*. Leuven.
Winlock, H. E. (1936), *Ed Dakhleh Oasis*. New York.
— (1941), *The Temple of Hibis in El Khargeh Oasis*. New York.
Winlock, H. E. and W. E. Crum (1926), *The Monastery of Epiphanius at Thebes: Part I: The Archaeological Material; The Literary Material*. New York.
Winnicki, J. K. (1978), *Ptolemäerarmee in Thebais*. Warsaw.
Winter, E. (2003), 'Octavian/Augustus als Soter, Euergetes und Epiphanes: Die Datierung des Kalabscha-Tores,' *Zeitschrift für ägyptische Sprache und Altertumskunde* 130: 197–212.
Witt, R. E. (1971), *Isis in the Graeco-Roman World*. Ithaca NY.
Wuttmann, M. (2001), 'Les qanats de 'Ayn-Manâwîr', in P. Briant (ed.), *Irrigation et drainage dans l'Antiquité* (Paris):109–35.

Yoyotte, J. et al. (1997), *Strabon, Le voyage en Egypte: un regard romain*. Paris.

Ziermann, M. (1993), *Elephantine XVI*. Cairo.
Zitterkopf, R. E. and S. E. Sidebotham (1989), 'Stations and towers on the Quseir-Nile Road', *Journal of Egyptian Archaeology* 75: 155–89.
Zivie, C. M. (1980), 'Bousiris du Létopolite', in IFAO *Livre du Centenaire 1880–1980* (Cairo): 91–107.
— et al. (1982–92), *Le temple de Deir Chelouit*, 4 vols. Cairo.
Zuckerman, C. (1995), 'The hapless recruit Psois and the mighty anchorite, Apa John', *Bulletin of the American Society of Papyrologists* 32: 183–94.

ILLUSTRATION ACKNOWLEDGEMENTS

Acknowledgement is made to the following institutions for permission to reproduce illustrations of their objects or photographs from their archives:

Ägyptisches Museum, Berlin: 8.11.2.

British Museum, London: 1.1.1, 1.1.2, 1.1.3, 1.1.4, 1.3.1, 1.3.2, 1.4.1, 1.4.2, 1.4.4, 1.6.1, 1.6.2, 2.6.2, 5.1.2a–b, 5.2.3, 5.5.1, 6.2.3, 7.3.10.

Egypt Exploration Society, London: 3.4.8, 3.4.10, 5.3.4, 6.2.4, 6.3.9, 7.3.2.

Egyptian Museum, Cairo: 3.2.1, 3.2.2.

Fondation Egyptologique Reine Elisabeth, Brussels: 8.8.4.

Graeco-Roman Museum, Alexandria: 1.4.3, 2.2.1, 2.3.1, 2.4.3, 5.3.6.

IRPA-KIK, Brussels: 7.3.9.

Kelsey Museum, University of Michigan, Ann Arbor: 2.6.3a–b, 4.3.3, 5.2.1, 5.2.2, 5.2.4.

Louvre, Paris: 3.4.3.

Dipartimento di Scienze dell'Antichità, University of Padua: 5.4.6.

Oriental Institute, Chicago: 8.12.1.

Yale University, New Haven: 1.3.4a–b.

Acknowledgement is made to the following people for permission to reproduce their photographs:

S.-A. Ashton: 2.3.2.

R. S. Bagnall: 2.6.5, 4.4.1, 6.3.3, 6.3.6, 9.2.2, 9.2.4, 9.2.6, 9.2.8, 9.3.2, 9.4.2, 9.5.1, 9.5.3, 10.2.2, 10.2.3, 10.3.2, 10.3.3.

E. S. Bolman: 6.5.3.

A. K. Bowman: 2.2.5, 2.2.6, 2.2.8, 2.3.1, 2.4.1, 2.4.2, 2.5.2, 2.5.3, 7.3.3, 8.7.2, 8.9.2, 8.9.4.

W. Clarysse: 8.6.1, 8.8.2, 8.8.3, 8.9.5.

A. Cottry: 4.2.6.

J. G. Manning: 8.11.2.

P. T. Nicolson: 3.4.10.

D. W. Rathbone: 1.4.3, 2.2.7, 2.4.3, 3.2.1, 3.4.9, 5.3.6, 5.4.2, 6.2.1, 6.5.2, 8.2.3.

T. K. Thomas: 4.2.4, 4.3.2, 4.5.1.

D. J. Thompson: 3.4.4, 5.4.5, 8.2.1.

K. Vandorpe: 7.2.2, 7.2.3, 7.2.5, 7.3.6, 7.3.8, 7.4.1, 8.5.1.

T. G. Wilfong: 7.3.1.

INDEX